KANT AND THE TRANSCENDENTAL OBJECT:
A Hermeneutic Study

KANT
AND THE
TRANSCENDENTAL
OBJECT

A Hermeneutic Study

by
J. N. FINDLAY
FBA, FAAAS

CLARENDON PRESS · OXFORD
1981

Oxford University Press, Walton Street, Oxford OX2 6DP

OXFORD LONDON GLASGOW
NEW YORK TORONTO MELBOURNE WELLINGTON
KUALA LUMPUR SINGAPORE JAKARTA HONG KONG TOKYO
DELHI BOMBAY CALCUTTA MADRAS KARACHI
NAIROBI DAR ES SALAAM CAPE TOWN

Published in the United States by
Oxford University Press, New York

© *J. N. Findlay 1981*

British Library Cataloguing in Publication Data

Findlay, John Niemeyer
    Kant and the transcendental object.
    1. Kant, Immanuel
    I. Title
    110'.92'4   B2799.M5   80-41782

ISBN 0-19-824638-2

Typeset by Anne Joshua Associates, Oxford

To
John Silber,
Lover of Kant,
Scholar, and Friend

A gramophone record, the musical idea, the written notes, and the sound-waves, all stand to one another in the same internal relation of depicting that holds between language and the world. They are all constructed according to a common logical pattern.

Wittgenstein, Tractatus, 4.014.

Foreword

This book is an attempt to conduct a comprehensive examination of Kant's metaphysic of Transcendental Idealism, which is everywhere presupposed by his critical theory of knowledge, his theory of the moral and the aesthetic judgement, and his rational approach to religion. It will attempt to show that this metaphysic is profoundly coherent, despite frequent inconsistencies of expression, and that it throws an indispensable light on his critical enquiries. Kant's philosophy throughout draws a deep distinction between knowing and thinking, the former of which, in the human case, involves conceptions which find their fulfilment in *Anschauung*, or intuitive encounter, and which lead to what is called experience, whereas the latter is empty, and involves conception alone. That conception may be empty does not, however, deprive it of interest or profit, since it sets before us the formal structure of what in our case often transcends knowledge, but which must, for the purposes of knowledge, and of enterprises more important than knowledge, none the less be thought. Kant's philosophy is throughout concerned to illuminate the region where knowledge is possible, and to set forth its conditions, principles, and limits, but he is only able to illuminate it by bringing in agencies and acts, both subjective and objective, which transcend knowledge altogether, and of which we can only think in unfulfilled, formal fashion.

It is widely held that these Kantian procedures are unreasonable, and that it is absurd, both in itself and on Kant's principles, to make assertions, intended to produce conviction, regarding acts and agencies which are held to be unknowable. This view is, however, mistaken, since Kant conceives of knowledge in especially narrow terms, and there is nothing absurd in the view that thinkables must, in his sense, extend far more widely than knowables. Kant also goes further than most who have thought in his fashion in holding that, not only the qualities of the senses, but also the space and time in which we place them, have non-sensuous, non-spatial, and non-temporal foundations in relations among thinkables which transcend empirical knowledge. This contention also reposes on important arguments, and can be given a sense that will render it interesting and consistent.

It will be the task of this book to explore this sense, and also to connect it with the thought of Kant's immediate predecessors in the great German scholastic movement which began with Leibniz: this scholasticism, it will be held, is throughout preserved as the unspoken background of Kant's critical developments, whose great innovation really consisted in pushing it out of the region of the knowable, into the region of what is permissively or, in some cases, obligatorily, thinkable. Kant further spoke of himself as if he had been the author of a thought-revolution in which the subject suddenly assumed the place of the Copernican sun. This book will argue that he was in fact rather the author of a thought-revolution in which the subject assumed the place of the humble earth, from which, however, everything had to be viewed, while heliocentric pictures, admirable in themselves, could only be sketched in firm but formal outline, without the detail inserted by the speculative metaphysicians.

The content and development of Kant's thought also displays many interesting analogies with the content and development of the thought of Wittgenstein, though it proceeded in an opposite direction. For while Wittgenstein progressed from earlier views of thought and language in which non-empirical objects, a non-empirical subject, and non-empirical relations among these, still had a place, to later views in which there were no objects and no subjects but the ones recognized in ordinary language-performances; Kant, in his critical phase, progressed rather from views in which non-empirical thinkables practically only enjoyed a marginal, limiting role, to positions in which their governing role became more and more prominent. The relation of Kant to Wittgenstein and to other contemporary thinkers will be considered in the last chapter of this book.

My own thought-relations to Kant have continued throughout my philosophical life. While I began by interpreting Kant in terms of an idealism which saw all knowledge as springing from the spontaneous thought-acts of the pure subject into which there could be no external intrusion — the Thing-in-itself being merely a senseless survival — I was led to see and feel the many absurdities of trying to account for the content of knowledge, and for agreement among knowers, on such a purely constructive basis, and was also deeply influenced by Prichard's book, *Kant's Theory of Knowledge* (1911), in my perception of profound error in any opinions which assimilated knowledge to making. I see moral as well as intellectual error in such opinions, since they tend to destroy the deep respect for existent fact and being without which men cannot be decent or courageous. And I also saw much that seemed both incredible and reprehensible in the reported proceedings of the Productive Imagination in Kantian theory.

Deeper study of Kant has, however, convinced me that the Productive Imagination is, for him, an innocuous faculty, which operates altogether out of time, and which works hand-in-glove with Things-in-themselves to produce a translation of their unknowable order into the symbolism and syntax of sense, time, and space. I am now in fact happily persuaded that not only Kant, but none of the philosophers I greatly admire, for example, Hegel, deserves to be called an idealist in the epistemological sense, at least not in the more significant phases of their thought. Genuine epistemological idealism could flourish only in the cushioned comfort of late nineteenth-century Bismarckian Germany or imperial Britain.

I wish in conclusion to thank my friends Professor Klaus Hartmann of Tübingen University and Dr Arend Kulenkampff of Frankfurt University for reading my manuscript, and for making many helpful comments on it. They do not, of course, agree with many of my opinions. I owe a similar debt to Professor W. H. Walsh of Edinburgh University.

J. N. FINDLAY
Boston University,
1980

PS I have profited greatly from the writings of Professor Erich Adickes, who died in 1929, on the Kantian Thing-in-itself. Since his monumental analysis of Kant's *Opus Postumum*, in a 1920 Supplementary Volume of *Kant-Studien*, is not widely known in England, I have summarized much of its content in the eighth chapter of this work.

NOTE

My references to Kant's works in the present work are incorporated in the text and not put in footnotes, and have
involved little abbreviation beyond *CPR* for the *Critique of
Pure Reason* and *CPrR* for the *Critique of Practical Reason*.
I have distinguished Kant's two importantly different works
on the Metaphysic of Morals, of 1785 and 1797 respectively,
by using the term *Grundlegung*, Groundwork or Foundation,
which occurs in its title, for the former work, and have mentioned the date, when not clear by context, in the case of the
latter. I have not for the rest worried with Kant's immensely
long titles, especially in the case of his earlier and minor pub-
lications, as these can readily be found in standard histories,
which it is not my purpose to write. I have also made no attempt
to refer to all that Kant wrote on all the matters with which
I was concerned, and the same applies to my treatments of
Kant's predecessors and successors. The translations of passages
from Kant given in the text are always my own, though not
at all novel and controversial, and my references are either
to the numbered paragraphs given in all editions, or to the
pagination of the early editions which is always printed in
the margin of all good Kantian translations and editions, including the standard German Academy Edition, which I have
mainly used.

Analytical Table of Contents

Note: The compression necessary in the following Analytical Table has led to some inaccuracies of statement. The full text should be consulted where necessary.

expounded. It distinguishes the sensible world, consisting of everything as it affects our senses, from the intelligible world consisting of everything as it is, or would be for an understanding capable in principle of representing things *as they are*. Both worlds have a matter consisting of all things that are their parts, and a form consisting in the relational organization which binds those parts into a world. The form of the intelligible world consists of certain pure concepts (later called categories), e.g. substance, cause, possibility, etc., used to bind sense-based and other concepts together: the forms of the sensible world are its time and its space. Time and space are universal forms in which everything must be sensed by us, but which are independent of particular sensible content. The forms of the sensible and the intelligible worlds must *not* be confused (error of subreption). What is intelligible need not be sensible, e.g. simple substances, infinite totalities, etc., while what is sensible need not be intelligible, e.g. forms which correspond to no logical category, relations without *relata*, diversities without differences, etc. But we must posit inherent laws of the mind in virtue of which real and intelligible patterns (*species*) are systematically represented by sensible ones. The Dissertation makes plain that experience is never a free improvisation, but a controlled translation.

iii. Examination of Kant's arguments in the Aesthetic for the *a priori* and the intuitive character of the space and time of our experience. It was a mistake to regard time as primarily a form of inner experience, and only derivatively of phenomena in space. The notion of intuition must be taken as covering much that is a matter of readiness, or that is obscurely 'felt in our bones', e.g. space as an infinite whole. The basic arguments for the phenomenal status of space and time are ontological rather than epistemological. The doctrine is best interpreted as affirming the parasitism of what is spatial and temporal on deeper structures which are neither.

CHAPTER IV. THE ANALYTIC OF CONCEPTS

i. Complementarity of thought and intuition in human knowledge, relation of concepts to rules and the

contrast with objectivity, as an inbuilt property of itself. A relation of contrast is not, however, a relation of co-incidence or identity, and there must be a place for *both* arbitrarily subjective, and objectively necessitated syntheses. These are both in fact recognized in the Analytic of Principles. The unity of self-consciousness is not therefore a sufficient condition for the applicability of the categories, but requires co-operation from another source. The requirement is intrinsic, but also involves what is extrinsic. 140

vi. The Transcendental Deduction of the Second Edition is a vastly confused document involving most of the logical faults of the First Edition Deduction, without its illuminating excursions into transcendental psychology. It is the source of all the purely idealistic interpretations of Kantianism. 156

CHAPTER V. THE ANALYTIC OF PRINCIPLES 158

i. Nature of the transcendental schemata. Stress on their dispositional aspect. Kant over-emphasizes their time-aspect at the expense of their space-aspect. 158

ii. The Axioms of Intuition: there are no indivisible simples in the realm of spatio-temporal phenomena, and they are phenomena for that reason. The Anticipations of Perception: need of intensive, qualitative magnitude to differentiate occupied space-time from void. Kant's vacillating attitude to the void. 162

iii. The Analogies of Experience. These stress the necessity of being able to distinguish such syntheses as are arbitrary and subjective, from such as are necessary and objective, and so bring out the contrast between self-ascription and object-ascription, which the Transcendental Deduction obscures. Interesting doctrine of the three modes of time: permanence, succession, and simultaneity. Question: in what sense is time held to be permanent? 163

iv. First Analogy of substantial permanence. Is substance in this principle something phenomenally given or transcendentally thought? Answer: it represents a transcendent thought-identity pinned down by a phenomenal constancy. 166

CHAPTER VI. THE DIALECTIC OF THE SOUL
AND THE WORLD

Chapter I

Introductory

i

The aim of this book is to interpret and criticize the thought contained in the major writings of Kant from the special standpoint of three centrally important, sometimes divergent, but also often coincident concepts: that of the Transcendental Object, that of the Noumenon, and that of the Thing-in-itself. The philosophy of Kant lays central stress on what appears to the senses, and is seen in the embracing frames of space and time, and also on the formation and use of concepts which enable us, through the continued synthesis of appearances, to arrive at knowledge of what thus appears. But it is also teased by the thought of something which lies beyond or beneath such appearances and their syntheses, and which is, by its underlying presence, somehow able to impart content and necessity to their interconnections, and to prevent us from putting them together in a wholly arbitrary and fanciful manner (see, e.g., *CPR*, A. 104). This object is not for Kant *different* from the object or objects which appear to the senses and which we can judge about and know — innumerable references can be cited to attest such non-difference (see, e.g., *CPR*, A. 538-9) — but it is the *same* object or objects conceived in respect of certain intrinsically unapparent features, and which is in such respects incapable of being judged about or known. It is, in the terminology of Kant, an object of which, in these respects, we can form only an *empty* or sensuously unfulfilled conception: it has to be thought of as an X, a something-or-other, of whose unapparent character, or make-up, or relationships we can know nothing, since knowledge, on the Kantian account, always involves the actual or possible marriage of conceptions with intuitively sensuous presentations.

But though thus conceived emptily, and without the sort of meaning that looks to the possible presence to sense of something we can see or intuit, it is not, in a broader sense, devoid of significance or even of cognitive import. For we *must*, in Kant's view, conceive of there being something that appears, and whose being is not exhausted in such appearance, if the appearance of anything is to be conceivable at all (see, e.g., *Prolegomena*, §32, p. 314). And we must also conceive of what is thus non-apparent as so *affecting* us that it can appear before us, or be variously given in experience; it being absurd to conceive of things as apparent or experienced if they are not also, in their non-apparent aspect, thus affecting us (see *CPR*, A. 19). And Kant speaks of this our affection by unapparent objects with so little argumentative preamble, that he plainly does not regard it as involving any difficult, problematic step: it is rather, if one so likes to call it, a primordial certainty which stands in no need of justification, even if its lack of empirical content means that it can never be ranked as knowledge. And, as we have said, the whole compulsive, non-arbitrary content-element in appearances and experiences has to be attributed to the action of what thus affects us from without, even if it also fits in with our own deep need for such imposed regularity; and the object which is thus appearing to us, and affecting us, could certainly, we conceive, have been there, at least in its non-apparent aspects, even if it were not thus appearing to us, or affecting us at all. But our knowledge and judgement, though not *of* objects in their non-apparent capacity, none the less presupposes the latter: we cannot but conceive of, and believe in, such non-apparent objects or aspects of objects, even though we can have no knowledge of them. It is here important to stress that, while Kant insists that our concepts and categories can only contribute to *knowledge* where they have a connection with appearances to the senses; he also insists, in a great number of places, that as empty thoughts they are not thus restricted, and can range with complete freedom far beyond the bounds of sensible intuition (see, e.g., *CPR*, B. 167 *n*.). It must be in some such empty but profound way, which Kant certainly does not elucidate, that we can be primordially aware of objects as affecting our sensibility, though retaining aspects that are not capable of affecting us.

It is also important to stress here that, for Kant, our own thinking selves, as the agents who perform all our perceptual and conceptual syntheses, and who present us with our picture of a coherent, real world, and of whose regular action we are at all times capable of being conscious, are themselves objects of which no intuitive, sensuous presentation is possible, and which are accordingly, in their non-apparent aspects, wholly beyond knowledge (*CPR*, B. 157-8). It is only of the inwardly sensed thoughts, feelings, desires, and so on, with which this unknowable object or subject affects itself, and in which it consciously appears to itself, that we can be said to have knowledge. And this unknowable, thinking subject must further be credited, in virtue of certain moral demands which will be examined in a later chapter, with the power to initiate changes in itself and the world, to which no adequately determining, previously existent causal factor can be assigned. Such a power is not only *not* illustrated by anything given to sensible intuition: it is also, in Kant's view, incapable of being thus illustrated. And similar demands of morality lead Kant to postulate the unending temporal existence of the unknown subject responsible for our thoughts and volitions, as well as its performance of some such acts out of time altogether. And they also lead him to postulate the existence of an all-possible, all-real, all-perfect God, who exists of necessity, and who makes possible endless moral progress and its ultimate reward: all of these postulations employ concepts going beyond all limits of possible sensible fulfilment, and so beyond all knowledge.

Kant therefore regularly operates with the conception of objects which transcend knowledge, and which are none the less necessary to the understanding of morality and also of knowledge; and he may, in respect of such objects, be termed a problematic realist, since there is nothing in respect of such objects that is not also a problem for him, or regarding which he can intuitively *fulfil* his conceptions. And he mainly uses the term 'Transcendental Object' when he conceives of such objects — the Transcendental Subject, of course, is merely one of them — as being what *we* have to conceive as being the underlying, unknown ground of appearance and experience; while the term 'Thing-in-itself' is mainly employed when he conceives of them as existing *independently* of whatever we may conceive or believe (see, e.g., *CPR*, A. 190-1). And in very many contexts the two concepts are interchangeable, the former merely stressing a relation to our own subjectivity which the latter prefers to ignore. The term 'Noumenon', or object of pure thought, is also employed in both contexts, though, at times, with the additional feature that it is the appropriate object of a type of awareness not called into action by sensuous affections, but in some manner directly constitutive of its object, or at least directly apprehending it, in the very act of conceiving it (see, e.g., *CPR*, A. 251-2; B. 306). The Thing-in-itself, the Noumenon, and the Transcendental Object therefore all point to the same sort of unapparent source of all that is apparent, in which Kant profoundly believes, and our task in this book will be to interpret the Kantian writings in terms of these three conceptions, and particularly of the last. It will be our contention that these conceptions admit of a significant and valuable interpretation, and that they are, moreover, essential to the structure of Kantian theory, and of theories of the same type as Kant's. And it will also be our contention that there is indeed a noble and profitable use of such essentially empty concepts as Kant employs in his theory, and that no full understanding of our knowledge or our practice will be possible without them.

ii

That Kant regarded the Transcendental Object as essential to his teaching admits of no doubt: that he was right to do so has been widely questioned. There have been interpretations of Kant that have emphasized his severe restriction, only rarely lifted, of knowledge to what can be experienced through outer or inner sensibility, and his not infrequent denial even of meaning (*Bedeutung*) to judgements which go beyond the possibility of experience, or which try to make use of categories like number, causation, substance, necessity, and so on, in regard to things that could never appear sensibly (see, e.g., *CPR*, A. 242). These interpretations, which certainly do justice to a great deal that Kant says, and at times thinks, may be broadly covered by the name 'positivist', and have certainly been vastly influential in recent times. And they have also certainly dwelt on a vastly important and illuminating side of Kant's teaching. They all, however, forget that Kant's limitation of knowledge to what can be given in sensible experience itself rests on arguments involving a vast amount of what we may *call* transcendental machinery, which certainly go far beyond the limits of possible experience. For Kant's theory holds to the presence, in all our intuitively fulfilled or intuitively based experience, of an element contributed by the thinking self which is necessary to its counting as 'experience' at all, and that this element, and its necessity, and its source in the thinking self-itself — a Transcendental Object — are all matters which, since they make experience and learning from experience possible, are not themselves matters that can be given in experience, or that can be learned from it. Our examination of the feelings and conceptually slanted symbols that process unceasingly through our thoughts can indeed provide us with *instances* of this universally present, necessary, categorial thought-element, but they cannot distinguish it from other thought-elements and connections which are merely arbitrary and personal. They are unable to show that this element *must* be present in all our experience and thought-life, and that it must spring from the activity of a unifying agent which is not itself given to us in them. And there must further, Kant holds, have been certain 'transcendental acts', acts mainly ranged under the rubric of the 'Productive' or 'Transcendental Imagination' (see, e.g., *CPR*, A. 123), which must have been performed unconsciously, or in some manner prior to experience, or perhaps out of time altogether, in order that the well-arranged world should stand before us as it does, and should be amenable to our judgements and our inferences. And of course, as we have said, Transcendental Objects other than our transcendental selves must, by affecting our sensibility, have somehow helped to determine the character and arrangement of what is given to us in experience, though in ways that transcend experience and are necessarily beyond knowledge. Kant's account of experience and knowledge therefore presupposes the existence of agents and acts that cannot be empirically known, since they are the preconditions of empirical knowledge, and it also presumes that we can form just notions of such agents and acts even though we can never have experience or knowledge of them. If Kant's theory of knowledge and meaningful judgement thus has aspects that can with justice be called 'positivist', it is not at all positivist in its account of the necessary underpinnings of such knowledge and judgement. These underpinnings have to be *conceived* if we are to understand how knowledge and empirically based judgement are possible, but they are not themselves matters of knowledge or empirically based judgement.

It may, however, be argued that all Kant's transcendental underpinnings are unnecessary to his theory, and that he was deeply confused in introducing them. It may also be held that

they can be excised from Kant's theories without damage to
its essential structures. For the existence of empirical knowledge as a series of successful syntheses of appearances, falling
within a limited number of types of synthesis, is arguably
a plain fact, if taken, that is, within the limits of what has
actually appeared. We have certainly achieved the awareness
of a large number of enduring, classifiable things interacting
regularly with one another around us, and of ourselves as
manifest in a series of 'inner' states in time, which are regularly
related to one another, and to the appearances of other things.
And it has been possible for us, through extensions from
phenomenal cases, to frame conjectures regarding things and
states of things which have never appeared to us, some of
which conjectures have been afterwards confirmed by what
did appear to us, and so came to count as knowledge. It is
legitimate, it may be argued, to ask how such phenomenal
knowledge is *possible*, if our enquiry is confined to what
such knowledge actually and phenomenally *is*, to an *analysis*
of it *qua* phenomenon; and this, it may be argued, is what
Kant brilliantly did in many of his treatments in such sections
as the Analogies of Experience. But it is neither legitimate nor
necessary to establish the possibility of such phenomenal
knowledge by assembling non-phenomenal machinery to
account for it, nor by attributing what thus unmysteriously
appears to mysterious and unknowable subjects and objects,
and to unknowable encounters among them. All this non-
phenomenal machinery must be dropped: this will not affect
the well-demarcated, well-ordered world of phenomenal things,
whether objective or subjective. Moreover, Kant's theory will
profit by such a transcendental excision, becoming thereby
the sort of theory that our own recent, highly enlightened
phenomenalists might have propounded.

Kant would not, however, have tolerated such an excision,
and it is clear that a view which seeks to tolerate it cannot
claim to be Kantian. And there are further good reasons why
Kant would, and should, have found it hard to accept such a
case of Hume without scepticism. For, as in the doctrine of
Hume, it would offer us no *guarantee* that the vanishing appearances will continue to deliver the epistemological goods, that
they will not at any moment degenerate into the disorderly
phantasmagoria which seems to have filled Kant with peculiar
terror. For Kant's approach to phenomenally based knowledge

is not hypothetical, but categorical. He does not merely say that, *if* phenomenally based knowledge is to be possible, such and such conditions must obtain. He, on the contrary, says that, *since* phenomenally based knowledge *is* possible, such and such conditions *do* obtain, and among these conditions there are many going beyond the bounds of possible appearance. For it is only, he holds, if there is a unitary subject, who never appears, nor is known to himself, but can none the less conceive himself, and who belongs to a whole class of similar subjects — for Kant always presupposes community — and if this subject is such as to harbour certain highly general expectations as to how things will appear to him, and is ready to fit appearances together into a picture of enduring things regularly interacting in the world, that there can be such phenomenal knowledge. And he also of course holds, though he emphasizes it less, that it is only if there are things, also not in their intrinsic character apparent or known to us, which are such as to be capable of appearing to us in manners which meet our cognitive expectations and enable us to perform the required syntheses, that phenomenal knowledge is possible. Kant certainly uses the word 'knowledge' eccentrically in holding that what we regard as a *necessary* condition of a certain sort of knowledge is not itself capable of being known; but for Kant we can never be said to know what we only conceive emptily and without fulfilling intuition. We cannot therefore be said to know that there is a Transcendental Subject or that there are Transcendental Objects, though both are necessary to the existence of empirical knowledge.

What is important in both these types of postulated entity is their *unitary* character, that they are single and simple. They can thus be thought of as holding appearances together, and also, by being the *same* in a large number of successive situations, giving them *constancy* of character. Kant is, of course, in all this, harking back to the monadic simples of the Leibnizian–Wolffian tradition, from which we shall see reason to hold that he never really departed. But what distinguishes Kant from this tradition is that he does not believe that we can have *knowledge* of any such simple entities, even in the case of ourselves, since such a non-phenomenal unity cannot reveal itself intuitively. In the appearances, of course, there is only synthetic multiplicity, never simple unity. We shall, however, argue that Kant is profoundly right in recognizing that our thought simply cannot do without such pervasive, underlying unities, which are the required complement to the externality and the vanishingness of appearances.

If we now ask what we are to do about the many passages (see, e.g., *CPR*, A. 242) where Kant plainly says that we cannot even intelligibly *mean* objects which are confessedly non-intuitable, the answer is that Kant operates throughout with *two* conceptions of meaning. The one is epistemological, and applies only where intuitive verification and fulfilment is possible. The other, wider kind of significance, applies even in the case of the necessarily empty reference, for we can certainly think of *something* as qualified in *some* way or other, or as being related in *some* (if Quine forbids such quantification, so much the worse for Quine) way to *something* else, or being such that its existence is a necessary condition of *certain* other existences, and so on. And what is referred to in such an emptily formal or logical way can also, in Kant's view, be truly connected with something that appears to intuition. But in such cases we do not, according to Kant's usage, have knowledge, only a rational presupposition of knowledge. There is no reason to reform Kant's usage, provided we clearly understand it.

That there are objects that appear to us in various ways, and that so affect us that we experience them as thus appearing, while having intrinsic natures which are not thereby made apparent; and that we ourselves are such objects, and affect ourselves as being thus affected, while having an intrinsic nature which does not thereby become apparent: all these are propositions necessary to the Kantian account of empirical knowledge, while yet transcending the knowledge and experience which their postulation helps us to explain. And to attempt to dispense with them in an interpretation of Kantianism is certainly to modify it so vastly that the name 'interpretation' scarcely would apply to it at all. Kant admittedly says in many places that we ought not to apply such categories as those of number, underlying substance, causation, possibility, existence, and necessity to matters that transcend possible experience, and this might seem to destroy the meaning of all talk of Things-in-themselves (or, for that matter, of selves-in-themselves) in the plural, or talk about them as affecting or as being affected by one another, and so on. It is, however, best to interpret such statements as implying only that such a use of categories is in a valuable sense empty, and cannot in any circumstances amount to what Kant calls 'knowledge'. Kant's theory of knowledge cannot, therefore, be called positivistic, though it is quite right to see something like positivism in his account of what we can effectively know.

iii

If Kant's theory of knowledge is not, therefore, rightly regarded as positivistic (with a few shards of metaphysic left clinging to it from an earlier dispensation), it is also wrong to regard it as basically idealistic, with a few realistic vestiges similarly clinging to it. It is true that Kant describes his theory as an empirical realism which is also a transcendental idealism (see, e.g., *CPR*, A. 28, 36), but this transcendental idealism is not idealistic in the sense of Berkeley or Husserl, for whom only our conscious selves and their conscious acts exist absolutely, while all other things exist only in so far as they are perceived or conceived, or as they are 'posited' or 'intended', by such selves. Much less does it hold to any solipsistic idealism which conceives that selves, other than a single one, exist only in being conceived by that one self. Nor is it idealistic in the even stronger sense of Fichte, who believes that even such a single self only exists in the act of being 'posited' or given to consciousness. Now Kant does indeed believe that our own thinking self must, at all times, at least be capable of being consciously thought of, or made present to consciousness, whether as a pure subject, or in respect of its concrete, inner states. And he also does believe that the phenomenal objects that appear before us when our senses seem to be affected from without, and our understandings seem stimulated to perceive such objects around us, that all such apparent objects have, *qua* apparent, no being apart from the sensations aroused in us, or from the ways in which these are actively interrelated and connected by our interpretative intelligences; and that even the great frameworks of space and time in which they are all located are themselves intuitive projections of the native machinery of our minds. The empirically real world — whether we consider the objects we perceive in space around us, or that we *would* perceive if we were better placed or more sensitive, or the feelings, stirrings, images, presentations, and so on that we are aware of as going on in ourselves — is, therefore, in all its immense variety and indefinite extension, no more than a show called into being before consciousness by the acts and undergoings of the sensitive, perceptive, cogitative subject; of which acts and undergoings, and of the subject that has them, there is often a perception or at least a consciousness. If this is not absolute idealism, what else is?

It is, however, all-important to stress that Kant believes that there absolutely *is* such a sensitive, perceptive, thinking subject, before which objects display themselves in experience, and that it is present and active even when we are much too object-absorbed to be conscious of it, and that there are properties that it has 'in itself', with which we are necessarily unacquainted. It may even, as far as we can tell, be the very same being that appears to us as the brain or the nerves in the body (see, e.g., *CPR*, B. 72). We attribute, and must attribute, our objectively oriented, as well as our disorderly, personal thoughts to it, and must see in it the source of the immense symphonic unity, mixed with discords, that orchestrates all our experience, but it remains, and always must remain, an *éminence grise* behind all such orchestration; something we must conceive of and believe in, but of which we cannot know who or what it is. The idealism of Kant, therefore, believes in a Transcendental Subject, which is itself a Transcendental Object, posited indeed, but not constituted or given being by such an act of positing, and which must be correctly thought of as transcending experience and knowledge. Kant's transcendental self, unlike Fichte's ego, does not confer being on itself by positing itself: it is only able to posit itself because it already exists. Such a transcendental idealism is plainly, in some respects, a transcendent realism, even if Kant prefers to call it 'problematic'. And it is plain, further, that Kant accepts without question the existence of countless *other* subjects, all constituting phenomena around them in much the same way as this subject does: he does not doubt that what he says about the structure and content of a single, conscious experience can be generalized to cover countless others (see, e.g., *CPR*, B. 72). Almost, we may say, he makes a presumption of the existence of other subjects an *a priori* condition of the possibility of experience, though he seems not to be fully aware of this very modern issue. Altogether, however, it is plain that here too he is a realist rather than an idealist.

It is plain, further, that Kant thinks that there are many acts and proceedings, through which appearances are constituted by and for the Transcendental Subject, of which there is either no consciousness, or only a very dim consciousness. The subject must have located, or must have helped to locate, phenomenal qualities in particular regions of space or periods of time, yet of such location it can have no consciousness whatever, since phenomenal experience is never of empty space or time, nor of unlocated qualities. Once phenomenal objects are given as located in space and time, it will no doubt be possible for the Transcendental Subject to *extend* and *enrich* the phenomenal picture, and of such proceedings it may no doubt be dimly conscious; but of the original constitution of spatio-temporal appearances, whatever this may have involved, there can have been no conscious experiences. Such a pre-empirical constitution of appearances, necessarily thought of but not knowable, is what Kant seems to have covered in his all too obscure concept of the Productive Imagination. And even in the case of such acts and undergoings as are fully conscious, it may be doubted whether their spontaneous agency or their contrasting passivity, can, in Kant's view, be intuitively given to consciousness. We have, Kant holds, some sort of immediate sense of our own spontaneous causality in acts of free choice, particularly in those of moral decision, but the sort of freedom of which we are then conscious is nothing that we can clearly understand (e.g., *CPR*, B. xxix), and of which he only once or twice dares to say that we can have knowledge. And such transcendence *of* knowledge will *a fortiori* obtain in the case of the spontaneity attributed by Kant to certain syntheses which occur *in* knowledge (*CPR*, B. 130). And it must be by the failure of this non-epistemic sense of spontaneity that we are non-epistemically made aware of being passively *affected* in sensation. Feelings, stirrings, glimpses, visions certainly parade in a constant phantasmagoria before our internal self-awareness, and can become materials for knowledge, but the dynamism which informs them can be phenomenally represented only by the same sort of empirical regularities that are given in the case of external things. As Hume said, association plays the same role in the inner world that gravitation plays in the outer, and can in both cases be reduced to phenomenal regularity. The true agency and passivity that we attribute to ourselves, must therefore, for Kant, be thought of as something which transcends experience and knowledge. Here too, then, we have a case of a problematic realism: something exists, and must be thought of as existing, even though we can know nothing about it, and *need* not have been thinking of it.

It is clear, further, that, despite all the spontaneous efficacy and energy that Kant attributes to the Transcendental Subject, there are yet other functions which he attributes to transcendental entities other than the subject in question. For Transcendental Objects, not ourselves, are definitely said to be responsible for the material or content of experiences or appearances (*CPR*, A. and B. 1-2), however much *we* may carry about with us the space-time frameworks into which we project them, and the categories and thought-principles to which we make them conform. And Transcendental Objects beyond ourselves are also said by Kant in a crucial passage (*CPR*, A. 104, 109) to be what we have to think of as responsible for the element of *necessity* in all our experiences, the necessity which forces us to put sensory elements together in one way and not in another, and that prevents us from synthesizing them in a fashion which is in any degree arbitrary. (It is important to realize that there might be *many* ways of putting appearances together so as to satisfy the structure of space and time, and likewise the demands of the categories.) The general *style* in which such elements are put together is of course our own, and involves our own active spontaneity: it is *we* who schematize the categories in a *temporal* and *spatial* fashion, and who, therefore, must give to phenomenal objects their precise distances, positions, configurations, orderly successions, and so forth. But the transcendental sources beneath such phenomenal objects must certainly also be thought of as having their own characteristic *Zusammenhang* or mode of interconnection, even if we can form no intuitively fulfilled conception of the same, and it is to the unknown and unknowable character of their interconnection, as a crucial passage in the First Critique teaches (*CPR*, A. 494-5), that the interconnection of empirical objects must be in some measure ascribed. We must, in short, in some manner *translate* the structure of what does not, and cannot, appear into the phenomenal structure of experienced spatio-temporality. And while, in such translations, we moderns would say that we at least *knew* the formal, logical structure of Things-in-themselves, we do not, in Kant's sense of knowledge, *know* anything about this structure at all, since we are not acquainted with the actual elements or the relations which enter into it. In

Kant's view, general conceptions which we cannot apply to sensibly intuited instances are empty, and cannot by themselves yield us knowledge of anything (*CPR*, A. 51). How much more will this be the case when such concepts are purely formal, and merely inform us that a manifold of unspecified entities are ordered in a certain number of unspecified dimensions by relations having certain abstract logical properties?

Kant's failure to insist that his ascription of an 'affective' role to the transcendental elements behind our perceptions involves at least some parallelism of structure between objects-in-themselves and objects as perceived, has made sad havoc of his expositions. For they have been taken to mean that his objects-in-themselves only contribute a disjoined *congeries* of elements to experience, and that the subject has then complete liberty to locate them or to assemble them as and where it likes, provided only that it respects the exigencies of space-time structure, and the requirements of substantial permanence and causal regularity which are, in Kant's view, built into its subjectivity. This bizarre view is part of the bad heritage of Lockean empiricism, modified but still retained by Leibniz, according to which whatever the senses admit, they admit 'simple and unmixed', and their data can only become part of a complex, relational unity through an activity that Locke calls 'compounding', and that Kant speaks of as 'synthesis'. A modern empiricist would concede the central importance of perceptual and conceptual synthesis in knowledge, without accepting the unstructured character of what enters into it: synthesis would for him merely *extend* the structure found in unsynthesized parts, practise interpolation and extrapolation upon them, not *impose* a structure on unstructured simples. It is plain, however, that objects-in-themselves could only be said to 'affect' us in our sensations if we supposed that there was some *correlation* between the differences and relations in the former and those in the latter. It would at least be necessary to credit the transcendent sources of experiences with as many distinct and independent *powers* as there are distinctions within experience, and with degrees of difference and resemblance among such powers corresponding to the degrees of difference and resemblance found among phenomena, and with dependences and collocations corresponding to phenomenal dependences and collocations, and so on. To speak of anything as affecting anything in manners ABCDE must be at least to credit it with as many distinct 'moving forces', to use Kant's term, as there are distinctions met with in phenomena. We must not, of course, fail to say that the original 'affections' and synthetic projections which led to the presence of phenomena in the frameworks of space and time, cannot themselves have occurred in space and time at all, since it was precisely *their* task to render the non-spatial spatially, and the non-temporal temporally. In so far, therefore, as Kant speaks of 'affections' and 'syntheses' in such ultimate contexts, he is at best using such terms analogically, and in respect of a parallelism of logical structure which transcends knowledge. He of course often talks as if there were 'pure syntheses' in time by which time and space were themselves constituted (see, e.g., *CPR*, A. 99–100), and such slips into nonsense have deluded many interpreters.

It is clear, further, that if there were no correlation between the phenomenal relations of sensible objects, and the non-phenomenal relations of their sources, there would necessarily be much arbitrary variation in the former, and not the non-arbitrariness and restrictive necessity which we attribute to the action of transcendental objects. It is baseless to believe that conformity to geo-chronometrical and categorial restrictions would be sufficient to limit such variety. Given a 'manifold' of disordered, atomistic sense-elements, and a demand that they be distributed through space and time in a manner which satisfied the requirements of phenomenal permanence and causal regularity, there would still be indefinitely many ways in which such a distribution and regularization might be carried out. Different subjects might inhabit considerably different phenomenal worlds, and there might have been no single, common world such as Kant unquestionably believes in (see, e.g., *Prolegomena*, §319). These difficulties were met in the case of a genuinely idealistic thinker like Fichte by 'positing' the existence of a single pure ego common to all of us, whose imaginative 'positing' covers all objects and all subjects. This view is not, however, entertained by Kant, who at best comes close to it by at times supposing that all spiritual substances depend on God, and may in some manner be said to see all things in God (*Dissertation*, §22, Scholium). Without such a supposition, which altogether goes beyond the appearances, there is no reason why the phenomenal worlds of different transcendental selves might not be vastly diverse, and out of rapport with one another, though all might be applying the same conceptual and spatio-temporal programme to a like manifold of disordered data. Kant does not entertain any of these possibilities, though they were often enough raised by his early critics. He at most entertains the possibility of a systematic divergence among subjects in the *general way* in which they structure appearances (see, e.g., *CPR*, B. 72), and not in the manner in which they distribute and assemble its contents.

Kant's whole procedure is, therefore, such as to suggest, and at one or two crucial points to assert, a thoroughgoing correlation between the structures of phenomenal givens and those of their transcendent sources. Only he is unwilling to allow that such correlations can ever lead to knowledge. We can only form an empty, logical picture of them, and of their relation to appearances, and such an empty, logical picture has no use in knowledge. It is clear, therefore, that the Transcendental Object or Thing-in-itself plays an essential role in Kantian theory, both in the case of the Transcendental Subject, which is only one Transcendental Object among others, and in the case of *other* Transcendental Objects. It has also been shown that the Transcendental Subject, though all-important for *us* because it is ourselves, is not always accorded the superior importance for conception and knowledge that would seem to be its prerogative. For, Kant is disposed, in the difficult Refutation of Idealism in Edition II of the First Critique (*CPR*, B. 274-9), to accord such a prerogative to the Transcendental Object and its phenomenal representative. For it is only, he holds, in so far as our Transcendental Subject is affected by *other* objects which appear to it as in space, that it can also be affected by *itself* as so affected, and can accordingly become aware of itself as having ideas, beliefs, desires, and feelings directed to the outward, sensible objects which are its main concern. And it is only in relation to such acts and objects that it can have the thought of itself as the active centre of them all. There is, therefore, no consciousness of ourselves, or of anything else, except in so far as independently real Things-in-themselves act upon us, and by so acting evoke those conscious orientations in which our whole phenomenal being consists. All these points confirm the problematically realistic character of Kantianism, and its remoteness from complete idealism.

iv

The introduction of a transcendent, and to a degree unknowable, object into what is none the less a theory of knowledge, is not of course a Kantian innovation. For, the doctrine of the primary and secondary qualities, with its roots in ancient atomism, and its espousal by Descartes and Locke, certainly offers us a world which underlies and grounds the world with which we are acquainted, and with which, in its stripped, disqualified form, we can never hope to be acquainted. If we could only be said to know what could sensibly appear to us, and what could thus be an object of possible experience, this stripped, disqualified world could certainly not be known. It is, however, thought of as having characters of extension, figure, motion, duration, and so on, which are met with in appearance and experience, and so is not stripped down to the empirically empty, logically skeletal status of the Kantian Thing-in-itself. Kant, in fact, elaborated a theory of nature as reduced to purely spatial and temporal determinations which is to be found in his *Metaphysical Foundations of Natural Science* (see chapter VIII of this book). Only, this world, though inferred by argument from the world of our common experience, is still characterized by him as phenomenal. It is, for him, a world of *primary* appearances, first fruit perhaps of the commerce of the Transcendental Subject with Things-in-themselves, and inferred by us as lying beneath the secondary appearances, or appearances of appearances, that we encounter in ordinary life. Ordinary sensuous appearances are appearances of these primary appearances, which, in their turn, refer us back to the unknown characters and structures of Things-in-themselves (Kant's *Opus Postumum* has a great deal to say on these matters). But that Things-in-themselves are *not* spatio-temporal is a point on which Kant strongly insists, and for which he offers a large number of weighty arguments, which will be considered in their place. Only a dynamic structure sufficient to produce the actual structure of appearance and experience need be postulated, but such a postulation will remain emptily analytic: it will only parallel the arithmetical multiplicity and the relational connectivity of what appears.

Unapparent objects behind appearances and experience are also part of the Leibnizian tradition, which, as modified by Christian Wolff and his school, provided the true background against which all Kant's teaching must be understood. To

Leibniz, as to Kant, space was only a well-founded phenomenon, the expression of parallelisms and affinities among monadic substances, some apperceptive and rational, some irrationally conscious, and some dizzily confused, which make up the true world. To this view Kant always shows deference: it tells us, he says, what Things-in-themselves would have to be like if we could have any knowledge of them (see *CPR*, A. 267; *MFNS*, 507–8). Leibniz, however, thought that we *did* have such knowledge: that our conscious and self-conscious *Moi* or Ego was at least perfectly known to us, and that it was in fact the model on which we might conceive the 'true unities' which underlie the spatially extended and spatially distant appearances in the world. And though the Leibnizian monad, in its interior economy, is programmed to press on to all that it will do and experience in the whole of its history, and so in a sense transcends succession, it must still carry out this internal programme *in time*, which is thus not regarded as something wholly phenomenal. For Kant, however, the phases of the inner life which appear in time are not the true acts of the tran-scendental self, but are only appearances of those true acts to itself; having set various objects before itself in varying lights and manners, and having had various active responses to such objects, it then sets these acts, responses, and objects before itself in a fashion which none the less leaves much of their deep structure unapparent. Kant's phenomenalism is therefore an infinitely more radical theory than the phenomenalism of primary and secondary qualities, or the panpsychistic Leibnizian metaphysics. It empties the Transcendental Subject and Tran-scendental Object, not only of all sensory and affective content, but also of the basic spatio-temporality which we surrender far more reluctantly. We are left, in the end, with an empty array of logical variables, linked with similar terms by wholly variable relations, for which no constant meaning can be sub-stituted, and of which, accordingly, no knowledge can be consummated.

It may be asked, however, though the question cannot be fully answered at this stage, whether there is not something absurd about a phenomenalism as radical as the Kantian. Prichard and Ryle and others have made such an objection, and there seems at first sight to be substance in it. In ordinary usage appearances may at least in *some* cases coincide with what is real: an object may, in certain standard circumstances, *seem* to be just as it is. Thus an object in space may appear to be just as far away as it actually is, and it may seem to have the very shape that it actually has, and it is often taken as axiomatic that our own thoughts, feelings, mental images, and so on must appear to us, if they do appear to us, as they truly are. There are appearances which deviate from the real, but it only makes sense to talk of them as thus deviant, since there are also cases in which such deviations can be made to vanish. No one, for example, would think that the sight of a knife and a fork on a table could be a false appearance of a decanter and a piece of cheese, and it is to some such wild supposition that Kant's phenomenalism seems committed. It seems to want to make use of a concept of 'appearance' in which the appearances are so widely deviant from the reality that it makes no sense to connect them with one another.

Kant does, however, connect his transcendental 'appearances' with an irremovable feature of the human predicament, which gives them an analogy to the removable 'appearances' of ordinary discourse. This irremovable feature is our passive subjection to affections stemming from things outside of us and so giving rise to an experience which is as much an expression — Kant would hold it to be even *more* of an expression — of our *own* inherent nature than of the nature of the things thus acting upon us. This sort of extension of the ordinary use of 'appearance' to irremovable features of the human predicament, has, as we have said, been less radically used in the doctrine of the secondary qualities. Kant *does*, however, conceive of a situation in which the appearances, irremovable in the human condition, might none the less drop away, and in which what was before the subject would *coincide* with what a thing was in itself. Such a situation would be one in which an intuitive understanding was not trying to fit its concepts to data compulsively imposed on it from without, but was itself in some way spontaneously generating such data, living through conceptions which were in some fashion self-fulfilling, and constitutive of what they conceived (see, e.g., *CPR*, B. 138-9). It would be an archetypal, primal understanding, and not, like ours, an ectypal, derivative one, and it would belong properly to an archetypal being, whose nature comprehended all positive possibilities, and which could not be separated from its own existence or the existence of anything. Of such a being Kant believes that we have a flawless conception, in terms of which everything in our moral or intellectual life can best be understood, but of which we can have no intuitive or demonstrative knowledge, since it transcends possible experience. Ectypal understandings like our own, entirely dependent on external, sensuous intrusions, cannot form more than the most empty conception of the archetypal understanding in question: we must, however, frame the problematic concept of a *Noumenon*, the object of such an archetypal understanding (see, e.g., *CPR*, A. 254-5), to cover what we cannot but think, but cannot hope to know. And we can certainly think of ourselves as able, in some problematic state, whether projected into the future or the past, but properly placed out of time altogether, to achieve some sort of participation in such intellectual vision. We should then perhaps experience the dynamic agencies which underlie and are responsible for all appearances, though this is not possible for us as things are. Kant, however, also says, in not a few places, that in our sense of our own free spontaneity we have some sort of an access, once or twice spoken of as 'knowledge', to a kind of causality which differs essentially from the Humean causality which governs experience. And he also holds that we must have exercised such causality in the free choice of the whole life that we are now laboriously living out in time, which free choice must have taken place, or must be taking place, out of time altogether (see *CPR*, A. 539-40). Kant, therefore, does try to give sense, even in the case of his transcendental appearances, to the same sort of ultimate coincidence of appearance with reality which obtains in the case of ordinary appearances. The coincidence in question is, however, eschatological and theological, though dimly prefigured in our present experience, and we shall certainly have to wait for its full realization.

Kant does not, however, simply reject a full coincidence between ordinary appearances and noumenal realities. He offers a vast number of arguments to prove it, some resting on Leibnizian, Wolffian, and Platonic grounds, others on highly original grounds of his own. We can in the present chapter only indicate the general scope and nature of these arguments. The principle of these arguments is that what appears before us in experience is in certain respects inconceivable, and may even violate basic logical laws: things cannot really *be* as they are given in experience as being. There is in these arguments always the secret reference to the conception of things as they would be revealed to be, if we could have access to them as they in themselves are. What they appear to be is condemned as appearance because it fails to square with such a conception, and a guiding notion of the Noumenon or Thing-in-itself is always the unasserted ground for asserting the phenomenal character of whatever is held to be phenomenal. Without such a positive notion of what Things-in-themselves would or could be like, Kant would have no reason to regard certain features of experience as phenomenal.

Kant's arguments for the phenomenal character of all experience are based, first of all, on the continuous flux of content which is a prime feature of conscious experience, and which spills over from conscious experience to the external things which appear in it, and which are all given as in motion, or in perpetual change of state. Kant, like Plato, thinks that there is something inconceivable, illogical about such flux. We can in fact only conceive of it by projecting it on to a line which is not imagined as being in flux, and on which all the instants of the flux are imagined *together* (*CPR*, A. 33; B. 154–5). All conscious synthesis is in fact an attempt to overcome the sheer supersessiveness of such flux (*CPR*, A. 99). Since we cannot understand how what is the case suddenly should not be the case and vice versa, we overcome these difficulties by thinking of all these phases *together*, and projecting them on to imaginary lines, in which each of these otherwise contradictory conditions can without contradiction find a place. The sheer succession which lies at the root of the projection known as time, cannot therefore characterize things as they in themselves are, but only things as they appear. There is nothing self-contradictory in supposing that the same things should appear to be A and also not A if we can posit non-apparent distinctions which enable them to be both. Kant therefore supposes, with Spinoza, that behind the appearance of things as in time, there is always their intrinsic reality *sub quadam specie aeternitatis*, and many of the most mysterious passages in his moral philosophy rest on this transcendent assumption. And it is, moreover, because phenomena are in supersessive flux, that they also are phenomenal. They are only appearances because they fail to live up to a prime requirement of intrinsic being: that they should be what they are, not piecemeal, but together. And it is because Kant believes in the illogical, essentially phenomenal character of flux, that he even goes beyond Leibniz, that he sees our inner life in time as being as much phenomenal as outer appearances in space. It is in fact *more* phenomenal, since it has absolutely no last-ingness of character, and only conjures up some semblance of lastingness by concerning itself with the more durable appearances of objects in space (*CPR*, B. 275-6).

We may here speak up briefly in support of such a Platonic and Spinozistic and Kantian doctrine of the phenomenal character of supersessive time. Time is, *qua* supersession, phenomenal, not in the sense that it does not characterize the world and ourselves as we experience them, but rather in the sense that it requires to be supplemented by something *else*, which has the antithetical property of eternity or non-passage, and which is rightly held to be what we think of and believe in, rather than what we actually can experience. Such supplementation of passage by non-passage is to be found in the modern theories of the physicists who incorporate all the patterns of supersessive local and empirical times in a single, inclusive space-time order, in which all time's local, ordinal properties are preserved, but their local supersessiveness done away with. And it is also present in Husserl's marvellous de-lineation of the time-consciousness, where the form of time-experience is as invariant as its contents are always shifting. Time certainly has its Bergsonian aspects, of which no one was more clearly conscious than Kant, but he rightly held that these had to be supplemented by Eleatic-Platonic aspects of permanence, which yield the 'reality' of which the Bergsonian aspects are only the appearance.

Space is for Kant as essentially phenomenal as time, but for somewhat other reasons. It can only be an appearance, since its logico-metaphysical status is obscure. It is not a predicate, nor a relation of the things found in it, since its contents can be indefinitely varied and attenuated (*CPR*, A. 24). It is not, however, a substance or an underlying subject of predicates, since, when emptied of contents, it does not seem to differ from nothing (*CPR*, B. 70). It is also complex, without per-mitting resolution into simple parts, as each complex Thing-in-itself must of necessity do (*CPR*, A. 441). For the points we imagine as in space are rather its limits than its elements (*CPR*, A. 438, 440). And it is essentially continuous, infinite, and total, so that spaces are rather limitations carved out in it, than elements from which it is composed (*CPR*, A. 25); but yet, though thus continuous and total, we can never imagine the whole of it, but only more and more of it (*CPR*, A. 432). Such things are indeed possible if space is only how objects appear to us: they are not possible if space is either a Thing-in-itself, or a feature of Things-in-themselves. Space has further the logically queer property of differentiating things in which no intrinsic difference is discoverable: an indefinite number of quite similar things can be imagined, but not conceived, as existing outside of one another in space (*CPR*, A. 272). And there are, further, some sophisticated absurdities concerning the difference without difference of left-handed and right-handed symmetry, which, in Kant's view, establish the phenomenal character of space and also of time, since we saw that time must, to be conceived at all, be projected on to a line in space. These arguments, too, are more respectable than many moderns would allow. For space, with its mutual externality and distances of parts, obviously requires supplementation by unapparent factors that bridge its distances and that give it genuine continuity. In the equations of modern field-theory and the theorems of Gestalt psychology we are perhaps reaching towards the something more of which phenomena in space are the mere appearances.

And to all these impressive reasons for holding space and time to be phenomenal, Kant adds the further reason that there are a great many axiomatic principles which govern things in space and time, which are not logically necessary, since there is no plain contradiction in supposing them unsatisfied, but of which we can none the less not *imagine* an empirical counter-example. We cannot, for example, imagine a case of two straight lines enclosing a space, or of a number of lines parallel to a given straight line intersecting in a point, or of an event which came both before and after another event, and so on. If these are principles governing Things-in-themselves, it is not, Kant holds, understandable how we can be sure of them in advance of exhaustive experience of their cases; whereas if they rest only on the manner in which things appear to us, it is understandable how we can establish them by conducting imaginative experiments on our imaginations, which, since they are our own, can exhaustively assure us of the purely subjective necessity of such axioms. This argument, by far the feeblest in the Kantian armoury, but the most insisted on in the Introduction to the *Critique of Pure Reason*, has been found defective by many critics, and even Kant's contemporary, Crusius, saw that our imaginations might well have been so preformed by God or nature as to conform to the pre-existent patterns of reality (*CPR*, B. 167-8). And it is indeed strange that the thinker who held that we could never learn anything from experience without bringing to it general principles that were not learned from experience, should also have found it strange that such principles were not, after all, learned from experience, which would, on his own showing, have been unable to establish them. There is no presumption of subjectivity in the fact that we have to establish things in the only way in which they could have been established by us. An intuitive understanding, which could range over all the possible cases of certain concepts, would of course have done better, but there is no reason why our unlearned presumptions should not dimly prefigure its insights.

A stronger argument shows that the type of explanation, the causal, which we above all use with vast success in interpreting natural phenomena, is also such as to presuppose the existence of something which it is unable to offer us. For, explanations are nothing if they cannot be completed, if they do not terminate in something which is self-explanatory, and which points to the existence of *nothing* beyond itself. The self-explanatory is, however, such that it can never be given empirically. To achieve it, we should either have to have a total awareness of a single condition which, without prior conditions, existed of necessity, or the awareness of a condition which could spontaneously initiate a whole causal series, and which required no prior condition to provoke such initiation (*CPR*, A. 446). Causal explanation, as practised on phenomena, therefore demands a completion which transcends phenomena: if we are to dispense with such a completion, we can only be sure how things seem. It is because we live in a sphere where there are no phenomenal sum-totals, and no absolutely necessary or spontaneous phenomenal first conditions, that we necessarily inhabit a world of appearances, of which we can never know the real roots. Again we find the concept of the transcendentally real being used to show that the world about us is not thus real. The concept of the Transcendental Object is therefore negatively at work in all

Kant's characterizations of the experienced world as phenomenal. Without some definite idea of the logical character of what could be independently real, we should not be able to characterize our experienced world as being merely phenomenal. And if a phenomenal world is one whose essential presuppositions are necessarily unrepresented in it, then Kant has given quite good grounds for calling our empirical world merely phenomenal. It has to be thought of by us as containing much that it cannot in principle show us.

v

We now come to a final point in which Kant's philosophical genius is supremely apparent: his use of the *unknowability* of the Transcendental Object to explain how we can and do know what we know regarding the phenomenal realm. For, since the Transcendental Object can never, *qua* transcendent, be directly given to us, and since we can at best have a problematic concept of it, which will only enable us to treat it as if existent, and as if responsible for the compulsive, connective element in our experience, it has to be represented in experience by a number of purely phenomenal criteria, whose use is a built-in property of our own subjectivity, and which can perfectly do duty for it in an experience like our own. For something can only be as if something else existed, if it involves definite *marks* which link it logically to what is spoken of in this as-if fashion. And since temporal flux, and its irremediably supersessive, piecemeal character, is the main stigma of our phenomenal condition, it follows that the criteria which do duty for a noumenal presence in experience will all be connected with the piecemeal, supersessive character of time. Such is, indeed, the lesson of the Transcendental Deduction, of the Schematism of the Categories, and of the Analytic of Principles, all of which offer us phenomenal substitutes for the absent, but as-if, presence of the Transcendental Object. We shall deal with these Kantian treatments in a later chapter of the present book: here we can only expound their conclusions in a general manner.

Space, we may first say, with its lack of intrinsic succession, and the comprehensive togetherness of all it contains, may be regarded as the phenomenal stand-in for the interconnection and interdependence of noumenal entities, for their constituting a world at all, and this is why we have to imagine even temporal succession as a sort of fourth dimension to space. But, since we have no contact with the individual noumenal substances behind phenomena in space, they have to be represented to us by permanences of phenomenal character, associated with the only phenomenal substrate for such permanences, that is, definite regions in space. Such permanences of phenomenal character must in some cases be wholly generic and common to all phenomenal substances, for example, the laws of motion, in other cases more specific, and perhaps involving the lasting collocation of a great number of distinct characters. These regular associations, originally given in the instant 'translations' of the Productive Imagination from unknown noumenal texts, must be carried yet further by the Reproductive Imagination. It must acquire habits of perceptual and imaginative synthesis, which the understanding must carry yet further in its concepts, and their synthetic products will then do duty for the noumenal substrates which lie for ever beyond our knowledge. Phenomenally, we seem to do everything, simply because it is only what *we* do that *we* know.

The changing states of a phenomenal substance will, further, be attached to its permanent phenomenal characters in no random manner. They will have to develop in definite phenomenal circumstances according to a rule characteristic of the phenomenal substance in question, which rule is one of the phenomenal criteria for its being the sort of substance that it is. It will further be necessary that we shall be able to disentangle the changes in appearance due to different substantial agents, and in particular the omnipresent changes due to our own agency as experiencing subjects. This will only be possible if we can distinguish the rules followed by one phenomenal substance from those followed by another, and above all if we can distinguish the empirical sequences due to our own bodily movements, our own wishes, feelings, and imaginative habits, from those determined by the nature of phenomenal objects outside of us in space. If the sequence of states in the phenomenal environment were not determined by rules, such and such a state following uniformly upon such and such a state in the same or another phenomenal object, we should not be able to distinguish phenomenal objects from one another, nor from our own phenomenal subjectivity. We should not be able to say that this or that phenomenal change was merely due to the order in which *we* chose to consider, or had to consider, objects or parts of objects one after the other, but that in other cases the order of a sequence of phenomenal states was based on a relation in the objects themselves (see *CPR*, A. 201–2).

Phenomenal substances can, accordingly, only be discovered to have their own history in time, according as there are rules, distinct from those governing our own changes of interest, attention, and so on, which govern the sequence of their states, and gear them in with the similar changes of other substances. The phenomenal world is like some immense cocktail party, at which we and others are making our own contributions to the deafening clamour: it is only by qualities of voice, and coherence in what is said, that we can sort out distinct speakers and conversations, and give each its appropriate due. It is therefore only by a set of fixed rules of phenomenal persistence and succession that we can give time a filling of phenomenal substances, a succession of phenomenal states in each, and a relation of the states of one phenomenal substance to those of another. Without such a filling, phenomenal time would vanish into a mere flux of states in which nothing phenomenally objective or subjective could be discerned. There would, in fact, be no such thing as phenomenal time at all.

We must say, further, that phenomenal space likewise depends on something more than the glimpses of pattern which perception and imagination offer us: it depends on the rules which govern the phenomenal commerce of one phenomenal substance with another, and on our own subjective rules which enable us to vary the way in which phenomenal data are surveyed one after the other, thus revealing what is *objectively* coexistent about them. Rules in the collocation and succession of phenomenal characters are, therefore, the criteria through which we distinguish phenomenal substances — including ourselves *qua* phenomenal — from one another, and also determine such of their coexistences and successions as do not depend on ourselves or on what we do. It is further by considering the rules that we look for and follow in finding our own way about in the world, that we become aware of the higher activities of our own subjectivity, activities which Kant sums up in the word 'synthesis'. We become aware of our own activity in bringing phenomenal data to apprehension in a rule-obedient manner, in the extended bringing of them thus together in imagination, and in the conceptual unities which are the outcomes of all such syntheses (see *CPR*, A. 98–103). And we become aware of our own activity in trying to subordinate such conceptual outcomes to one another in the great edifice of reason. In such a consciousness we also learn to distinguish between the rules which are logical and aim at knowledge, and those which are merely personal and associative. Our own phenomenal subjectivity, and also our own transcendental subjectivity, are therefore only known to, or thought of, by us, to the extent that they are seen as at work in the structuring and arrangement of our concepts, and they are therefore throughout dependent on the phenomena and the rules which constitute and integrate them.

It might be thought at this point that transcendental objectivity and transcendental subjectivity could be altogether dispensed with, and that all that are required are their phenomenal surrogates, and particularly the synthetic activities through which objects are pinned down and identified. This is in fact the line taken by the many forms of Neo-Kantianism and Neo-Hegelianism that have held the Thing-in-itself to be superfluous. But, as we have seen, the Transcendental Object expresses the element in experience which makes it compulsive and non-arbitrary, and which is not exhausted by the subjective forms postulated by Kant: it is the element of *control* in all our experience. To believe in unities, not themselves in flux, which underlie the flux of phenomena, and are revealed in its regularities, is really the same thing as believing that future phenomena will continue the pattern of previous ones, and expresses precisely the same confidence; for a chance regularity that might be interrupted at any moment is really no regularity at all.

We have so far merely attempted to gather together the various strands of Kantian doctrine and to consider them all from the standpoint of a single conception: that of the Transcendental Object, or Noumenon, or Thing-in-itself. It is our view that, considered in the light of this conception, the strands of Kant's doctrine form a coherent fabric, and that only a very few of his utterances have to be treated as ill knit or aberrant. There is a great deal of brash writing in the *Critique of Pure Reason*, and an exaggerated repudiation of the magnificent metaphysical tradition in which Kant grew up, and which is really always in the background of his thought. But this brash writing has been greatly admired by many, particularly in recent times, and has been given a false importance which a careful study of Kant will dispel. We shall seek to dispel it in the chapter-and-verse examination of Kant's doctrine which will follow: we have avoided this in an introduction. It is our concern to show that Kant's radical form of phenomenalism has much more to be said for it than has been usually supposed: it is a uniquely illuminating, inspiring form of problematic realism. But it is not our concern to argue that there are not serious objections, and many interesting alternatives, to an approach so radical. Kant's reasons for holding being in space and time to involve many profound inconceivabilities, which demand their relegation to appearance, are far from cogent; possibly we must follow the moderns and try to see what is wrong with some of our conceptual approaches rather than with spatio-temporal appearances. But possibly also Kant's basic mistake was in drawing too firm a line between how things are and how they appear. Perhaps, as some of his utterances suggest, there is a continuous spectrum from appearances which depart far from the reality of Things-in-themselves to appearances in which Things-in-themselves declare themselves more adequately. If the deliverances of sense and their spatio-temporal framework lie at the one end of this spectrum, the awareness of ourselves as agents, and of our own practical and intellectual spontaneity, may lie near the other. And though we can have no knowledge of the kingdom of ends in which all our moral endeavours terminate, nor of the architectonic reason which presides over it and holds it together, our faith in it may not be so remote from being an intuitive vision of it as Kant takes it to be. These points will, however, concern us later, and then only marginally. Our main concern will be to interpret a great philosopher in terms of his own central conceptions.

Chapter II

The Historical Background of Kant's Critical Teaching

i

We shall, in the present chapter, which is not concerned with details of history, give a brief account of three major influences which shaped Kant's opinions, which provided the background from which he dissented, and which he in great part transposed and restructured. The influences we shall consider are those of Leibniz, of Christian Wolff, and of Christian August Crusius. (We shall not consider Baumgarten, a very compressed, derivative writer, even though Kant, limited by the prescriptions of the Prussian Ministry of Education, regularly based his metaphysical lectures on his dull treatises.) Wolff and Crusius were only two among the large number of contributors to the steady stream of metaphysical thought, all originating in Leibniz, that flowed through the German universities in the eighteenth century, and which was, in its way, as valuable and as interesting a scholasticism as any that had its source in Aristotle. Christian Wolff, now vastly neglected, can in fact be regarded as an eighteenth-century German Aquinas, of much the same stature and originality as his great predecessor. This eighteenth-century scholasticism was, however, short-lived, and Kant himself, with his intemperate criticisms of the 'old metaphysics', was largely responsible for its early demise. But it was, as a scholasticism, immensely respectable, and an age which values formalism and formalization should not conceive too meanly of it. There is often as much profundity in the would-be exactitudes and trivializing demonstrations of Christian Wolff as in the argumentations of such moderns as have set up axioms for 'tense-logic', or for 'possible worlds', or suchlike. Kant himself disowned all that he had written prior to his major critical writings, but this very disowning shows the extent of his debt to the thinkers that had shaped his thought. It was in fact because spatio-temporal experience, now central in the new critical dispensation, failed to live up to the conceptual demands of the old metaphysics, that such experience had to be regarded as merely phenomenal: the concepts of elementary simplicity, of substantial unity, of absolute necessity, of sufficient ground, and so on, that the old metaphysicians had used so confidently, had no application to such experience, and it was the sheer impossibility of such application that forced Kant to relegate our experience and knowledge to the merely phenomenal, and to seek phenomenal replacements for the old metaphysical categories. The old metaphysics, with its characteristic presumptions and methods, therefore retained its dominance over the new phenomenal picture: it told us what things *would* be like if we could only know them as they were in themselves, and it therefore also established that we cannot so know them, and that we must therefore rest content with such phenomenal surrogates as we can and do actually apply empirically.

It is usual to suppose that the British empiricists, and particularly Hume, were very great influences in the development of Kant's thought, and that he in a sense reconciled their empiricism with the rationalism of the continental tradition. Such at least is the well-established story regarding these matters. It is clear, however, that Kant's acquaintance with the British empiricists was at many points indirect and inaccurate, and that, in the case of some such as Berkeley, it was wholly wide of the mark. The voice of Hume, whether original or quoted, was said by Kant to have awakened him from his dogmatic slumbers, but it seems reasonable to hold that he was already well on the way to such an awakening when that voice was distantly heard. What the voice communicated to Kant was not, further, the psychologistic view of causal connection as due to mental habit, but the fact that this was all that could be laid hold of at the phenomenal level, and that to understand why we had to think causally we should have to penetrate to deep structures that underlie appearances, whether in ourselves or beyond ourselves, and which make certain connections among appearances unavoidable. In the same way, the immensely persuasive voice of Newton, which Kant had listened to attentively when he wrote the *General Natural History and Theory of the Heavens* in 1755, and later the *Metaphysical Fundamentals of Natural Science* in 1786, was not to convince him of the absoluteness of space and

time, or of the mechanistic determinism which governed events
in them, but rather to make him seek out the deep grounds for
such absoluteness and rigorous determinism at one level, while
also finding grounds for reinterpreting these deep grounds at
a deeper level. Kant's attitude to both philosophical and scientific
empiricism was thus anything but deferential: it urged him to
show how such learning from experience was possible, but in
terms of structures that transcended experience — that, for
example, of the transcendental, self-referring subject — and
whose existence and manner of working could not therefore
be learned from experience. Kant cannot, therefore, be said
to have been influenced by empiricism as he was influenced
by metaphysical rationalism. But he so developed the latter
that it wholly transformed and absorbed whatever was empirical,
while transforming itself in the process.

The influence of Leibniz on Kant, mainly mediated by
Christian Wolff, was of course immense: all of Kant's distinctions — that of the *a priori* and the *a posteriori*, that of
the *a priori* analytic and the *a priori* synthetic, that of the
phenomenal and the noumenal, that of the true unity of the
subject and the merely derivative unity of other things, that
of what ineluctably *must* be and that of what, less ineluctably,
only *ought* to be, or is morally necessary — all these distinctions
are to be found less clearly in Leibniz, though Kant has given
them other names and somewhat sharper, more extreme de-
lineations. Leibniz was, of course, one of the supreme, constructive geniuses of philosophy, even if he chose to hide his
light under a bushel of courtly charm, in the writing of a large
number of letters and special treatises for private individuals,
or in producing treatises of an edifying or relatively superficial
sort for second-rate intelligences. For our purposes, which also
involve the impact of his brilliant *persona* on the thought of
Kant, one of Leibniz's most important contributions was his
illumination of modal concepts, and his view of possibilities
as being, in their exhaustiveness and their permanence, in a
sense more actual than actualities. What they are the possibilities of, may not be actual, but, *qua* possibilities, they are
actual, and more so than their inconstant actualizations. No
one before him had made God do a preliminary survey of all
logically possible worlds, before deciding on which, among all
of them, he would realize. He was also original in his extension
of possibilities to the whole nature of concrete substances, each

of which would include everything that it would do or suffer in the whole of its history, so that time merely spelled out what was contained in the comprehensive possibility which was that individual's idea or essence, and we should, in his view, have a totally different individual if he, or the world to which he was related, were different. All these views are reflected in the constructions which Kant used to compass the all-reality and all-possibility of God, and also of the timeless being of the noumenal self, which, in one act, determines the whole life which it has to live out phenomenally in time. The Leibnizian stress on the possible is also mirrored in Kant's perennial enquiries into the *possibility* of this or that, of experience in general, of geometrical certainties, of applying categories to *sensibilia*, of moral freedom, and so forth. In all such cases he thinks in terms of permanent structures in which inconstant items are to be given a place, or in terms of which they are to be understood.

Original and important was also Leibniz's view that an individual substantial essence must be a *true unity*, profoundly simple despite a vast number of predicates and relational properties. Such an essence cannot have parts alongside of parts in the manner of extended unities: its true complexity must all be internal to it. This means that all relations that are really parts of its nature are relational properties: they do not import their *relata* into the unity of what has such relational properties, as this would involve breaking up and destroying the latter. We are, Leibniz thinks, directly acquainted with one such case of relativity without *relata* in the representations of conscious life: we can represent extended and divisible things to ourselves without thereby becoming extended and divisible, or in any way sacrificing or reducing our conscious simplicity. This will further enable us to conceive analogically not only of other fully conscious beings like ourselves, but also of beings having perhaps only a reduced form of the clear consciousness and self-consciousness that we enjoy. There may be simple substances other than ourselves which, after a fashion, represent divisible and extended things, without such representation being clearly conscious or self-conscious: a multiplicity of matters may be *there* for such simple substances in some dim or analogical fashion which does not amount to conscious recognition. The logical essence of what we call 'representation' is in fact, we may suggest, no more than the specific relationality without necessarily existent *relata* of which representation is a specific form, and there well may be other cases of such relationality which are quite unlike the case that we call 'consciously representative'. From the Leibnizian point of view of substantial simplicity, it at once follows that, since the many things represented in a simple substance cannot literally be parts of it, their representation can amount to no more than their appearance to, or for, the substance in question. And any relational rapports among such simple substances must be essentially phenomenal or ideal; it is only *for* the simple substances that they and other simple substances are given as together or are thought of together. It is plain further that, in these basic conceptions of Leibniz, we have the plain foundations of the view of space as phenomenal, since space does in fact make all its parts coexist or exist together, and since space nowhere affords us a specimen of the true unities in regard to which division is unimaginable: everything in space falls apart from everything else, without leading us to truly separable unities incapable of falling apart, since points have no such separability, nor any representation of the areas around them.

It is plain, therefore, that Kant, brought up in a Leibnizian school, could not fail to come to believe in the phenomenal character of space, and, by a natural extension, of time also, since time's phenomenal vanishingness made it necessary for him to represent it spatially. And he could not fail to see interpretative syntheses, which give intelligibility and structure to the phenomenal world, as an exercise of our own intrinsic subjectivity, and not of anything external. And all this *without* thereby excluding the unknowable possibility or truth that such syntheses might in some unknowable fashion be the translation into a phenomenal, spatio-temporal idiom of rapports among their non-phenomenal sources that could be known only to their transcendent harmonizer, God. Leibniz further credited his simple substances with inherent powers or forces which led them to pass on from one representative condition to another, and which led to a phenomenal law that force, as a measurable, active phenomenon, was always conserved. Kant's later theory of matter as consisting of simple force-centres, holding each other off through repulsion, and holding together through a countervailing attraction, is thoroughly Leibnizian, and one might ask whether Leibniz and Kant had not truly dug down to the deep essence of matter, that it compels, that it pushes and pulls, that it is nothing more than the hard element, the stiffening in or behind phenomena.

The influence of Leibniz is also betrayed by the magisterial centrality of the thinking and apperceiving self in the doctrine of Kant, the self which carries about both the categories and the forms of intuition as *its own* structuring principles, of which it cannot but be certain, and which can only be conscious of itself as a unitary and unitive principle, in so far as it uses these forms and categories in phenomenal projections. Leibniz also, in the *Avant-propos* to his *Nouveaux Essais*, says that we are so to speak innate to ourselves, and that we find in *ourselves* being, unity, substance, duration, change, action, perception, and countless other objects of our intellectual ideas. And he compares our minds to a block of marble in which there are already a large number of 'veins' or virtual lines of rupture, which naturally and inevitably give rise to arrangements and alignments in which these categorial notions will have application. The mind is not monolithically uniform and void of original structure, as the empiricistic metaphor of the *tabula rasa* would suggest. And Leibniz also asserts, in the first chapter of the second book of the same work, that we must add to the dictum *Nihil est in intellectu quod non fuerit in sensu* the qualifying words *nisi ipse intellectus*. The mind brings *itself*, and its canons of intelligibility, to the empirical table, and is not entirely dependent on such pabulum as the table offers. This is of course precisely the doctrine of the Kantian *a priori*. It may in fact be argued that Leibniz had perhaps *too great* an influence on Kant in his attribution of functions to the Transcendental Subject, as is particularly evident in what are, by general consent, Kant's two worst-written treatments: the Transcendental Deductions of the Categories in Editions One and Two of the *Critique of Pure Reason*. For there it is almost forgotten by Kant that Transcendental Objects *also* have a hand in the possibility of experience, as well as the Transcendental Subject, that experience is not a free composition, but rather a translation into the diction of space and time of a text framed in another idiom: the fact that we know nothing of this original text, apart perhaps from its empty logical structure, nor of the manner in which it was translated, makes no difference to this fact. It is, in these treatments, also largely forgotten by Kant, that the transcendental self can on his own view be as little known to us as the Transcendental Object, and that there is therefore no reason why he should follow Leibniz in according any special prerogatives to it. These are, however, points which will concern us later when we examine the twisted arguments of the two Transcendental Deductions. The distinction of the *A Priori Analytic* and the *A Priori Synthetic*, so central in Kant's theory, also has its roots in the teaching of Leibniz, who regards the law of contradiction as the governing principle of all logical axioms and all analytic truths, whereas the principle of sufficient reason — that wherever there are alternative possibilities, there is always a sufficient reason why one such possibility is realized rather than any other — is the governing principle of all contingent truths of existence and circumstance. For God, who always has a good reason for everything that He creates or permits, and who no doubt sees this principle as involved in His own essence, the two principles may perhaps come into coincidence: for the human intelligence, however, they must always remain distinct. Plainly, the Kantian view on these points is a direct descendant of the Leibnizian, and both sorts of principles are by both thinkers made part of the structure of the thinking subject. And the possibility of experience which Kant makes so central in his validation of synthetic principles is also plainly rather more of a justifying *reason* than a compelling axiom or cause.

Leibniz further taught a large number of doctrines which are faithfully taken over by Kant, except that, for Kant, they are not anything that we can know about, only something that we can conceive of, and must believe in. Like Leibniz he believes in the existence of a supreme substance or God, who is simply the omnipossibility, dynamic and not merely quiescent, from which all finite, contingent existences are mere extracts. But while for Leibniz this ordered, dynamic omnipossibility is necessarily an actuality, since its concept involves no contradiction, and also covers *all* possibilities, and cannot therefore in *any* circumstance be conceived as unrealized, Kant in effect discovers an inner contradiction in it, in so far, at least, as phenomenal *knowledge* is concerned. For possibility, as a *phenomenally* relevant category, is essentially bound up with the empirically discoverable ways of things, and cannot be extended, or only in an empty manner, to cover everything that is logically conceivable. That something exists or is possible is always, in the epistemic sense, a synthetic truth, and cannot without absurdity be made to follow from a mere definition. Kant, however, believes, like Leibniz, that the concept of the all-possible, and so necessarily existent, being is without an internal logical flaw, and that it therefore corresponds to an object, though not to one of which we can have knowledge. And moral considerations also buttress this persuasion. These points will concern us later when we consider the relevant tracts in the *Critique of Pure Reason*.

The realization of one definite possibility of existence rather than another depends, however, for Leibniz, on considerations of goodness or value: he adopts from the *Phaedo* the axiom that the ultimate reason why anything exists or is the case must be that it is *best* for it to be so. The omnipossible, necessary being must therefore have chosen, out of all systems of existence and fact that are possible, the one that is also the *best*: Leibniz takes no trouble to establish, as he has taken trouble in the case of the omnipossible being, that there is no self-contradiction in such a requirement. Kant likewise believes in an order of ends as the unknown backing of the whole phenomenal world, and for him this order culminates in what he calls a 'kingdom of ends' consisting of all the rational, self-conscious members of the transcendental order, presided over by the divine reason itself: this kingdom is of course not different from the Leibnizian realm of grace. And, like Leibniz, Kant believes both in a mechanistic phenomenal world, governed at all points by rigorous natural laws, and a teleological, noumenal order among free subjects, who have, by their common source in the divine reason, been put into a pre-established harmony with one another. Whatever a man does is, according to both views, a consequence of internal and external laws and circumstances; but according to both views the man, through being just what he essentially is, also freely decides on each and all of his acts that he performs in time. The only difference between Leibniz and Kant, if there is a difference, is that Leibniz conceives, somewhat Calvinistically, that the Creator has programmed finite, contingent beings to have the nature and history that they have, whereas Kant rather holds that they have in some sense spontaneously programmed themselves in this timeless fashion, the Creator being only responsible for their existence.

Kant also frequently makes use of the principle of sufficient reason in a thoroughly Leibnizian manner. Thus he repudiates the possibility of there having been a wholly empty space and time before the beginning of the world, since this would afford no reason for expecting the world to begin at one point in space and time rather than another. But he also repudiates the principle in certain phenomenal cases. Thus there are, he holds, possible existences in space and time which differ *solo numero*, and are quite indiscernible in respect of their intrinsic properties. This piece of profound perception leads however to the Leibnizian conclusion that this fact is only yet another proof of the phenomenal character of space and time.

It will, however, astonish the critical reader to find how Leibnizian Kant is and remains even in discussions directed mainly to the criticism of Leibniz. Thus, in the important Appendix to the Transcendental Analytic (*CPR*, A. 260–89), which Kant calls *The Amphiboly of Concepts of Reflection*, he repeatedly rejects Leibnizian conclusions as applied to empirical phenomena, while affirming that they *would* have a correct application to Things-in-themselves, if only we had some acquaintance with the latter. Thus, he says (A. 264): 'Leibniz took the appearances for Things-in-themselves, and so for *intelligibilia*, i.e. objects of the understanding (although on account of the confused character of our representations of them, he still gave them the name of phenomena), and on that assumption his principle of the identity of indiscernibles (*Principium identitatis indiscernibilium*) *certainly could not be disputed*.' He likewise says (A. 265–6): 'In an object of the pure understanding, that only is inward which has no relation to anything different from itself. It is quite different with a *substantia phaenomenon* in space: its inner determinations are nothing but relations . . . As object of pure understanding, on the other hand, *every substance must have inner determinations and powers which pertain to its inner reality. But what inner accidents can I entertain in thought save only those which my inner sense presents to me? They must be something which is either itself a thinking or something analogous to a thinking*.' He also says (A. 267): 'Consequently, in the concept of the pure understanding, matter is prior to form, and for this reason Leibniz first assumed things (monads), and within them a power of representation, in order afterwards to found on this their outer relations, and the community of their states . . . This in fact *is how it would necessarily be* if the pure understanding could be directed immediately to objects, and if space and time were determinations of Things-in-themselves.' He likewise says (A. 441): 'Though it may be true that when a whole made up of substances is thought by the pure understanding alone, we must, prior to all composition of it, have what is simple, this does not hold of the total substantial phenomenon as an empirical intuition in space.' And he says in the *Metaphysical Foundations of Natural Science* (p. 507) that this priority of simplicity does not at all belong to the explication of natural appearances, but *'is a correct concept in so far as the world is regarded not as an object of the senses, but as a Thing-in-itself, as an object of the understanding which underlies the appearances of the senses'*. From all these passages it is plain that Kant *accepts* the Leibnizian principles that composites presuppose simples, that relations presuppose intrinsic properties, that form presupposes material, and that distinct simple substances must differ in their intrinsic properties. Space and time, and things in space and time, do not, however, conform to these ontological rules, and it is for *this* reason, among others (for example, our strange prescience regarding their ungiven cases) that they are to be regarded as phenomenal.

ii

We now turn, in more detailed fashion, to the work of Christian Wolff. This we shall shamelessly summarize, since it is so little known and so much deserves to be known, and since long hours spent reading it up in the British Museum Library deserve to be made useful to others. In Christian Wolff we have a Leibniz purged of poetry, but also purged of some exaggerated conceptions, for example, the drowsy or slumbering monads, and the phenomenal character of space. All is built into an immense, systematic exposition, magnificent in its formal rigour and clarity, and building on, though also improving, the ontological, cosmological, and theological doctrines of the Aristotelian schoolmen and, in particular, of Suarez. (The improvements are possibly due to Platonizing influences, which modified the ingrained love of the individual instance so characteristic of the Aristotelians.) Christian Wolff expounded his systematization both in a German version (the *Logic, Metaphysics, Ethics, Politics, Natural Theology*, etc.), and also in a Latin version (a *Logic* (1728), an *Ontology* (1730), a *Cosmology* (1731), a *Psychology* (1732 and 1734), a *Natural*

Theology (1736-7), and a *Universal Practical Philosophy* (1738-9)). There are also many political writings of interest. To this vast system, with its innumerable *Epigonoi* — Bilfinger, Meier, Rüdiger, Baumgarten, Tetens, Crusius, and so on — Kant made his great emendations, which have been exaggerated into the idealisms, and later the positivisms, by which the thought and even the public policy of Europe has been bemused. What is, however, amazing is the immense volume and solid merit of Wolff's works, and the almost total misunderstanding and neglect that has since enshrouded them, so that copies of Wolffian books are hardly to be found in libraries outside of Germany. Wolff, it is true, is heavy, repetitive, over-exact, and dull, but so are the works of such a latter-day compatriot as Rudolf Carnap: both formalized an embracing philosophical outlook, in the one case metaphysical, and in the other linguistic and semantic. We have reached a stage where formalization of talk about necessary beings, simple substances, sufficient reasons, and so forth presents itself as no less respectable than formalizations of talk about basic propositions, logical content, metalanguages, material modes of speech, and so on. It, in fact, presents itself as in some ways more respectable than the latter, since, while obsessive simplifications characterize both sorts of formalization, the obsessive element is more honestly revealed in the procedures of Wolff than in the poorly-stated arguments of Carnap. (Many later formalists than Carnap might of course be mentioned here, but we have no wish to be needlessly odious.) The logical form through which Wolff worked was of course the syllogism, but nothing has shown that any immense philosophical advantage has gone with the use of more elaborate symbolic techniques. (Without the latter we should at least have been spared one supreme piece of symbolic arrogance, that to be is no more than to be the value of a variable.) This chapter will not, however, attempt to rehabilitate Wolff in detail, but merely to make plain that his thought, like the thoughts of Leibniz, was very estimable, and that Kant's great innovations, though they may have illuminated the Wolffian structures from many new angles — like the *Son et Lumière* playing over Heidelberg castle — have not demolished them in the way that they are commonly thought to have done.

Wolff's *Ontology* begins (§27) with the assertion of the two laws of contradiction and sufficient reason, both fundamental to the assertion that something is, or that it is not. The former requires that what is must be free from inner conflict, the latter that, if it does not, like a necessary being, have a reason for being in its own nature, it must depend on such a reason in something other than itself. The law of causation, as we ordinarily understand it, is for Wolff only a special form of the law of sufficient reason, pertinent to temporal, changeable things and their states (§71). From these principles Wolff proceeds to the consideration of the metaphysical modalities, of which the most fundamental is the possible, the negation of the self-contradictory, or logically impossible. Everything actual, he holds, is by the law of contradiction possible, but he here embraces some invalid theorems, for instance, that a possible consequence can only have possible premises. Obviously, modal logic is still insecure, though Wolff's treatment of apagogic proof in §98 is of some interest. From Wolffian principles it follows that the notion of an entity not wholly determinate is 'imaginary', and that the indeterminate is only what is *for us* determinable, and that it will have to be determined by a sufficient reason (§§111, 117). There is no room in Wolffianism, any more than in Leibnizianism, for radical alternativity: Kant, however, will diverge from this position under the influence of Crusius.

All this leads, however, to Wolff's treatment of what he calls an entity: an entity is defined as any thing which *can* exist, to which existence is not repugnant. Thus warmth in this stone is a something, *an entity*, since a stone certainly *can* be warm or a warm stone can exist. There does not need to be any *actual* stone-warmth for us to have an entity before us. An entity is, however, rightly called fictitious or imaginary, if it lacks existence, which does not, however, make it less of an entity. These near-Meinongian positions are of great contemporary interest, and form the spring-board for much of Kant's later criticisms of the ontological proof, which is Wolffian enough to treat 100 possible dollars as if they certainly were *something*. Wolff goes on to draw the distinctions of essential features and attributes, on the one hand, which always must belong to an entity, and its modes, on the other hand, which are merely the characters that it *can* have and also can *not* have. Obviously, however, something must be added to possibility to raise it to full existence, and this Wolff is simply content to call the possibility-complement (§174). It rather resembles the modal moment of Meinong. He proposes to deal with this possibility-complement separately in his discussions of different spheres, for example, theology, cosmology, and psychology, since the intrinsically sufficient reason which makes God an actual existent is not at all like the extrinsically sufficient reason which underlies existence in the cosmological sphere. It is deeply characteristic, and deeply interesting, that Wolff should make actuality a mere enrichment of the possible, not the latter an impoverished abstraction from the former. The efforts of Wittgenstein, Carnap, Ryle, Quine, and so on have shown the hopelessness of trying to elucidate the possible in terms of the actual: the traditional priority may well prove more successful. Both tendencies are of course manifest in Kant's treatments of possibility, the 'modern' in, for example, the Postulates of Empirical Thought, and the Wolffian in many 'transcendental' contexts. Individuation does not, for Wolff, represent a going beyond the possible. It merely occurs where we have the complete determination which the logico-ontological laws require, and there are, accordingly, imaginary and fictitious as well as real ones. The latter may be far more determinate than any characters in fiction, but they will still lack a final nuance of determination. There are, likewise, incompletely determinate specific and generic properties of individuals, all of which must rank among imaginary entities, though some, connected with actual instances, will obviously be less imaginary than others. Wolff has here developed points which Meinong was later to develop in his doctrine of complete and incomplete objects, and there are also many anticipations of the modern theory of possible worlds.

Modal differences have their apex in the necessary, the possibility which represents the *only* possibility, whose contrary is accordingly impossible, and which contrasts with the contingent, which always involves the two-pronged possibility of being when one is not, and not being when one is. Wolff has the insight to hold that the possible is also the necessarily possible, and the impossible the necessarily impossible (§§286-7): he implies, but does not clearly say, that the necessary is also the necessarily necessary. Certain confusions also lead him to hold that whatever is, as long as it is, necessarily is (§280), though hypothetical necessity, which is dependent on the possibilities of sufficient reasons, is suitably distinguished from absolute necessity (§302). Contingent entities can never by their existence provide a sufficient reason for the existence of any of their members, nor is any series of contingent entities anything but a huge contingency. Spinoza might have read this with profit. The pathway to theology is therefore correctly prepared by Wolff in the very structuring of our modal notions, and is highly relevant to Kant's later treatments. At the end Wolff modestly claims that his notion of the necessary and the contingent conforms to ordinary usage — *communi usui loquendi conformis* — as well as to the received notions of philosophers (§§326-7).

The notion of order, so essential in abstract and empirical thought, is connected with a notion very prominent in Kantianism: the rule (§487). Dreams in which a person changes into someone else as one looks at him or vanishes altogether, or in which a hall in which people are assembled suddenly changes into a garden, are given as examples of disordered presentations: Wolff holds, as Kant was to hold later, that *all* experience cannot possibly be of this character. Truth then emerges as an *intrinsic* order among entities: *Veritas adeo quae rebus ipsis intelligitur, est ordo in varietate eorum quae enti conveniunt* (§495). The treatments of Suarez are here treated as fumbling and redundant. And perfection emerges when order takes the form of a *consensus*, when a great number of separate features or devices tend to a single outcome (§503). Perfection is in fact a higher-order regularity which presides over rules: it is much the same as the embracing hierarchy of genera and species which Kant was later to elaborate in his Appendix to the Transcendental Dialectic, and to see as the phenomenal expression of God's absolute perfection.

In the second half of Wolff's *Ontology* we deal with the notions of simple and composite entities which are so fundamental in Leibnizian thought. Wolff begins, somewhat surprisingly, with complex entities, whose essence consists in the manner in which their parts are put together: to have knowledge of such an essence is to know what sort of parts it consists of and how they are mutually conjoined (§534). We move in the territory of Russell's *Principles* and Wittgenstein's *Tractutus*. Complex entities permit of a coming into being when their elements are conjoined, and a passing away when their elements are disjoined, a sort of intelligible origin and extinction that is quite impossible for simples. Diversity of entities is however held to be impossible without that mutual externality that we call spatial: Wolff seems not to follow Leibniz in regarding space as merely confused or phenomenal. The notion of extension is that of a complex unity of numerous entities external to one another (§548): anything which is a complex of parts external to one another is necessarily extended (§550). In such extended entities, the parts have no differences except those of number: qualitative distinctions are irrelevant (§551). The continuity of the extended is explained in terms of the impossibility of inserting alien elements between their parts: in an interrupted entity, for example, a meditation, such insertions may be made (§555). Distance is defined in terms of a minimum possibility of intercalation, that is, it is the shortest line between two separated parts (§561). Wolff takes great pains to show that his conceptions of the extended, the continuous, and the distant do not differ from those in ordinary usage, and involve no horror of the distinct as such (§§567–8). Equally, we may add, they avoid the horror of the unified, which is characteristic of some modern analyses.

After space we have time, as the order of such determinations of entities as are essentially and continuously successive: apart from the entities whose essence deploys itself in this successive manner there would be no such thing as time (§§522–4), though an imaginary time, abstracted from actual entities, may be a useful conception (§577). Duration is a sort of extent of the continuously successive, and has, like spatial extent, its measure (§580): simple existence defines the present, while past and future are defined by the having been or being about to be of actual existence. Wolff solemnly tells us that *Nullum ne fingi quidem potest tempus quod non fit vel praesens, vel praeteritum, vel futurum* (§584), but he has no theory regarding the systematic, higher-order *change* in these modalities, so that what *has* been present becomes *past*, and what *has* been future present, nor has he a theory of absolutely initial states which *never* have been future, nor of absolutely terminal states which *never* will be past. Space and time are for him alike abstracted imaginary orders, a truth well understood by Leibniz, but hidden, Wolff holds, from the profoundly unmetaphysical mind (*rigoris metaphysicae minime tenax*) of a certain English writer on the Principles of Natural Philosophy whose name Wolff does not deign to mention, and who wrote, Wolff wrongly thinks, in his own tongue (§607).

Complex entities have so far been accepted by Wolff without

a Leibnizian reduction to appearances; their existence is, however, held to be impossible without that of partlessly simple entities, their ultimate components (§686), on which Leibnizian theory is also built, and which Kant will acknowledge as unknowably peopling the noumenal sphere. Of simple entities none of the properties of extended things can be predicated: they are indivisible, without figure or magnitude, incapable of occupying space, or of being in external or internal motion. They cannot arise out of composite things, and must therefore either exist immutably, and of necessity, or have the ultimate reason for their existence in something else which exists of necessity, that is, God (§689). If they arise or pass away, they must do so in an instant, and out of, or into, nothing (§§91-9). Simple entities are not, however, incapable of a number of distinct determinations, some coexistent and others successive, and some intrinsic while others involve extrinsic relationships (§706). Wolff gives the name of *subject* (not *substance*) to an entity conceived as having an essence, and as capable of internal and external modifications: to everything that can be attributed to such a subject he gives the name of an *adjunct* (§711). He claims that his definition is quite free from imaginary elements, for example, that of conceiving of a subject as some sort of receptacle in which predicates can be deposited (§712), such as have haunted the Aristotelian tradition.

Acting and suffering exist, in so far as the sufficient reasons for such changes are to be found in the essence of a subject-entity, or in that of some other subject-entity. But, behind all changeable, sufficient reasons must always lie certain more enduring, sufficient reasons, which will consist in the potencies of certain sorts of subject to act or suffer in certain ways (§§715-16). All this leads to a centrally important concept, that of a *vis* or active force. Such a *vis*, Wolff holds, was never properly understood by the Aristotelians, who failed to distinguish it from the merely potential (§761). But just as there is a possibility–complement necessary to raise the possible to the actual, so there has to be a dynamic–complement necessary to raise a mere potency for action to active power. This complement is covered by the name of *vis* or active force (§§721-2). We experience such a *vis* inwardly when we try to push something that resists our efforts: remove such resistance, and the *vis* in our effort would result in appropriate action, which would not result were the active force absent (§724). Active forces, unimpeded, will result in continuous changes (§729), which seems to mean that they may also continuously change their expression. At a given time, however, a single active force will produce only one single action. Propositions follow which concern the measurement of active forces, and their amenability to mathematical treatment: the imaginary, yet useful, character of an abstraction which reduces a single, intense active force to a number of equal, yet less intense, components is fully recognized.

All this leads up to the Wolffian conception of a substance, an entity which is both *perdurable* and *modifiable*. It has enduring sides to its active-passive nature, and sides which are essentially modifiable, and it is thereby distinguished from an accident, which is not modifiable, but can at best arise, last, and perish (§768). This conception of a substance as something inherently modifiable is held to accord better with ordinary notions, and to be freer from obscurities, than the Aristotelian notion of an underlying subsistence and the support of accidents (§771), which do not in any case differentiate between what is modifiable and what is not. The modifiable nature of a substance involves, however, that it is always the seat of active forces which, whether remaining within one substance or passing from one substance to another, will continuously change the states of substances, unless resistances prevent (§778). Composite substances can, however, have no essences and no inherent forces, but such as rest on those of their simple parts, which are, accordingly, the only genuine substances, so-called composite substances being merely aggregates (§§793–4). Simple substances are then either finite or infinite, and, in the former case, dispose of only a limited amount of active force, which, determined by present factors, whether intrinsic or extrinsic, and meeting with no resistances, will push the substance on through the whole repertoire of modifications of which it is capable (§849). Infinite simple substances, however, of which there can only be one, that is, God, dispose of an unlimited amount of active force; they are not pushed on from one realization to another, but are all that they can be, *tout d'un coup* (§838). But the unlimited power and freedom of God does not prevent us from speaking of Him analogically, as of one substance among others. We are obviously moving over Leibnizian territory, and over territory that will in later discussions be traversed by Kant. Leibnizian, too, is the treatment of the relations of simple substances as in some manner imaginary, mirroring in part, certainly, the impact of the active powers of substances on one another, but also our own conscious references of the one *to* the other (§§856-7). The intricacies of joint causation, proximate and remote causation, instrumental and auxiliary causation, and so forth, are all treated exhaustively.

Final causes are then held to be a species of causes which depend on the active nature of *intelligent* substances, and which operate through common causes as their efficient means. There is, he holds, an indissoluble logical nexus between willing an end and willing its efficient means (§941). And in the web of efficient and final causation, linguistic and other artificial signs are shown to play an important part (§§958-67). What Wolff's remarkable ontology shows is the immense explanatory value of the conception of a *limited* number of wholly *simple* substantial units, characterized by *fixed dynamic* natures in terms of which their interactions can be predicted. He has successfully substituted a dynamic monadology for the conscious monadology of Leibniz. Kant does not, in fact, in any way seek to modify this Wolffian machinery. He merely removes it from the purview of knowledge, and replaces it with phenomenal substitutes which work as if the unknowable machinery were operating behind them, and were in gear with the deep machinery of our own intuitive, conceptual, and explanatory subjectivity.

iii

We shall not attempt to follow Wolff through the applications of his ontology to cosmology: the latter had, of course, a profound influence on Kant's dynamic theory of the foundations of physics. The arguments by which Wolff arrives at the measure of active force, as the product of a body's mass and the square of its velocity, are of interest for the history of science, not for philosophy. What is of philosophical interest is his view that, not only are extension, and all the secondary qualities necessarily connected with it, purely phenomenal, but also the empirical forces and resistances used to explain them (*Cosmology*, §145). The nature of the forces present in the *simple* substances underlying empirical appearances, eludes us entirely; and whether they truly act, or only appear to act on one another, is something that we can never hope to say. But in natural philosophy, Wolff holds, it is not essential to be able to answer ultimate questions, nor would a knowledge of their answers change our phenomenal explanations one whit, only provide a more adequate basis for them (*Cosmology*, §294). Obviously Wolff is not far from the Kantian doctrine of the unknowable, necessarily thinkable, Noumenon or Object-in-itself.

There are also doctrines profoundly important for the understanding of Kant in Wolff's *Rational Psychology*. His definition of rational psychology as covering the essential *possibilities* (§§4-5), as well as the empirical actualities, of psychic life also ranges him among the predecessors of Husserl's phenomenology, as does his recognition of the intentional character of psychic activity, inasmuch as in all perceptions the psyche must distinguish what it perceives from itself *qua* perceiving subject. He also stresses that apperception of self-consciousness can only arise where there is a consciousness of change in our mental activity (§12), a very Kantian point, and when this consciousness is not obscure, but clear. Obscure perceptions, which fail to present their objects lucidly, also fail to present themselves lucidly (§19). Wolff therefore holds, as Kant was later to hold, that all clear consciousness of objects, and of their distinctions and relations, is also clear consciousness of subjective activity, and of the distinction of the former from the latter (§§21-2). The retention of past states of objectivity and of concurrent subjective acts is also essential to self-consciousness, as in the Kantian doctrine of synthesis (§§24-5).

Since all bodies are complex aggregates of simple substances, and since a psychic entity has nothing of aggregation about it, it is a simple substance and necessarily incorporeal (§§48-9); materialistic monisms which hold all substances to be corporeal are therefore refuted (§50). Psychic substances must, however, have this in common with the simple substances underlying material aggregates, that they are endowed with a force which enables them to change their state continuously: they will at one time feel, at another time imagine, at another time attend to their perceptions, at another time abstract, or reason, or desire, or wish (§61), and will represent the whole universe to themselves from the standpoint of their organized bodies (§§62-3), the sensations from which provide the necessary foundation for all their other psychic changes (§§62–8). All the possible modifications of the psyche have, therefore, their essence in a representative force directed upon the whole universe from a definite bodily centre (§69): whatever does not have its point of origin in such bodily representation must be miraculous or supernatural (§§70–1). But, despite its close involvement with the composite body, the psyche as a simple, representative substance is quite different from anything composite, and obeys its own essential and peculiar laws.

From the vastly ramifying Wolffian treatments of sensation, imagination, memory, attention, and intellect a few extracts will suffice. Sensations represent the composite in the simplicity of the representing subject, but Wolff is happily free from the Lockean and Kantian mistake which attributes all *composition* to that subject. Sensuous composition stems from the bodily composition that is being represented, not from the subject, which only brings it to a focus (§84). Representation, however, proceeds only to a certain point, and beyond that there is only confused representation of minute bodily structure: such confused representation may, however, be, as such, clear, as witness our clear awareness of distinctions of colour (§96). The sensuous idea of continuous extension, clear as it is for geometrical purposes, none the less represents relations of simples which altogether transcend sense-experience (§103). The geometrical properties of space are all imaginary representations of the underlying coexistences of basic simples (§§106–7). Inertia and resistance are based on the passive properties of elementary simples, but we have a confused representation of them in the sensuous experience of resistance (§108). The motor force of elementary simples reveals itself confusedly, on the other hand, in the awareness of trends which our own body resists, as when we hold a heavy body in our hand (§109). Wolff then traces perceived structures back to other structures discoverable in such bodily organs as the retina, and says much that is well observed and to the point, but no longer interesting.

From sensation Wolff proceeds to imagination and memory, the former being regarded, in Leibnizian fashion, as a very confused representation, arising according to fixed laws, of all the previous states of the psyche's bodily aggregate, and through this of the whole past of the universe (§§182–4). But he also extends the range of the imagination, more confusedly, to all the *future* states of the psyche's body and the concurrent states of the whole universe (§§185-93). We dispose, in fact, in confused form, of an infinitely extended awareness of *all* past and future states of the world, thereby revealing ourselves to be an image, though infinitely confused, of God's clear awareness of everything (§186). In these Leibnizian doctrines Wolff is believing, as the modern phenomenologists believe, that our experience is always of a single, total world, extending as a horizon beyond whatever local fragments sensation and perception manage to pick out. He does not proceed, in a desperate empirical fashion, to construct the whole experienced world out of sensational fragments. Kant, we may say, shows a confusedly divided allegiance, in his doctrine of the Productive and the Reproductive Imagination, to both Locke and Leibniz–Wolff: would that he had clung whole-heartedly to the latter. The theory of imagination is further buttressed by a theory of cerebral 'images', similar to those produced by actual sense-impacts in the past (§206); and the presence of imagination, as a supplement to sensation, is, in Kantian fashion, everywhere acknowledged (§232). Memory is seen as a particular exercise of imagination, involving either a clear or a confused recognition of something as having been previously experienced (§§279-81): the latter is immensely aided by the use of words. The syntheses of successive acts of meaning into a single, total, but indistinct, memory-act are admirably sketched, and Wolff stresses that such meaning-synthesis of words is far clearer than any visual or other non-verbal synthesis (§§287-8). He also holds that syntheses must have a neural representation (§291), concerning which he makes interesting suggestions.

The higher mental processes are all based by Wolff on the special activity of attention, which has the power to give clarity and prominence to parts of what is presented and to keep them longer in such clarity and existence (§374). Such selective clarity has, of course, its neural representation, and is also connected with the movements and positions of the sense-organs (§375). But attention, which raises anything to special clarity, will necessarily also turn away from other parts and aspects of what is presented (§377). The intellect, a power essential to the human psyche, begins to function when singulars are compared, and when their universal sorts or kinds are brought to clarity by attention, and are given fixity by means of names (§392). The consciousness of the universal is not directly represented by anything corporeal, but the words which accompany it must have a neural representation (§395). The coverage of a universal term will be fixed by definition, but a real as opposed to a nominal definition will select the real essence and attributes of some sort of entity. This real essence is of course not to be confused with that of the individual essences of the simples underlying what is thus defined: it is only a confused, general representation of their organized outcome (§401). Next, as regards syllogistic and other types of reasoning, Wolff does not hesitate to give them a neural representation which anticipates a computer-type mechanism (§§415-16), but will of course avoid materialism through his acceptance of the pre-established harmony. In all reasoning about the world, the principle of sufficient reason will play a central role, everywhere discovering the *general* reasons in virtue of which what happens to one entity chimes in with what happens to others. The justification for assuming that reasons are general, rather than wholly individual, is nowhere discussed by Wolff, but the simplicity of substances perhaps guarantees their uniformity of operation, while their derivation from a single, supreme substance will likewise guarantee the ordered affinity of their essences.

The conative-affective side of psychic life is rather summarily dealt with by Wolff (§§480-529), and will be the foundation of his moral theory. His doctrine is predominantly hedonistic: the psyche is by nature such as to tend towards what is clearly discerned as pleasurable, that is, good, and away from what is clearly discerned as unpleasurable, that is, evil (§521). Freedom of will is simply determination by clear ideas which *seem* to correspond to what will truly give pleasure or displeasure, and is therefore always determined by a sufficient reason. Such a reason may, however, differ from one psyche to another, owing to the differing individuality of its inclinations and satisfactions (§528). Freedom, in the sense of being able to decide *without* an overriding reason, has no place in the Wolffian theory.

Wolff's *Rational Psychology* must, however, be completed by a consideration of the possible relation between the psyche, or simple representative substance, and the aggregated mass of non-representative units which amount phenomenally to its body. Is the relation between psyche and its phenomenal bodily aggregate to be interpreted as involving a *direct physical influx*, in which a change of state in the one is a sufficient reason for a change of state in the other? Or does the relation demand a circuit through the infinite agency of God, and is it then a case of an ever recurring, occasionalist miracle on God's part, or of a harmony pre-established by God for all possible occasions (§553)? Wolff is clear that these hypotheses are only acceptable if their consequences agree with observation, but he also asserts that, whichever of such hypotheses we adopt, the phenomenal facts will always be as if the psyche and the bodily aggregate regularly influenced one another. Phenomenal correlation of psyche with bodily aggregate is a given matter of fact, and a necessary presupposition of any metaphysical hypothesis. The hypothesis of a direct physical influx will, however, involve something like a *transfer* of force from one substance or set of substances to another, and of such a transfer we can frame no notion whatever, not even a confused one, since all that we can ever observe is psychic change following upon a bodily change or vice versa (§573). Wolff, we may note, has not needed to read Hume to arrive at this essentially Humean position. But from a hypothesis which involves something of which we can form no notion we can proceed neither to a confident assertion nor a rejection (§§574-5). We are dealing with an 'occult quality', a thing abhorred since the time of Descartes (§582). And, quite apart from this surd element, the hypothesis will involve an addition to, or a subtraction from, the total amount of active force in the universe; which is contrary to the order of physical nature, since it treats a force, not as a necessary apanage of some substance, but as itself a quasi-substantial packet which can be passed from one substance to another (§§578-81). To speak of a physical influx between soul and body is, in fact, to employ empty expressions, without intelligible sense or use (§§554-5), and without empirical testability (§587), and hence devoid of even a vestige of probability (§588).

The system of occasional causes is more favourably considered, since the operation of an omnipotent deity is not something of which it can be said that we can form no concept whatever. Difficulty, however, arises if divine interference increases the amount of active force in the universe: it has been argued that it can, at most, be able to alter its direction, but even this, as has been shown by Huyghens, requires an increment of active force (595-7). And, even so, the theory violates the principle of sufficient reason, since there is nothing, whether

in the soul or the bodily aggregate, which can justify such divine
interference (§606). The hypothesis, while not empty, involves
a set of perpetually repeated, inadequately motivated miracles.
All these difficulties are however avoided, Wolff holds, by the
Leibnizian theory of pre-established harmony. Active forces
are accidents chained to the substances which they characterize,
and cannot migrate from one substance to another (§613).
But bodily mechanisms and mental purposes may accord with
one another *without* mutual influence, and everything in either
could have happened just as it does, independently of what
happened in the other (§618). Everything, in fact, will then
happen naturally and not supernaturally (§§622-3). The
hypothesis depends, of course, on acceptance of an omniscient,
omnipotent God, and is therefore not available to atheists or
sceptics (§§626-8). But it is not to be regarded, as Newton
and Clarke thought, as involving a perpetual miracle, since
a perpetual miracle would be really no miracle at all.

iv

We may turn finally to Christian Wolff's remarkable *Natural
Theology*, in which will be found the foundations of many
of the positions which Kant criticized, yet with his own reserva-
tions, also accepted. The work consists of two parts, the first
a posteriori, the second *a priori*: the former corresponds to
Kant's cosmological approach to the divine existence, the latter
to his ontological approach. In the *a posteriori* treatment
Wolff, like Descartes in one of his arguments, begins by assuming the existence of the human psyche. This existence requires
a sufficient reason, which must ultimately reside in a being
which carries its own reason for existing in itself, and is accordingly a necessary being, one that has aseity or self-existence.
The psyche must then either itself be such a self-existent being,
or must depend on one (§§24-8). The existence of such a
necessary being could only be ruled out if it were inherently
impossible: it involves, however, no inner contradiction, and
so, being possible, and also the only possibility, is also actual
and necessary (§34). (Wolff does not, of course, consider
the Kantian argument that existence, being extrinsically attached
to essence, can never be necessarily connected with it.) The
self-existent is then proved to be without origin or termination
(§§35-43), and also to be essentially incomposite and unextended: from this it is clear that the *mundus adspectabilis* or

given world cannot be self-existent (§50). But even the simple elements which underlie this world cannot be self-existent, for, since such a world is wholly determined by their inherent forces, it would itself then be self-existent, which has been shown to be absurd (§52). But the soul itself cannot be held to be an *ens a se* (§59), since it is essentially representative of the existent world, and shares in its essential contingency. The *ens a se* is therefore wholly other than this adspectable world or its non-adspectable constituents (§62). None the less it must be by considering what is required to explain the existence of the adspectable world and its constituents that the properties of the *ens a se* can be ascertained (§65).

The very important proposition (§66) is then proved that, since *one* self-existent being *suffices* to explain the contingent existence of the adspectable world and its non-adspectable constituents, there can be no sufficient reason for the existence of *more than one* such being, who accordingly must be given the religious name of God (§67). A plurality of independent, adspectable worlds springing from such a being can next be rejected, because there could be no sufficient reason for making them wholly alike, and, if not wholly alike, no sufficient reason for giving them such unlikeness when they have nothing to do with one another. But, since God must have had something like an intellectual vision of *all* possible worlds, and a free will to realize one of them rather than another, He must without doubt be describable as having something analogous to an intelligence and a will, and so being something analogous to a spiritual being (§§121–5).

The intelligence, power, and goodness of God are then argued for in several long sections, and their deep difference from *our* intelligence, power, and goodness fully emphasized. The divine intelligence surveys the existent world in all its plenitude of systematic detail, and it surveys every other possible world in the same plenitude of detail as our own (§§146–9). But though thus exhaustively visionary, God's simplicity will prevent Him from having anything like a body, and hence anything like sense or imagination (§§164, 157–8). Such an intelligence must be wholly incomprehensible to such as ourselves (§172). Its ideas will be wholly necessary and unconfused, but it will understand all forms and degrees of confusion in its ideas of human and other possible souls (§198). Its cognition will extend over both the intelligible and the sensible worlds, the

former being the whole ordered aggregation of simple substances which constitute the world as it *re vera* is, the latter
the complex of appearances proceeding from the former, and
represented in the confused perceptions of souls (§203). Of
all such intelligible and sensible possibilities the divine intelligence will have a simultaneous, distinct, and self-conscious
awareness which Christian Wolff describes as 'intuitive'. He will,
of course, in these doctrines be faintly echoed by Kant. And
the divine intelligence will further be aware of a whole *a priori*
world of rational conceptions which will apply in every possible
world: God will in short, among cther things, be the supreme
philosopher (§268). And His knowledge will further embrace
all the possibilities of rational or irrational error of which
fallible men have been, or might be, capable (§§307–10).

From the divine intelligence Wolff then proceeds to the
divine power and will. God can only will the possible, but since
every possibility stands opposed to a counter-possibility, mere
possibility can never be a sufficient reason for being willed by
God (§315). What alone can serve as a sufficient reason for
willing the realization of one world rather than another, can
only be its superior degree of perfection, which is defined as
its resolution of all particular reasons for this or that case of
succession or coexistence into one comprehensive, unitary
reason (§324). God accordingly, we may say, has chosen to
realize the most intricately coherent of worlds rather than
any other: such maximal perfection is unaffected by the im-
perfections of countless of its parts (§§326–7). And God has
chosen to realize this best of all possible worlds because He
ought to have done so (§334), but it is also the world which
pleases Him best (§330), and which He has freely willed without outer or inner compulsion (§§323, 351). Wolff is bound
to admit that this most perfect of all worlds is also necessarily
the seat of much physical, metaphysical, and moral evil
(§§373–6). The absence of such evil would, however, make a
world less intrinsically eligible than ours, and hence God could
have had no sufficient reason to realize it (§§377–8). But the
limitation of human vision and understanding necessarily
imparts an element of the inscrutable to God's choice of the
best (§398).

In the second part of Christian Wolff's *Natural Theology*,
the being and attributes of God receive a purely *a priori* demonstration. This treatment corresponds to what Kant called an

ontological, as the previous *a posteriori* treatment corresponds to his cosmological, approach. Wolff begins with a definition of the Leibnizian concept of compossibility, compossibles being properties which can belong *together* to a single subject (§1). The essentials, the attributes, and modes of every substance are necessarily compossible (§§2, 3), and a most perfect being is defined as one in which all *real compossibilia*, that is, not merely confused, phenomenal properties such as colour, are present in the highest degree (§6). Reality is, however, *itself* something which admits of distinct degrees: either it is contingent, and could itself possibly not exist, or it is necessary, and could not possibly not exist. The latter sort of reality has also a *higher* degree of existence than the former (§20). A perfect being will, however, combine all compossible real attributes in their very highest degree, and will therefore also exist necessarily. There is, however, nothing impossible in the notion of a being thus comprehensively real (§§12-13, 19), which will therefore include the higher grade of being, that is, necessary being, among its perfections (§§20-1). Such a being is therefore in the unique position of being actual and necessarily actual if it is merely possible. Wolff correctly sees that it is only if there is some internal logical flaw in the conception of an all-perfect, necessary being — a flaw such as Kant was later to try to establish, at least as regards the phenomenal sense of existence — that its reality would not follow from its mere possibility: it could not be possible if it were not also real, since there is no possibility that its reality does not cover. God, therefore, an all-perfect, necessary being, necessarily exists (§21), and exists in virtue of His sheer essence and possibility (§§27-8). Granted its premisses, this conclusion is valid: if necessity of existence is possible, then necessity of existence obtains.

The eternity, simplicity, immateriality, eminent substantiality, and supercosmic status of God are then demonstrated in a manner that we need not go into, and so also is His eminent representation of all possible worlds, of which Wolff now gives a second, alternative treatment. The point is made that God's knowledge of all the primary possibilities of being is simply part of His own self-knowledge (§89), and that the secondary possibilities realized in finite things are merely limitations of what is contained in that self-knowledge (§§91, 102). This is the sort of reconciliation of transcendent theism with immanent pantheism which is also to be found in Aquinas. The essences of finite things are then all the compossible combinations of the limitations of the unlimited possibilities comprised in God's nature and self-knowledge (§94). To this, however, the principle of sufficient reason adds the demand that all such finite essences must be linked, as regards their possibility, with the possible realization of other finite essences which will serve as their hypothetically necessary pre-conditions (§95). What God can realize is therefore not only an internally self-consistent, but also a positively coherent and profoundly interdependent world of finite essences, whose unlimited forms all enter as aspects into His own essence (§96).

The eminent peculiarities of God's intelligence are then considered at vast length, and not very differently from what we had before. It is not very interesting to consider the analogical manner in which God can be said to have eyes, ears, a memory, and so forth. A long consideration is also given to the peculiarities of divine volition, which repeats most of what was previously established. We learn, among other things, that God is supremely pleased with Himself (§203), that He is never troubled or bored (§205), is only affected by the unconfused notion of the good (§213), and is deeply concerned for the felicity of finite beings such as men (§234), and that compassion, hatred, anger, and so on can in an analogical manner be attributed to Him, but not vacillation, shame, terror, hilarity, and so on.

We then pass on to consider creation, the bringing into being of contingent existences, whose properties are all limitations of the divine properties. Such creation is necessarily limited to simples, since, given simples, everything aggregated and derivative follows (§313); a different world would only be possible, if *all* its constituent simples were different (§322). There are no trans-world existences in the Wolffian unlike the Kripkean ontology. The intelligible world is simply the idea of all these simple essences as contained in the infinite intellect of God, and all consistent by virtue of the principle of contradiction, and all interlocking by virtue of the principle of sufficient reason. God was logically capable of not creating the simple substances underlying our present world (§355), but such creation had its sufficient reason in God's essence and attributes (§362). It was a good thing, in fact the best thing, to do, and so it behoved God to do it (§361).

Christian Wolff in fact reaches the Spinozistic conclusion that God could not have created the world otherwise than He has in fact created it, nor had He any wish to do so (§376).

v

We have dealt inadequately with the valuable, vastly under-valued scholastic system of Christian Wolff as providing the framework within which Kant developed his critical opinions. The doctrine of simple substances behind phenomena, of whose character and energies knowledge is impossible, the doctrine of the phenomenal character of space, and in some aspects of time, the reference of all contingently existent substances to an all-real, necessary being, of whom nothing like phenomenal knowledge and existence can be predicated: these and many other doctrinal points are part of the heritage within which Kant matured his critical doctrine, and which he continued to use in his quest for phenomenal substitutes and representatives of what he no longer believed we could know.

We now pass from Christian Wolff to his more profoundly neglected but brilliant successor, Christian August Crusius, whose criticism of the Wolffian foundations had a great influence on Kant. Kant described him, in a public dissertation given in 1755, as *acutissimus Crusius, quem inter Germaniae non dicam philosophos, sed philosophiae promotores profiteor vix cuiquam secundum*, and from whom he certainly took over certain important positions. The notion of certainties that were universal and necessary without being analytic, the connection of these with the structure and make-up of the investigating mind, the criticism of the principle of sufficient reason as providing a complete answer to most philosophical questions: all these and other points influenced Kant's thought profoundly, and it would have been well if at certain points, for example, the preformation epistemology, he had followed the lead of Crusius, instead of moving in directions that some-times savour of gratuitously constructive subjectivism. The most important works of Crusius are the *Entwurf der not-wendigen Vernunftwahrheiten* (*Sketch of the Necessary Truths of Reason*) of 1745, and the *Weg zur Gewissheit und Zuver-lässigkeit der menschlichen Erkenntnis* (*Way to the Certainty and Reliability of Human Knowledge*) of 1747. We shall briefly sketch the main points made in the former.

The *Entwurf* consists of four subordinate treatises, one on ontology, one on natural theology, one on cosmology, and one on pneumatology (Crusius's name for rational psychology). The ontology begins with the assertion that there are two species of truths, necessary and contingent, and that metaphysics is entirely concerned with the necessary species (§1). Such necessity is to be conceived not relatively to anyone's knowledge, but absolutely: the necessary truths of metaphysics must be truths in *any* possible world (§2). The concepts to which metaphysics must dig down, and which it must seek to combine in necessary truths, must, further, be the simple, absolutely basic concepts which are involved in *any* dealing with *anything* whatsoever, and must be as much present in utterly familiar and common material as in what is most elaborate and rare (§9).

From these reflections Crusius proceeds to consider the nature of a thing (*Ding*) as such, and distinguishes between things in a wide sense, as being anything of which we can think at all, and things in a narrower sense as being only such things in the wider sense as also have a being outside of our thought, and are such as we think them (§11). Things in the wide sense, however, assert themselves into the two species of possible and impossible things, the latter being frequently called unthings (*Undinge*). The criterion of the possible thing is that it can on some reflection be thought, whereas the unthing or impossible thing cannot on reflection be thought (§12). A thing involving a contradiction cannot be thought, but there are also things which involve no contradiction, and yet cannot be thought of or be, and there are things which combine properties which can, without contradiction, be separated, though their separation can neither be thought of nor be. The law of contradiction is *not* therefore the sole arbiter of the possible and the impossible: there are *impossibilia* which are not self-contradictory, and there are necessities whose negations are not self-contradictory (§14). In this important section Crusius is recognizing the existence of what Kant was later to call *a priori* synthetic truths. But in all such cases it is, for Crusius, our ability or inability to think certain propositions which determines their modal status (§15). Crusius further gives a psychologistic account of reality (*Wirklichkeit*) and connects it with sensation: the real is what some sensation, whether external or internal, compels us to think. This doctrine has left its trace in Kant, for example, in his Postulates of Empirical Thought. Crusius further distinguishes between *complete things* which require nothing beyond themselves in order to be, and *incomplete*, that is, abstracted *things*, which, though they may be real, require something beyond themselves in order to be, and which can only exist as properties, or in the setting, of something else (§18).

From the general notion of things, Crusius passes to consider their essence and their existence. The former consists, in a wide, metaphysical sense, of everything that has to be thought in the case of a thing, and that distinguishes it from other things (§19). In this wide sense of essence, many determinations are included, for which others might have been substituted, and a complete thing is of course fully determined in every respect, positive or negative. All positive determinations involve, however, an aspect of *power* which may be that of the thing itself, or which may spring from other things (§29). This leads on to a Crusian version of the principle of sufficient reason: that everything that at some time begins to have a property it did not have before, must necessarily owe this to the operative power of some other thing (§31), which is the real ground of this property. This principle is justified, not by any appeal to the principle of contradiction, which Crusius regards as empty, but by our inability to dispense with it in our thinking, though we may no doubt *try* to do so. But he refuses to hold that such a real ground is to be identified with an ideal or epistemic ground which will enable us to *know* what a thing will be like determinately. Crusius further holds that real grounds may be to some extent indeterminate in their working (§38), a conception that Kant was later to adopt in his notion of noumenal spontaneity. The necessary and contingent properties of a thing are distinguished by Crusius in the usual manner, and the former called the *Grundwesen* or basic essence of the thing: this is a narrower concept than its metaphysical essence, which, in Leibnizian fashion, includes *all* its accidental and relational properties.

From essence Crusius passes to existence, which he connects with position in space and time: a thing thought of, or essentially possible, will exist if it has a place *somewhere* and occurs *at a definite time* (§47). Crusius resists the objection that there is a covert circle in this definition, in that a thing which exists must be acknowledged to *be* somewhere or somewhen: he argues that being is a wider concept than existence, and that it includes essential or possible being and being for thought. To these, existence only adds a definite location in space and time. Crusius does not consider the difficulties raised by things which have only a *fictitious* position in space and time, for example, some characters in Sir Walter Scott's novels. But his view of the connection of space and time with all we can know or think to be phenomenally real or existent, is, of course, also the doctrine of Kant. Space, Crusius further argues, is not a property or relation inhering in existing things or substances: it is rather a basic something in which things or substances must inhere in order to exist at all (§49). The connection between real existence and spatial location is, moreover, *not* a trivial matter of definition: we can indeed distinguish existence from spatial location, but we cannot seriously think of the former without connecting it with the latter (§50). Crusius rejects the Leibnizian objection to space, as being neither a substance nor a property: his answer is that it exists in the sense of being an abstract aspect of existence, of which the substantial and the attributive are necessary aspects. Space is indeed no separate, complete thing, but it necessarily enters into every separate, complete thing, and God must everywhere occupy it, whether finite substances occupy it or not. Such divine occupation need not imply extension in the occupier, since extension only applies to divisible, complex substances (§51). Crusius's doctrine of time resembles his doctrine of space: time is not a substance; it is only an incomplete, but necessary, ingredient in whatever really exists (§54), and a substance can only really have properties if it has them at some time or other. But God, an eternal substance, must exist invariantly at all times, as He must at all places (§55).

After thus connecting existence with space and time, Crusius goes on to consider the conception of a real or causal ground, which he refuses to confuse with an epistemic or ideal ground which has no necessary connection with causation. If a thing begins at some time to manifest a property that it did not previously manifest, we have to connect this in thought with the active *power* of some other thing. Such a power can be either actually operative or *living*, or merely potential and inoperative. All this has to be thought, not by virtue of the empty principle of contradiction, but by virtue of a necessity of thought which compels us to connect ideas in a certain manner, even though it would not be self-contradictory not to connect them thus (§31). What is here extremely interesting is Crusius's view that a real ground may not serve us as a predictive, epistemic ground, because it may be such as to be capable of operating in alternative directions, without requiring any additional factor to determine in which of these it will operate. This particular sort of real ground is only to be found in exercises of rational freedom, and not in those of unconscious nature. But it remains perfectly intelligible and possible none the less, and we have a sufficient ground when we attribute a man's choice of A rather than B to his use of freedom, even though we then have no determining or epistemic ground. When we know that a man freely chose to do A rather than B, though he *could* have chosen either, we have an entirely adequate explanation of his action, which imports lucidity, not confusion, into our view of the world (see §§38, 82-3). This very illuminating conception of the spontaneous as a species, and not a violation, of causality, is of course one that Kant employed in his conception of noumenal freedom, even though the conceptual terror inspired in him by Newtonian physics made it impossible for him to hold to it in his conceptions of phenomenal nature.

After an interesting treatment (ch. VI), of unity, combination, diversity, and identity, Crusius goes on to the concept so important in the Leibnizian tradition, that of simplicity. Simplicity is defined, not as the absence of parts distinguishable in thought, which everything has and must have, but of parts separable in reality (§105). It is held to be evident that separability of parts goes together with extension, and vice versa (§108). And it is also taken as axiomatic that, wherever there are complex things, there necessarily are simple things which are their ultimate parts, and from whose powers all the powers of the complex things must be derived (§111). Such ultimate simples are not, however, to be identified with mathematical points, which are unreal abstractions: their simplicity is rather to be seen in the indivisibility of their powers (§116), which is not incompatible with their pervasion of a finite region, or their possession of distinct sides (§117). Obviously, Crusius is working towards the idea of dynamic atoms, each holding sway over a definite territory, a notion to which many other philosophers, including Kant, have argued.

Chapter VIII of Crusius's Ontology deals with the concepts of the necessary and the contingent, as applying to existence and to the possession of properties. Something is held to be necessary when it is, or is the case, and when there could not be anything that could make it not be, or not be the case, whereas it is contingent if it depends on causes that might have operated differently (§121). This account does not of course escape circularity. But we can also define the necessary and the contingent psychologically, and say that something is necessary if its negation *cannot be thought*, and contingent if its negation *can be thought*. (The circularity is here very evident.) It is held to be important to distinguish unconditional necessity from conditioned or hypothetical necessity (§125), and Crusius, like Kant, applies the concept of the hypothetically necessary where the absolute freedom of an initial decision still leaves all its hypothetically necessary consequences quite open (§126). He holds it to be axiomatically true, as Kant was to argue in the Thesis of his Third Antinomy, that states of affairs which have a merely hypothetical necessity must go back to acts of freedom which are without absolute necessity, though they are exercises of causality, and so provide sufficient reasons for what issues from them (§129). The *simplicity* of God, taken as a being that exists with absolute necessity, is held to be evident, since only a simple being can be independent of any coming together of prior parts (§130).

The Ontology ends with a discussion of perfection, which is measured dynamically by the sum total of the effects which a thing *can* produce, or, what is the same, by the sum total of the positive reality that can be ascribed to it (§180). This sum total may be finite or infinite, and it may or may not be relative to the thing's essential capacities. A thing may be perfect of its kind, and yet imperfect relatively to a larger or to an infinite capacity (§142). Crusius is well aware of the difficulties involved in determining what the essential capacities of a thing are, and when it can be said to be exercising them perfectly: he holds, however, that we can, by a careful study of the observable structure and behaviour of things, frame reliable judgements as to the degree to which they are being perfectly or imperfectly actual or active (§183). And he believes that rational theology and ethics are sufficiently clear to enable us to state the ends in terms of which human and divine perfection can be determined.

vi

The Ontology leads on to a Theology which is not of particular originality or interest: the most important sections are those dealing with arguments in support of the divine existence. Crusius is here somewhat inconsistent, for, while he has been willing at one point (§137), to deduce the divine existence ontologically from the mere notion of a perfect being, he at a later point turns his back on all such approaches, and holds it to be impossible to argue to the divine existence from anything but God's *putative works* (§235). The ontological proof, he holds, confuses a being merely entertained in thought with a real being independent of thinking, and tries to argue from the former to the latter. Of theistic arguments based on putative works an endless number are possible, some demonstrative, some practically demonstrative, some only of finite probability. *All* of these arguments should be canvassed, since even a strict demonstration need not always be experienced as cogent, and since there are apparent as well as genuine cogencies (§207). Of such arguments Crusius gives as an instance one that argues from the contingent existence of the vastly many *simple* substances, which must underlie all natural being, to the existence of a sufficient cause, which will have to be both simple and also necessary, that is, God (§209). A similar argument bases itself on the whole series of changes of which the world consists, and which necessarily point to a first, spontaneously active cause without whose freedom there would be no sufficient cause for the total series (§213). Crusius rings the changes on similar arguments from the contingency of the cosmos as a whole (§217), from the preservation of species (§218), and from the continued existence of individuals, of which we ourselves are the most poignant instance. In all these cases Crusius appeals to necessities of thought which are not guaranteed by the law of contradiction. Tacitly he assumes the pre-Reformation principle which Kant is later to question: that what we are unable to think is also what cannot be, or that the structure of our minds must be accommodated to the structure of the real.

From Theology Crusius proceeds to Cosmology, the doctrine of the essential properties of Worlds (§347). He admits the basic difficulties of the enterprise, since we cannot be sure that certain things found in our world belong to its necessary or to its contingent structure, for example, the presence of light and colours, of animals, and so on; and so will, or will not be found, in every possible world (§348). The law of contradiction alone will not decide such questions: we have also to determine carefully what we can and cannot think. Modern possible-worlds logic experiences similar difficulties. Crusius thinks that the following are at least some necessary properties of any and every world: (a) that the existence of a world is contingent, and not, like that of God, necessary; (b) that a world cannot consist of a single individual creature; (c) that a world must necessarily combine and unify the things that are in it, and do so in a real, and not merely ideal, manner; (d) that a world must be comprehensive, and not merely part of some more comprehensive unity. This does not, he argues, exclude the possibility that there might be a plurality of real worlds, whose contents would have only an ideal relation to one another in the thinking of God (§349).

Crusius's principle of contingency excludes the possibility that a world, being contingent, could always have existed. Every world must therefore have had its beginning in an act of creation, before which there was no such world at all (§351). The notion of an eternal, but contingent world, is regarded by Crusius as self-contradictory. Every world must likewise be kept in being at all times by an act of divine preservation (§352). Every world must also comprehend a finite number of simple components and be spatially finite: the mathematically infinite and infinitesmal can have only an ideal, not a real being (§353). Every world must also have a final end, to which everything else is subsidiary, and this must be the existence, in a real space and time, of a class of free, rational creatures (§354). The identity of a world depends, further, on the essences of the substances that enter into it, and on the character of their reciprocal relations, since it is on these that its capacity to fulfil its end depends: the same world could accordingly have been in many respects different, a point particularly important, in that every world must contain rational beings, whose causality is disjunctive, and might have taken other directions than those it did (§§35–8). Crusius has therefore criteria for world-identity different from those of Leibniz, and not the same as those of modern possible-world theorists.

A world must, further, be a system in which the real relations among things include the possibility of their acting on one another (§369), a demand preserved in Kant's principle of community or reciprocal interaction. Crusius goes on to hold that this interaction of natural substances must involve motion, and that it presupposes the impenetrability of one finite natural substance by another: two such substances cannot occupy the same territory. But some simple substances are active in ways besides those which involve motion: they are spiritual substances, capable of thoughts and volitions, as well as motions. There are therefore in every world both spiritual and material substances, the latter energetic and mobile, but destitute of thought. Crusius is, however, not quite clear whether a world of purely thinking substances may not be possible (§362). But he *is* clear that there must be interaction between thinking and material substances, if they are to belong to a common world (§363): merely ideal relations among them such as are postulated in the doctrine of pre-established harmony do not suffice. He holds, therefore, that there have to be *three* different sorts of causal laws: physical laws concerned solely with sequences of motion, pneumatic laws concerned solely with sequences of thought and volition, and physico-pneumatic laws which concern both (§365). For all this to be possible, every world must involve empty space which will allow substances, including such as are spiritual, to move about without hindrance, and the occupation of such space must be capable of being enlarged or reduced, and of being heterogeneous as well as homogeneous. A world cannot be quite unvariegated. Certain organized aggregations of heterogeneous materials constitute natural machines, such as are the bodies of rational spirits, which those spirits both regularly act upon and by which they are acted upon (§372). The purely mechanical is, however, limited to purely corporeal aggregates, and the world cannot, as a whole, be regarded as a machine (§382).

Crusius rounds off these treatments by courageously rejecting certain Leibnizian dogmas. He rejects the dogma of the identity of indiscernibles, for he holds that the dogma rests on a confusion of the true principle of sufficient reason with the false principle of a completely determining reason. God as a perfectly free being may elect to locate, without any completely determining motive, precisely similar simples or aggregates of simples in different regions of space or periods of time. The simple substances of which the world consists may in fact be wholly similar; only the way in which they are organized, and the consequent unfolding of their dynamic powers, may differ (§383). Crusius also questions the Leibnizian dogma that our world is necessarily the best of all possible worlds (§385). He holds that a world, being finite, is necessarily limited in its achievement of perfection: other existences, performances, and so on could always be added to it, which would raise its perfection to higher degrees. There is no way in which what is finite can rise to a perfection which transcends all finitude (§387). Since therefore there can be no best of all possible worlds, there is no determining reason why God should have chosen this world in preference to all others: there can only be a *sufficient* reason for His choice, which must be sought in His complete freedom, on the one hand, and in the entire goodness (not bestness) of what He chooses, on the other (§389). Crusius's treatments of motion further lead him to a spirited rejection of what would in later times be called the dogma of internal relations: there are, he holds, many changes in the state of certain things in the world which make no real difference to the state of other things (§423). For the comparing mind there will of course be an ideal difference. Crusian cosmology is replete with plain common sense, and with a refusal to be bulldozed by *a priori* principles: some of this common sense penetrated to Kant, but one would perhaps wish that more had done so.

The Crusian *Sketch of the Necessary Truths of Reason* ends up with a Pneumatology or Rational Psychology, which deals with the necessary properties of the rational spirits, which have been shown to be necessary to any world (§§281, 334, 425). We are, Crusius asserts, aware of the fact that we think, and that in some of these thoughts we also have sensations of things other than such thoughts, some being of states of ourselves as thinkers (inner sensations), others of things other than our thinking selves (outer sensations). We also have thoughts which bring before us previously enjoyed thoughts and their objects, and which are called cases of memory. We are also aware of certain other, non-sensational thoughts, which count as cases of imagining or dreaming, or as cases of judgement with its attendant *assertibilia*. In all these cases we are aware of doing something called thinking that is very distinctive, and that demands a distinctive inquiry we may call noology. But we are also conscious in ourselves of states that we call desires and aversions and decisions and acts of will, states which, though bound up with thoughts, reveal themselves as being of a wholly different, dynamic sort, and which must therefore be made the theme of another discipline called thelematology (§427). Crusius argues that the themes of both these disciplines are essentially irreducible to the mere motions we observe in outer things, however much motion may enter into their essence, and that the substances which have powers of thought and volition must therefore be quite different from substances which merely have powers of motion (§432). Such thinking-willing substances are arguably present in animals as well as in men (§433), and there must be a supremely perfect thinking-willing substance, whose infinity, however, forbids it to move or be moved.

Crusius discusses the two ground-powers of understanding and volition at great length. His treatment of freedom, and of the extent to which it presupposes partial determination by the understanding and by pre-existent desires, and of its possible triumph over, or its defeat by, the collective strength of the latter, is valuable and intelligent (§§450–1). So also is his doctrine of the priority of the practical (§454), and his frank confession that he does not understand how the will produces motions (§456).

vii

We have now completed our summary sketch of two of the major influences on Kant's pre-critical and critical thinking, Christian Wolff, whom he always mentions with immense respect, and Christian August Crusius, whom, as a promoter of philosophy, he thinks second to none. These two men are also philosophical thinkers of the highest originality and performance, the former being perhaps rateable as an eighteenth-century Germanic Aquinas, and the latter as an eighteenth-century Germanic G. E. Moore. There are many other thinkers in the great forest of eighteenth-century German metaphysics who influenced Kant considerably — Baumgarten and Tetens are such — but it would not be profitable for us to penetrate further into that forest and its many *Holzwege*. An exemplary penetration was, however, essential in order to combat a major delusion, for which Kant himself is largely responsible: the delusion of the great light which dawned with the advent of the critical philosophy, a light which dispelled the vain shadows of all previous thought, and made them irrelevant for subsequent philosophizing. The words of Dilthey, in the Introduction to the 1902 Academy Edition of Kant's works, are good expressions of this notion: 'The mighty genius of Kant dissolved the old German metaphysics, founded the critical standpoint, and sought in the self-active, pure ego unshakeable foundations for the empirical sciences, and for the unconditional validity of basic moral propositions.' Certainly a great light dawned when Kant began to formulate his critical philosophy, but it was not a light that dissolved the old German metaphysics, nor one that based all certainties on the self-active, pure ego. It was rather a light that relegated the structures of the old German metaphysics to regions where they could only be thought but not known, and where one had to find a directly experienced, phenomenal surrogate for what so transcended experience and knowledge. Thus the simple soul-substance believed in by Wolff and Crusius had as its surrogate merely various forms of objective and subjective synthesis; the simple objects behind phenomena had their representation only in the steady invariances of their phenomenal manifestations, their inherent forces only the regularities of phenomenal succession; the source of all things in God only their ever-expanding scientific arrangement in genera and species, and so on. What Kant was to do in the critical philosophy was therefore very much what Husserl was to do in his phenomenology, though neither fully understood what he was doing: to suspend transcendent affirmations in order fully to understand the complex experiential and cogitative mechanisms which alone give them a working reality. The transcendental note of the 'as if' can, however, not be eliminated in either type of thought, for, in default of it, the whole structure of intentional reference will crumble and the self-active subject will become a plant torn from the rude soil in which alone it can flourish and burgeon. All this will, however, be argued in detail as we comment on the detail of Kant's critical system. It was, however, necessary to explain why we saw fit to linger in its pronaos and its propylaea, before plunging into its sometimes overdark interior.

Chapter III

Kant's Pre-Critical Writings and the Transcendental Aesthetic

i

We shall, in the present chapter, attempt to sketch the philosophical content of Kant's more important writings from 1747, when, at the age of twenty-three, he wrote his first essay on the nature of *vis viva* or active force, up to 1770 when, on taking up his Chair of Philosophy at Königsberg, he produced his great inaugural Dissertation, *On the Form and Principles of the Sensible and Intelligible World*. The *Dissertation* anticipates many points in the Transcendental Aesthetic, the first part of the *Critique of Pure Reason*; and, since this 'Aesthetic'-doctrine — the term 'Aesthetic' has not here the modern meaning — has more links with the Dissertation-doctrine than with many later parts of the *Critique*, we shall deal with the two writings together. Kant's pre-critical writings perhaps include nothing of the first philosophical importance, but they everywhere move in novel and exciting directions, remaining well within the bounds set by the Leibnizian and Wolffian metaphysic, on the one hand, and by Newtonian physics, on the other, but everywhere making suggestions that will later transform this matrix of origin. In comparison with the exhaustive care of an exponent like Wolff, they can perhaps be described as slapdash — all Kant's writings can be called such — but their most hasty passages betray a penetrative insight to which Wolffian scholasticism never rises.

The 1747 essay deals with the True Estimation of *Vis Viva* or Active Force, and boldly passes judgement on the arguments of Leibniz and other philosophical physicists, including Descartes, regarding it. (The German title of this essay is *Gedanken von der wahren Schätzung der lebendigen Kräfte und Beurtheilung der Beweise deren sich Herr von Leibniz und andere Mechaniker in dieser Streitsache bedient haben*.) Leibniz, Kant tells us, to whom human reason owes so much, thinks

that bodies are tenanted by an essential power, more fundamental to them even than their extension (§1). This active
force reveals itself in the motions which bodies impart to
other bodies: it is also revealed in the changes in conscious
representations which either lead up to, or are led up to by
such motions. A world only exists to the extent that there
are such active forces connecting bodies and souls with other
bodies and souls; to the extent that such active forces are
absent, we do not have one world, even if the divine understanding were to institute bonds of comparison between the
contents of such separated systems (§8). (This point was
also made by Crusius in 1745.) Even more interestingly,
Kant maintains that space *itself* depends on these dynamic
interactions, a point later taken up in the Third Analogy of
Experience in the *Critique of Pure Reason*. That space has
three, and only three dimensions has no foundation in logic
or mathematics: it is based entirely on the dynamic properties
of bodies, which through divine appointment also obey
the law of the inverse square. Were these dynamic properties
different, there might be spaces of four or five or any number
of dimensions (§§10–11). Space, he holds, is entirely a
phenomenal order in which dynamic relations make themselves manifest: we therefore already have the unknown structure of Things-in-themselves in some manner translated into
spatial relationships. Kant further objects interestingly to
the Cartesian attempt to connect *vis viva* with *actual* motion:
this would lead to its vanishing or its reduction in many
cases of impact. An active force must be a constant behind
appearances, governed in its manifestations by a complex
rule, but not to be identified with anything apparent. He
takes the Crusian view that to have a location in space proves
that one is a substance exerting force upon other substances, and the soul, being located in space, therefore necessarily acts on bodies, and is acted on by them (§6). The
article contains many other points of interest, many too technical for our purposes.

The very important *Natural History and Theory of the
Heavens* belongs to 1755, and is interesting as involving a
completely mechanical theory of the origins of the solar system,
based on original forces of attraction and repulsion, and extending to a theory of the Milky Way and of more comprehensive galaxies. What is philosophically interesting is the view

that it accords better with divine teleology to have let the solar system construct *itself*, as a consequence of general laws of gravitation and so on, than to have constructed it by special acts of shaping and intervention, such as the piety of Newton had found quite acceptable. God did not *have* to construct a cosmos out of materials whose natures pre-existed, and which therefore required further manipulation: He was able to *give* His materials natures that were obedient to laws that would lead mechanically to the ends that He proposed (see the Preface to the article). This was, in fact, a far greater exhibition of divine providence and creativity than any arrangement which required constant tampering. Kant's magnificent cosmology of course anticipated the even more celebrated cosmology of Laplace: it successfully extended even to such details as the rings of Saturn. In the third part of the article, Kant deals perspicaciously with problems concerning the habitation of other planets, and hazards speculations regarding transmigrations to other planets in the everlasting progress of men's souls towards intellectual and moral perfection. These speculative beliefs remain, though only as beliefs, even in Kant's latest writings.

A Public Dissertation of 1755, written in Kant's inimitably unreadable Latin, was called *A New Elucidation of the First Principles of Metaphysical Cognition*. It adheres to the Leibnizian doctrine of the laws of contradiction and sufficient reason, as being the first principles of all reasoning. But for the former Kant prefers to substitute *two* formulae of identity, that whatever is, is and that whatever is not, is not; while, in regard to the latter, he follows Crusius in distinguishing a determining from a sufficient reason, but, unlike Crusius, holds the former to be necessary as well as the latter: there must always be something which determines something to be A, by excluding the possibility that it should be not-A. This leads on to a Theorem (VII) that there must be something, that is, God, whose real existence underlies the possibility of all possibilities, and so is a necessary, and not a contingent existence, an argument further developed in a full-fledged, theistic Demonstration in 1763. From these premises Kant proceeds to prove, in opposition to Crusius, that there must be determining reasons even for our free actions, and that God, having foreknowledge of them, also knows what we shall freely do. He also argues for the Leibnizian view (XIII) that no relations between finite substances hold between them directly, but only by way of God. It cannot be said that there is anything of great consequence in this curious *mélange* of theorems and proofs, but they reveal the directions in which Kant's thoughts were then moving.

In 1756 Kant gave another Public Dissertation in Latin on the topic of a *Physical Monadology*. Since the Leibnizian monad was always the model for Kant's Thing-in-itself, this Dissertation is of some interest. Kant defines a monad as a simple substance not consisting of many parts, and capable of existing apart from all other similar substances. Bodies, it is affirmed, must consist of such monads. Space, however, is infinitely divisible, and has no simple, ultimate parts. The monads, therefore, must fill whole regions of space, without being divided. A given region of space may accordingly be the sphere of action of one monad, which is a Crusian doctrine (VI), and the impenetrability of a lump of matter is the phenomenal sign of such a monadic presence (VIII). But the territorial occupancy of a monad is not only shown by keeping other monads out of its territory, but by an internal, attractive force (X). All matter is therefore the seat of repulsive forces, which hold its parts asunder, and attractive forces, which bring and keep them together, forces revealed more remotely in gravity, more intimately in cohesion. All portions of matter, endued with the same repulsive and attractive forces, will, whatever their phenomenal qualities, swell out to occupy the same volume (X Corollary). The force of inertia, added to these two primal forces, is needed to account for differences of bodily mass (XI Cor.) and density (XII). All in all, we see the phenomenal world underlaid by a vast number of dynamic centres, most of them objects rather than subjects, of which extension and motion are the phenomenal expression. This picture is still at work in the later critical theory, which will not make sense without it.

Further treatments of inertia and impact occur in a paper on *A New Doctrinal Conception (Lehrbegriff) of Motion and Rest* (1758), and are dealt with in terms of the Leibnizian conception of the absolute continuity of all change and motion. The 1762 paper on *The Misleading Subtlety of the Four Syllogistic Figures* also makes several logical and epistemological points important to the understanding of the *Critique of Pure Reason*. These may be summarized as: (1) All mediate inference really reduces to the first figure: the other figures merely supplement it with immediate transformations. (2) It is in mediate inference alone that the full sense of our judgements reveals itself, that is, a judgement essentially ranges particulars under ever more generic headings. (3) It is in judgements alone that the full sense of our concepts reveals itself: a judgement, Kant says, is the act through which a concept becomes actual. This opinion is of course central to Kant's later Metaphysical and Transcendental Deduction of the Categories, but it is also responsible for some of their basic mistakes. For it is obvious that there are thought-syntheses which merely run through items in an *enumerative* and *listing* manner — this and that and that — ships and shoes and sealing-wax and so on — and pronounce no judgement upon them. It is even arguable that enumerative syntheses are more basic than judgemental ones: our eyes and minds wander idly from item to item, before we proceed to sort them out and to say things about them. Hence a great deal of our thought, though synthetically unified, owes no allegiance to the categories, a point which Kant himself not infrequently recognizes, but not for a moment in his two infinitely ill-written Transcendental Deductions, where all synthetic unity goes hand in hand with the application of the categories in judgements. (A similar over-exaltation of the judgement and proposition is present in the transition from Platonic science, which is arguably a mere matter of the division of concepts, to Aristotelian science, which is all a matter of deducing propositions from other propositions.) Propositions and judgements are not all that important: concepts can surely be contemplated and enjoyed as well as used in assertions and reasoning.

In 1763 Kant produced a full-length treatise on *The only possible Ground on which a Proof of God's Existence can be based* (*Der einzig mögliche Beweisgrund des Daseins Gottes*). This expands some theological points in the *Nova Dilucidatio* of 1755, and anticipates some of the arguments in the Transcendental Dialectic. Kant repudiates an ontological or Cartesian proof of the divine existence, which reasons from the *possible* existence of a perfect being to the necessary and actual existence of the same being. Real existence, Kant argues, is not a genuine predicate, and can add nothing to the perfect round of predicates through which God is conceived (I. i. 1, 2; I. iii. 2). But he also repudiates a cosmological proof from the existence of contingent things to the existence of a God as their necessary foundation. For, while the principle of sufficient reason suffices to prove the existence of *some* sort of necessary being, as the ground of all contingent existences, it does not suffice to equate such a being with the perfect being of theology, unless we assume existence to be part of perfection, which we have refused to allow. This subtle but questionable argument, which reads the ontological proof back into the cosmological, is of -course repeated in the Transcendental Dialectic, and will concern us later. From these unsatisfactory lines of proof, Kant proceeds to his own more satisfactory line: that the existence of a God is necessary, not in order to account for the *existence* of contingent things, but for their *possibility*. The possible, Kant argues, must be grounded in the actual: there must *be* something or other which can be such and such, or could be responsible for something's being such and such, if there is to be any such possibility at all (I. ii. 2–4). In this argument Kant characteristically recognizes the empty meaninglessness of mere logical possibilities, so much beloved in our own modern scholasticism: there must *be* a realm of things, and sorts of things, if any possibility is to be asserted. For p to assert a possibility, it is not enough that it should involve no inner contradiction: it must assert something of something, and this is only possible in a context where there are predicable contents, and instances of which they could be predicated. But, Kant argues, we cannot without absurdity try to conceive of a situation in which all existence, and with it all possibility, will be liquidated: that there should be no possibilities is itself impossible. It follows that, since contingent existence is not sufficient to guarantee the being of possibilities, necessary existence is needed to guarantee that being. There must, therefore, be a being in whose description, whether attributively or consequentially, all possibilities are included. Only a unique, simple, eternal, intelligent, and therefore spiritual, being is capable of ranging over every possibility, and there is therefore no possibility that such a being should not exist. This extraordinary argument, half-ontological and resting on cosmo-possibility rather than cosmo-actuality, has not, to my knowledge been carefully examined by anyone, though it certainly deserves close consideration. If not quite nonsensical, it is perhaps one of those very simple arguments, which, under an appearance of fallacy, conceals the ultimate truth about the world. It is not, however, a truth that will ever recommend itself to those who believe, with Aristotle, that actuality is in all respects prior to possibility. Kant himself, however, grew away from it, and does not resuscitate it in his treatment of theistic proofs in the *Critique of Pure Reason*. The view of God as an intelligence presupposed by the whole ordered realm of essence, and guaranteeing its structure, is, however, retained in Kant's view of God as a necessary, regulative Ideal of Pure Reason (see the Appendix to the Transcendental Dialectic). God, in fact, becomes, for theoretical purposes not so much the guarantor of the well-ordered realm of possibilities, as rather that very realm itself. He is, in short, the omnitude of possibility, the logical space within which we have at all times to conduct our conceiving, our judging, and our reasoning. Kant goes on to show the advantages of his proof in that it makes God the Creator of the laws and patterns of being as well as of their instances. Such a God can shape nature to suit His purposes, and has no occasion to interfere miraculously with it.

In the same year, 1763, Kant wrote his very interesting *Attempt to introduce the Notion of Negative Quantities into Philosophy*. If the previous treatise subordinated empty logical possibilities to the real, comprehensive realm of the possible, so the present essay subordinates empty logical negations to negations which involve content, and genuine opposition. Logical contradictions produce nothing by their combination, but real opposites either cancel each other out completely, or reduce each other's force: they are, in a real sense, capable of combination. And a real opposite is as positive as what it cancels out. Kant shows how pain is in this sense the real opposite of pleasure, aversion of love, vice of virtue, and how polar opposites in physics are never merely the logical negations of one another. Philosophy, however, he holds, has insufficiently recognized the difference, and has often tried to reduce opposition to contradiction. Kant suggests various cosmic principles guaranteeing both the constancy and the equality of all cosmic opposites, and their capacity to cancel out in an algebraic sum which always amounts to zero (Section III). The negations of formal logic must in some way ultimately depend on such non-formal, real negations. Obviously we are moving in the conceptual ambience of some of the pre-Socratic philosophers, as well as in that of Schelling and Hegel and of modern physics.

Ignoring the disappointing, superficial, anecdotal *Observations on the Feeling for the Beautiful and Sublime* (1764), we pass on to the very important, *Dreams of a Spirit-Seer seen in the light of the Dreams of Metaphysics* of 1766. This is one of the first critical considerations of supernormal or 'psychic' phenomena, both from a metaphysical and an epistemological standpoint. The work was touched off by the writings of Emmanuel Swedenborg, a theosophical Swede of great charisma, who had managed to convince many that he enjoyed visiting rights into an incorporeal, spiritual world, and that he also exercised clairvoyant powers in regard to much that was happening in this one. His obvious personal integrity was such as to recommend itself to Kant, and so was the mystical rationalism of his religious teachings, his spiritual world being perhaps the original of Kant's 'kingdom of ends', and there are passages in Kant, particularly in his last writings, which are somewhat Swedenborgian. Kant's rational mysticism was, however, a matter of moral faith, and disdained the aid of clairvoyance: he desired there to be a high wall between what we could see now and what we could know hereafter. And he had also obviously been incited to write the treatise by sceptical friends, and wrote in a much more scoffing, polemical style than really accorded with his feelings (Academy Edition, vol. II, pp. 367–8). No one who reads the treatise carefully can doubt that Kant felt the same, wistful half-sympathy for Swedenborg's dreams that he also felt for the dreams of metaphysics. He regretted his certainty that one could frame no reliable judgement on what transcended the deliverances of the senses.

The treatise begins by sketching the hypothetical structure of a spiritual world, in which, however, we have no reason at all to believe. Kant acknowledges that there is an ultimate mystery in the way in which the simple elements, of which matter must consist, occupy extended territories and repel other elements from them: we do, however, know that they somehow manage to do this, but we have no analogous knowledge in regard to the spiritual simples which must underlie thoughts, reasonings, and so on. It is not clear *how* they can find room for their action in a space seemingly pre-empted by the elements of matter, and while it seems natural to locate them in the *whole* organized body, the empirical evidence tends to restrict them, if they exist at all, to some obscure region of the brain, where their role must be similar to that of the elementary substances underlying matter. Kant confesses at this point (Academy Edition, vol. II, p. 327) that he is strongly inclined to believe that there *are* such immaterial natures, mixed up with the material elements in the cosmos, but that he has great difficulty in accepting such a piebald conception. It constructs the world out of two radically different sorts of interacting agents, some underlying the activities of thought and perhaps life, while the others only underlie the phenomenal behaviour of inert matter. We have in fact two worlds, one material and one immaterial. Once this conception is tolerated, however, we easily slide over into holding that immaterial substances may not only influence one another by way of their bodies, but also *directly*, a conception which can be used to account for our deep concern for another's weal and woe, from which all morality develops. This moral feeling will then play the same sort of pervasive role in the spiritual world that Newtonian gravitation plays in the material, and we may expect that, when our association with our bodies ends, we may enter into a realm dominated by this moral gravitation, which will no doubt bring about the happiness of the unselfishly good and the pain of the selfishly wicked. The problem of reconciling the divine goodness with the way of the world will not arise in that other world (ibid.). We are obviously here anticipating the kingdom of ends of which so much is made in the *Metaphysic of Morals*, and it is pleasing to know that this conception, though rational, is also mystical and Swedenborgian. The conception of a spiritual world further involves, according to Swedenborg, that material likenesses can be made use of by disembodied spirits in a symbolic manner: they will communicate with each other through bodily images (pp. 339–40). Similar bodily images and visions occur also in the case of embodied spirits, and especially in the case of those, like Swedenborg, who are abnormally sensitive to spiritual influences. The phenomena of clairvoyance, telepathy, and so on therefore involve many quasi-sensible appearances, but these, like normal sensible appearances, will often be well-founded and informative.

Kant expounds the Swedenborgian doctrine with so much understanding that he obviously feels deep sympathy for it. But his objections to it are that there is nothing intersubjective about its visions, nothing that can be tested by others, nothing, therefore, involving the essential parallax of objectivity (see p. 349). The Swedenborgian visionary is a waking dreamer, who projects his dreams and fantasies into the intersubjective world revealed to us in normal sensation. He should with more justice project them into some region of his brain, as we normally do when we recognize certain appearances to be delusive. Once such projection is freely practised, anything whatever can be envisaged and asserted, and the adepts of the spirit-world will lose all credit with us. Such adepts should not be burnt, but they should be got rid of (p. 348). Their reports are, however, of greater interest than the speculations of many metaphysicians, since profound disturbances of the senses are much rarer and much harder to explain than the aberrations of reason. It will be noted that Kant nowhere accuses Swedenborg of confabulation or simulation: he believes in his abnormal experiences. And he is deeply interested in the alleged quasi-publicity of other-world images, the alleged entry into the mental pictures of other spirits, the translation of their thoughts into languages better understood by the subject, and the gathering together of spirits into societies dominated by the thoughts and images of a single, great spirit, and so forth (pp. 365–6). If all this material is fictional, it has enough coherent detail to be factual. The role of philosophy is not, however, to encourage such uncontrolled, visionary excursions into regions beyond intersubjective testing, but rather to remain within the bounds of the latter. We do not understand how our will moves our members, or how anything causes anything, but this does not mean that we do not know what to expect, and that we are free to fabricate any sort of force or connection of which we have absolutely no experience. Kant believes that the hope of a future life has its roots in our moral experience and practice, but that our moral practice does not depend on such hopes, much less require the help of insights like the Swedenborgian. As regards the life to come, it will be best to wait till it comes. All this does not prevent Kant in his later work from having many definite thoughts with regard to the life that will be lived in the communion of rational spirits and in fellowship with the divine reason, even though he does not regard such thoughts as forming a part of knowledge.

The last pre-critical writing that we shall consider, before going on to the 1770 *Dissertation*, is the very illuminating

On the Prime Ground of the Distinction of the Regions in Space (1768). This is concerned with the problems raised by incongruous counterparts, of which the right hand and the left hand, or a man's body and its mirror-image, are salient examples. Obviously there is a thoroughgoing analogy, yet also a systematic difference, between cases like those just mentioned: they are in a sense exactly alike, and yet so different that one could not be fitted into the place occupied by the other. This difference in some manner eludes conception: we cannot tell ourselves exactly what it is, in general terms, but have to have recourse to ostensive methods. It is similar to the fundamental difference between the here and the there which is also interesting to Kant: obviously what is here can be exactly like what is there, and, if a pattern is repeated indefinitely, there can be indefinitely many distinct cases of precisely the same properties and relationships. (The fundamental difference between the I and the Thou presents the same teasing obscurity, but has had to wait till quite recent times to be deeply experienced.) The Leibnizian identity of indiscernibles is by all such examples strained: only an appeal to the principle of sufficient reason can prevent God or the world from being thus repetitive.

Kant's strategy at this stage of his development is to maintain the inadequacy of our conceptions to the intuitively given structures of space, rather than the other way round. Space is not merely some general manner in which extended parts and their limiting points are related to one another: if it were, there would be no such difference as that between the left hand and the right hand. Space has to be an actual structure of regions even in the absence of matter; it is the prime ground of the possibility of combining material parts. This fact shows itself in innumerable physical and biological differences: the difference between screws which turn to the right and screws which turn to the left, between hops which wind to the right and beans which wind to the left, and so on. Obviously Kant has here chosen a strategy of subordinating conception to intuition: intuition reveals differences of which conception knows nothing. Hegel and Bergson will follow him on this path, particularly in regard to the continuous and the developing. But he could equally well have chosen the strategy of subordinating intuition to conception, after the fashion of Leibniz and Wolff, and he does in fact do so in the *Dissertation* and in the critical writings. For there, space and time, on account of their inconceivable properties, are firmly relegated to the status of mere appearances.

ii

The 1770 Dissertation *On the Form and Principles of the Sensible and Intelligible World* is one of Kant's most weighty writings, though written in a German-styled Latin which it is a sustained agony to read. Its arguments for the phenomenal character of space and time are repeated with little change in the Transcendental Aesthetic, the first part of the *Critique of Pure Reason*, which is very imperfectly adjusted to what is later said in that work. The *Dissertation*-treatment is, however, clearer and better than the Aesthetic-treatment, and gives time the priority which space has in the Aesthetic. For, it is plainly the most basic property of our thinking minds that we have always to run through items *in succession*, and *then* piece or weave them together. The *Dissertation* does not advance to the critical standpoint, which limits knowledge, as well as sensibility, to phenomena in space and time: it still presumes it possible, though it does not itself attempt much of the sort, to advance on the wings of thought to the contemplation of Things-in-themselves. But it implicitly involves the whole critical standpoint, inasmuch as the critical limitation of knowledge to phenomena does not rest, at least in Kant's more considered utterances, on anything presumed wrong in our concepts as such, but solely in their necessary involvement with sensuous intuition, and with the time and space which are its pervasive forms. In default of such sensibility, our concepts, however well-framed and coherent, will be epistemologically empty and senseless, and unable to provide more than vague scientific regulation or moral inspiration. In the doctrine of the *Dissertation* the whole teaching of the *Critique* is, therefore, implicit, though the consequences for conception and knowledge of all we see around us or within us are not drawn out at all.

The *Dissertation* begins in its first section by establishing two limiting notions, that of a world, or a whole which is not a real part of anything larger, and that of a simple, or a part which is not a whole to anything smaller: 'In a substantial composite, just as analysis does not end except in a part which is not a whole, i.e. a simple, so synthesis only ends in a whole which is not a part, i.e. a world.' The understanding, or the reason, or the mind, has not, Kant thinks, the slightest difficulty in framing either concept, or in grasping its possibility: the formation of both concepts involves no more than the mind's native capacity to distinguish parts within wholes and its capacity to fit parts together so as to form wholes. (That the parts and wholes must be substantial and real, and not merely ideal, will be emphasized later.) But when, however, the mind tries to *intuit* or *envisage* an actual instance of either concept, it comes up against an absolute barrier, in the form of an infinite series of divisions or augmentations which can never be completed in time, and which also characterizes space. For time and space are alike such that their division can be continued indefinitely without yielding us simple elements — points and instants are not isolable elements, but merely boundaries — while augmentation by successive addition can likewise be carried on indefinitely, without yielding us the cosmic whole that we are trying to compass: 'For since in a continuum there is no term to the regress from a whole to its giveable parts, and in the infinite no term to the progress from the parts to a given whole, a complete analysis is in the former case impossible, and a complete synthesis in the latter case, nor can the whole be completely thought out in conformity with the laws of intuition, whether as regards its composition, in the former case, or as regards its totality, in the latter.' This intuitive barrier is not, however, a conceptual barrier, and it is quite mistaken to confuse the intuitively unillustrable or unimaginable with the conceptually unthinkable, a doctrine from which Kant never deviates: 'For whatever violates the laws of the understanding and the reason is certainly impossible, but not so when, being an object of pure reason, it simply is not subject to the laws of intuitive cognition.' A footnote further informs us that the infinite has only been wrongly held to be unintelligible because it has been misdefined as the greatest of numbers, rather than as something that surpasses all number. And such an infinite would be accessible to the intuition of a being like God, who did not estimate multitude by successive counting of items, but could take it all in, in a single glance (*uno obtutu*, N. 2, p. 388 — Prussian Academy Edition). Kant plainly grasps all that Cantor later worked out in his theory of transfinite numbers, and his definition of infinity as transcending all number is merely another way of hiving it off from the finite, inductive cardinals. He has also, in God's timeless intuition, given something like a verifiable content to the whole conception.

Kant then says, in §2 of the first section, that there are *three* essential aspects to what we understand by a world. The first is its *matter*, which consists of all the distinct *substances* that enter into it as parts, not, however, their attributes, successive states, and so on. For, if we included the latter, even the most simple substance might, in respect of its attributes, be rated a world, as a man's egoistic or private world of thoughts, feelings, images, and so on often is. The second essential aspect of a world is its *form*, which consists in the *real* manner in which its constituent substances are co-ordinated or brought together, so as to make of them a single, total world. The *reality* of this manner of co-ordination is important: substances do not make up a world merely because they are arbitrarily put together in someone's thought, as Leibniz imagined that the diamond of the Grand Duke might in someone's thought be put together with the diamond of the Great Mogul. The connection of the substances in a world, must in some sense be objective, and not merely based on external reflection or comparison: 'This co-ordination is conceived as real and objective, not as ideal and based on the mere whim of the subject, according to which, by enumerating any plurality one would at will generate a whole. For by comprehending many things together, you without difficulty produce the totality of a representation, but not therefore the representation of a totality.' It is also essential that the form of a world should be a *co*-ordination, and not a *sub*ordination: the constituents of the world must all be on a *like* footing, not some one-sidedly dependent on others. It is for this reason that actual causal connections between substances will not suffice to cement them into a common world, since causal connections do not run symmetrically from all world-substances to all, but only from some to some. What we require is rather a principle which will condition the *possibility* of causal interaction among substances, whether they are actually interacting or not. Kant holds further that a world only can be a world if it has a *permanent* nature, which, in its turn, depends on the permanent existence of its substantial parts and on *their* permanent natures: it cannot, therefore, be held together by actual causal interactions, which are essentially impermanent, and in many cases non-existent. Space and time are by most thinkers thought to constitute the universal form which binds all substances together, and makes interaction among them possible: Kant can only allow them to provide a *phenomenal* connection among all mundane substances, which may indeed point to some common connective principle, but cannot itself constitute it. And, in the third place, the substances in one world must have the third necessary property of exhaustive omnitude (*universitas*), of being *all* the substances that are brought together by the form in question, and so constituting its total world. Such exhaustive omnitude can quite readily be conceived, not however intuited or imagined through the sort of piecemeal synthesis we are able to perform in time. Only a being like God, who can embrace an infinity of items in a single glance, could carry out such a synthesis intuitively, but Kant objects to our using even the temporal notion of simultaneity in the case of such a divine oversight.

Section II of the *Dissertation* goes on to deal with the differences between sensibility and understanding and their objects. Sensibility is said (§3) to be an essentially *receptive* mode of representation, in which the subject is passively affected by the actual presence of its object. Understanding, on the other hand, goes beyond all such passive affections, to such matters as are not of such quality as to enter its sensitive life. The object of sensibility is thus a phenomenon, of intelligence or reason a Noumenon. To this he adds (§4) that sensibility always depends on some special subjective condition (*indoles*) which may differ from one subject to another, and so can only represent objects as they *appear* to a subject, whereas intelligence, being free from any such special subjective condition, can represent objects as they are (*sicuti sunt*). The freedom of intelligence from such a subjective condition seems for Kant practically a matter of definition. Kant then goes on to make an all-important distinction of matter and form, both in the case of what is sensible and what is intelligible. The matter of sense is what is qualitative about our sensitive representations, and it differs according to the sensitive disposition of the subject: the form, however, is the *species*, the configuration or pattern of what is sensed, and this depends on a certain law of co-ordination which is natural to the mind. (*Repraesentationi autem sensus primo inest quiddam, quod diceres materiam nempe sensatio, praeterea autem aliquid, quod vocari potest*

forma, quae animi lege coordinantur.) In other words, there is
an inner law of the mind which results in the spatial and
temporal patterning of what is thus sensed, in the *species* or
resultant look which the various sense-qualities thus assume.
But Kant goes on to say in the next sentence, that just as a
sensible quality bears witness to the presence of something
sensible, though not of the same quality as our subjective
modification, so the form or pattern of our sensible representation bears witness to *some relation* or respect among the things
sensed, that is, among their noumenal sources, but is not,
however, an adumbration or schema of the object, but only
of an internal law in the mind which governs its co-ordination
of whatever is sensed as a result of the presence of the object.
(*Porro, quemadmodum sensatio, quae sensualis repraesentationis materiam constituit, praesentiam quidem sensibilis
alicuius arguit, sed quoad qualitatem pendet a natura subiecti,
quatenus ab isto obiecto est modificabilis; ita etiam eiusdem
repraesentationis forma testatur utique quendam sensorum
respectum aut relationem, verum proprie non est adumbratio
aut schema quoddam obiecti, sed nonnisi lex quaedam menti
insita, sensa ab obiecti praesentia orta sibimet coordinandi.*)
This passage (which involves many obscurities on account of
its use of the ambiguous term *sensa*, which may mean either
things *qua* given to sense, or the non-sensuous, real things
which are sensuously thus given) can none the less be held
to teach us that, just as the subject translates noumenal characters into the quite different qualities of his own sense-
experiences, so he also translates noumenal relations, which
are neither spatial nor temporal, into the spatio-temporal
relations which are what are seen to hold among objects *qua*
apparent. The next sentence may appear to refute this interpretation, for Kant there says that objects do *not* strike the
senses in virtue of their form or pattern (*species*), and that
the mind therefore has need of its own stable, innate laws
to make the varied things affecting the senses coalesce into
a representational whole or pattern. (*Nam per formam seu
speciem obiecta sensus non feriunt: ideoque, ut varia obiecti
sensum afficientia in totum aliquod repraesentationis coalescant,
opus est interno mentis principio, per quod varia illa secundum
stabiles et innatas leges speciem quandam induant.*) This sentence
seems to suggest that the species or pattern of arrangement of
objects as appearing to sense, bears *no* relation whatever to the

species or pattern of arrangement among those objects as they really are. If this were Kant's view, then it would certainly involve all the purely productive constructivism of Fichtean and other idealistic interpretations, in which Things-in-themselves really play no meaningful role. It seems clear, however, that all that Kant is here saying is that objects as they are in themselves do not communicate their actual relational pattern to their appearances, and that the mind therefore has need of its own relational patterns in order to organize its sensations into a patterned whole. All this does not exclude the presumption that the relations among Things-in-themselves are the *transcendental sources* of the relations among things as they appear to the senses, and that the law of the mind is one that in some sense 'translates' the former into the latter. There could, in fact, be no law about the whole proceeding if this were not the case. That the process of such 'translation' is logically prior to all experience, is, of course, only the general *presumption* of all Kantianism.

Just, however, as sensuous cognition has a matter and a form, so intellectual or conceptual cognition has the same. Its matter consists of empirical concepts, all of which have their ultimate origin in intuitive encounters with sense-given individuals (in space and time): the intellect or understanding has, however, a power or a use which enables it by reflection to abstract common conceptual marks from such sense-given individuals, and to range such individuals under such common conceptual marks. It has also the power to range such common concepts under other more widely generic concepts. Both these powers or uses are called by Kant cases of the *logical* use of the intellect, and are common to all the sciences. But, however far the generalizing intellect may depart from intuitively given individuals in its logical use, the concepts that it elaborates are still to be reckoned as intuitively based or empirical: they have resulted from the action of external objects on the intelligence, and are not the intelligence's own, spontaneous product:

For when a cognition has been given in some manner or other, it is either seen as falling under some mark common to many cases, or as opposed to such a mark, and that either quite immediately, as happens in judgements leading to a distinct cognition, or mediately, as in reasonings leading to adequate knowledge. For when sensitive cognitions are given, they are subordinated through the logical use of the intellect to other sensitive cognitions as their common concepts, and phenomena are subordinated to more general laws of phenomena. It is all-important to note, however, that cognitions are always to be regarded as sensitive, no matter how much there has been a logical use of the intellect in regard to them. For they are called 'sensitive' on account of their origin, and not in respect of comparisons which establish identity or opposition (§5).

There are, however, *other* concepts which are not abstracted from sense-given individuals or cognitions of any sort, but in which it is rather the case that, in framing them, it is we who abstract from, or turn our backs on, sensuously given materials of every sort. They are not isolated *within* what is sensuously given, but are given when we ignore *all* that is sensuously given. 'Hence', as Kant says, 'the intellectual concept *abstracts* from all that is sensitive, and is *not abstracted* from what is sensitive, and should perhaps rather be called *abstracting* (*abstrahens*) than *abstract* (*abstractus*)' (§6).

Such pure concepts are isolated by what Kant calls the *real use* of the understanding or intellect: they arise when the intellect reflects, not on the sense-given material that it organizes, but on the manner in which it organizes that sense-given material, whether by subsuming one sense-given concept under another in judgement, or one judgement under another in reasoning. It is thus that all the pure concepts of metaphysics arise, and of these Kant gives as examples: possibility, existence, necessity, substance, cause (§8). These are the pure concepts of the understanding, which give judgements their Form without entering into their empirical material, and to these Kant was later, in the *Critique of Pure Reason*, to give the name of categories. 'Since, therefore, empirical principles are not to be found in metaphysics, the concepts which confront us in metaphysics are not to be sought in the senses, but in the very nature of the pure intellect, not, however, as innate notions, but as notions abstracted from the inherent laws of the mind, by paying attention to its actions on empirical occasions, and therefore *acquired* (*Non tanquam conceptus connati, sed e legibus menti insitis, attendendo ad eius actiones abstracti, adeoque acquisiti*). Of this kind are possibility, existence, necessity, substance, cause etc. with their opposites and correlates' (§8). Kant further makes the important point that such concepts, though pure, require much clarification: he rejects the view of Leibniz and Wolff that a pure concept is necessarily a clear one, as a sensuously based concept must be confused. Geometrical concepts, though sensuously based, are paradigms of clarity, while a pure concept like substance is desperately obscure (§7).

Among such pure concepts, Kant however also lists certain concepts of absolute perfection, that we now call Ideals, though Plato gave them the name of Ideas, and that Kant himself was later to call Transcendental Ideas. Such Ideals are either theoretical or practical. The former Ideal is that of a God who has, in the highest degree, all the perfections that occur in lesser, limited degrees in all lesser things: such an Ideal is moreover not merely an Ideal for knowledge, but is also conceived as the source of the becoming (*principium fiendi*) of all such lesser things. The second Ideal, on the other hand, is that of purely moral perfection. This is an Ideal framed by pure practical reason and is in no manner derived from the sensuous notion of the voluptuous or the tedious, as in the misguided, empiricistic ethical systems of such as Epicurus and Shaftesbury (§9). Kant says that, of such Ideals of ontological or moral perfection, we can have only a symbolic cognition, one by way of general concepts in the abstract, and not by way of a singular concept in the concrete. Our intuitions are passive, and depend on the way things affect our senses: we can, therefore, never have intuitions of the things themselves that are thus affecting us. A divine intuition, which is the independent archetype of our dependent intuitions, and which is also the active principle behind objects, and not merely something deriving from such a principle, can be purely and perfectly intellectual, as our sort of intuition and intellect cannot (§10). Kant's position here is exactly the same as in the later, critical writings, with the sole distinction that the symbolic cognition he is here describing still counts as a form of *knowledge*, whereas in the later critical writings it is only a legitimate exercise of conception, which cannot count as knowledge. The change is more trivial than it is usually thought to have been.

Kant ends up section II by stressing that phenomenal knowledge is not false and delusive because it is phenomenal: we can truly discover how things regularly appear to us, and the things thus appearing to us are moreover really present and really acting upon us (§11). And he divides sensibility into the outer senses which receive the impact of real objects external to us, that appear before us as in space, and the inner or introspective sense, in which we are affected by ourselves, and by our own subjective acts, in so far as they appear to us as in time. Our own selves, and their noumenal acts are, of course, not given to us introspectively. And because space and time are forms of appearance, they further give rise to two pure sciences which are independent of detailed empirical content: geometry and pure mechanics are the sciences in question. But arithmetic, though it has a purely conceptual content, only acquires concreteness when countable phenomena come before us in space and time (§12). The position here is superior to that of the *Critique*, where number is unacceptably tied down to the empirical activity of counting, and to the temporality of the activity in question.

Section III of the *Dissertation* then deals with the principles of the sensible, phenomenal world. These principles, we learn in §13, apply to everything as it appears to us, but not to matters that transcend all appearance, for example, our own selves as spiritual substances, or God as universal, noumenal cause of all. Then, §14 deals with time, and attempts to prove that time can be nothing but a universal form of appearance. Kant says that (1) seeing things after one another, or as simultaneous with one another, *presupposes* an idea of the time in which things are thus seen. Unless we already had this idea, we could not see the things that we successively sense *as* successive: our experience would then presumably be no more than an unimaginable flux, if indeed it could be anything. Kant presumes that we have to have an idea, or the readiness to form an idea, of something that spills over beyond the immediate present, in the vague direction of the 'past' and the 'future', in order to be able to fit what we thus experience successively into a definite time-order. We cannot come by the idea of succession through experience, because we have to have it in order to have experience. It is possible to teach people the use of tenses and temporal expressions by showing them things that happen one after the other, as is picturesquely set forth in §§49–51 of Wittgenstein's *Brown Book*, but the teaching will only be effective, on Kantian principles, if the pupils already dispose of a vague vision of the indefinitely extended temporal order into which such teaching can be fitted. And who can doubt (to use Wittgenstein's technique of the rhetorical question) that Kant has really illuminated a question that Wittgenstein, with a wonderful appearance of illuminating it, has altogether begged?

Kant then tells us in (2) that time is given to us in a single overview, as a single, infinite, individual whole in which all limited time-lapses must find their places, and not as some generic relational structure abstractable from many distinct time-lapses. In other words, it is only because there is something like a primordial And So On attaching to all experienced successions, that we can be taught to extend the map of the past and the future indefinitely. This leads on to the important point (3) that time, though it precedes all sensation, is intuitively, not conceptually presented, and that its presentation is a *pure*, not a sensuous intuition. In other words, time, as extending vaguely into the past and future, is so absolutely *integrated* with the sensible contents beyond which it is felt to extend, that it must be said to share their individuality, and to be intuitively 'there' in the same way that they are, and yet, since it is certainly felt as a horizon extending beyond them, it has also to be said to be the object of a *pure* intuition, one that needs to be complemented by sensory content, but which does not wholly depend upon the latter. Our awareness of time is certainly something intermediate between our awareness of some highly generic feature and the manner in which a sensuous quality like redness seems to strike upon our senses.

Kant then tells us in (4) that time raises difficulties for conception in virtue of its absolute continuity: we cannot break it up into simple parts, moments being merely limits to processes in time. Kant thinks with Leibniz that this continuity also conditions processes in time, which can therefore never involve wholly abrupt transitions. But all this leads on to (5), where he says that time cannot be anything absolutely real in the noumenal order, since it is neither a substance, nor an attribute, nor a relation. It is, in short, for logical and metaphysical reasons that Kant rejects the absolute reality of time; and the later critical system, while making great play with the notion of synthetic *a priori* knowledge, really rests on the same logico-metaphysical grounds as the *Dissertation*, which are those that Kant inherited from Leibniz and Wolff. Time is therefore held to be only a way in which what is real makes itself sensible to such as ourselves: it is 'a subjective condition necessary by the nature of the human mind in its co-ordination of any sensibles to itself according to a fixed law, and a pure intuition'. And though this pure intuition may not exist ready-made in us as an innate idea, it represents the response to external, sensory prodding of an inner law of the mind, through which all that we see comes to be arranged in a definite time-order, and to occupy differing lengths of time, and so becomes for us either a motion outside of us or a sequence of thoughts within us. So pervasive is the influence of this law, that even the pure laws of logic only acquire concrete significance through it. The not-A which A excludes must be moored to the concrete situation by the temporal relation of simultaneity: there is no incompatibility of A and not-A if they are not predicated simultaneously. Then (6) adds the codicil that time, despite its conceptual difficulties, is truly the form of phenomena, and cannot be argued out of existence by so-called contradictions which themselves presuppose it. To which (7) adds that time is therefore the ineliminable form of the whole sensible world.

It is clear from these passages that Kant's conception of a pure intuition does not exclude many obscure and dispositional elements. He makes unoccupied time live on the fringes of occupied time, into which the latter can and does constantly extrude itself, rather than be something that we can envisage as *totally* empty. Of *totally* empty time there can obviously be no intuitive envisagements, as the *Critique* will later argue: it is on the fringes of movements and changes that we also envisage the empty medium in which they take place. And the endlessness of time obviously involves only the conscious experience of being able to go on indefinitely: Kant does not however, like Wittgenstein, banish the dispositional from the concrete stuff of experience. Dispositions are for him arguably more 'real' than vanishing sense-contents. Kant's treatment of the imagination and its schemata in the *Critique* involves the same sort of 'ontologization' of the dispositional, an accordance of actuality to our readiness to form images rather than to actual image-formations, and it is in this sense that we must understand Kant's intuitive envisagement of the infinitely lasting, divisible, and all-compassing time. It is something whose possibility we feel 'in our bones' rather than in what is actually seen or seeable.

Having dealt with time under seven heads in §14, Kant proceeds to deal with space in §15 under five more or less similar heads. He argues (A) that seeing things outside of ourselves, and outside of one another, presupposes the comprehensive spatial order in which things are cast or seen. (B) says that space is unique and singular, and given us in a single over-view as the *whole* in which everything finds its place. Plainly if we had not the idea of this unique, singular order we should not locate what we see at this definite point in space, and we should not locate what we do not as yet see, or what we no longer see, as some *other* point in space. There is no empiricist build-up to a comprehensive space from the fragments offered us by sensory intuition. (C) adds that space is, therefore, in virtue of its individuality, a part of our intuitions, but of its pure, formal or non-sensuous part: it is not an object of abstrac-tive conception. Kant must here *not* be taken to mean that we dispose of a completely worked out intuition of the whole of infinite, empty space, but that whatever we sensibly intuit has to be seen in a spatial horizon which *could* be explored in-definitely. Here again the dispositional element is quite as real as the content-element which variegates it, and cannot be simply *analysed* in terms of the latter. The whole science of geometry, Kant further tells us, involves intuitive construction as well as conception, and also many odd features such as the incongruity of exact counterparts, and the three-dimensionality of space, which cannot be conceptually explained. (The in-tuition here involved cannot of course be limited by the accuracy of the circles, triangles, and so on that we actually see or draw, but by an imagination which bases itself on what we thus see, and which moves towards an indefinitely enhanced, limiting accuracy.) (D) then tells us that space is not a substance, nor an attribute, nor a relation, and hence not anything objec-tively real, but that it is something subjective and ideal which flows unchangeably from the nature of the mind, thereby providing a schema in which all external phenomena can be viewed. An empty, substantial space, as believed in by the English, is plainly a fiction, whereas an empirical, relational space, as believed in by the Germans, violates the certainty of geometrical insights, and opens up the possibility that we may one day meet with a bilineal rectangle. Kant assumes throughout that we can be quite sure of whatever flows from our mind's permanent nature, and can be sure that it does flow from that nature, an axiom that is, of course, open to question. (E) then argues that, since space is a structuring form of our sensitivity, we can be sure that its structuring principles will apply to everything which that sensitivity can ever experience. Kant ends the section by commenting on the manner in which we tend to construct linear, spatial images of time, a device that the *Critique* will argue is unavoidable. He also points out, however, that time has this priority over space: that it applies to all phenomena whatsoever, whether external or internal, whereas space only applies to what is external. Of the later doctrine that time is primarily the form of inner sense, and is only derivatively the form of outer sensibility, which would give motion a strange position in the material world, there is here happily no trace. Time further has the superior importance of conditioning the application of the law of contradiction, of the conceptions of cause and effect, and, through the procedure of counting, of the concepts of number. The forms of time and space, not being abstracted from sensory data, are for that reason not empirically acquired, yet without being innate. They spring rather from the activity of mind itself, which binds its sensations together according to laws of its own, which action can itself be cognized intuitively. 'Without doubt', Kant remarks at the end of section III, 'either concept (i.e. of time and space) is acquired, but not abstracted from our sensing of objects, for sensation only provides the material, not the form of human cognition. It is abstracted from the mind's own action, in co-ordinating whatever it senses according to perpetual laws. Each concept is therefore an immutable type which for that reason can be intuitively known.' It is of course clear that Kant does not here clearly distinguish between the spatializing and temporalizing 'actions' of 'the mind', and the resultant order they impart to phenomena, nor does he clearly recognize that the actions in question cannot have taken place in time at all, since temporal order is their outcome.

Section IV of the *Dissertation* then deals somewhat sketchily with the formal principles of the intelligible world. Once space and time have been removed from the connective tissue of this world, we are at once faced with the problem as to how its component substances are joined together so as to form a world which appears to us in a spatio-temporal guise. As Kant puts it: '*Manet quaestio, non nisi intellectui solubilis, quonam principio ipsa haec relatio omnium substantiarum nitatur, quae intuitive spectata vocatur spatium*' (The question remains, soluble only by the understanding, on what principle does *this relation of all substances rest, a relation which, intuitively regarded, we call space* [my italics]). This brief passage is of immense importance, since it shows that Kant believed that there were *relations* among Things-in-themselves that *corresponded* one for one, and in their logical properties, to the spatio-temporal order of phenomena, and that the law of the mind, whereby it spatialized and temporalized its sensuous impacts, was in a sense a *law of translation or transposition* which enabled it to *project* the noumenal order on to the surface of appearance, and that it was not the free improvisation that it has often been conceived to be — an improvisation, of course, insufficiently restrained by geometry and causality, and so on — and which assorts ill with the very notion of a law. Here, as in the later *Critique*, we are simply unacquainted with Things-in-themselves, whether in their individuality, their characters, or their relations, but the unknown differences and relations of these unknown things none the less carry over into the manners in which the mind orders and relates its data in space and time, and which are a logical picture of the former. Time and time again we find Kant anticipating the Wittgenstein of the *Tractatus*, whether in his unknowable simple objects, to which we none the less in some way unknowingly refer, or, as here, in the unknowable concatenations which are somehow reflected in the structure of our sentences. The statement or aphorism *4.014* in the *Tractatus* is thoroughly Kantian: 'A gramophone record, the musical idea, the written notes, and the sound-waves, all stand to one another in the same internal relation of depicting that holds between language and the world. They are all constructed according to a common logical pattern. (Like the two youths in the fairy-tale, their two horses, and their lilies. They are all in a certain sense one.)'

Kant refuses, however, to base the unity of the intelligible world on the mere fact that its substantial components interact causally. Causality is a relation of *sub*ordination, of one-sided dependence, while what we require is a *co*-ordinating relation which brings substances *together*, which makes interaction among them possible (§17). Kant finds this co-ordinating relation in the common dependence of all contingently existing substances on a single, necessarily existent substance, that is, God. They form the created, the contingent world, and their necessarily existent Creator must be external to this world (§§18–20). (Kant toys with the notion of a plurality of self-existent Creators, each responsible for a single world, but does not proceed far with its refutation.) The accommodations of the states of one created substance to those of another must then all stem from their common derivation from a divine source. Kant does not, however, decide whether such an accommodation is generic and ideal, as in the Leibnizian pre-established harmony, or whether it depends on countless divine interferences as in occasionalist theories, or whether, lastly, it is generic but *real*, in which case created substances can be held to have been so created as to be able directly to influence one another. This last theory of direct physical influence is the one that commends itself most strongly to Kant, though he concedes that God is always the remote artificer of all such interactions. He prefers also to attribute our *knowledge* of the things which appear around us in space to the direct action upon us of those things themselves, rather than to hold mystically with Malebranche, that we see all things in God (§22, Scholion). What has emerged from Kant's discussion of the intelligible world is simply a very radical form of the Leibnizian doctrine, in which time and the psyche have gone the way of space. The intelligible world can only be known in and through the sensible order which is its appearance. The critical writings will simply carry these conclusions a little further, though at a few points much too far.

The remainder of the *Dissertation* is wholly occupied with warding off the metaphysical errors which arise out of combining and confusing the intuitive and sensible, on the one hand, with the noumenal and intelligible on the other. Such errors are said by Kant to involve *subreption*, stealthy conversion. The logical use of concepts in subsuming particulars under concepts, and concepts under more general concepts, gives rise to no such subreptic errors. It is only when we consider conceptual contents *by themselves*, that is, make a real or hypostatic use of them, that such subreption becomes possible, and has to be guarded against by a special docimastic art, whose first principle is that nothing spatio-temporal must be predicated of Things-in-themselves, but only of things as they appear to us (§§24-5). Here we have a perfect metaphysical licence to *think* of things which do not conform to the axioms of space and time (§25). It is not metaphysically necessary to hold, with Crusius, that whatever exists must exist somewhere and at some time: this need not be true of immaterial substances, nor of the supreme cause of all such substances, God. God is not literally everywhere, nor is there any problem in His awareness of what is for us future (§27). It is likewise subreptic to argue that all *quanta* must be finite in number and measure: this only applies to such as appear to us in time. And it is subreptic to assume that whatever is without conceptual contradiction is phenomenally possible, or that what is phenomenally inconceivable may not be noumenally possible (§28). Nor should we regard what *always* exists in time as having an absolute necessity: the world, for example, is a contingent whole, even though it may be phenomenally everlasting (§29). Kant, lastly, thinks that there are principles of convenience which we, as working intelligences, must hypothetically act upon, though they are without any absolute, noumenal warrant, for example, that everything in the universe takes place according to the order of nature, that principles are not to be multiplied beyond necessity, that matter neither comes into being nor passes away, and so forth. We could not find our way among the intricate confusion of phenomena if we did not accept these as pragmatic principles, but it would be wrong to assume that the working of Things-in-themselves may not be more intricate and devious than would admit of any phenomenal sorting out.

It will be seen how most of the basic positions of Kant's critical writings have been worked out in the *Dissertation*, sometimes with much greater clarity. What has not been clearly worked out there is the limitation of verifiable certainty to what is phenomenal, and the consideration of the phenomenal criteria which will have to do duty for unreachable noumenal differences. And the importance of Transcendental Objects, as regulative Ideals of thought and practice, will, of course, only be raised once the phenomenal restriction has been accepted. We now turn to the consideration of space and time in the Transcendental Aesthetic, the first part of the *Critique of Reason*. This in all essential points follows the lead of the *Dissertation*.

iii

The opening paragraphs of the Transcendental Aesthetic inform us that *Anschauung*, intuition, direct envisagement, is the means whereby knowledge directs itself *immediately* to objects, and that it is also the preferred means to its goal. Intuition can, however, only arise in so far as an object is actually *given* to us, and this, in its turn, can only happen, at least in the case of us men, in so far as the object *affects* our minds in a given manner. Sensibility (*Sinnlichkeit*) is the name we give to the receptive faculty which enables us to have presentations (*Vorstellungen*) as the result of being thus affected, and it alone yields us intuitions. These, however, have to be thought by the understanding (*Verstand*), and from this faculty concepts (*Begriffe*) will arise. All thinking must, however, relate, whether directly or indirectly — in the latter case through general marks — to intuitions, which are in our case sensible, since sensibility is the one manner in which objects can be given to us. Sensation (*Empfindung*) is the operation of an object on our capacity for presentations, which latter is thereby affected, and the intuition which thus relates to the object through sensation is said to be empirical. The undetermined object of an empirical intuition is called by Kant an appearance (*Erscheinung*). (A. 19–20, B. 33–4.)

The hermeneutic difficulties of these opening paragraphs are considerable, but we may confidently assert that sensation for Kant is not only an experienced affection, but also, in some primitive fashion, the 'reference' of that affection to an affecting object, the latter being thereby *given* to us, and given to us as being of a certain quality. Such a quality can then, in its turn, become the basis of an empirical concept, empirical, since it arises out of sensation, but able thereafter to be applied to many objects, or be kept in readiness for such a use. The kind of causality expressed by the word 'affection' cannot be the sophisticated causality afterwards analysed in terms of regular succession: we cannot, in sensation, be making elaborate causal inferences. It can only be a primitively experienced impact of a thing not ourselves upon ourselves, having a character which at once reflects ourselves and the thing which is thus affecting us. It is important to realize that Kant never thinks in terms of substantialized sensations or sense-data as British empiricists have become trained to do: always he deals with things acting upon, and affecting other things, and sensations can never be more for him than the products of such commerce. The thing-analysis, we may say, forms the basis of his conceptions both of the phenomenal and the noumenal order: in neither case does he think in terms of discrete fragments or a messy continuum.

Kant goes on to say, in the next paragraphs, that what corresponds to sensation in an appearance will be called its matter, whereas what is responsible for the relational ordering of the many items in such an appearance, will be called its form. This form, he maintains, being the manner in which sensational materials are ordered, cannot itself be sensational, but must lie ready to hand in the mind, in advance of all sensation, and so must permit of being treated independently. (We, of course, who have read William James and the Gestalt-psychologists, will not here be impressed by this too confident, Lockean relegation of all relations to the 'work of the mind'.) Kant calls presentations 'pure', or describes them as pure intuitions, when they have been purged from anything which belongs to sensation, when they retain only the forms, the general relational patterns, in which the 'manifold' of sensational material has been or can be envisaged. Transcendental Aesthetic will be the name given by Kant to the study which will isolate these ordering forms or patterns in which whatever we directly intuit or envisage will be viewed. It will be 'transcendental', in that it will abstract from whatever is due to the affection of the knowing mind from without, and from what is not part of its inherent mode of action, and it will be 'aesthetic' in that it will abstract from the purely cogitative or conceptual side of this action, and will consider only the function of direct, intuitive envisagement. (Ἀίσϑησις is Greek for sensation or perception, and Kant is here using the term in the original Greek manner, and not connecting it with our feeling for the beautiful, as was the new fashion set by Baumgarten in 1750, and followed ever since.) And Kant will of course argue that space and time are the two ordering forms representing the inherent mode of action of the intuiting mind on the manifold material offered to it by sensation.

Before we consider the arguments set forth in the Aesthetic, we must, however, criticize certain general suggestions in this preliminary account, which are not acceptable even from a point of view sympathetic to Kant's, and which will be profoundly revised in the course of Kant's later expositions. Kant here talks as if the life of the knowing mind is a three-stage process: *first* we receive a manifold of disordered sensations, which are the direct outcome of impacts from Things-in-themselves, *next* we order such sensations in the empty relational cadres of space and time, which exist ready to hand in our conscious apparatus, and then, *lastly*, we proceed to interpret or think the sensations that we have thus envisaged, and to

apply certain general concepts to them, for example, by recognizing them to be substances of a certain sort, having states
of this or that sort, and so forth. It is plain that this three-stage
story is profoundly absurd, and it is afterwards clearly realized
to be such by Kant. For, since space and time are confessedly
the pervasive forms in which, by an inherent law of the mind,
all sensuous content must be cast, if it is to be intuited or
viewed by us at all, it is nonsense to suppose that we were
first confronted by detached sensory contents, and *then* found
a place for them somewhere in space and time. Our sensations
must indeed spring from the impacts of Transcendental Objects
on our own transcendental subjectivity, but the outcome of
such encounters must have been spatialized and temporalized
from the start, even if such a spatialization and temporalization
is thereafter an ever-developing activity, and is always adding
new ranges of vision to what was originally given. The act of
accommodating the impacts of objects-in-themselves to the
forms of vision lying ready to hand in the subject himself,
and so generating appearances in space and time, must therefore have been a *pre*-conscious, rather than a conscious accommodation, and must have been a single package-deal rather
than a two-stage process. (The use of the term 'pre-conscious',
and all other terms suggestive of proceedings in time, must of
course be interpreted as pointing to logical pre-conditions out
of time altogether.) Once appearances have been given, they
can, no doubt, be extended indefinitely by inferences, but there
can be no untemporalized, unspatialized, conscious items on
which spatiality and temporality are *afterwards* imposed. It
is just as clearly the case that there can be no intuitive envisagements in which no interpretative concepts are present. We
must see whatever we do see, as being something or other,
however vaguely or indefinitely we do so, if we are to see it
at all. A restricted accommodation of conception to intuitive
envisagement must therefore be present in the very origins of
such envisagement, together with an unlimited possibility of
extending this later, and the accommodation of the pre-
conscious impacts of objects to our own intuitive requirements
and thought-requirements must have been present from the very
start. One could not have been faced by a disordered intuitive
manifold on which one *then* imposed conceptual order. All
this is in fact conceded by Kant in his difficult and obscure
doctrine of the Productive Imagination, which will concern

us later. The whole perceived world, with its indefinite possibilities of imaginative extension and conceptual interpretation, must be the product of what may be called by analogy an 'act', but which never in truth took place in time at all. It may be called 'imaginative', since the appearances it generates are quite unlike any of the real sources from which they spring, and 'productive', since it reproduces nothing previously apparent. Its phenomenal products and their phenomenal relations may have one-to-one correspondence, and similarity of logical properties, with their noumenal originals, but by and large they are a new, productive, imaginative creation. This creation is the outcome of a single creative act in which sensible content, spatio-temporal order, and conceptual amenability are all present, though they of course require, and permit of, indefinite enlargement and refinement. The Aesthetic is therefore not so much the study of a *stage* in our conscious orientation to knowable objectivity, as the study of one pervasive *aspect* of such orientation. Kant's contention is that this aspect is entirely rooted in the necessary relations of ourselves as envisaging subjects to the objects that we envisage, and not at all in what we ourselves, or our objects themselves, independently are. The arguments for this difficult form of perceptual relativism will now be considered.

We shall, in the following exposition, conflate Kant's arguments for the transcendental ideality of space and time, though they are not completely parallel in the text; we shall also follow the treatment of the Second Edition, which does not, however, depart fundamentally from the First. Kant divides his treatment into a Metaphysical and a Transcendental Exposition of space and time, the former setting forth what the concepts of space and time themselves involve, the latter the consequences for knowledge that result from the nature of these concepts. There are four heads to the Metaphysical Exposition, which may be summarized and briefly commented upon as follows:

(1) tells us that space, with its mutually external regions, is presupposed by any location of perceived objects outside of my own body or outside and alongside of other perceived objects. It is not an empirical concept garnered from the relations perceived in, or between, bodies, but is presupposed by all such relations and first renders them possible. And time is, in precisely the same way, not an empirical concept abstracted

from what we see as existing simultaneously or successively around us or within us, nor from their relations, but is presupposed by all such relations and first renders them possible. In other words, to borrow the language of the *Dissertation*, there must be an inner law of the mind which regularly translates the mind's affections by Things-in-themselves, ordered in manners of which we know nothing, into instances of sensible qualities spatially and temporally arranged; such an ordering being the manner in which what is external to, and other than the self, or what is internal to it and proper to it, *must* appear to it. The internally based, presuppositional character of such an ordering is further shown by its absolutely pervasive character — absolutely *all* objects appear to us either in space and in time or in time alone — and also by the fact that it is always seen or felt to extend *beyond* the definite contents that it orders, or to fill in their interstices, and so to act, in some sort, as a connective tissue between them. Kant is, in short, recognizing the plain phenomenological fact that space and time are always vaguely given as the embracing horizons and media of all that we perceive, and not merely as patterned structures among or within the latter. And he is very arguably giving this priority a metaphysical foundation in the unknowable relations of the subject to objects-in-themselves.

(2) tells us that space differs from the contents seen in it by having an absolute irremovability, a necessity for the direct intuition of whatever is other than, and outside of, ourselves, which is absent from all such contents. Even if we move towards a point where all sensible content vanishes from space — Kant does not believe that we can absolutely reach such a point — we still do not think or feel that space itself would then also cease to be. Space is therefore an advance or *a priori* presupposition, built into our possible perception of whatever will act on our senses by an internal law of the mind, and so remains, as a presupposition or predisposition, even when actual sensations are not present. In much the same way, time is a necessary background idea, always generated by an inner law of the mind, which conditions the possibility of all our perceptions, whether internal or external, and which is therefore not removed even if we move in imagination to the unreachable point where all temporal appearances would vanish. Kant in these assertions shows the profoundest phenomenological penetration. Plainly we do feel, in some inexpugnable, if obscure, fashion, that even

if all spatial appearances were to vanish there would still remain the bare *room* for them, and that, similarly, if all temporal appearances were to vanish, there would still remain the *time* for them. Empty space and time, given aš a background to what is grossly given, are in fact as solid a datum, phenomenologically speaking, as they are in the axioms of Newton. We have them before us, we experience their immensity, in a manner indeed less palpable than the manner in which we experience their contents, but which remains most definite and compulsive, whether or not we yield to it philosophically. And while to yield to it would be by many condemned as 'picture-thinking', it remains questionable whether our thought is not much more pictorial if we believe only in vanishing sense-contents. Kant recognizes all these plain phenomenological facts in his doctrine of pure or *a priori* intuition, but this in no wise commits him to the view that we could have this deep sense of the two great media in the absence of all contrasting contents, much less that they could *exist* in the total absence of all such material.

(3) tells us that space is not some *general* concept of the relationships of things based on our noting what is common to many separate spaces. Space is always before us as a unitary, individual whole of which all separate spaces are merely the limited extracts (*Einschränkungen*). Time likewise is not some mere abstraction from definite, finite times, but is presupposed by them all as the individual whole of which they are only partial excerpts. Kant infers from this that, since space and time share the individuality of their contents, and are not given as generic features of them, our awareness of them must be intuitive and not merely conceptual. They are, we may say, the single, unique instances of the structures they embody, and so are not strictly separable from those structures, or those from them. This means, in effect, that the intuition we are said to have of space and time will always range an indefinite, impalpable penumbra about its palpable, definite core-elements, and that not all of it can be palpably given in the manner in which limited extracts from it certainly are.

(4) tells us that space and also time come before us as *unlimited* or *infinite* wholes: they are given as going on *endlessly* beyond the limited contents that palpably appear in them. This too shows that they are intuitively, not conceptually, given, since no concept, even if it may have application to an unlimited number of instances, can have an unlimited inner

articulation of content. But space and time in some sense set a whole, fully realized infinity before us, as the analysis of no concept could ever involve. Kant here again shows his phenomenological penetration: he does not, like a dogmatic empiricist, for example, Berkeley, hold that whatever is given, whether to sense or imagination, must in every respect be definite and clear. Kant plainly does not believe that we can *see* the whole of infinite space and time as we can see some limited datum in it. Kantian intuition includes much that is marginal and half-lit and only ready to become clear. For Kant, we may say, the *possibility* of what is not actually given is an actual element in what is given, without which the latter would be nothing at all.

In the Transcendental Exposition which follows Kant argues that the acceptance of space and time as the ineliminable, structuring forms of all our experiences, and so of all direct appearances to us, very readily explains how we can assert and prove all sorts of necessary axioms and theorems about what can appear to us as in space and time. Kant here instances such geo-chronometrical axioms or theorems as that space has three and only three dimensions, and time only one; that in a triangle two sides taken together are always greater than the third; and that, while many distinct events can happen at the same time and not successively, distinct times are necessarily successive, and so on. There would, Kant holds, be no self-contradiction in denying these axioms and principles, but we are sure none the less that they hold, not only of the instances that we have examined or experienced, but also of all the instances that will ever be examined or experienced, or that are or can be. If the way things appeared to us depended solely on what they intrinsically were, we should not expect them to appear so uniformly, or for us to be so confident of their structuring laws as we in fact are. Whereas, if the way things appear to us as spatially and temporally structured rests not on their intrinsic nature or structuring alone, but also on some inner law of the mind which systematically translates their intrinsic differences and arrangements into spatio-temporal differences and arrangements, then we can well explain how we can have such an absolute confidence in regard to such things *qua* apparent, and how such a confidence can very well be justified.

It has not, to my knowledge, been observed that this famous

argument is covertly inductive and scientific, and in no sense depends on transcendental insight. For Kant does not here argue that we can know the ways of our intuiting minds in some vastly superior way to the manner in which we apprehend the ways of the things that they reveal to us, and which we distinguish from ourselves. He does not argue that it is intrinsically clearer that *we* cannot imagine a bilineal figure than that there cannot *be*, as a given phenomenon, such a bilineal figure: the two certainties are precisely on the same level, and are in fact two aspects of the same certainty. And if we can think, without contradiction, of a bilineal figure, then we can also think, without contradiction, of someone imagining or perceiving it. The strength of the argument rests on the strange *uniformity* of our spatio-temporal certainties: we bring them ready-made to experience, and are never disappointed in our confidence in them, even if there is nothing analytically necessary about them. This uniformity points to their certainly having their roots in *ourselves* as intuiting subjects, whether or not they may not also have their roots in the intrinsic natures of the things that may appear to us. And it is arguable that beings constituted as we are, who depend for their knowledge of objects, including themselves, on the way that those objects *affect* them, must of necessity envisage those objects in the systematic externality of space or in the piecemeal progressiveness of time. Kant's view on these points is an explanatory, scientific hypothesis rather than an *a priori* certainty, and rests on a presumed substructure of things affecting other things, and so becoming apparent to one another, while their intrinsic natures are not thereby rendered apparent.

Two general conclusions are then held to arise from the Metaphysical and Transcendental Expositions that have just been rehearsed: (a) that space and time are not to be regarded as properties or relations of things as they exist in themselves, independently of the manner in which they appear to us; for it is not understandable that we should have definite and certain general intimations of such properties and relations prior to an exhaustive encounter with their actual cases; (b) space and time are to be regarded as the manners in which things appear to us, or are intuitively given to us; for, on this assumption, it is understandable that we should have general advance intimations as to the laws limiting what can be the case in space and time, prior to exhaustive encounter with the cases of such laws. Kant further holds, in the case of time, that it is primarily the structuring form of *inner* appearances, that is, of our own conscious states as given to introspection or inner sense. These states, he takes it, are themselves never spatial nor extended, though they may present objects and states of objects in space. Since, however, all objects and states of objects in space are presented to states of mind which are in time, time is *indirectly* a universal structuring form of external as well as internal phenomena (A. 34-5; B. 50-2). This view represents a regrettable departure from the *Dissertation* position, and would make it difficult for Kant to distinguish changes in objects that we judge to be objective, and changes in objects that we judge merely to depend on the order in which *we* apprehend them: in the Analogies of Experience in the *Critique of Pure Reason*, these distinctions play an all-important role. Motion is further for Kant one of the most centrally important features in phenomenal nature, as witnessed in the *Metaphysical Foundations of Natural Science* of 1786, and motion can only be understood if time is regarded as being as much a form of external, spatial phenomena as of internal, psychic ones.

Kant further holds that, though space, the form of outer appearance, has to borrow something from time for its motions, time likewise has to borrow something from space in order to have anything like a figure or a position (A. 33). It is only by projecting successive temporal states on to an imaginary line that we can be clearly aware of their sequence, and of the varying lengths of time that they occupy. This view is on the surface false, since it is certainly possible to be aware of duration, rhythm, and so on without representing it spatially, and the need to frame spatial pictures of time-patterns would seem to be peculiar to certain psychological types. Kant, however, also lays great stress at varying points in the *Critique* (e.g. in B. 75-6) on the vanishing, supersessive character of phenomena in time, and the need to give them a measure of permanence by connecting them with phenomena in space. It is arguable, however, that evanescence is as much a character of appearances in space as of appearances in time, and that constancy can sometimes be a character of phenomena in time as much as of those in space. Witness, for example, a continuous state of profound depression. What seems, however, to be the case is that time, in a most enigmatic fashion, combines ordinal properties, which do not alter, with supersessive properties, which are always in flux: its restless shuttle is always weaving a fabric that endures. How this is possible we cannot hope to understand: it is one of the places where Kantian or Bergsonian intuition outsoars the nimble understanding, and can perhaps only hope to be captured in such a C-series as that of McTaggart, which is not very different from Kant's own final solution for Noumena. The ordinal properties of time are, however, such as to lend themselves to representation in space, whereas its supersessive properties do not, and this perhaps is the reason that Kant thinks that time's permanent, ordinal structure has to borrow a non-supersessive representation from space.

The outcome of Kant's two conclusions is that space and time are empirically and phenomenally real, but transcendentally ideal: they are genuinely the manners in which things, with their characters and relations, whether within or without ourselves, must appear to beings like ourselves, and their laws must apply to whatever such beings have before them in experience; but it would none the less be a subreption, an invalid conversion, to treat them as the forms of Things-in-themselves (A. 27–30, 35–6). They translate, we may say metaphorically, the differences and other relations of Things-as-they-are-in-themselves into the special language of appearances in space and time, but such a translation yields only an empty conception, and no true knowledge, of the original. It would even be subreptive to apply them with certainty to the way that things might appear to other sorts of finite being (A. 27, 42), though it is quite conceivable that all finite beings perceive things as we do (B. 72). God, however, being conceived as perfect, and inclusive of all possibility, must assuredly be able to intuit things as they in themselves are, and not as they affect Him, or appear to Him. His intuition must therefore be of an archetypal and active sort, which *puts* things there, rather than receives impressions of them once they are there, and must therefore be quite different from our own derivative, ectypal intuition. But, though thus wholly phenomenal, time and space are not to be thought of as delusive or illusory, in the manner of certain sensuous shows which depend on other, more basic, phenomenal conditions. Thus a rainbow is taken to be illusory, since it is a special phenomenon which has its basis in sunlight, a more permanent phenomenon, when this shines upon rain. In such a situation we rightly take the rain and the sunlight to be the underlying realities of which the

rainbow is only the appearance. To the transcendental philosopher this distinction remains a valid one, even though for
him the sunlight and rain, since given in space and time, are
in a deeper sense ideal and phenomenal, and not to be treated
as belonging to Things-in-themselves (A. 6). The same applies
to all the secondary qualities of colour, warmth, sound, and
so on, which are limited to the perceptions of those having
sense-organs constituted in certain ways, such as need not, and
do not, obtain in the case of all sensitive beings. These secondary
qualities are, therefore, rightly to be regarded as the appearances
of movements, special spatio-temporal configurations, and so
on, which for *this* purpose count as realities. For the transcendentalist, however, the latter are *also* merely phenomenal,
and a mere half-way house towards the properties and relations of genuine Things-in-themselves (A. 29–30). In the
Metaphysical Foundations of Natural Science, and also in
Kant's *Opus Postumum*, the nature of this phenomenal half-
way house is richly canvassed, and in the latter writing Kant
puts forward the fascinating theory of a double affection,
the mind or *Gemüt* being first confronted by a *primary* phenomenal world of pure spatio-temporality, as a result of its *primary*
affection by Things-in-themselves, and then, at a second gasp,
being confronted by a secondary phenomenal world decked
out in all the sensory qualities, as the result of the mind's
affection by its own primary creation, very much as in orthodox physical theories of perception. Transcendental phenomenalism, therefore, leaves all ordinary distinctions between
reality and appearance intact, whether these be those of the
scientist or the ordinary percipient. The 'appearances' recognized by the latter are then rightly to be regarded as appearances of appearances; a designation actually used by Kant
in the last period of his theorizing.

Kant notes that, while many are willing to accept transcendental phenomenalism in regard to the objects and states
of outer sense, they experience the greatest difficulty in accepting it in regard to the mental states revealed by inner sense,
and in regard to the time which counts as the form of inner
sense. The things that I perceive as in space may not really
be in space at all, there may not really be any spatial things,
only things which appear to be in space; but it cannot be
doubted, the objection runs, that I do so perceive them, and
that my perceptions of things as in space are therefore real. Those

perceptions are, however, certainly given as following upon one another in time, and succession is therefore a real character or relation of real things, so that time at least cannot be the merely phenomenal form that the transcendental philosopher holds it to be. Kant's reply to this widely felt objection, first formulated in a letter from J. H. Lambert in 1770, is characteristically paradoxical, but it is also logically unassailable. He accepts the general Cartesian position that, when I doubt whether what I perceive or think is real, I cannot really doubt that my perception or thought of it (or, we may add, my doubt regarding what I thus perceive or think, or my own existence as percipient, thinker, and doubter) are all of them real. What I *can* doubt, however, is whether my perception, or thought, or doubt, or my own self as percipient, thinker, and doubter, are in all respects *as* I perceive or think them to be. If it *can* be contended that, while I certainly perceive real objects as in space, though absolutely they are not in space at all, then it *can* with equal justice be contended that, while my real perceptions of objects as in space are certainly perceived as in time, they may none the less absolutely not be in time at all. It is a mistake, in Kant's view, to confuse the *reality* of a mental act, and of the subject that performs it, with the *appearance* of that act on the stage of reflection or introspection, and to imagine that the two must necessarily coincide in their content. States of mind *as* they are introspected, or are given to inner sense, may *not* be quite as they are in themselves. Only in the case of a God, who is in all ways perfect, will the intellectual intuition of objects as they are in themselves necessarily go together with an intellectual intuition of *that* intellectual intuition as it is in itself; they may in fact merely be aspects of one and the same intuition. In *our* case, however, this may not be so at all.

Kant's views on these points have often been regarded as absurd. There cannot, it has been held, be misleading appearances of misleading appearances; this would, among other things, lead to an infinite regress. But if there can be such things as misleading appearances at all, then there is nothing to stop them from being misleading appearances of misleading appearances, and so on indefinitely: the logical possibility of an infinite regress will not, however, point to its actuality. And there can be little doubt that introspection, whatever it covers, is not an incorrigible process. It has, in fact, been

argued, by Wittgenstein, Titchener, and others, that many of
the mental acts of believing, intending, expecting, and so on,
which some claim to observe inwardly, are not, on a more
careful examination, really there at all: what are really there
are only a paltry set of images, feelings, and so on, not at all
relevant to public discourse, plus a readiness to react or to use
signs in certain characterizable ways. But equally well, it may
be contended, there may be an infinite number of subjective
actions which do not as such reveal themselves to introspection
at all, though their outcome is written large on the world as
we see it, and as it comes before us, which are responsible,
in short, for the world's phenomenology without themselves
forming part of the latter. Thus we may be continuously
projecting causal relations, valuations, significant interpretations, and so on into the phenomenal world, without having
the least awareness of the projective activities in question. It
is the second point of view that Kant subscribes to in his
transcendental psychology, and it is arguably the better way
to deal with such matters. For, if the physical world is nothing
without its 'deep structures', the same may arguably be true
of the life of the mind. And it is perfectly possible to hold that,
at a sufficiently deep level, the life of the mind no longer
involves the supersessively progressive, piecemeal character
inseparable from time, and that a whole life-career may be
projected and decided upon in a single, comprehensive act
of vision and free decision, which is neither before nor after
anything else, but out of time altogether. Kant's whole moral
philosophy is built on this difficult, seemingly mystical conception; and we may hold that, if the exigencies of modern
physics demand revision of some of the most fundamental
of our temporal intuitions, for example, those regarding simultaneity, there is no reason why the exigencies of our moral
imperatives should not also demand such revisions. If decisions
can only be free on the assumption that we have also decided
freely on the whole course of our practical life out of time
altogether, so that causal conditions are irrelevant to such
noumenal choices, then it may well be reasonable to believe
with Kant that decisions, even if taken out of time altogether,
have a definite, if not intuitively illustrable, sense. We can
mean and think them, even if we can neither know them
nor know anything about them (see A. 37–8; B. 67–9).

Kant's defence of phenomenalism in the Aesthetic mainly

rests on epistemological or, as he styles it, transcendental grounds; on the difficulty of understanding how we can know so much about the whole of space and time and their possible contents, and be so unshakeably confident regarding them, if they are forms of things as they exist independently of ourselves and of our mental constitution, and are not merely the ways in which, by that very constitution, we must necessarily perceive or envisage things. But to these transcendental difficulties Kant adds metaphysical or ontological difficulties, though he does not develop these at all as fully as he did in the *Dissertation*. Space and time, he argues, must be merely phenomenal, since it would be absurd to believe in the real existence of two such eternal, infinite, self-existent nothings (*Undinge*), which are believed to exist even in the absence of real contents, only in order to perform the function of containing (*befassen*) all real contents in themselves (A. 39). He also points to the fact that all that we see in space and time are relations, and that we cannot intuit the terms, presumably Leibnizian simples, between which such relations hold, nor pronounce on their inner character (B. 66–7). Time and space exhibit the basic difficulty, more fully canvassed in the *Dissertation*, of being neither substantial things, nor characters of substantial things, nor relations among substantial things. Falling under no metaphysical or logical category, they can only be subjective forms of appearance. Things can appear *as* in space and time, but they cannot simply *be* in space and time, nor can space and time themselves simply *be*.

Kant's belief in the merely phenomenal character of space and time is so central to his whole transcendental theory, and so puzzling in many of its contentions, that it will be well to examine it more fully, and to explore the basic reasons which led him to such conclusions. We may at first briefly contend that Kant has not been successful in *proving* the purely phenomenal character of space and time, whether by his transcendental or his metaphysical lines of agrument. That we can only perceive or imagine things other than ourselves as in space and time, and ourselves and our own states as in time, and that there are definite laws limiting what can be thus perceived or imagined, certainly proves, or is the same as saying, that space and time are built-in ways in which objects appear to us or are intuitively given to us: it does not, however, prove, as a long line of critics from Eberhard and Trendelenburg to

Bertrand Russell have argued, that they are not *also* the ways in which objects are ordered quite independently of our ways of knowing and perceiving them. For the grammar of the verb appearance is such that, while a thing may appear to be other than it is, it may also appear exactly as it is: how and what it is may, in short, simply appear. Perhaps we cannot certainly know that how things appear to us is also how they are, that their relational structures correspond or coincide, but it is not absurd or self-contradictory to suppose this, and it may in fact be quite reasonable to do so. And since Kant does hold that things other than ourselves do affect us, and give rise to appearances in space and time, and that we ourselves do affect ourselves and give rise to appearances in time, it is clear that there must be some sort of regular correlation between the differences and relations of what thus affects us and the differences and relations in its spatial and temporal appearance to us, if the notion of 'affection' is in fact to have any meaning at all. And what better correlation can there be than one in which the two structures are *identical*, at least in the main, so that things appear to us as ordered in space and time, when they are in fact actually so ordered? Things may in short appear to us, at least in the main, or in a special set of cases, to be just as they independently are, and they may both appear to us to be spatio-temporally ordered and also be so. It may in fact be argued that this is what it is rational to suppose.

Kant's motives for rejecting such a natural supposition are, however, threefold, and it is a little hard to understand why certain prejudices should have remained so deeply ingrained in a mind so perceptive, when the whole trend of his philosophy was to eliminate or overcome them. We may say that Kant, despite his defiant, if problematic, realism, is a crypto-idealist, and that, despite his stress on certainties which are both non-analytic and non-empirical, he is also a crypto-logicist and a crypto-empiricist. For, to take up the first charge, while Kant thoroughly recognizes the intentional nature of all conscious reference, and its direction to objects which need in no sense be parts of *itself*, and while for him the object *par excellence* transcends all of our perception and conception; he, yet, often confuses the sensational effects through which we perceive objects with the objects perceived through their means, and the thought-acts through which we conceive and know objects with the objects that we thus conceive or know. He therefore sometimes feels it to be a problem, as he does, for example, in that popular treatise, *Prolegomena to Any Future Metaphysic* (§9), that a property of something external to us should literally have to *migrate* (*wandern*) into our presentative faculty, in order that we should be able to perceive or conceive it. Plainly, Kant recognizes this sort of facile, idealistic argument to be a μετάβασις εἰς ἀλλὸ γένος, and his whole notion of appearance likewise refutes it, since space and time are not held to be *really* present in the intuitions which undoubtedly present them. Kant also throughout makes confident assumptions regarding other people's experiences, or about future or possible experiences, without thereby conceiving that such experiences have to 'migrate' into his own idea of them. There is, therefore, no reason why what we have to perceive or conceive, as belonging to objects, should not also really belong to them, and the spatio-temporal order, in which we cannot help seeing whatever we do see, may thus very well be an order which belongs to them (with some detailed modifications) as Things-in-themselves.

The second deep prepossession in Kant is what we call his crypto-logicism: his strange persuasion that there is a mystery in our knowing something, not guaranteed by empirical encounters with individual objects, when such knowledge is also not 'purely analytic', when it clearly merely elicits something already presupposed in some concept we are applying. There is, therefore, for the cryptologicist, a mystery in our knowledge of the three-dimensionality of whatever exists externally to ourselves, since it is not self-contradictory to conceive of it as having any number of dimensions. Kant has, however, done more than any philosopher to lessen the exaltation of the law of contradiction so prominent in his predecessors, and to show that it requires to be supplemented by non-formal compatibilities and incompatibilities to have any concrete meaning. We have, for example, to know such things as that X cannot move to the right and to the left at once, in order to give some concrete sense to the empty requirement that X cannot be both A and not A. And with this crypto-logicism, goes, as a third deep prepossession, Kant's crypto-empiricism, his belief that there is something puzzling about our knowledge of things if, not being analytic, it goes beyond what is met with in the individual case, if we know, for example, that movements to the right and to the left will always cancel each other out. This third prepossession is above all baseless, since Kant is certainly the philosopher who has shown that we cannot learn anything from the experience of particular instances, unless we bring to such experience a knowledge that extends infinitely beyond such instances, unless we know, for example, as argued in the Transcendental Analytic, that all that happens is subject to rigorous causal laws. (The validity of the general principles to which Kant appeals in order to justify our ability to learn from experience will be considered in the next chapter.) Here it will only be contended that it is very strange to see mystery in our ability to know non-trivial general principles in advance of experience, if experience could never teach us non-trivial general truths without making covert use of such principles. If *a posteriori* knowledge that is not of particular immediate empirical fact always demands *a priori* knowledge of certain non-trivial general principles, then it is absurd to lament that we are unable to learn *these* from experience. It can also here be objected, as has been done by Russell and others, that non-trivial knowledge of the general ways of our minds raises precisely the same problems as non-trivial knowledge of the general ways of anything else, and cannot therefore be used to make the latter more intelligible.

But if we now turn from Kant's transcendental arguments to his metaphysical arguments for the purely phenomenal status of space and time, it is again clear that, while in no way cogent, they have a much greater persuasive force. Kant has difficulty in believing in the independent reality of such empty 'nothings' as space and time, or in discovering the simple terms between which spatial and temporal relations ultimately hold, or in finding the logical 'category' to which space and time belong, since they are plainly not self-subsistent substances, nor attributes, nor relations. But it is plain that we *need* not think of space and time as pure nothings, and that we *may* construct theories basing them on the simple force-centres that are operative in them, and that we may also readily assign them to a peculiar category of their own, which is neither that of a concrete substance, nor that of an attribute, nor that of a relation. There are, in fact, a vast variety of ways in which it is possible to believe in a real spatio-temporal world, and we are not compelled to hold a subjectivist or phenomenalist view of it. And those theories of modern physics which resolve the occupying contents of space and time into mere unevennesses in space–time structure certainly deserve to be carefully examined and reformulated, even if they have hitherto been so poorly conceived and set forth.

On the other hand, Kant's view of space and time as purely phenomenal does arguably point to a certain ontological incompleteness in them. His basic objection to space, which applies also to time, is the Leibnizian objection that it never offers us true unities of any sort, whether in the direction of the small or the great. We cannot get to such unities in the direction of the small, where we merely regress on and on towards an unreachable limit, and we never reach them in the direction of the great, which likewise always pushes us on to an unreachable limit. And yet, we are not satisfied with the intermediate positions, which are arbitrarily demarcated, and have nothing complete about them. These, we may note, are also the objections of Plato to the Great and Small, the Pythagorean principle of the quantitatively indefinite, which only can achieve sense or worth when it is limited by the principle of unity or definite form. Kant, in regarding space and time as phenomenal, is thus, in effect, demanding that they should in some way be completed by true unities of some sort, that they should in some manner be taken to be 'expansions' or 'fluxions' of such unities, and that the latter should be indivisibly present in their divisibility, and unmanifestly active in their manifestations. And he is ultimately demanding that all such unities should stem from a single supreme unity, which sums up the possibility of them all as well as of anything else: only so can they give rise to a concatenated world, and not to a mere phantasmagoria. To rule that space and time are phenomenal is not, therefore, to extrude them wholly from reality; but to make them parasitic upon deeper, real structures, to relegate them to a manifest periphery beneath, or within, which we must locate various unmanifest unities, whether psychic or merely dynamic, whose permanent natures explain all surface modification and variegation. To talk thus is indeed to talk metaphorically, but not all metaphors permit of an exact, literal reformulation. And, from the point of view of human knowledge and volition, the underlying unity of the greatest importance to Kant is the unmanifest transcendental self which must be thought of as active in all our conscious postures.

Time, further, has metaphysical weaknesses which it does not share with its sister medium, space, and so is, in a sense, more incontestably phenomenal than the latter. For while time has permanent, ordinal properties resembling those of space, it also has what may be called its supersessive properties, which involve that, even in its smallest tracts, one content is always in process of replacing another. Such supersession is only intelligible if supplemented by an unmanifest unity in which nothing ever replaces anything. The supersessive aspects of time are, thus, peripheral and phenomenal, whereas its ordinal aspects are invariant and noumenal; even physicists have been forced to conceive of the latter when they locate all their variable local times in an invariant space–time, which is the same for all instruments and observers. There is then a good defence that can be put up for Kant's views of space and time as phenomenal. For, in and by themselves they offer us nothing that can be understood or that can be: they are like a sentence that trails off in an aposiopesis. Supplemented by indivisible, permanent unities and natures, they can, however, very well be, and be understood. And if these hermeneutic statements do not conform to the exact letter of Kant's text, they are arguably true to its spirit.

Chapter IV

The Analytic of Concepts

i

We have seen how Kant came to hold that the ways in which objects appear to us, and the ways in which we ourselves appear to ourselves, do not represent what such objects in themselves are, or what we ourselves absolutely are: there is an absolute and necessary divergence between the forms of intuition, the guises in which things are encountered by the senses or by introspection, and the ways in which they are qualified or structured as existing independently of sensory and introspective encounter. The *Dissertation*, however, argued that our conceptions and thoughts could successfully penetrate to things as they were in themselves, and that we could apply to them such pure concepts as substance, existence, number, causation, possibility, and so on; and could at least formulate such basic truths as that the world in itself consists of simple substances, that its components form an interacting causal community, that they all spring from a single, necessarily existent source, and so on. The *Critique of Pure Reason*, however, while continuing to allow such exercises of *thought* beyond the bounds of appearance and experience (see, e.g., Note to B. xxvi), and allowing them to be both unavoidable, and to have important inspirational and regulative uses, nevertheless believes them to be incapable of achieving anything like a fulfilment of their meaning, much less anything that would deserve to count as knowledge. Our thought, therefore, is as much a part of the way in which objects appear to us, and are represented by us, as are our more direct, intuitive encounters, and as little revelatory of what things may be 'in themselves'.

This phenomenal restriction of thought, as much as intuitive encounter, depends, moreover, on the necessary complementarity of the two subjective functions, at least in the case of beings organized as we are. The two cognitive functions may both spring from a (to us unknown and unknowable) common root (A. 15), and there may be forms of transcendent cognition in which such a common root functions alone; but, in beings like ourselves, the two functions have to work in harness, if they are to achieve anything like fulfillable reference or knowledge. Intuitive encounter, moreover, represents the receptive, passive element in our experience, the side stemming from the impacts or impressions of things actually affecting us, in virtue of which something comes to be *given* to us; while thought, on the other hand, represents the spontaneously active side of our experience, which interprets or thinks whatever we have before us. Intuitive encounter, unilluminated by thought or understanding, would be *blind* (A. 51; B. 75): and would not amount to the experience or knowledge or epistemically relevant reference to any object. It would at best contribute indirectly to knowledge, in so far as what it offered *could* be thought, interpreted, or understood. But, likewise, thought unrelated to intuitive encounter, whether actual or possible, would have the opposed defect of *emptiness*: it would also not amount to the experience or knowledge of anything. Such a defect does not for Kant have the connotation of a sheer meaninglessness that it has for the positivistically oriented: Kant, like Husserl, assigns important functions to the unfulfilled, or even unfulfillable, cognitive reference, for example a reference to God or to the transcendental self. He does not, however, give it meaning in his special epistemological sense: it cannot contribute to our knowledge of anything. All our knowledge, further, begins with experience, but such experience, Kant assures us, need not be taken to be an original passive givenness as some have regarded it. Experience must from the start involve rudimentary acts of combining, distinguishing, comparing, and so on, on which countless further acts of thought can be superimposed. (And, logically, prior to even such rudimentary acts, Kant, in his doctrine of the Transcendental Imagination, holds to the existence of a pre-experiential, pre-conscious preparation of the whole experiential field, which has rendered it as much amenable to our thinking as it is to our intuition.) In the same way, all thoughts must at least seek to fulfil themselves in intuitive encounter (A. 50-2; B. 1-2). Only in God might there be nothing of the antithesis between the thinking and the intuitive approaches to objects, since God must be credited with originating objects through

His clear thought of them, and with knowing them, not by passively submitting to their impacts, but by being spontaneously responsible for their very existence and nature (A. 252-6; B. 71-2). But, in *our* knowledge and experience, objects are not originated, only derivatively reconceived, and such reconception is always geared, even if only remotely, to the impacts such objects did or might have on our senses, and so to the manner in which they appear to us and not to what they may be in themselves.

Kant's conception of thought, as opposed to intuition, is based throughout on logic: it distinguishes between the three categories of the concept (*Begriff*), the judgement (*Urteil*), and the inference (*Schluss*). A concept, for Kant, arises out of an act or function of assembling a number of distinct presentations, and ranging them all under a single presentation, which is the common universal of which they are the specific or the individual cases. 'All intuitions', he tells us, 'as sensible, rest upon affections, but concepts rest on functions. I understand by functions the unity of the act of ordering different presentations under a single common one' (A. 68). Thus, to recognize something we see before us as a metal, is to range it under a concept, to apply a notion to it which either has been, or could be, applied to other sensible objects: the concept then applies mediately or indirectly to the object which is directly intuited or seen. But a concept can also be thought of as ranging over other concepts, as when we consider metals as cases of bodies, and bodies as substances: we then have a more remotely mediate relation of a concept, through other concepts, to the individual cases given in actual or in possible sense-encounter. Kant assumes that, for a concept to play a part in knowledge, it must at least be capable of application, whether directly or by way of other concepts, to individual cases given in intuition. Only by being so capable, can it avoid the stigma of being an empty, an epistemically useless, concept.

A further character of a concept must here be noted, though Kant leaves it imperfectly clarified: that a concept always conjoins a plurality of features, which are not, however, a mere aggregate, but a genuine unity involving an organizing *rule*. Thus, a triangle is conceived as consisting of three straight lines combined according to a definite rule which permits of intuitive illustration (A. 105). The concept of a rule itself combines two features which Kant does not clearly separate:

that of producing a unity among the items it combines, so that what we have before us counts as one thing, and our awareness of it as a single thought; and that of being readily repeatable, so that innumerable different things can be ranged under the same concept. This second feature depends on the first. For it is only because concepts are simplifying, integrating unities that they can readily be carried over from one case to another: a mere assemblage of features would not be so transferable. This equation of concepts with rules is fundamental for Kantian theory: it entails that a set of features or items that obeyed no rules would never amount to an object or set of objects that could be located in a real or an imaginary world. The conception of a rule is, of course, infinitely obscure, but few have elucidated it any better than Kant.

A judgement is now characterized by Kant as being precisely the act of ranging presentations under higher, more general presentations or concepts, whether as individual cases given directly in intuition, or as general concepts which rank as specific cases of yet more general concepts (e.g. *Every body is changeable*). A judgement is therefore described as 'the mediate knowledge of an object, i.e. the presentation of a presentation of it', and it is held that 'in every judgement there is a concept applicable to many, among which a given presentation is included, which latter relates directly to the object. So, e.g., in the judgement "All bodies are changeable", the concept of the changeable relates to various other concepts, and here specifically to the concept of body, and this in its turn to certain phenomena which come before us' (A. 68-9). A *Schluss* or inference, on the other hand, is characterized, at a much later stage in the *Critique*, as a complex act of thinking, in which, by ranging a presented case, whether intuited or conceived, under a given concept, and that under yet another, we proceed to range the first case under the last concept. (See, e.g., A. 321-2: Caius is a man, Men are mortal, so Caius is mortal.)

We must, however, not attach too narrow a meaning to these logical rubrics introduced by Kant. His concepts must be taken to include much that is very vaguely and confusedly conceived, and much that requires philosophical analysis and perhaps emendation (A. 7). A man who can see the meaning of 'there being people in the moon' in all that would be encountered in the 'empirical advance' involved in going there to see

(A. 492–3), or who discovers deep difficulties in the concept of the soul as a simple substance (A. 355), cannot be held to have identified a concept with anything clearly definable. And by a 'judgement' Kant plainly covers all sorts of vague presumptions, and takings for granted, as well as clearly formulated pronouncements, and something quietly at work in imagination and perception, as much as in self-conscious assessments. He also includes in it acts of entertainment and surmise as well as acts of assertion, as when he says that the hypothetical judgement includes two 'judgements', whose truth is, however, undetermined (A. 73). The whole activity of imagination, however remote from reality in its objects, and however little involving fully developed assertion or belief, would also involve 'judgements' in the very wide Kantian sense. For in all its activities there is an application, or intended application, of concepts to imagined instances: it is as if something or other exemplified a certain concept, or was of a certain sort. Plainly also Kant does not limit inferences (*Schlüsse*) to syllogistic reasonings, precisely formulated or rigorously deduced: Kant's own work contains hardly any of the clear syllogisms of his great predecessor, Christian Wolff. It may be held, therefore, that in his concepts, judgements, and inferences Kant included much that was penumbral and marginally vague, much that was tentative and confused, and much that a modern sensualist would describe as 'dispositional'. It is a great point of strength in Kant that his inner acts and experiences are always living, burgeoning structures, not reduced, strengthless appearances, *à la* Hume, Titchener, or Wittgenstein, trailing past in a bloodless masquerade or only given meaning by what we outwardly do or say.

We must, however, note at this point that Kant gives to judgement too central a place in the life of thought, and one that we shall show affects his arguments in the Transcendental Deduction. He assumes without question that 'the understanding can make no other use of concepts but to judge by them' and that 'All acts of the understanding can be reduced to judgements, so that the understanding can in general be presented as a faculty of judging' (A. 93–4). This view leads Kant to connect the very unity of consciousness with the connection of all items we are aware of through judgements, and so to deduce the categories from this unity of consciousness, the main point of the Transcendental Deduction. It is clear, however, that there are other uses of concepts than the judgemental, uses that Kant himself very often recognizes: there is the straying from concept to cognate concept in wandering thought, there is the Platonic determination of the relations of concepts to other concepts, which is certainly not oriented to their application to instances, and there is lastly, and of central importance, the assembling of items, whether concepts or individuals, in an enumeration or set, which need have nothing to do with their subsumption under higher concepts. It has often been contended, for example, by Frege, that such enumeration is always conceptual: we only have sets where there are common properties. It is clear, however, that there are arbitrary as well as conceptually limited enumerations: the Kohinoor diamond, chastity, and the number five form a triad; and ships, shoes, sealing-wax, cabbages, and kings form a pentad, though there need be no attempt to judge about them or through them. The unity of consciousness plainly extends to other operations besides judging, even though judging may have an all-important place in it. And it is misleading to suggest that the thinking mind has no other or better occupation than to apply its notions to specific cases or examples, that it is only there, in the last instance, to determine what happens to exist or be the case.

ii

Kant further makes the momentous assumption that our concepts, our judgements, and our inferences, like our intuitions, bring certain structuring forms to experience and knowledge, by means of which all that is perceived or imagined by us as in space or time, whether in outer objects or in ourselves, and all that is more remotely conceived, believed, or reasoned about, has to be ordered or structured. Such subjectively imported structuring features are said by Kant to be *a priori*, ready for activation *in advance of* experience, as opposed to other elements which derive directly from our exposure to the impacts of Things-in-themselves (ourselves included), and which are said by Kant to be *a posteriori*, or arising only *after*, or *as a result of*, empirical encounter. (The temporal implications of this 'afterness' are of course highly misleading, since *both* what is *a priori*, and what is *a posteriori* only become fully actual together, as parts of a fully actualized experience, while the impacts of Things-in-themselves really fall outside of time altogether.) Kant further assumes that these *a priori* elements in conception, judgement, and inference will reveal themselves, not so much when we reflect on what we are thinking *about*, or on the *subject-matters* we are considering; but rather when we reflect on the *manner* or *manners* in which we think about such subject-matters, how we prize them apart, and put them together again; or on what the *Dissertation* described as the inner laws which the mind follows in the ordering of its materials, though then we were only concerned with an intuitive ordering in space and time, whereas now we are concerned with their ordering in and for thought. Such an ordering can, however, become fully conscious, and will then reveal the higher-order, *a priori* concepts or ideas which the mind brings to experience and knowledge, and which are used and followed, rather than consciously thought of, in our ordinary thought-procedures. But though thus brought by us to experience, it is important to note that the *a priori* concepts, judgements, and ideas in question are not for Kant merely subjective: they structure objects as understood or reasoned about, and so are, in an important sense, as much objective as subjective. There is nothing in Kant which excludes the thoroughgoing 'objectification' which we find, for example, in Husserl's *Logical Investigations*.

We shall now give a brief preliminary survey of the *a priori* conceptual, judgemental, and ideal elements which Kant will treat of in many places all over the *Critique of Pure Reason*. Among our *a priori* concepts there are those that are derived, not from contentful, empirical intuition, but from pure intuition, that is, concepts of the purely spatial and temporal, such as contact, right, and left, the straight, succession, duration, the past, and the future, and so on. It is in constructing figures in space, or in representing time by linear diagrams, that such concepts arise. They are in an ambiguous position, not being *a priori qua* concepts, since they are based on intuitive constructions, but being *a priori*, since their source is *a priori*, not empirical. More important, however, are the pure concepts which Kant listed in the *Dissertation*, and of which he is, in later parts of the Analytic, to offer a listing and an impressive deduction, and which will be known as 'categories'. For our purposes it will be sufficient, in this preliminary section, to list the categories of number and quantity, the categories of the positive and the negative, those of substance and causality, and those, finally, of the possible, the actual, and the necessary. Kant's listing and deduction of these categories will shortly concern us. But, in addition to these categorial concepts, which the understanding can regularly apply to its material, there are also notions which Kant calls Transcendental Ideas, and which arise out of a need to extend our inferences to first grounds and unconditioned conditions. Here we may mention the Ideas of the soul or Transcendental Subject, and of its unconditioned freedom or spontaneity, and its essential perdurability in time. We may also mention the Idea of the omnireal, omnipossible, necessarily existent God, which Kant calls the Ideal of Pure Reason. These Transcendental Ideas, though indispensable, as the imaginary foci of all explanation, quite transcend possible experience. Their role will be considered, and be purged of mistakes, in Kant's Transcendental Dialectic.

The most important *a priori* aspect of our thinking is, however, Kant thinks, to be found in our *judgements*, and particularly in those which are both *a priori* and synthetic, and not merely analytic. Kant's treatment of these topics is mainly in the Second Edition Introduction to the *Critique*, and has given rise to a vast critical literature, whose outcome is, however, somewhat exiguous. Kant distinguishes three classes of judgement important for his purpose: (1) judgements which are *synthetic* and *a posteriori*, which are, that is, substantial, and not trivial, but which rest on experience; (2) judgements which are *a priori* but analytic, which are not based on experience, but which also give us no substantial information about the empirical world; (3) judgements which are both synthetic and *a priori*, which give us substantial information about the empirical world, but which are not based on our experience of it. These preliminary characterizations will be explained as we proceed. We may here point to an important class of judgements which Kant ignores, those which we learn *a posteriori* from our experience of particular cases, but which can nevertheless be shown, on profounder conceptual examination, to be purely analytic. Thus, to use an example which would not accord with Kant's synthetic views of arithmetic, a man might discover by experience and problematic induction that the sum of the first *n* odd numbers was always a perfect square: he might then afterwards advance to a proof of this remarkable proposition, which would, on a modern view of arithmetic, be purely analytic. It is even arguable that Kant's whole theory of knowledge, as resting on deep-laid subjective structures, is a judgement of this sort: it starts by being an empirical hypothesis to account for certain remarkable cases of prescience, and it ends by being an analytic consequence of the sort of knowledge that we humans can possess. Perhaps most valuable philosophy is a transformation of what seem remarkable contingent matters of fact into consequences that follow analytically from the only right set of concepts. There must, of course, be a material of brute facticity that no set of structuring concepts will ever reduce to order, but it is arguable that its range is much more definitely restricted than has been supposed.

Kant bases his distinction between analytic and synthetic judgements on a somewhat clumsy concept of conceptual containment. Judgements are analytic if the concepts connected in them with a given concept can be regarded as perhaps obscurely (*versteckterweise*) or confusedly (*verworren*) contained (*enthalten*) in the concept in question, and as emerging when that concept is broken up into its constituent concepts (*durch Zergliederung in seine Teilbegriffe*); whereas they are synthetic if the concepts connected in them with a given concept add something that is not thought in the latter at all, and which could not have been extracted from it by any process of analysis (*welches in jenem gar nicht gedacht war, und durch keine Zergliederung desselben hätte können herausgezogen werden*) (A. 7). Kant limits his treatment to the special case of the subject-predicate judgement, and gives 'All bodies are extended' as a case of an analytic judgement, since I need not, Kant thinks, go beyond what I think when I judge anything to be a body in order to think of it as extended; but he gives 'All bodies are heavy' as a case of a synthetic judgement, since I *do* have to go beyond what I think in judging anything to be a body when I remark that bodies are heavy (A. 7). Analytic judgements are, therefore, judgements where the predicate-concept adds nothing to what is thought in the subject-concept, whereas synthetic judgements do amplify what is thought in the subject-concept with something that is not contained in it.

Objection has, of course, been raised to the subject-predicate restriction of this account, but Kant certainly does not *mean* to be thus restrictive. He admits other forms of judgement than the subject-predicate form, and would certainly wish to apply his distinction to them, for example, to judgements stating a reciprocity of relations among a plurality of terms.

Thus 'Everyone loves everyone' would plainly be a synthetic judgement, since it is not part of what we understand by a person that he should love any or all persons, whereas 'Every magnitude is either equal or unequal to every magnitude' is quite as obviously analytic. And there are of course other distinctions based on the variability and marginal vagueness of the concepts connected with certain words, for example, body, experience, judgement, and so on, of which Kant certainly took full cognizance, even if he may not have taken great pains to spell them out. The petty problems of the exact analyst or logician, worried as to just what to say in a given situation, are not the problems that engaged so richly concrete a thinker as Kant. Of course it is true that what is, at one time or for one man, not part of the conceptual content of a term, can, at another time or for another man, be made part of it, or vice versa, and that what is synthetic can thus in a sense be made analytic, and vice versa. And of course we can so fatten a set of concepts with meaning as to make it hard for us to move them about in discourse, or make them so lean and spare that the most preposterous alignments become open to us. There are, in fact, thought-contexts where a policy of emaciation and reduction seems best, and where 'logical possibilities' become rampant, and there are other thought-contexts where concrete enrichment seems the better policy. And it is a matter for philosophical insight to decide where abstractive emaciation really becomes senseless, or where concrete enrichment gives a false necessity to the merely factual.

For Kant, any judgement which rests on the concrete arrangements met with in empirical encounter, and which is capable, therefore, of being true or untrue according to what we thus encounter, is both synthetic and *a posteriori*. It is synthetic because the concepts which it brings together are not such, *qua* concepts, that they have to be brought together, and it is *a posteriori* since we are only in fact able to connect them in our judgements *after* they have been offered to us together in a given empirical case or set of cases. And the synthetic *a posteriori* will be *certain* only in respect of the cases on which it has thus been founded, and will be highly problematic in regard to all further cases. *A posteriori* judgements therefore never have necessity and strict universality, that is, application to all possible cases, since they depend for their truth on actual cases, and not merely on concepts. *A priori* judgements, on the other hand, have their foundation in concepts and not in cases, and they are therefore such that they can be known in advance of particular cases: the concepts they involve are such that they *must* be connected wherever they apply, and so must apply in all *possible* cases. But of such *a priori* judgements there are the two sorts we have mentioned: the analytic sort, where a concept connects with other concepts simply because it is part of their content, and so only serves to elucidate that content; and the synthetic sort where a concept is connected with other concepts, not merely because it is part of their content, and not merely because we have encountered them together in particular cases, but because the concepts concerned, though distinct in their content, must none the less be judged to belong together, and to belong together in all possible cases, by anyone who is acquainted with them. Such non-trivial, non-case-based insight certainly is remarkable, and Kant recognizes its importance by making it the central problem of the *Critique* (see particularly the Second Edition *Introduction*).

Kant gives several examples of the sort of non-trivial, non-case-based conceptual connections in question, all of which are highly controversial. Arithmetic is held by him unquestionably to involve such connections in all the specific relations it establishes among numbers, for example, $7 + 5 = 12$. Amounting to 12 is not part of what we understand by being the sum of 7 and 5, and it is only by imaginatively constructing, or being ready to construct, aggregates instantiating the separate numbers concerned and their sum, and also recognizing the universal possibility of such aggregation, involved in our consciousness of items in time, and also perhaps in space, that the resultant connection establishes itself. In the same way, many of the axiomatic principles of geometry can only be established by our willingness to play about with the intuitively given medium of space and to see that it connects invariance of direction, that is, straightness, with maximum brevity, and that it also only permits lines to lie in three wholly independent directions, and so on. Natural science, likewise, involves the regular application of principles whose universality is not trivially analytic: that there must, for example, be something permanent in space whose amount admits neither of increase nor decrease, that every alteration must have a cause (B. 5); as well as more detailed principles, such as that action and reaction must be equal and opposite, and all the Leibnizian-Newtonian laws later elaborated in the *Metaphysical Foundations of Natural Science* of 1787 (see A. xxi; B. 18). Metaphysics, also, as a science of non-phenomenal being, at least *aspires* to non-trivial *a priori* truths: that all composition must terminate in the absolutely simple, that the contingencies of existence must depend on an existence which embraces all possibilities, and hence is absolutely necessary, and so forth. There is then, for Kant, no field of knowledge, or would-be knowledge, that can be purely empirical. We can only learn from experience by invoking principles which make such learning possible, which give us an advance, general intimation of what we may hope to find, and so enable us to put the right questions to nature. As Kant puts it in a well-known passage: 'Reason only has insight into what it itself projects and produces . . . and must compel nature to answer reason's own questions, and not, as it were, dangle along tied to nature's leading-strings' (B. xiii).

We shall not, in the present work, add to the immense volume of detailed criticism of Kant's examples of the synthetic *a priori*. It is obvious that, if arithmetical concepts are built up in a formalized deductive system like that of Russell, Frege, or Peano, a proposition like 7 + 5 = 12 can have no claim to state a synthetic truth. Even Hegel held all arithmetic to be analytic. There are also, on the other side, eccentric arithmetics, such as those worked out by Wittgenstein in his 1939 Lectures, in which some arithmetical concepts behave differently from the way they do in orthodox arithmetic. It is likewise clear that certain geometrical axioms and theorems hold only in certain sorts of space, and that other sorts of space are not only conceivable, but also, with a little difficulty, imaginable. (The optical phenomenology of a finite, spherical space can, for example, be successfully worked out.) And as regards the *a priori* synthetic principles underlying natural science, it is highly arguable that Kant has been too rigorous, too Newtonian, and that he has been blind to many laxer, more probabilistic views of the rules connecting natural phenomena with one another. All this does not affect his general insight that one must have some advance intimation of regional structures, in order to ask detailed questions regarding a given region, and to receive empirical answers to one's questions. And though such advance intimations are corrigible by further experience, it may yet be the case that some part of them survives uncorrected, and becomes less and less open to correction. There may, for example, be a geometry which will cover every possible geometry. And such a consilience of the inductive with the *a priori* approach might affect even the august science of logic: Kant himself suggests as much in his bringing in of questions of succession, and of the cancellation of opposites, if one is to give concrete sense to the logical notion of negation. The logic that is wholly formal, and that applies to all subject-matters whatever, is then, arguably, something that will only emerge when one has explored the regional *a priori* of every subject-matter, and has become clear as to the universally structuring principles which obtain in them all. It may then have many of the features that are now thought of as extralogical.

Husserl and others have sought to show that every field of empirical investigation must have its own regional *a priori*, its governing body of concepts and principles which make it the field that it is, and that make it possible for us to locate empirical details in such a scheme, and to learn something from them. The *formal a priori*, which applies to material from *all* regions, is then also, from such a point of view, merely one very abstract, regional *a priori* among others less abstract. But what Husserl did not see, and what Kant only imperfectly grasped in his practice, is that one can only arrive at the presuppositional *a priori* which enables one to learn from experience by oneself learning from experience how one learns from experience, and what the principles are which quietly guide one's investigations in a variety of fields. One's pronouncements on such principles are therefore open to correction by careful reflection upon one's actual investigative procedures, and one's resourceful changes in strategy when faced by new problems; and have, therefore, always a certain note of the presumptive or probable about them. And what Kant and Husserl have alike never considered is that even the emergent *a priori* which distinguishes itself in a certain field, may in some cases remain irreducibly probabilistic. It would, in fact, appear that the transcendental *a priori* of the mind is itself in this case, and that we can only hope to establish laws of tendency in this field, not laws that are absolutely apodictic. Thus, desire for an end must necessarily determine desire for what is seen to be a means to that end, but may not necessarily *succeed* in determining action.

Leaving aside these questions, which range far beyond the explicit thought of Kant, we may notice how, in his own transcendental theory, he first adopts, as a quasi-scientific hypothesis, the 'Copernican' view that objects, as we know them, must be such as to conform to the requirements of our intuitive faculty, and to those of the understanding, which interprets the materials offered by that faculty; rather than that our intuitive faculty and our understanding must have to conform themselves to independently real objects. Copernicus found it hard to explain apparent stellar motions on the hypothesis that all the stars revolved around us, and around the earth beneath us: he found it simpler to suppose that we ourselves, and the earth beneath us, revolved uniformly in a certain direction, which made all the stars *seem* to move together in a contrary manner. This argument, we may note, was guided by parsimony: it was simpler to suppose that *one* body was moving in a certain manner, than that a congeries of independent bodies were all doing so. Kant, following Copernicus, will explain our advance knowledge of many non-trivial principles, governing all we shall afterwards have to intuit or interpret, by supposing, not that we thereby accommodate ourselves to countless independently real objects, but that they, in so far as they appear before us, have to accommodate themselves to our own intuitive and conceptual requirements. 'If intuition', Kant says, 'must conform itself to the character of its objects, I cannot see how one could have any *a priori* knowledge of this character, but if the object (*qua* object of the senses) conforms itself to the character of my intuitive faculty, I can very well conceive this possibility. But . . . since I cannot rest with such intuitions, which must be made into acts of knowing, and be referred as presentations to something or other as the object that they determine, I can either assume that the concepts through which I manage to arrange such a reference conform themselves to their object . . . or I can assume that the objects, or, what is the same, the experience in which alone, as given objects, they can be known, conforms itself to these concepts' (B. xvii). The second hypothesis is again preferred, since it is harder to see how I should have an advance accommodation to countless independent objects, than it is to see how all objects that affect me intuitively, and that provoke my interpretations, should be accommodated to my own intuitive and conceptual requirements. Kant claims, however, in an important Note to page xxii of the Second Edition Preface, that, though his transcendental theory may start very much as an explanatory scientific hypothesis, exactly on a level with the Copernican theory, it will end by being established apodictically from the nature of our sort of understanding, experience, and knowledge, in which all thought has to refer itself to affectively received intuitions. That Kant really succeeded in this apodictic establishment may well be questioned, but he certainly did construct a set of very fundamental, well-integrated concepts which range far beyond those of a scientific hypothesis.

We may, however, further note that Kant, in his transcendental theorizing, has forgotten the fact that, in his view, we know as little of ourselves in ourselves, as the ultimate dynamic sources of all our mental workings, as we know of the Things-in-themselves which underlie all external, phenomenal manifestations. We are indeed *almost always* being affected by ourselves through inner sense, as we are *not* always being affected by given external things through outer sense, and we can accordingly acquire more familiarity with our own phenomenal workings than with those of external substances. But all this will not justify Kant's almost Cartesian exaggeration of the degree to which we can know ourselves, which at times almost amounts to holding that we know ourselves as we in ourselves truly are. This Cartesian exaggeration expresses itself in utterances like the following: 'Nothing in the systematic inventory of all our possessions through pure reason can escape us, for what reason brings forth entirely from itself, cannot be hidden from reason, but must itself be brought to light by reason' (A. xx). Or again: 'This critical science of reason cannot be of terrifically wide range, since it has not to do with objects of reason, whose variety is infinite, but only with itself, with tasks that spring from its own bosom, and are not prescribed to it by the nature of things other than itself, but by its own nature' (B. 23). Such utterances plainly represent a relapse into a kind of thought which Kant himself has repudiated: the old Cartesian approach to consciousness as presenting us with acts and agents more indubitably real than anything in the non-subjective sphere. And it also represents a relapse, since it *unhesitatingly* accepts a *synthetic a priori* in the subjective field, while finding this hard to understand in other fields. Obviously such utterances are profoundly un-Kantian, since the phenomenal laws of our own subjectivity are as empirical, as incapable of strict universality and necessity, as are the phenomenal laws governing external objects. We can indeed argue conceptually that, *if* there is to be such a thing as experience and knowledge in beings of a certain intuitive-conceptual organization, then it follows analytically that such and such conditions must prevail, for example, regularities of succession must be discoverable. But a proof from the mere possibility of knowledge and experience, in beings of a certain constitution, does not guarantee the continued actualization of such a possibility, nor of the unknown conditions that render it possible. But if, however, Kant really wishes to maintain that we can have a non-empirical knowledge of ourselves, and of our inbuilt ways of working, which does not rest on the manner in which we affect ourselves inwardly; then, a similar possibility is plainly open in the case of objects in space and time, which may, by the combined efforts of the geometer and the physical scientist, come to be laid bare just as they are in themselves. Geometry and space–time physics are certainly disciplines that achieve a higher degree of lucidity and cogency than does transcendental psychology.

It is also important to note that Kant's 'Copernican' explanation of *a priori* synthetic knowledge really applies primarily to our intuitive faculties, and only secondarily to our faculties of conception. It is only because our conceptual faculties have to complete their objective references through intuitions which are in some sort external and alien to themselves, that they are incapable of envisaging objects as they are in themselves. Space and time, and the pure intuition which presents them, are always the nigger in the woodpile in Kantian epistemology, and conception is only prejudicially infected through its association with them. Could we, like God, complete our references without being externally affected, there would be nothing subjective or phenomenal about them. There are, indeed, a few ill-considered passages in which Kant does suggest that conception may suffer from inherent distortions as much as does intuition — B. 145 may be such a passage — but, by and large, this is not presumed, and the use of the word 'Noumenon', as a thought-object which is also an independently real object, establishes this fact. The position of the *Dissertation* is therefore fundamentally sustained. And space and time are held to be subjectively grounded, *not* because they obey *a priori* synthetic principles which are also built into the nature of our minds, but because they fail to reveal the true logical subjects or substrates for their manifestations and structures which our understanding requires. Space only offers us relations without *relata*, and a confused phenomenal *mélange* in which we can only problematically disentangle the substantial agencies operative in the latter. And time only offers us sequences infected with vanishingness, which cannot best suggest the presence of permanent underlying agencies. Since we are only ectypal and not archetypal intelligences, we must, however, make do with phenomenal substitutes for the explanatory unities which for us must remain inaccessible.

Kant has accordingly, in the Prefaces and Introductions to the *Critique*, shown that our knowledge of things through empirical encounter always involves a mixture of sensuous intuition and cogitative interpretation, but also a tacit acceptance in both of principles ranging infinitely beyond empirical encounter, and which alone make learning from the latter possible. And he has made the use of such principles a built-in character of intelligences organized as ours are, though it requires a careful reflection on our actual imaginative procedures and thought-procedures to lay them bare. And he has argued that, while our purely cogitative procedures are not unfitted to mediate an empty logical sketch of things quite independent of ourselves, they are unable to give concrete application to such a sketch, and, in their commerce with objects, have to have recourse to sensuous and imaginative encounters or constructions, which latter, in virtue of certain inherent defects, can be seen to be incapable of introducing us to things as they themselves are. The consequences of these assumptions will now be worked out in the Analytic of Concepts, which will be dealt with in this chapter, and in the Analytic of Principles, which will be dealt with in the next.

iii

The Analytic of Concepts undertakes two tasks: (a) to establish an exhaustive list of all the basic *a priori* concepts involved in the interpretation of phenomena by our understandings or thinking minds — the Metaphysical Deduction of the Categories; (b) a proof that this list can and must have a valid application to what comes before us phenomenally, and cannot ever fail of such application — the Transcendental Deduction of the Categories, of which there are two different versions. These tasks will then lead on to an Analytic of Principles, which will argue for a series of axiomatic principles relating the categories to the forms and materials of intuition. The portions of the *Critique* that we are now about to consider, though at many points confusedly and at times absurdly written, are admittedly the most important and fascinatingly profound parts of Kant's whole phenomenology of reason.

The Metaphysical Deduction of the Categories or Pure Concepts of the Understanding makes the assumption that these will reveal themselves in the connective forms of our judgements, rather than in any objective or conceptual contents that enter into such judgements. The work of the understanding does not lie in any immediate relation to objects — intuition alone can effect this — but in bringing whatever is, or could be, intuitively presented, under suitable concepts, ranging those concepts under higher concepts in an indefinite hierarchy, and then also connecting the connections thus established in higher judgemental complexes. (This last function of the understanding is understressed in Kant: there are, e.g., said to be *two* connected judgemental members in a hypothetical judgement (see A. 73).) It will not therefore be in our intuitions of objects, nor in concepts stemming from such intuitions, that the pure concepts of the understanding will reveal themselves, but in the connective acts of the understanding itself, the acts which connect intuitions with concepts, or concepts with other concepts, or which connect connections of these elements with other similar connections (A. 68–9). Judgement, in a very wide sense, which includes entertainment, surmise, supposition, presumption, and so on, is therefore for Kant the typical act of the understanding in which all its *a priori* concepts will reveal themselves, but they will only do so in a sort of metaconsideration of their form. We shall have to see, for example, that our judgements in a sense implicitly presume that what we judge about will meet certain conceptual requirements, will consist of distinguishable, denumerable items, will be bound together by certain comprehensive forms of togetherness, and so forth. There is nothing to be criticized in this judgemental approach to the categories: Husserl's Phenomenology and other related theories of mind and its objects (those, e.g., of Brentano and Meinong) have laid a similar stress on judgemental synthesis. It is only a little regrettable that Kant has not sufficiently stressed the distinct existence of syntheses *other* than the judgemental, for example, the purely enumerative, and that he has not achieved the fine sense of the difference between intentional acts and the intentional objects that they constitute for us, that these later thinkers have led one to expect.

We shall not involve ourselves in any elaborate discussion of the list of twelve categories set forth in Kant's Metaphysical Deduction, and in the many difficult questions as to their derivation, detailed interpretation, and so on. For, the foundations of Kant's would-be irrefragable architectonic everywhere abound in quaint anomalies and obscurities which have been sufficiently exposed in the past. By and large, however, there is little to object to in his list, though it requires, as the study of modern logic would show, some reordering and considerable supplementation. There can, in the first place, obviously be no such thing as thinking, unless, through our concepts, we can *refer* to their cases, which in the privileged case will confront us in intuition. And reference can obviously be to some *single* instance of a concept, or to an *indeterminate number* of such instances, or to *all* the instances of the concept in question. These judgemental differences correspond to Kant's three categories of quantity: singularity, plurality, and totality. The conception of a class, a set, covering all the cases of a single concept, lies ready to hand: we cannot blame Kant for having failed to explore it further. And obviously, in the second place, reference to objects may or may not involve the presence of negation, that most mysterious, all-pervasive character of our thinking, of which Kant here distinguishes *two* varieties, the kind which simply cancels or eliminates a thought-determination, and the kind which then makes a vaguely 'infinite' reference to all other, uncancelled possibilities. (The Soul, for example, belongs to the infinite remainder-class of non-mortal things.) It is a pity that Kant does not here find a place for his own conception (and Hegel's) of the negation of internal conflict, where the negation is not thought of as eliminating its opposing positive, but as merely struggling against it. Obviously, we may say, concepts must be capable of having a strictly limited coverage, and this involves the possibility of counter-concepts which cover whatever they exclude or tend to exclude. Kant's three categories of the positively real, its sheer negation, and its limitation by an infinite environing field of positive possibilities, are therefore quite necessary to thought.

And, if we turn to the categories of relation, the position is similar. To the categorical judgement, for example, 'This lump of gold is heavy', corresponds the function of applying either *one* or *more* concepts or characters to a given logical subject, which, in the paradigm case, is one of the substantial things — this hand, this lump of gold, and so on — recognized by common sense. In this category there also lurks, though Kant ignores it here, the conjunctive function which makes a single concept out of a variety of distinct attributes; and it also involves the distinction between the permanently identifying or essential properties, which Kant will later refer to as *substantia phaenomenon* and the variable, contingent properties which are predicated of it as its states. Plainly all these functions are essential to what we call 'thinking', and are carried over from substantial things to almost anything, however tenuously abstract, that we choose to speak of. In the same way, thought certainly involves the constant use of conditional or hypothetical assertions, of which causal assertions represent the most concrete, paradigm case. For, having determined what will or would happen to things in certain concrete circumstances, we can carry over this mode of thinking to the most abstract and metempirical contexts. Kant, for example, in his moral theory, applies the category of causation to situations altogether out of time: it is plain that he is here dealing with a form of dependence of which ordinary causal conditioning represents a phenomenal example. Modern semantic and logical discussion has distinguished many varieties of conditional dependence that Kant has not considered: this does not affect the importance of what he has considered, nor its prime connection with causal dependence. And there is obviously deep insight in Kant's connection of the disjunctive judgement with the spelling out of a generic conception into a variety of mutually exclusive alternatives, in the treating of it as constructing a sort of *Spielraum* in which many forms of possible, or actual, being coexist, and perhaps interact. Plainly this is one of the nobler, more intelligent uses of disjunction, even if a large number of its more trivial uses are of greater interest to the formal logician.

There is, finally, an immense importance for thought in the

modal distinctions of the possible, the actual, and the necessary (together with their contraries): these plainly lie ready to hand when we assert something tentatively or hypothetically, or when we assert it simply and without qualification, or when we assert it with an implicit refusal to entertain anything else. And Kant seems right in looking for the prime use of such modals in situations where *experience* has taught us what is likely to happen or not to happen, what certainly is the case or is not the case, or what should be asserted or denied in all circumstances whatever. And once introduced in this empirical fashion, the use of the modals is extended by deeper insight to the analytically possible, contingent, and necessary, and their contraries; to what is a possibility, a mere fact, or a necessity, or their contraries, from the *a priori*, synthetic standpoint; and to what is a possibility, a fact, or a necessity, or their contraries, from the standpoint of transcendental psychology; or what, lastly, is a possibility, a fact, or a necessity from the subjective standpoint of a certain individual's actual knowledge. All these senses of the modals are to be found in different places in Kant, and there are even some references to probability. It would not be fair to object that Kant has not systematically ordered this complex thought-material, which is still only imperfectly ordered by our better contemporary logicians and wickedly neglected by others. Kant's Table of Categories, with its four dimensions of the quantificational, the positive-negative, the connective, and the modal, has therefore established itself sufficiently, even if there are some dimensions, for example, the intentional and the intensional, which he has not clearly distinguished.

iv

We must now turn to Kant's two Transcendental Deductions of the Categories, the most difficult and controversial of all his treatments. It will be contended in this section that some of the most astonishing and much admired theses in these Deductions, in particular those connecting the categories with the unity of self-consciousness, are quite unacceptable if read in isolation, as they very often have been read. They permit, however, of a very illuminating interpretation if read in the context of later utterances in the Analytic of Principles, and with due respect to what Kant takes for granted regarding the indispensable background role of the Transcendental

Object or Thing-in-itself. The First Edition Deduction was written in the afflatus generated by a 'great light', which dazzled and blinded Kant as well as illuminated him, and made him lose sight of some of the essentials of his own theory, whereas the Second Edition Deduction turned the results of what should have been a temporary blinding into a seductively written, falsely simplified picture. In view of their great importance, we shall consider what the two Transcendental Deductions say in a more detailed, paragraph-by-paragraph manner than we have hitherto followed.

Before turning to this task, we may, however, attempt to set forth, in a general manner, what Kant's two Deductions were trying to establish. Their problem is that understanding and intuition are disparate faculties, and that, though the categories are the only concepts in terms of which we can understand and know the phenomenal order, this order might none the less be such that it would not be possible for us to apply our categories to it: it might be quite unintelligible, nothing of which we could make sense. As Kant puts the point in A. 90 (B. 122-3):

That objects of sensuous intuition should conform to the formal conditions of sensibility, which exist *a priori* in our minds, is clear, in that
they would not otherwise be objects for us. But that they should further
conform to the conditions which the understanding needs for the synthetic unity of thinking, is not so evident a consequence. For appearances
might very well be of such a sort that the understanding did not find
them in harmony with the conditions of its unity, and that all was so
confused that, e.g., in the succession of appearances there was nothing
to help us towards a rule of synthesis that would accord with the concepts
of cause and effect, which concepts would therefore become quite empty,
nugatory, and meaningless.

Kant's problem is, of course, perfectly genuine, on the assump-
tion of the radical disparity of sensuous intuition, on the one hand, and conceptual interpretation on the other, an assump-
tion on which he has so far proceeded. For, if the intuitive order stands ready-made in advance of conceptual interpretation, the latter might very well find no purchase, no ποῦ στῶ in the former. And, even if some conceptualization could find some united purchase, this might be quite differently exercised by different subjects, so that there would not need to be the uniform, intersubjective world that the categories aim at educing (for intersubjectivity see, e.g., *Prolegomena*, §18).

Kant's strategy in the face of this problem is to revise his conception of the radical disparity of intuition and conception: he has, in fact, previously suggested that they both might spring from some unknown, common root (A. 15; B. 29). He has to suppose that what we intuit comes before us, not indeed fully conceptualized, but fully conceptualizable, and in a manner that can be shared by others, so that intuition and conception have in some fashion been working in harness to achieve a common outcome. How has this working in harness been effected? The answer is to invoke the action of a *third* agency, the Productive or Transcendental Imagination, an action and agency which, because it conditions the very possibility of experience, must, in its basic work at least, lie wholly beyond experience, and so have absolutely no phenomenal representation either in space or in time. The *primal* acts by which phenomena are constituted and ordered for us must be what Kant calls 'transcendental acts', though the term 'transcendent' might be much more appropriate; and the agent that accomplishes them must be not the empirical, but the transcendental self, the unknown and unknowable I which is the source of all our intuitions and acts of thought, but which we can only posit and think of as existent, and cannot put before us intuitively. Once these primal acts have been consummated, and the original appearances constituted, the further extensions of such appearances may indeed at times reveal themselves to introspection, though even their 'real essence' remains beyond introspection: we are certainly sometimes aware of filling in gaps in the perceived order, or of letting our imaginations stray beyond it. But of the *basic* acts which underlie both perception and introspection we *cannot* be introspectively aware: they have to be thought of, believed in, not known or seen. That Kant seriously believed in such timeless, noumenal acts is even more clear in his moral theory (see, e.g., A. 538-9) where a man's whole life-pattern is decided upon out of time. Noumenal determination here merely means the existential dependence of one state of affairs on another, and has nothing to do with phenomenal happenings, though it may appear to itself in the latter.

Kant does not, however, make it crystal clear that his basic, transcendental, imaginative acts are not acts of the self *qua* empirical, but of the same self *qua* noumenal; and so inferior commentators, infected by Cartesian notions of self-consciousness, have accordingly hastened to make the Productive Imagination some sort of empirically familiar, but semi-somnolent faculty, which merely tidies up, and fills in, the gaps left by the senses. And Kant has himself sometimes encouraged such interpreters by such a passage as we meet with in A. 78 (B. 103), where he says that a certain synthesis 'is the mere effect of the imagination, a blind but indispensable function of the soul, without which we should have no knowledge whatever, but of which we are seldom conscious'. It is also more than probable that Kant started in Lockean fashion, by conceiving of the primordial imaginative synthesis, which occurs even in sense-perception (see A. 121, Note), as some sort of a *conscious* process of compounding simple ideas together so as to form complex ones; and that only the force of his principles forced him to abandon this impossible view, as is shown by his intro-duction of the new terms 'productive' and 'transcendental'. There is even a very perplexing passage (A. 102) where a *reproductive* synthesis is treated as among the 'transcendental acts of the mind', though perhaps this only means that there are underlying transcendental acts of the mind even beneath our *reproductive* activities. The same noumenal self which projects phenomena must also extend them, and can, *qua* phenomenal, be phenomenally given as doing so.

By and large it cannot, however, be doubted that the acts which constitute experience are for Kant metempirical acts, just as the self which performs them is, in its relevant character, a metempirical entity. It is on account of these metempirical acts, which combine conception, and a use of the categories, with sensuous intuition in space and time, that we can be *sure*, even in advance of experience, that whatever we will experience will also conform to the categories. We are *sure*, in advance of experience, that the phenomenal world will be intelligible to us, because we presume and know 'in our bones', though we cannot in the *strict* sense know at all, that we ourselves, in our supraphenomenal capacity, and by supra-phenomenal acts, must have made this be so (see, e.g., A. 114, 125). It is, in fact, to quote a very well-worn, but remarkable, almost mystical passage (A. 79), Kant's view that 'the same function which gives unity to the different presentations in *one judgement* also gives unity to the mere synthesis of pre-sentations in *one intuition* . . . The same understanding, there-fore, and through the very same acts through which, by way of an analytical unity among concepts, it gives rise to the logical form of a judgement, also imports a transcendental content into its presentations, owing to the synthetic unity of the manifold in intuition.' The Productive Imagination is therefore simply the understanding operating under an alias, and producing by acts out of time, appearances in space and time, which can then be patiently unravelled in its judgements.

We must not, however, let the suggestions of a term like 'production' intoxicate us. It must not be conceived that the arrangements of phenomenal data to suit categorial requirements lack an element of *external* control and necessitation, which can be attributed to nothing but the Transcendental Object or Thing-in-itself. This *too* has 'to be conceived of, though not known, if the phenomenal picture is to be understood. For though the spatio-temporality and categorial conformity of whatever we experience reflects the free spontaneity of our intuitive and thinking nature, experience is always a *translation* of metempirical characterizations and orderings, and never a free composition. It can only be the unknown and unknowable aggregate of Transcendental Objects, geared into one another, and also with ourselves, in unknown and unknowable ways, that can give rise, or assist in giving rise, to intuitive materials which will fit in with our cognitive demands, and that will continue to provide such materials as long as our conscious experience persists. And, if Things-in-themselves ceased to act on us in such a way as to produce such materials, then there could, on Kantian principles, be no thought and no experience at all. We can in fact be as sure that we shall never experience a discrepancy between experience and our categories, as we can be sure that we shall never experience our own deaths: we could not, *qua* experients, be there to experience either.

Such, we shall try to contend, are the central contentions of Kant's Transcendental Deductions, though it must be confessed that he has not spelled all these points out satisfactorily. But if the imaginative ordering of phenomena in space and time were as unilaterally free as some commentators have imagined, it would lack the element of necessitation which Kant regards as essential to objectivity. Mere categories with disordered materials tend to no single, definite, necessary outcome. And it would also necessarily lack the intersubjectivity which Kant regards as essential to all that is objective. We should then have to have recourse to the transcendental exercises of a Fichte, where a *single*, unique ego first posits a non-ego which seems to confront it imaginatively, and then also practises a wide range of discrepant impersonations in order, in the end, to be able to consummate its own complex self-consciousness. The constructions of a Fichte are not to be despised — they are perhaps the only completely coherent elaboration of a thorough-going subjectivism — but they were rejected by Kant as 'spooky', and certainly do not agree with his profound, if problematic, realism. We shall now attempt to comment on the main points in Kant's two Transcendental Deductions.

v

Kant's First Edition Transcendental Deduction involves a brief preliminary transition in the paragraphs (A. 94–5) where it is said that *three* forms of unification or synthesis are neces-sary for the possibility of experience. These are (a) a synoptic viewing of whatever is intuitively given, (b) an imaginative synthesis of all its details, (c) a unification of the synthesis through 'original apperception'. The term 'apperception' is Leibnizian: in a curious fashion its sense combines a con-ceptualization of the given with a self-consciousness in respect of such conceptualization. The thinking self, Kant is saying, must be able, in a single view, to sum up whatever it has in-tuited and imagined, to register its whole character conceptually, and to be fully conscious of having done both. Kant then adds that there must be a transcendental, as well as an empirical, employment of these three forms of synthesis. This must be taken to mean, on our previous showing, that there must have been, or must timelessly be, an act projecting a unified spatio-temporal framework before the self, an act filling this up with sensible content corresponding in some unknown manner to the unknown impacts of Things-in-themselves, and an act which arranges this content so as to satisfy categorial applica-tions. These three 'operations', being out of time, really coalesce into a single operation: it is only in time that they split up into three distinct operations. The transcendental operations in question must, of course, transcend experience and know-ledge: the thought of them as *having been* merely expresses, by an analogical use of the past tense, the necessary presupposi-tions of the fact that an intelligible, contentful, spatio-temporal world is appearing before us.

Kant now proceeds to work out a preliminary, tentative

Subjective Deduction, which reaches out to the transcendental through much that is empirical (A. 95). Kant confesses in the First Edition Preface (A. xvii–xviii) that there is much that is hypothetical and debatable in this section. For the three forms of unification briefly mentioned in A. 94–5 Kant will substitute a threefold synthesis: this, it must be emphasized, will cover an empirical series of acts, acts that can be introspectively given, but which will point, Kant hopes, to metempirical, transcendental acts of the pure subject which have rendered them possible. The first form of synthesis is that of apprehension in intuition (A. 98–100): intuition presents us with a manifold of impressions, but such a manifold can only be consciously given in so far as we break it up into elements that we can run through singly, and then grasp them all together. The possibility of such an empirical synthesis of apprehension points, however, to a transcendental, timeless act of synthesis, which, responding conjointly to a number of impacts from Things-in-themselves, translates them into a unified, spatio-temporal picture, which can then be consciously run through, analysed, and synthesized. In this transcendental act of synthesis, Kant tells us, space and time are also themselves made into possible objects of conscious apprehension: they then exhibit that form of parts outside of parts, and of parts coming after parts, which are a pre-condition of successive synthesis. Kant's pure synthesis of apprehension does *not* mean, as has been supposed by some who have failed to grasp Kant's consistent use of timelessness, that the conscious subject has to put space and time together, in Lockean fashion, like a set of stage-flats, in a series of shuffling extensions from perceived fragments. Kant knows that space and time are *always* given as unitary, total, and of infinite extent: the transcendental self has seen to that.

Kant's second form of synthesis is that of the Reproductive Imagination (A. 100–2). In order to have experience, we must not only be able to apprehend brief successions of items in a single view, but must also be able to reconstitute past successions in imagination, and to recur to other cases of the same or similar things or happenings, and to the setting with which they were associated. The whole mechanism of associative recall is, in fact, *necessary* to the constitution of experience. Kant then suggests that there is a transcendental act necessary for the success of imaginative reproduction. The phenomena which parade themselves before us must display a certain regularity, a certain affinity, or community, or continuity, of nature, if the apprehension of one of them is to lead our imagination on to that of another. They must be inherently associable, if they are to be associated. There must therefore be a transcendental act which *gives* them their affinity or associability, on which the Reproductive Imagination merely cashes in; and this act must, of course, have occurred, or be occurring, *out of time*: plainly we never in time dreamt up a complex scenario for the appearances to follow. The transcendental faculty which performs the transcendental act in question is by Kant usually called the *Pro*ductive Imagination, though even the *re*productive synthesis of the imagination cannot succeed without its background prodding. (This is perhaps the explanation of the puzzling reference to a transcendental, *re*productive synthesis at the end of A. 102.) And it would be un-Kantian to think that Things-in-themselves play no part in such associability, though we know nothing of their secret links of affinity which make our phenomenal affinities possible. We may, and we must, emptily conceive of them as noumenally linked, but we cannot give flesh and blood to this conception. For us it must suffice that, since experience and knowledge and thought exist, these unknowable linkages must have been propitious: had they not been, there could have been no experience and no knowledge and no thought at all, a situation which blessedly transcends our significant consideration.

Kant's third synthesis is that of recognition in a concept (A. 103–6). We must be aware of some unifying pattern, some rule, linking apprehended or imagined items or features together, and enabling us to grasp them as a whole; whether these patterns be extremely simple like the rule which engenders a straight line or a triangle, or a complex rule such as that shown forth in a body, or in a particular sort of body, or in some individual body before us. (Kant does not consider questions as to the *degree* of affinity or connectivity among distinct features or items which entitles us to speak of a rule in their case: rules are obviously very open-textured concepts.) There must, accordingly, be some transcendental act which has made it possible for us to abstract concepts from empirical instances: such concepts must, as it were, have been lying ready in them from the start. In what follows only *one* transcendental faculty will suffice to perform all these syntheses, and that faculty is the Productive Imagination, which is merely the understanding acting out of time, and conditioning what will appear to it in time. Metempirically it injects into the tissue of experience what will afterwards have to be teased out of experience through conception and judgement.

Kant, however, passes at this point to a very difficult excursus involving *both* the Transcendental *Object*, or *external* Thing-in-itself, and the Transcendental *Subject*, or *internal* Thing-in-itself. Neither of these entities can be intuited or known, but the empty *thought* of them, and of their existence, none the less underlies the possibility of experience (A. 104–10). The Transcendental Object must be thought of as what prevents us from thinking of an object just as we please, and which brings into our thought an element of necessitation, which compels us to synthesize what we think of in a given manner. 'For we find that our thought of the relation of all knowledge to its object carries an element of necessity with it, since this relation is what prevents our acts of knowledge from being haphazard or arbitrary, and which determines them *a priori* in a definite manner. For, in so far as they are to be referred to an object, they must also necessarily accord with one another, i.e. have the particular unity which makes up the concept of an object' (A. 104–5). Thus a triangle is an object of thought since in it certain spatial possibilities are combined according to a definite rule, a body is an object since in it extension, shape, impenetrability, and so on are synthetically combined. The Transcendental Object which necessitates such syntheses is, of course, not given to us, but remains an empty X on which our synthesis is taken to be dependent.

All this might appear very clear and self-sufficient, but Kant immediately passes to several very unclear theses regarding the Transcendental *Subject*. He has already argued (A. 103–4) that in all synthetic consciousness of an object, as combining several features successively considered, there must also be a concurrent consciousness, which may be extremely feeble and dim, of the subjective activities by which such a synthetic consciousness is generated. This thesis is, of course, doubtful, and is later replaced by the weaker assertion that such a concurrent awareness of our own synthetic activity must always be *possible* (A. 116; B. 134). He now argues that the subjective acts and agency in question could never reveal themselves to introspection or inner sense, since this can only reveal our contingent, experiential states in time, whereas the acts and agency in question are *necessary* to all awareness of objects, and such necessity necessarily points to a transcendental condition (A. 106). It must, that is, be possible for us to attribute the synthetic activities constitutive of objects to a subject which cannot be itself given in temporal experience (though it may no doubt *appear* temporally), and whose constitutive acts must also be located out of time.

Kant now has recourse to a very old and respectable argument which goes back to Plato, but which was also often canvassed in the Leibnizian-Wolffian metaphysic, and which Kant himself later criticizes as involving a paralogism. This is an argument which bases itself on the unity of consciousness, on the need that all our sensations, images, thoughts, and so on should be brought together in a common conscious focus, if the whole they form is to be an object of consciousness at all; and if they are to be compared with one another, and the relations that hold between them brought to consciousness. This argument led the metaphysicians of the period to posit the existence of a single, simple, substantial soul, which can be present simultaneously in a variety of acts directed to a variety of objects, and which can also persist from one conscious act to another, so that a summation of them all becomes possible. This argument is, as we say, highly respectable and there can be little doubt that Kant himself always continued to think in terms of it (see, e.g., A. 267, B. 323, and elsewhere), even when he came to hold that the existence of such an enduring, simple soul-substance could not be *known* or *proved*. Here, however, he does not base himself on its unprovable existence, but on our inexpugnable need to *think* in terms of it. We *have* to refer all our perceptions, thoughts, and so on to a single, co-ordinating self; and, since such a reference is *necessary*, this self cannot be merely the changeable, empirical self of inner intuition, but must also have metempirical or transcendental aspects. As Kant puts it: 'There could be no states of knowledge in us, and no connection and unity among the same, without this unity of consciousness which precedes all data of intuition, and in relation to which all representation of objects is alone possible. To this pure, original, unchangeable consciousness I give the name of Transcendental Apperception'

(A. 107). Let us not argue against Kant's argument. Plainly a unity of consciousness is essential to any awareness of objective unity and interconnection, and if we like to call it the Transcendental Unity of Apperception, and to connect it with some unclearly conceived Leibnizian simple, there is nothing unreasonable about such a step.

Kant is not, however, content to regard his Transcendental Unity of Apperception as a *necessary* condition for the awareness of rule-governed, conceptualizable, phenomenal objectivity: he also wants to regard it as a *sufficient* condition of the latter. He wants to argue that, if we can say, 'I am aware of all these things', we can also always say, 'All these things are bound together by objective laws'. He even wishes to go further, and to argue that:

> the original and necessary consciousness of the identity of Self is *at the same time* (*zugleich*) a consciousness of just as necessary a unity in the synthesis of all phenomena according to concepts, i.e. rules, which does not merely make phenomena necessarily reproducible, but also thereby determines an object for their intuition, i.e. the concept of something in which they cohere necessarily. For the mind could not possibly conceive of its own identity in the multitude of its presentations, and do so *a priori*, were it not aware of the identity of its action in subordinating all empirical synthesis of apprehension to a transcendental unity, which is the *a priori* basis of their possible interconnection through rules (A. 108).

The unity of consciousness is therefore the *same* as the interconnection of phenomena according to rules, or they are at most two sides of the same transcendental state of affairs. Kant even says in the next paragraph (A. 109) that the reference of all appearances to the X of transcendental objectivity is 'nothing else' than the necessary unity of consciousness, and so also of the synthesis of multiplicity, through the mind's common function, into one presentation. And, having thus supposedly shown the *identity* of the unity of consciousness with the unification of phenomena according to rules, Kant is at once in a position to take the next step: to identify the categories, or pure forms of conceptual unity, with the sort of unity involved in self-consciousness. 'The *a priori* conditions of a possible experience as such are', he remarks, 'at the same time, the conditions of the possibility of empirical objects. Now I assert that the categories I have introduced are nothing beyond the conditions of thought in a possible experience, just as space and time are the conditions of intuition in the same.

These categories are therefore the fundamental concepts through which objects are at all thinkable in relation to appearances, and so have an *a priori*, objective validity, which is just what we wanted to know' (A. 111). If Kant's simple identification of the necessary unity of consciousness with the interconnection of phenomena according to pure concepts or rules were valid, he would indeed have succeeded in his Transcendental Deduction of the Categories and of the *a priori* synthetic principles which their use will be shown to involve.

The arguments we have just examined have impressed many, but it is plain that, as they stand, they will not do. They are, in fact, scandalous arguments, paralogisms far worse than any which Kant afterwards exposes. For were they valid, they would certainly prove too much. It is, in fact, plain that the unity of consciousness, the integral togetherness of all that we are aware of, including our awareness of our own awareness, in one single, embracing state or experience, is (however we may choose to analyse it) quite necessary to *all* states that form part of a mental history; and not merely to those in which objects are being constituted according to neccesary rules, or in which objective permanences and dependences are being discriminated. Kant has simply been deluded by the often concurrent presence of two quite different necessities, one of which has a wider application than the other: the subjective necessity of conscious unity, which applies to *all* states of mind, and the necessity of categorial interconnection, which applies only to such states of mind as are attempting to know something, or to conceive of something by analogy with what is known. Kant is indeed fully aware of the distinction: it is central and crucial to his Analogies of Experience, which will be dealt with in our next chapter. There is, he perceives, a conscious unity which reflects only our own subjectively grounded integrations and our often arbitrary meanderings, which absolutely contrasts, and must contrast, with the objective unity which involves an application of the categories. Kant, however, seems to think that he can dismiss this former sort of conscious unity as applying only within the realm of empirical apperception or inner sense; that it is as empirically contingent as the contents it embraces. This is, however, not the case. It is quite as *necessary* to put a manifold of terms together and to contemplate them all together, if one is to have any awareness of them all, when the items thus unified are wildly incoherent, and have no rhyme or reason governing their joint presentation, as when they are duly integrated aspects of objects. There is as authentic and necessary a unity of consciousness in contemplating the sequence represented by the words, ships and shoes and sealing-wax and cabbages and kings, as there is in considering the crime-rate or the structure of DNA. And the transcendental self, we may add, for all its august inaccessibility, is as much implicated in the existence of the former as in that of the latter. It is certainly possible for us to combine features or items in an unprincipled manner, and to be aware of ourselves as doing so, and of the irregular, sometimes self-contradictory, objects which such syntheses would involve: we need only cite Kant's own examples (A. 100, 101) of a situation in which cinnabar were sometimes red, sometimes black; or in which men could change over into animal forms; or in which on the longest day in summer we sometimes had fruit, sometimes ice and snow, and so on. And it is indeed possible to argue that such incoherences would not be possible were there not also discoverable, objective regularities on which they were parasitic: this is one of the central messages of Kant. And it is also possible to argue that there are hidden subjective regularities underlying the most incoherent thought-sequences. But neither of these considerations alters the fact that, whatever their conditions, such unprincipled syntheses do exist, and as much evince the action of the transcendental self as our most rule-governed syntheses. If Kant's arguments were valid, there would simply be no room for the arbitrary, unprincipled sector in human experience and thought: we should always be trying to make out something objective, and, if we relaxed for a moment and simply meandered, we would fall apart into disjoined fragments, and cease to be conscious of anything at all. Whereas it is arguable that our sense of self is *enhanced*, not abated, when we integrate matters subjectively, and according to our own sweet will, rather than when we defer to the compulsions of objective categories. The idle association, the playful and perhaps nonsensical comparison, the happy ranging over things in general: all these give us a profounder sense of self than any application of the venerable categories. And we do not have to identify ourselves by applying a concept or rule to ourselves, as we do have to in the case of external objects.

Why, then, we may ask, has Kant seemingly subordinated our

consciousness of objects to our consciousness of the subject? Both, in Kant's view, have a substrate which transcends phenomenal experience, and both substrates are essential to the constitution of such experiences. And both have to be thought of, though not known to exist, whenever we seek to understand how experience is possible. Experience is a subject-object matter, and the metempirical source of experience must likewise be thought of as a subject-object matter. Why then does Kant exalt one transcendental substrate at the cost of another, and explain experience in terms of what our wholly unknown selves have put into it, rather than in terms of what equally unknown substrates other than ourselves have put into it, thereby giving undeserved comfort to an absolute idealism which he himself rejects? The answer to this question is not easy to give, but, when it is given, it will not be such as to satisfy, but rather to disappoint, the absolute idealism that has built itself on Kant. It is natural to attribute the structure of experience to ourselves as substrates, rather than to the substrates of other objects, since *we*, and not objects, have experiences, and are witnesses of phenomena, and the structures which make experience possible are therefore more importantly in ourselves, than in the objects that provoke them. This peculiar thing that we call mind, consciousness, and thought, may depend on external as well as internal substrate-conditions, but its salient peculiarities make it more correct to attribute it to internal substrates than to anything external. Even if, contrary to Kant's theory, time and space and spatio-temporal substance and causation were present in metempirical objectivity, it would still be necessary to attribute to us an *a priori* readiness to intuit and interpret things in terms of them; since this readiness translates a structure of *being* into a structure of conscious *understanding*, and since it always goes infinitely beyond the limited intuitive detail that fits in with it, and that stems from the actual impacts of Things-in-themselves. Spatiality, temporality, substantiality, causality, and so on are certainly built-in requirements for our sort of intuitively geared understanding, whether or not they are objective, structuring forms elsewhere. And if the impacts of external substrates could not yield materials that could be fitted into such forms, then the life of the conscious subject could not arise at all, any more than organic life could arise on a planet where there was neither air nor water.

There is, however, a deeper ground why the categorial forms of objectivity must be connected with the Transcendental Subject rather than with the Transcendental Object. For, as Kant will try to show, subjectivity requires objectivity in order to be aware of its own subjectivity, and even to *be* a subject, whereas objectivity does not so obviously require subjectivity in order to be as, and what, it is. The absolute idealist makes objectivity wholly parasitic upon subjectivity, and, from such a point of view, it is seemingly conceivable that the conscious subject should simply live a life of playful fantasy, and not trouble to set any law-governed objects before it at all. But the Kantian transcendentalist rather makes subjectivity parasitic upon objectivity, and it is only if the Transcendental Object awakens the life of the conscious subject through impacts which it can then translate into a spatio-temporal order governed by categories, that the conscious subject can become aware of itself and the phenomena of its conscious life at all, that it can in fact be the conscious being it is. For it is only by translating, or by having timelessly translated, the impacts of Things-in-themselves into its own phenomenal diction, that it can then become aware, not only of the categorially governed acts necessary for the consciousness of objects, but also of the arbitrarily subjective and personal acts which are just as necessary to its being a conscious person, and which, by their contrast with what is objectively necessary, enable us to be aware of *either*. We are perhaps first simply aware of objects; then of our own arbitrary, subjective activity in its opposition to given objects; then of our own deeper, transcendental activities that have made both sorts of awareness possible; then, in a quite derivative manner, of the action on us of Things-in-themselves without which we should have no thinking life at all. The most fundamental conditioning stratum is therefore the one of which we are least adequately conscious. Whether or not this is a correct spelling out of what Kant presupposes, the Transcendental Deduction is to be faulted; in that, by its failure to stress the necessary *contrast* between an objective and a subjective synthesis — whether or not the existence of the one entails the existence of the other — and by its attempt simply to *identify* the two types of synthesis, or to regard them as but two sides of the same mental activity, it has encouraged the development of all that idealistic constructivism which involves in Kant's view, a deep misunderstanding of the nature of knowledge. In the divine understanding something like that constructivism may indeed take the place of our contrast between a subjectively wanton and an objectively necessitated order — God in knowing and being Himself may also know all other things, as Aquinas teaches — but, in the human condition, *both* are essential, and subjectivity has its inbuilt need for what is compulsively objective, only because it depends upon and grows out of the latter.

The so-called Objective Deduction, which follows in Edition I (A. 115–30), traverses much the same territory as the Subjective Deduction just considered. It starts, however, with the Transcendental Unity of Apperception, arguing that whatever we conceive or intuit must be unified in a single consciousness, in which there can also always be a consciousness *of* such unification. The long Note to p. 117 spells this out in detail. But such a possible reference to one's own, conscious, unifying activities has a transcendental condition. There must have been an *a priori* or transcendental synthesis which preceded (no doubt only in an analogically temporal sense) all the analytic activities and subsequent syntheses of consciousness. This transcendental synthesis must be attributed to the Productive Imagination (A. 118); the reproductive synthesis of the imagination depends on this prior productive synthesis. Kant then says (A. 119) that what we call the understanding is simply the unifying self-consciousness which makes all our conscious acts belong to *us*, and that the categories are simply the various ways in which the understanding or pure self-consciousness has made such appropriation possible, when, acting as the Productive Imagination, it united the items of sense.

Kant then goes on (A. 121–2) to dwell on the necessary affinity of appearances which underlies their associability, and to ascribe this affinity and associability to the transcendental self. He again stresses the strangeness of his conclusion, that is, that the order and regularity in the appearances we call nature has really been introduced by ourselves. 'We could never find them in appearances, had we not ourselves, or the nature of our mind, originally put them there.' 'If the objects which our knowledge has to deal with were Things-in-themselves, we could have no *a priori* concepts of them' (A. 128). But if, in God, absolute subjectivity and objectivity have a common root, Things-in-themselves may very well have

as much to do with the structure of appearances as the
built-in forms of intuition and categories of our understanding.

vi

The Transcendental Deduction of the Second Edition offers
no fundamental novelties. But its condensation of content
and smoothness of style render it far more misleading than
the First Edition Deduction. The Transcendental Unity of
Apperception is by it, not by merit, raised to the bad emin-
ence that it has ever since occupied in idealistic thought.
We shall comment on its carefully styled paragraphs one
by one.

It is argued in §15 that a togetherness of items for consciousness can never come about through passive intuition,
whether sensuous or pure, but only through a 'spontaneous'
act of consciousness. Things cannot be presented to us as
bound together unless we ourselves have bound them together.
This doctrine, acceptable if applied to the pre-conscious
structuring of phenomena in the wake of transcendental impacts, of course makes nonsense if applied to the world of our
primitive sense-awareness, and it did not require the observation of a Köhler or a Koffka to point this out. It was merely
the non-empirical dogmatism of a Locke which could hold
that each idea must enter the mind simple and unmixed, and
be only afterwards compounded and related through our
mental activities. Kant's Productive Imagination which, timelessly and metempirically, has conjured up the whole chequered,
phenomenal scene out of what *may* have been a set of quite
different, differently related jerks from Things-in-themselves,
is precisely equal to projecting such a continuous, complex
scene before us; one involving neither empirical analysis nor
synthesis, but permitting the development of either. Obviously
the phenomena set before us by the Productive Imagination
were honeycombed with built-in relations from the start,
relations which invited our judgemental, fully self-conscious
analyses and syntheses, but presupposed neither. We never
consciously built up our roses out of a scent, a hue, and a
soft touch, but we certainly can build up our lucid knowledge
of roses in something like this manner, and Kant cannot have
been so deeply muddled as to have thought anything else.
And of course, as he maintains, the unity of consciousness
is a necessary condition both of our first, as yet unanalysed

imaginative projection, as well as of our subsequent conceptually analysed and resynthesized awareness.

In §16 he then goes on to maintain the necessary existence of this pure, original apperception, which involves no intuition, and is accordingly not a case of knowing, but which is spontaneous and not passively receptive, and which (or its possibility) accompanies all our conscious presentations (B. 134). If it could not thus accompany them all, we should, *per absurdum*, have as many-coloured a self as we have presentations: it is therefore an analytic truth that it should be able to accompany all our presentations, if they are to be ours. Kant believes, however, that his analytic principle will be rich in consequences, and, in §17, he goes on to assert that the possibility of such a synthetic self-consciousness is a *necessary* condition of all understanding and knowledge. Conscious reference to objects involves both the distinction and the unification of their parts and aspects, and of these it is self-evident that there *can* be an accompanying consciousness. What Kant does not show is that such a possible synthesis is a *sufficient* condition of understanding and knowledge, since the unity of consciousness, and the awareness of such a unity, must be possible even in the case of the most arbitrary listings and transitions. Kant further observes that, in an intuitive understanding like God's, there would not need to be that possible putting together of distinct aspects or elements which is necessary to a receptive intelligence like our own (B. 138-9).

In §18 he makes the further point that the Transcendental Unity of Apperception must be distinguished from the *subjective* unity of consciousness: the latter is merely a matter of inner sense, and depends on contingent personal peculiarities and empirical circumstances. Only the original, *a priori* unity is objectively valid: the empirical unity of apperception, which Kant says merely derives from it in given circumstances (B. 140), has merely subjective validity. The distinction drawn in this paragraph cannot, however, be sustained. For the Transcendental Subject, the unknowable source of *all* our conscious orientations, is plainly as much at work in what Kant calls a subjective as in what he calls an objective synthesis. And it must be at work in both of them metempirically, or out of time, since *all* of our subjective life in time expresses it equally, and also, since *both* our objectively valid syntheses and our arbitrary personal syntheses can be equally revealed to inner sense. What Kant really believes will be later shown in the Analytic of Principles, where he will show that *both* the possibility of objective and subjective syntheses are necessary to self-consciousness, whether empirical or transcendental: we are the sort of beings who *can* think according to the categories, but who can also *not* think according to the categories, and who are only conscious of our own subjective spontaneity in being capable of both. We have, in fact, to have both a categorially obedient and a personally arbitrary side in order to be aware of either of them, and both are involved in our transcendental essence. In the same way, it will be later argued in the moral theory, our transcendental freedom must have both a legislative and an elective aspect: we must prescribe a moral order to ourselves, and we can also, by defect, fail to implement it. The contentions of §18 therefore involve an immense mistake, and it is hard to understand how Kant could have perpetrated it, or his followers piously swallowed it.

In §19 Kant continues to stress his valid distinction between a synthesis which is purely subjective, and which only expresses how presentations are combined for us, and a synthesis where the combined features are judged to belong together with objective necessity. The *Prolegomena*, in a closely parallel passage (§§18–20), draws a similar distinction between judgements of perception, which merely connect items or features as they hold together *for us*, for example, The room is warm, sugar sweet, wormwood bitter and so on, and judgements which connect them objectively and necessarily, for example, Air is elastic. Kant, also in §19, connects his objective synthesis with the use of the copula 'is', and plainly the emphatic use of the copula *does* express objective connection. But he again connects this necessary, objective use with the transcendental unity of self-consciousness, failing to see that self-consciousness is as much involved in the one case as in the other, and in fact requires the contrast of both. The statements in §19 then enable Kant, in §20, to connect the categories with the Transcendental Unity of Apperception, as in the First Edition. They are indeed so connected, as the Analytic of Principles will make plain, but not in the direct, simple manner that is here suggested. We distinguish ourselves from objects in the pregnant sense of the word 'object', in that, while *they* are necessarily obedient to the categories, *we*, at least in the direction of our thoughts, can also disobey them.

In §21 Kant suggests that the categories, since they apply only in the case of judgements which synthesize a pre-existent manifold, would not apply to the divine understanding, which does not order and unify pre-existent intuitions. Plainly, if something like the categories subsists in the divine intelligence, it must do so in a sublimated version. God through His own simple, infinitely creative essence, must, after a fashion, 'conceive' all that we derivatively think, but without the affective ballast which is necessary in our case.

In §22 Kant says that a category has no other application *in knowledge* than to objects of experience. This does not entail, as some have supposed, that we cannot emptily *think* of objects that transcend experience, and can even *be sure* of their possibility or their reality, though we can never *know this*. And, in §23, he says that we do not know whether the category of substance has a possible application to Things-in-themselves. It may again be stressed that only our *knowledge* is limited in this fashion. The transcendental self must, for example, be conceived as a subject of various thought-predicates, and so corresponds, with admirable emptiness, to the conception of a substance, even if to a necessarily unknowable one. Our thought of it, though empty, is also, in Kant's view, obligatory, and the same amounts to our thought of the Transcendental Object. Kant's fine distinction between knowledge and obligatory conception is arguably a little hair-splitting.

In §24 Kant points to the possibility of a specious or figural synthesis in which the categories are applied to the pure forms of time and space in the absence of sensuous material: this specious synthesis must obviously be a stage in the work of the Transcendental Imagination, which does not, in reality, occur *before* the other stages. In an added excursus (B. 152–6) he explains how the transcendental self acts on itself, and so generates the apparent or phenomenal self, whose life is given as stretched out in time. Obviously all the acts of the pure subject, which occur metempirically and timelessly, will also occur phenomenally, and vice versa: there is no place in Kantian theory for the sort of bifurcation of the noumenal and the phenomenal self which the Second Edition Deduction has suggested. (Kant will show later, in his treatments of morality and religion, that the choice of the bad, as much as the choice of the good, must take place out of time, as much as it also seems to take place in time.) 'How the I that thinks', Kant says, 'can be distinct from the I that intuits itself, and yet, as being the same subject, can be identical with the latter, is a question which raises no greater nor less difficulty than how I can be an object to myself at all' (B. 155). Kant argues at this point, as he also does later, that *outer* phenomena are the preconditions of inner phenomena, and that the latter have to be pictured as if along a line strung out in space (B. 156). And he goes on, in §25, to argue that transcendental self-consciousness allows us to *think* of ourselves as existents, as centres of synthesis, not to know *what* we are in ourselves, nor even to *know that* we exist, since we can have no intuition of our transcendental being.

In §26 Kant argues that nature, in its material concreteness of content, has no basic laws of connection but those which the Transcendental Imagination, that is, the understanding in its primordial, timeless syntheses, has imposed on it. Things-in-themselves, Kant informs us, must necessarily be bound together by *laws of their own* (B. 164, l. 10), grounded in their unknown essences. But, as mere presentations, they will have to be subordinated to the laws which our connective faculty prescribes. This faculty is the (Productive) Imagination, which depends on the understanding for the unity of its intellectual syntheses, and on sensation for the multiplicity of data that it apprehends. Special laws are not, of course, deducible from the categories: they rest on experience, and must further rest, though Kant does not here specially stress the point, on the unknown natures and laws of connection among Things-in-themselves, which must all somehow be translated into our phenomenal arrangements.

In §27 Kant makes two points that merit attention: the first very clearly, in an important footnote to p. 166a, that the use of the categories can be extended *without limit* beyond the intuitive field, and that this use has true and valuable consequences. It is only the *knowledge* of what we thus think, the precise determination of its object, that requires intuition. The second is a somewhat hasty rejection of the Leibnizian view of Crusius, that there is a sort of pre-established harmony, a divine preformation, of the principles necessary to our understanding of the natural world, and the principles governing that world itself. Our Creator has, according to this view, from the very first moment of our creation, implanted dispositions in us, dispositions having neither an empirical nor a personal (*selbstgedachte*) origin, which are none the less in complete harmony with the basic laws on which nature proceeds. Kant rejects this preformation-hypothesis because he thinks it would destroy the *necessity* of the categories, and also their *objectivity*. They would depend on the divine pleasure, and their necessity and objectivity might seem dubious to some. There does not seem to be great weight in Kant's criticisms of Crusius. Arguably something very like his view is the one that Kant actually accepts. He is right in arguing that the Things-in-themselves which act on us as Transcendental Subjects, and which so come to appear to us, *may* not themselves have the spatio-temporal ordering, let alone the sensuous qualities, of phenomenal things. There are, as Kant shows, serious logical and ontological objections to space and time, which make their demotion to purely phenomenal structures at least arguable. But, even if this is admitted, there must, if the thesis of the causation of phenomena by Things-in-themselves is to be significant, be some sort of emptily formal, logical correlation between the elements in the phenomenal and those in the noumenal order — they must, as Wittgenstein observes (*Tractatus* 4.0412), have the same mathematical multiplicity, and there must also be a one-to-one correspondence between their structural relations. Kant, in fact, despite his denial of the knowability of Things-in-themselves, throughout supposes that they must have this sort of formal correlation with appearances, a point particularly clear in his treatment of the acts of the special Noumena called selves or subjects. The Kantian theory, therefore, involves the same sort of harmony between phenomenal *natura formaliter spectata* and noumenal *natura formaliter spectata* that Crusius wishes to extend to nature's material constitution. To attribute such a harmony to divine action is also unobjectionable. For, Kant's God, and the Enlightenment's God, is not an arbitrary, personal being, but the comprehensive source of all positive possibilities, which at all points combines rationality with goodness. Such a being is no more than a guarantor or guarantee of the rational enterprises, and must plainly have 'willed' the conformity of our basic rational expectations to the governing principles of nature. Kant's theory of knowledge, if it is not to be as much steeped in contingency and subjectivity as he accuses Crusius's theory of being, must plainly postulate that, if the categories and forms of intuition are entirely our own, our affections by Things-in-themselves must also be so structured as to conform to them, or we and our intelligences would not be there at all. Kant, we may argue, is more Crusian than he thinks. We often hate theories when we feel that our theories are really very like them.

In concluding our examination of the Second Edition Transcendental Deduction we cannot help stressing its quite painful unsatisfactoriness. While both Deductions involve the same unwarranted *identification* of categorial with self-conscious synthesis, which plainly proves too much, and simply does not work; the Second Edition Deduction proclaims these mistakes more overtly, and is responsible for all that epistemological constructivism which simply fails to understand the place of knowledge among our rational enterprises. Knowing is not making, Prichard said, and Kant would not really want to deny this. But, here as elsewhere, Kant is really his own best critic, and the Analytic of Principles, to which we next turn, builds throughout upon the necessary contrast between our subjectively motivated and our objectively oriented syntheses, and so avoids the subjectivistic exaggerations of Kant's two Transcendental Deductions.

Chapter V

The Analytic of Principles

i

From the Deduction of the Categories or Pure Concepts of the Understanding, Kant proceeds to the deduction of the *a priori* synthetic principles which govern their application in judgements. We must try to see how the pure concepts of quantification, of positive and negative characterization, of substantiality, causality, and reciprocal interaction, and, lastly, of the possible, the existent, and the necessary, can be applied to what intuitively appears before us, so as to yield empirical or phenomenal *knowledge*. Such an application in judgement is ultimately, Kant says, a matter of 'spotting', of mother wit (A. 133), but there are none the less general guide-lines which will tell our mother wit how and where to look, and which will thereby also provide it with an advance intimation of what it will find.

Before embarking on this investigation, perhaps the most important in the *Critique*, Kant studies the manner in which the imagination must modify the categories in order that they should be applicable to phenomena in space and time, the forms in which our sensibility operates. Pure categories are of no use if they remain empty logical forms: they must be geared to possible appearances in the two great media of appearance. This gearing involves the emergence of a sort of amphibious, conscious orientation, which is at once conceptual and also spatio-temporal. The Productive Imagination, in its metempirical constructions, must have shaped appearances to suit such an orientation, and the Reproductive Imagination and the interpretative understanding must then have elicited from appearances what the Productive Imagination put into them. The amphibious, conscious orientation in question is called by Kant a transcendental *schema*: it is not so much a specific act of imaging, as a *readiness* to form images, to *illustrate* a pure concept by a considerable range of intuitively given matters. Kant, like Husserl, makes this sort of psychic readiness a *real* factor in experience, not something that a mind-theorist merely postulates. And he believes that such schematism operates both at an empirical and at a transcendental level. With the concept of a dog or a triangle goes the readiness to fulfil it in appropriate intuitions, whether pure or sensuous: it is the general rule under which such imagining operates. As Kant has put it:

It is schemata, not images, which underlie our pure sensible concepts. No image of a triangle would be adequate to the concept of a triangle. For it would not rise to the universality of the concept which makes it hold of all right-angled, or acute-angled, triangles, etc., but would always be restricted to some part of the field . . . Much less can an empirical object or image rise to the empirical concept . . . the concept of a dog stands for a rule, according to which my imagination can in general depict a four-footed animal, without being restricted to any particular shape offered by experience, nor to any possible image I can concretely picture. This schematism of our understanding in respect of appearances and their mere form, is an art hidden in the depths of the human soul, whose true knacks we shall probably never extort from nature, nor lay them bare before our gaze (A. 141).

The schemata in which Kant is now interested are not, however, specifically intuitive or empirical, but such as correspond to the pure concepts of the understanding that he has been deducing. And the intuitions with which he is trying to marry these pure concepts are simply the *pure* intuitions of time and space.

In the treatment that follows Kant gives a rather strange preference to time, perhaps because, being the formal condition of inner sense, it is also a formal condition for *all* phenomena, whether these be motions in space or emotions in the soul (A. 38–9). This one-sided emphasis is misleading, since spatial coexistence, as well as temporal succession, figures later in his schematizing principles, and since time can, in any case, only be pictured by projecting it on to a line in space (B. 292). But perhaps the one-sided stress on time is due to the fact that time presupposes and involves space in its presentation, just as the one-sided stress on the Transcendental Subject is due precisely to the fact that it presupposes references to the Transcendental Object as that from which it distinguishes itself. However this may be, Kant has the insight to see that the two structuring forms of experience necessarily work in harness, and would be meaningless apart from each other.

The schemata of the categories are then outlined in somewhat summary fashion. Number, or what is constructed when a set of homogeneous units are added imaginatively to one another in time, and whose prime illustrations are certainly spatial, is said to be the schema of the quantifying categories: it gives exactness to the pure concepts of one, many, and all (A. 142). Sensible content, or whatever is imagined as *filling* time with a certain qualitative intensity, which can then be imaginatively diminished till one comes indefinitely near to total emptiness, becomes, with its contrary, the schema of the categories of reality and negation (A. 143). Continuous permanence of sense-content in space and time becomes the phenomenal schema for the category of substance (A. 143), while regular time-sequence among the temporary characters of the same or different phenomenal permanents becomes the phenomenal schema of the category of cause and effect (A. 144). When such phenomenal cause-effect relations are reciprocal, we have the schema of disjoined, coexistent community (A. 144). The schema of the modal character of possibility is existence at some time or another, of actuality existence at a definite point of time, and of necessity existence at all times whatever. Number is therefore, we may say, the quantitative aspect of phenomena; sensuous intensity their degree of reality; phenomenal permanence their substantiality; regularity of succession their causality; joint regularity their coexistence; while differences in the degree of their transience constitute their possibility, their actuality, and their necessity (A. 144-5). It is helpful to realize that all these schematizations are phenomenal substitutes for what we call the true multiplicities and differences of nature, the true dependences and independences, and the true demarcations of the possible and the impossible, which we can only attribute to Things-in-themselves, and which are inaccessible to our phenomenally restricted knowledge. The schematized categories do not, according to Kant's view, yield us what we would supremely wish to know, that is, the transcendental structures accessible only to the vision of a God; but it is because we *think* of them as deriving from such transcendental structures, and as in some fashion representing them or doing duty for them, that they have for us any epistemic reliability at all. Vanishing appearances can never of themselves generate even the appearance of knowledge, but vanishing appearances thought to spring from non-vanishing sources, whether within or beyond ourselves, can, according to Kant's view, very well do so.

The full meaning of the schematized categories is, however, only made plain in the principles which follow, and in the transcendental arguments for them. These arguments show what Kant really meant by his view of the categories as involved in the possibility of any experience, whether subjective or objective, and correct the one-sided exaggerations of the Transcendental Deductions. For, what Kant's transcendental proofs all show is that conscious experience, like the transcendent reality which underlies it, is a two-sided, a subject-object affair, in which we must be able to distinguish what is objective by its invariant necessity of connection; whereas what is subjective is distinguished by its *Beliebigkeit*, its free arbitrariness, which can *either* elect to follow objective necessities in knowledge, or unite things non-epistemically, and for its own weighty or wayward reasons. These acts of personal freedom will, of course, exhibit necessities of temperament, habit, general orientation, and so on, but they may be quite indifferent to the *objective* connections they skim over; and it is through this power to be affected or unaffected by such objective connections that they both reveal their own presence and the objective connections in question. All conscious experience, in short, involves the use of something like the methods of agreement, difference, and so on, so well worked out by Mill; which not only distinguish the rule-governed contributions of one phenomenal object from those of another, but also distinguish all of these contributions from those of the subject, to which they all, and also the subject itself, are apparent; and which apperceives itself in relation to them all, but always also in *opposition* to them all. This is the true Transcendental Deduction of the Categories from the Transcendental Unity of Apperception: it is because there is *opposition* and *independence* among the phenomenal contributions of differing Transcendental Objects, and because the transcendental self is just one among the Transcendental Objects in question, that such things as appearances and the knowledge of objects, and also of the subject, are possible at all. Without these categorial distinctions, no object would be distinguishable from any other, and no object could be opposed to a subject which could be conscious of that object or of itself. As opposed to this true Transcendental Deduction given in the remarkable arguments we are about to study, Kant's official Deductions would lead neither to a consciousness of objects, nor to a consciousness of empirical or transcendental subjectivity.

ii

The multiplicative activities through which the imagination
schematizes the quantificative categories give rise to what
Kant calls the Axioms of Intuition, whose general principle
is stated in the formula: All phenomena are, *qua* intuited,
extensive magnitudes. The import of this principle is really
to exclude the absolute simples which Leibniz and Wolff
believe are the necessary components of all things complex,
and in which Kant is willing to believe as the necessary components of Things-in-themselves (A. 274). But in the spatio-
temporal media of intuition we encounter no simples, except
as limits (A. 169). Whatever we encounter is always capable
of resolution into parts, and into parts of parts, without end;
and into parts, moreover, which can be equalized with one
another, so that measurement in terms of units is always possible. Even in the case of intensive magnitudes such measurement may be *indirectly* possible: thus the intensity of the
illumination of sunshine can be equated with 200 000 illumina-
tions by moonlight (A. 179). All this means that quantitative
science has unlimited scope for its operations, and that there
can be no substance to views which deny the infinite divisibility of space and time. It is plain, in this case as in others,
that Kant's *a priori* assertions are a little too strong: science
has learned to live with the actuality of quanta and units of
which further division is impossible.

The Axioms of Intuition are succeeded by the Anticipations
of Perception, which make a principle out of the schematized
concept of the sensibly real. Empty space and time are not
possible objects of experience: the statements in the Aesthetic
that we can think of them void of appearances (A. 24, 31)
must now be taken to mean that we can go on as far as we
like in thinning out their contents, or perhaps in leaving gaps
among them, but that we cannot empty them of all contents
whatever. Kant goes further, and holds that it is not even
legitimate to *infer* the existence of wholly empty space or
time from any empirical datum (A. 172), an *a priori* assertion
that certainly seems much too strong. Kant holds that reality,
qua phenomenon, must always have a content as well as a
form, and that even when our senses fail to discover content
in any tract of space and time, we still have to postulate that,
were our senses more refined, we should be able to sense
occupants of space that now wholly elude us. Thus, from the

perceived attraction among iron filings, we are forced to postulate the existence of a pervasive magnetic medium, which our senses are incapable of perceiving (A. 226). Kant therefore lays it down as an *a priori* anticipation of perception that all phenomenal realities will have intensive magnitude, a magnitude which is given whole and entire at a given time, and is not assembled out of parts (A. 168), but which none the less varies continuously from an upper limit to an unattainable lower limit of emptiness. That intensive magnitude contains no parts does not mean, however, that it cannot be measured indirectly, as we saw in the case of sunlight. Kant is bound to reject the views of all those physicists who explain densities and other causes of variable pervasion by an assumption of uniform pervasion plus differing amounts of void (A. 173-4). It is certainly not easy to see why such an explanatory use of the void is to be excluded, or how Kant would take, for example, modern reductions of material occupancy to simple differences in empty space-curvature. Plainly Kant's views on these matters are archaically narrow, and no longer merit profound attention.

iii

The Axioms of Intuition and Anticipations of Perception are called by Kant *mathematical* principles (A. 162), and are also said to be directly *constitutive* of our intuitions (A. 160, 180). They are, that is, quantitative principles, and they are *always* to be found in whatever comes before us in space and time. The principles to which we now turn, the Analogies of Experience and the Postulates of Empirical Thought, which correspond to the relational and the modal categories respectively, are said by contrast to be *dynamic*, and also to be *discursive* and merely *regulative*. They are also said to be concerned with the *existence* (A. 160) of what is intuited, rather than presumably with its intuited content (A. 179-80). These characterizations appear to mean that the principles in question are concerned with the conditioning of phenomena by other phenomena, and so direct us to *look* for the phenomenal conditions of certain phenomena, without enabling us to say in advance what they are. This contrasts with the sort of advance certainty possible in mathematical cases. We not only know that there *is* a number which stands to 8 in the ratio of 3 : 4: we can also calculate that this number is 6.

But in the case of a cause-effect relation, while we are absolutely clear that a certain happening must have *a* cause, we cannot, without consulting experience, determine *what* that cause is. We can, that is, always think of a cause discursively, but only know its precise character empirically. The Analogies of Experience, which correspond to the three schematized categories of substantial permanence, causal sequence, and communal interaction, are rather like a proportion in which there is no *a priori* method of determining the fourth proportional, as there is in the case of the mathematical categories. They only tell us, for example, that *something* stands to this thing as cause stands to effect, but what this something is experience must reveal.

The Analogies of Experience, the three most important members of Kant's transcendental principles of judgement, are all concerned with the *necessary* connection of perceptions (i.e. phenomenal data) in time. All recognition of objects as being of a certain sort presupposes the ability to distinguish features in them and put them together: the Productive Imagination may have performed its primordial synthesis non-successively, and out of time, but *we* can only achieve a clear awareness of anything successively, and in time. To have experience it is, however, necessary to be able to draw a distinction between such successions of features and elements as reflect only our own subjective approaches, and such as stem from the empirical objects we are perceiving and judging about; that is, such as stem from successions that occur in those objects. Time is not, however, knowable apart from its contents, and hence it can only be the ineluctable necessity and invariance of certain successions which distinguishes them, as objective, from the variability which stamps other successions as subjective. As Kant puts his difficult point:

in experience perceptions only occur accidentally, so that no necessity in their connection is, or can be, evident from the perceptions themselves, since apprehension only assembles a manifold of empirical intuition, without providing an idea of the necessity which binds such phenomena together in space and time. But since experience is knowledge of objects through perceptions, and so must conceive of the interrelated existence of the manifold, not as it is put together (by us) in time, but as it objectively *is* in time, and since time itself cannot be perceived, the determination of the existence of objects in time can only occur through their connection in time as such, and so only through concepts that connect them *a priori*. Since these, however, always involve necessity, experience is only possible through the idea of a necessary connection among perceptions (B. 219).

In this passage we have the plain recognition of the two modes of synthetic togetherness, one of which is contingent and subjective, and the other invariant and objective. It is only in so far as *both* are present, and bring out one another by contrast, that there can be either a rendering unto the object of what is objective, or to the subject of what is subjective. The obscurities of the Transcendental Deductions therefore vanish in this better, fuller account.

The necessary connections to be studied must, however, be differentiated by *three* modes, which Kant now distinguishes, in pure time. Pure time has a mode of permanence or continuous duration (*Beharrlichkeit*); it has a mode of succession or supersession (*Folge*); and it has, lastly, a mode of coexistent simultaneity (*Zugleichsein*). Since time is, as an empty structure, neither intuitable or knowable, there must be necessary connections among the phenomenal contents of time which enable us to give an objective sense to each of these modes (B. 219). The meaning of these three temporal modes is, however, enigmatic. That time involves a perpetual succession of phases by phases is certainly part of its ordinary notion, and so also is the notion that there is room, in one phase of time, for a large number of things to coexist, perhaps in different regions of space, and so give time a certain lateral spread. But what on earth does Kant mean by saying that time has an aspect of permanence, that it involves something that does not change at all? Is this permanence of time no more than the fact that the supersession of temporal phases by phases will go on indefinitely? Or is it the fact that we always project time's successive phases into a vast, space-like map, in which all are depicted together, and so acquire unchanging relations of precedence and subsequence, relations which derive from, but which are not the same as, the vanishing supersession of one phase by another? For, in bare succession, Kant tells us in A. 183, existence is always vanishing and recommencing, and never has the least magnitude. Or, is the permanent aspect of time the fact that it always seems to involve a central focus of the present, the enduring now of Aristotle, as well as indefinite, ordered ranges of the past and the future surrounding this, while events in time merely hurry through this permanent framework, and always occupy different positions in it? McTaggart, in his analyses of time, has distinguished *two* permanent temporal series, one, the B-series, in which events occupy unchanging positions, and the other, the A-series, in which they are always changing their positions. Which of these two permanent frameworks had Kant in mind when he talked of the permanence of pure time, or was he perhaps confusedly thinking of both? The answer that we shall give is that the permanence of time is basically *none* of these: it is that of the Transcendental Objects (including the Transcendental Subject) which, being intrinsically out of time, but manifest in time, are able to exist invariantly throughout time, and can accordingly hold time's vanishing phases together, and so give a unity and an order to those phases. This unity and order are given both to sensibly filled time and to the pure time which we conceive as underlying it. Pure time is therefore only the *mediate* substrate of filled time, the *ultimate* substrate being the unchangeable system of Things-in-themselves, which are out of time altogether. For both this mediate and this ultimate substrate we have to find a phenomenal substitute which can be a real object of experience. This phenomenal substitute can only consist in certain basic constancies of character in phenomenal objects, for example, mass, inertia, conscious unity, and so on, with which all their variable characters are invariably associated, and upon which they are found to depend. These phenomenal constancies in time are therefore the necessary phenomenal stand-ins for non-phenomenal unities outside of time. The thought of substances which are Things-in-themselves, and which, being out of time, operate invariantly in time, is therefore necessary both for the persistent identity of phenomenal things, and of time itself as more than a mere flux of phases.

iv

In Kant's First Analogy (A. 182–9; B. 225–32) we are offered a transcendental proof, based on the possibility of experience, of the need to postulate the existence of something phenomenally constant in that experience, that will serve as the phenomenal substrate for all that is empirically variable and successive, and so furnish an empirical stand-in for the aspect of permanence in pure time. The First Edition states the principle of this analogy in the words: 'All appearances contain the permanent (substance) as the object itself, and the variable as its mere determination, i.e. as a manner in which the object exists'; a statement which leaves it a little unclear whether this permanent is something phenomenal, or a merely postulated thing of thought. The Second Edition formulation is more specific, but not more lucid as to what is meant by 'substance': 'In all change of appearances substance is constant: its quantum in nature is neither augmented nor diminished.' The Second Edition (B. 225) begins the proof by a paragraph in which it is argued that time, as the permanent form of intuition, necessarily underlies all change in appearance: it is the substrate in which all relations of succession and simultaneity have to find their place. This substrate cannot, however, be independently perceived. We must therefore discover a *second* substrate *in* the data of perception, which will serve as a phenomenal surrogate for the pure substrate which is time itself. This phenomenal representative of pure time is substance, which is 'the substrate of everything real that pertains to the existence of things', and which is such that 'everything which pertains to this existence can only be thought of as a determination of Substance'. This again does not make it crystal clear whether substance is actually to be *found* in the sensibly real, or is merely *thought* of as being in it. The solution seems to be that substance is thought of as a timeless unity behind phenomena in time, which is necessary to hold such phenomena and the phases of time together, but which is also manifest *in* time in the form of certain phenomenal constancies of character. It is then argued that, since substance is the unchangeable substrate of all change, its amount in nature can neither be increased nor diminished.

This somewhat obscure paragraph is followed by eight paragraphs which are common to both Editions, but which, to yield full clarity, must be supplemented with things said in later parts of the Analytic. Our apprehension of phenomenal multiplicity, Kant tells us in the first of these paragraphs, is always changing, and will not suffice to tell us whether what is experienced is objectively successive or simultaneous. To determine this, we must find something which is *always* there, and which will serve as the permanent substrate of all changeable appearances, of which change and simultaneity are merely different modes of existence. This constant element must express (*ausdrücken*) time itself, which (as a formal map) cannot itself be thought of as changing, since, if it did, it would require another time in which it could change. Without this constant substrate, temporal existence could never achieve duration; for, in mere succession, we have nothing but vanishing and recommencing, and never build up the smallest magnitude. Since pure time (as a formal map) is, however, unobservable, this constant element in experience must serve as the empirical substrate of all appearances, and do duty for the unobservable constancy of the pure time-map itself. This paragraph (which we have dolled up here and there) makes plain that the substantial substrate required is something empirical, not merely conceptual: we must have something discoverably constant in experience to which what is empirically variable necessarily attaches; and which can accordingly serve as a phenomenal representative of a non-phenomenal, non-successive constancy, which, being out of time, can be thought of as holding together successive states in time and time's own empty stages.

The next paragraph (A. 184–5) notes how in all ages common men, as well as philosophers, have believed in substantial permanence, but have been unable to prove it transcendentally, as Kant now believes himself to be doing. And, in the following paragraph (A. 185–6), he gives a valuable example of the application of this belief. A philosopher, asked how much smoke weighs, suggested that one should deduct from the weight of unburnt wood the weight of its subsequent ashes: the remainder would be the weight of the smoke. This example shows that the philosopher had, by examining appearances, come to the conclusion that *weight*, a difficult, higher-order character, not evident on the surface of appearance, was the true representative of underlying permanence, and hence of pure time. Plainly philosophers go about *looking* for what is constant in appearances, and, when they find some character that does not phenomenally vary, they take it to be the criterion of what is substantial. Obviously, shape, colour, smell, taste, and so on, will not qualify for this role, but weight, Kant suggests, may be suitable. Whatever appears, we know that new permanents cannot come into existence, nor old ones vanish; but by what characters we shall identify such permanents only experience can suggest. In A. 188, Kant further says that changes can only be *perceived* in enduring substances, and that an absolute origination *ex nihilo* or an absolute annihilation cannot be a possible object of experience, since it would presuppose the existence of a wholly empty time. Plainly Kant here means that, where things are perceived as simply arising or vanishing, we are sure that such absolute origin or cessation is impossible, and can therefore look for the enduring sources of such deceptive appearances. As it stands, however, his statement seems a little too strong.

Some statements made in the Second Analogy throw further light on Kant's doctrine of the permanence of substance. He there makes it plain that the criteria for substantial permanence consist in uniformities of *action* and causal influence, rather than in any simple phenomenal constancy, for example, of shape, colour, and so on. He says in A. 204-5: 'Where there is action, and so activity and power, we also have substance, and in this alone must seek for the seat of the fruitful source of appearances ... Action is a sufficient criterion to establish substantiality without the need to establish the permanence of such a subject by comparing perceptions, a procedure which could never achieve the exhaustiveness necessary for so weighty and universally valid a concept.' And to this passage we may add a passage from the Refutation of Idealism (B. 277-8), which makes it plain that phenomenal permanence involves continuous presence *in space*, and changing relations to other permanents in space; and that it is the absence of spatial position in the data of our inner life which prevents us from discovering anything empirically permanent there: 'Not only is it the case that we can only undertake the determination of time through changes in external relations, i.e. motions, relative to what is constant in space — the movement of the sun in relation to objects on earth — but we have nothing permanent that can serve as an intuitive foundation for the concept of substance, but only matter, and even its permanence is not derived from external experience, but from being the *a priori* and necessary condition of all time-determination.' These two passages enable us to say that, for Kant, the existence of substances, *qua* empirical, is reducible to the existence of indefinitely lasting, spatially distributed centres of action, which we pin down, not so much by their surface look, as by the regular ways in which they *behave*, whether on their own, or in conjunction with other similar centres. The full criteria for the identification of phenomenal substances will therefore only emerge when the principle of the permanence of substance is taken *together* with the other two principles of causal regularity and reciprocal interaction.

Kant's difficult treatment of phenomenal substantiality is much more intelligible when we see its roots in the Leibnizian-Wolffian world of dynamic simples, whose interactions or pre-established harmonizations underlie the spatio-temporal order of nature. In this world Kant never ceased to believe, though he held that it could only be thought, never known. We could only hope to discover phenomenal interrelations that would, after a fashion, serve to represent the unknowable interrelations of these non-phenomenal substances, and their individual and specific differences. But pure space and pure time themselves, in so far as they are given an objective meaning, can also only distinguish themselves by systematic interrelations among phenomena. Time, in particular, with its permanent structure of possible events on either side of the present, and with its permanent focus of the present through which phenomenal contents pass, can only be envisaged if we can discover enduring phenomenal centres, with constant rules of behaviour, which will enable us to project the contents of time beyond the vanishing present. The same would apply to space, as will be established in the Second Analogy. Pure time and pure space are therefore half-way houses on the road to the unknowable relations of Things-in-themselves, and they too, like those Things-in-themselves, require specific phenomenal interrelations to make themselves phenomenally evident.

v

Kant has therefore shown that continuous presence in space, together with regularity of manifest behaviour, is essential to the substantial units which are the subjects of phenomenal discourse. He has therefore given a prime place in phenomenal being to causal regularity, which is the theme of his second Analogy of Experience (A. 189–211). This is called the principle of generation (*Erzeugung*) in Edition I, and is formulated as: 'Everything that happens (begins to be) presupposes something from which it follows according to a rule.' In Edition II it is called 'principle of temporal succession according to the law of causality', and is formulated as: 'All changes take place according to the law of the connection of cause and effect.' What follows is common to the two Editions, with the exception of the first two paragraphs, which are Second Edition additions. The complex, wordy treatment of the proof deals again and again with much the same considerations, regarded from slightly different points of view. Too much has been made of its many confusions, and of the supposedly distinct proofs which it involves. We shall, following Vaihinger and Kemp-Smith, divide it into six substantial sections, of which the two introductory paragraphs of the Second Edition will count as the last, followed by three passages which deal with side-issues.

In the first of these sections (A. 189–94) Kant argues that, while the apprehension of phenomenal many-sidedness and multiplicity is always successive, this does not mean that there will always be an *objective* succession in what is thus apprehended. In a very wide sense anything apprehended is objective, but in the sense relevant for experience and knowledge this is not the case. If appearances coincided with Things-in-themselves, and were not merely referred to such objects, they could throw no light on any order other than their own. But, since appearances do not coincide with Things-in-themselves, and none the less have to be referred to the latter, we can only distinguish what can properly be so referred from what cannot properly be so referred on some basis inherent in the appearances themselves, and particularly in their order. Such a basis is to be sought in the *necessary*, that is, the invariable time-order of certain appearances, as opposed to the *arbitrary* (*beliebig*) time-order of others; such invariability and necessity in a sequence being taken to be the mark of an objective ordering, whereas variability and arbitrariness in a sequence are seen as marks of a subjective ordering. Kant then goes on to give his lightly sketched, infinitely discussed, example of a boat seen as objectively moving downstream, and a house seen as only subjectively ordered, as my eyes wander over its parts in various directions. The former type of succession is taken as necessary – I do not think it would be possible for me to perceive the boat in a downstream position, and *then* in an upstream position – whereas in the case of the house I am not constrained to look it over from top to basement rather than the other way round, but look it over as I please. The former type of succession illustrates a rule of succession – Kant does not of course think that this rule lies on the surface, and has not to be excavated from the highly specific material on hand – whereas the latter illustrates no such rule, but can be varied at will. (If there are psychological rules involved in the sequence, they are not relevant to the object, i.e. the house.) 'In the former case, therefore', that is, the case of the

boat, Kant says, 'I must make the subjective order of apprehension depend on the objective order of appearances, for
the former would otherwise be entirely undetermined, and
would not distinguish any appearance from another. The subjective order reveals nothing of the combination of multiplicity
in the object, since it is entirely arbitrary. The objective order
will therefore consist in an order of phenomenal multiplicity
which dictates that the apprehension of one happening will
follow upon the apprehension of another that precedes it,
according *to a rule.* For in this way only am I justified in
saying of the phenomenon itself, and not merely of my apprehension of it, that there is a sequence to be met with in it'
(A. 193).

It will be seen how clearly Kant, in this passage, shows *both*
a necessary and a non-necessary synthesis to be necessary for
all reference to objects, and to the consciousness of myself
as subject. And it is arguable that, in his conception of *objective*
succession, there is involved the implicit *thought*, though not,
of course, the least knowledge, of the simple, indestructible,
underlying unities whose interrelations make themselves phenomenally manifest in the shape of rules. These rules are the
only possible phenomenal manifestation of the simple unities
behind them, and of their unmanifest accord. That this is
dimly in Kant's mind reveals itself when he says (A. 190-1)
that appearances are not Things-in-themselves, but point to
the X of transcendental objectivity through their systematic
interrelations (cf. also what he says in A. 104-5).

In A. 194-6, Kant approaches his point from a slightly
different angle. He imagines a situation in which nothing in
our perception follows upon what precedes it according to a
rule. In such a situation there would be nothing to distinguish
our subjective order of apprehension from any objective order
in the objects themselves. 'We should then', Kant says (A. 194),
'have nothing beyond a play of presentations that related to
nothing objective.' Rules governing the sequence of phenomena
are therefore necessary to there being anything objective that
can be known through phenomena; which contradicts the
empiricistic assumption that rules of sequence are wholly based
upon an inductive extension of experienced uniformities. The
general presence of rules cannot, Kant argues, have such a
dubious foundation, but must have an *a priori* validity. This is
only possible because *we*, or rather our Productive Imaginations,

have injected the necessary element of rule-obedience into experience, in co-operation, no doubt, though Kant is not explicit about it, with the wholly simple, and therefore connection-imposing, objects-in-themselves.

In A. 196–9, Kant points out that, whenever we do distinguish an objective from a subjective order of succession, we do so in terms of a rule which governs the former. There is in fact no other way in which we can pass from our subjective presentations to what is objective. Relation to an object is, phenomenally speaking, nothing beyond subjection to a rule. Kant then makes the additional point that it is only causal rules that give phenomena a definite place in the permanent order of temporal events. Vanishing events only acquire a lasting place in history by being necessarily related to such and such things as their prior causes, and to such and such things as their subsequent effects.

In A. 199–201, he then relates the whole of time, as an embracing formal structure, to the rules of succession which connect the phenomena we locate in it. Without such rules they would have no definite place in time, and time itself would become an empty and inapplicable form. 'Since absolute time is not an object of perception, the fixing of a place in time can borrow nothing from the relation of appearances to such time. Appearances must, on the contrary, themselves determine their mutual positions in time . . . [and] the principle of sufficient reason is thus the ground of possible experience, i.e. of the objective knowledge of appearances as regards their relation to the temporal series' (A. 200–1).

In A. 201–2, Kant merely repeats his argument that successive synthesis cannot reveal anything that can claim objectivity unless its order is mandatory and irreversible. 'If my perception is to contain knowledge of an event, that something is really happening, it must be an empirical judgement that thinks of a succession as determined, i.e. as presupposing another appearance in time on which it follows necessarily, according to a rule. Otherwise, if I posited the antecedent and the consequent did not necessarily follow, I would have to regard it as merely a subjective play of my imagination, and if I thought anything objective about it, would have to call it a mere dream.'

We may now consider the opening paragraphs in Edition II (B. 232–4), which were added after the others were written. They build on the previously established principle of the necessary presence in phenomena of something abiding, to which changeable states must attach: all coming into being and passing away really pertains only to such changeable states, and not to their abiding substrates. The imagination can, however, connect such states in two opposed ways, one in which A comes before B, and one in which B comes before A. To achieve objectivity, we have therefore to decide in favour of one of these incompatible orders. This involves the application of the transcendental concept of cause and effect, which amounts to the determination of succession according to fixed and irreversible rules.

Three subsidiary comments accompany these transcendental asseverations. The first (A. 202-4) deals with the difficulty raised by the fact that the causes of an event are often taken to be *simultaneous* with, and not prior to, that event; for example, the heat radiating from a stove is contemporary with, and not prior to, the resultant warmth in a room. Kant resolves this difficulty in a manner afterwards followed by W. E. Johnson. A causal event A may be contemporary with its effect B, but it will then be the last term in a continuous process which started *before* B began to be produced, and without whose prior continuance B would not have arisen. The second comment (A. 204-7) stresses the connection of causality with action and force, and these latter with substance, as we have already mentioned. The permanent nature of a substance consists in its *readiness* to act in certain ways, and to do so necessarily in appropriate circumstances. Substances themselves cannot be phenomenally caused: they may, however, be noumenally dependent on a metempirical divine cause. Kant stresses that only experience can acquaint us with the causal powers of substances: it cannot enable us to understand them further. The third comment (A. 207-9) argues for the absolute continuity of all causal action. Every cause evinces its causality over a whole period, and produces an effect over that whole period. The effect will accordingly be produced with infinite gradualness, and never instantaneously or abruptly. This Kantian principle is Leibnizian, but it seems to involve dialectical difficulties that had best be avoided. It is not clear why there should not be 'mnemic causation', as in the theories of Semon, where causality operates over a gap of time as well as in the immediately successive. It would also seem, to our modern thought-habits, that Kant is a little too Newtonian in the strictness with which he believes in the reign of causal law. Considerable openness to alternatives in the behaviour of phenomenal substances would not reduce them, or their behaviour, to a mere dream. If noumenal options are admitted by Kant, occasioning great difficulty in his phenomenal explanations, it is not clear why he should not have admitted a limited range of phenomenal options as well, as men of science now contentedly do.

Kant's Second Analogy is really the fundamental one: the assertion that it is the law-governed character of certain sequences in time which enables us to distinguish what is objective from what is arbitrary and subjective. (That the latter, *qua* presentations, may obey regularities of their own, is not relevant to their character as presentative of objects.) It is this governance by rules which has to do duty for an acquaintance with those simple, dynamic units which underlie and are manifest in phenomenal connections, and which, by their simple invariance, render them necessary. In such underlying monadic entities Kant never ceased to believe, but he also assumed that they were forever beyond knowledge, except as the target of empty logical references.

vi

In his Third Analogy of Experience (A. 211-18) Kant extends to space the transcendentally necessary interconnections which the Second Analogy has attributed to time, and which prevent it from being a wholly inapplicable, empty form. These interconnections are not, however, among events or states of substances, or not so primarily, but among permanent substances themselves. These have to be perennially acting on one another, and revealing their presence to one another in characteristic, regular ways. Only in this manner does the coexistent, spatial world become a real community, in which all substances and their workings have their definite place. This, as the 1770 *Dissertation* made plain, is the characteristic unity of the sensible world: the intelligible world must be characterized by a very different sort of unity among harmonized simples. The principle of the Third Analogy is called the principle of community (*Gemeinschaft*) in the First Edition, and its formulation runs: 'All substances, in so far as they coexist, stand in thoroughgoing community, i.e. mutual interaction, in relation to one another.' In the Second Edition it is called the

'principle of coexistence in accordance with the laws of reciprocal action or community', and its formula runs: 'All
substances, to the extent that they can all be perceived as
coexisting in space, are in thoroughgoing reciprocal interaction.'

The Second Edition version starts with a paragraph peculiar
to itself, which is followed by paragraphs common to both
Editions. This new paragraph tells us that substantial things
coexist, if my perception can pass from one to the other in
either direction in time, as is not possible in the case of causes
and their effects. The moon and the earth are in this position:
I can readily pass from either to the perception of the other.
The coexistence of substances means, however, their joint
existence at one and the same time. (Since Kantian substances
are perennial, they exist throughout the whole of time, and
also throughout ever lesser phases of time: they of course also
coexist in space, and Kant shows a strange, double tendency,
sometimes to exclude coexistence from time, and make it
merely spatial, while time is strictly a one-tract affair (A. 183),
sometimes to regard it as a sort of extra, lateral dimension of
time, as in the present Analogy.) Since pure time is unobservable, only the reversible passage from one substance to another
in perception reveals coexistence, and this passage involves
the action of both substances on the perceiving subject, and
so, less directly, on one another.

From this rather tenuous example, Kant proceeds to postulate the necessity of *universal* reciprocal action among phenomenal substances, if all are to be observed and known as existing at the same time, and tenanting the same empirical, spatial
world. He supposes (A. 212) the coexistence of a number
of totally isolated substances, separated by empty spaces, none
of which in any way acts upon, or is acted upon by any other.
Such a coexistent world would not, he argues, be a possible
object of experience. We might indeed flash from one substance to the other, and so experience a time-order among
their states, but this would not tell us whether this time-order
were not merely subjective, or involved objective coexistence
among such states. Only if there were regular routes of influence
leading continuously from one substance to the other, that
could be travelled in both directions, could we establish time-
correlations among states, and coexistence among substances.
'There must therefore be something beyond mere existence
which gives A its place in time in relation to B, or B in the

opposite case in relation to A, since only substances thought of on such conditions can be empirically represented as co-existing' (A. 212). The mere *communio* or common existence in space would therefore be empirically meaningless without a *commercium* among them. 'Without community each perception (of a phenomenon in time) would be cut off from others, and the chain of empirical presentations, i.e. experience, would have to start anew with each new object, without the least coherence with what went before, or the possibility of putting the former into time-relations with the latter' (A. 214).

The claims in this passage are certainly impressive, but must not be given too rigorous an interpretation. Kant does not mean to maintain that *every* state of *every* coexistent substance must make some difference to *every* other: some states of some substances may be without influence on some states of some others. Nor must the word 'thoroughgoing' (*durchgängig*) be taken to mean that every substance is *always* actually acting on every other: it is enough if there are definite routes along which influences *could* be transmitted in either direction. Kant's principle of community has been turned, by Anglo-American idealists, into a doctrine of entirely universal, inter-locking coherence among substances and their states, which would preclude anything from being in any way other than it is. Kant's principle does not, however, require that every state of every substance always has repercussions on every state of every other, whether directly or indirectly: it would seem to permit subsidiary failures of communication. Provided there are *major* causal bonds that tie every substance in with every other substance, whether directly, or through common effects or causes, the principle should be satisfied.

Kant here comments (A. 216–18) on the total failure of all who have hitherto attempted to prove his three principles of substantial permanence, universal causal determination, and thoroughgoing reciprocal action *dogmatically*, and not, as he has tried to do, transcendentally, that is, from the possibility of experience and knowledge. These principles must certainly hold for *us* if we are to be able to have experience of objects, and of our own wayward selves; and our Productive Imaginations must have managed to impose such principles on their systematic transpositions of the unknown impacts from sources which transcend experience into the empirical, that is, spatio-temporal, idiom.

vii

Kant's fourth set of principles are called the Postulates of
Empirical Thought in General, and are concerned with the
phenomenal meaning of the modal categories of the possible,
the actual, and the necessary. These Postulates set forth the
use of these categories in relation to empirical knowledge:
they do not seek to define any use they might have in relation
to *thinkable* objects which transcend experience, or which
have no specifiable links with what we have hitherto experienced. Such transcendent uses of the modal categories will
come up for discussion in the Transcendental Dialectic, which
will follow upon the Analytic: some of such uses will be held
to be regulatively profitable, others unprofitable. But the
uses of the possible and the necessary, which occur in Kant's
own transcendental expositions, including the present, are
also not here in question, for example, Kant's talk about the
possibility of experience, or about the necessity of referring
presentations to the Transcendental Subject. Such uses of
the possible and the necessary help to state basic principles
involved in the very possibility of experience, and of the
empirical uses of concepts, and do not therefore themselves
form part of their empirical use. There are, Kant later makes
plain, many metempirical and transcendental uses of the modal
categories which are *not* here in question at all (see A. 232).
The postulates now to be stated are called postulates, not
because Kant thinks he can offer no justification of them,
but because they are of the same arbitrary sort that occurs
in certain geometrical constructions, for example, the treatment of a circle as 'generated' by the rotation of a straight
line about a point. We can, in the same way, 'generate' the
three principles we are about to state by considering the relation of · the objects of experience and knowledge to our
cognitive powers, the possible then being what we are empirically entitled to entertain, the actual what we are empirically
entitled to believe, and the necessary what we are not empirically entitled to doubt.

The formulation of the postulates is interesting, but does
not altogether accord with the long explanations that follow.
This formulation runs as follows (A. 218):

1. Whatever agrees with the formal conditions of experience
(i.e. of intuition and concepts) is *possible*.

2. Whatever accords with the material conditions of experience, i.e. of sensation, is *actual*.

3. Whatever is connected with what is actual, according to the universal conditions of experience, is, or exists, necessarily.

The definition of the possible just given would allow anything to be possible if it were not self-contradictory, and accorded with the axioms definitory of space and time, and also with the extremely loose and general requirements represented by the categories. In the following explanation, however, Kant goes much further in requiring that what is possible should have a definite foundation, not merely in the general possibility of experience, but also in actual specific, empirical findings. Thus he rules that:

if one should seek to construct quite new concepts of substances, of powers, and of interactions from the stuff which perception offers, without borrowing an instance of their connection from experience itself, one would be weaving fantasies for whose possibility there are absolutely no criteria, since one would not in them have consulted experience as one's instructress, nor borrowed one's notions from her . . . A substance which was enduringly present in space, but without filling it (like the thing intermediate between matter and thinking being which some have tried to introduce), or a special, fundamental power of seeing into the future, independent of inferences, or, finally, a power to enter into communion with the thoughts of others, however distant: these are concepts whose possibility is quite groundless, since they cannot be based on experience and its known laws. Without these, they are idle thought-combinations which, though involving no contradiction, can make no claim to objective reality, and so not to the possibility of the sort of thing they are conceiving (A. 222-3).

It is obvious that Kant is here making possibility not merely dependent on analytic and transcendental conditions, but on the accepted corpus of scientific fact and law. He is therefore unwarrantably restricting the boldness and creativity of the scientist, and also of the philosopher, which has never advanced except by trying out radically new conceptions, of which current experience and theory afford only the merest suggestion. Plainly Kant is here the victim of the eighteenth-century bedazzlement by Newtonian physics, but he is perhaps venturing uncertainly in the direction of a Popperian refutability, which is certainly a requirement of the empirically possible.

As regards what is actual, Kant is careful to say that we need not actually have observed it. Reliable connection with what has been actually observed, according to the preceding Analogies of Experience, will be sufficient. Kant's own elaborate theory of the underlying structures of nature, as worked out in the *Metaphysical Foundations of Natural Science*, is certainly meant to deal with what is empirically actual, though unobservable. And he does not hesitate, in the section under examination, to speak of the existence of a magnetic matter pervading all bodies, which the grossness of our senses will not enable us to observe, but of which the attraction of iron filings affords reliable evidence (A. 226). One wonders why Kant thinks that there could not be reliable evidence of precognition and telepathy, which, as in his earlier discussions of Swedenborg, he dismisses out of hand.

As regards the empirical sense of necessity, Kant makes it wholly hypothetical and conditional. Something is empirically necessary if it follows from well-established causal laws and well-attested fringe-conditions. Necessities of substantial existence, and Kant's own transcendental necessities, are not here in question. The determinism of Newtonian science also makes Kant reject the existence of a realm of *possibilia* extending far beyond the actual, and, *a fortiori*, beyond the necessary. Such a realm can indeed be *thought* without fallacy, and sometimes with cognitive or moral profit, but it can never make phenomenal sense. The possible, which is wider than the actual, can only be admitted in the sense that we may not as yet be apprised of all the empirical facts and laws necessary to establish the existence or non-existence of some connection. It therefore merely expresses the relation of such a connection to our cognitive faculties. 'What is only possible on conditions that are themselves merely possible is not in all respects possible' (A. 232). What is, in the ultimate, possible, must wholly coincide with the actual and the necessary. But Kant immediately points out, as noted before, that there are metempirical uses of the modal categories, which are not here in question, and which will be discussed later (A. 232). Kant is not the natural father of logical positivism: he is merely its adoptive father by holding something that faintly anticipates it.

viii

Right in the middle of his treatment of the Postulates of Empirical Knowledge, Kant, in the Second Edition of the *Critique*, inserted a short section entitled Refutation of Idealism (B. 274–9).

This passage must be read in close connection with the Note on pp. xxxix–xliii of the *Vorrede* to the Second Edition, and also with the passage B. 291–4 in that Edition, and with the whole treatment of the psychological paralogisms in the Transcendental Dialectic, which will be discussed later. *The Refutation of Idealism* is of crucial importance, as well as being perhaps the only added section of crucial importance in the whole Second Edition. In this section Kant refutes the opinion that we are in some way more certainly apprised of our own existence, as percipient and thinking subjects, and of our own perceptions and thoughts in time, than of the existence and properties of substances external to ourselves, and phenomenally located in space. Phenomenally, he argues, both sorts of substances and their states are in like case, and those which are external and spatial have even a certain priority, as being the necessary conditions of an apprehension of those that are internal and non-spatial. And, transcendentally and metempirically, both are in like case: we have to posit the existence of a timeless substance underlying our mental acts in time, and we have to posit the existence of other timeless substances provocative of those mental activities. In neither case, however, are we acquainted with what underlies the relevant appearances, though we are, no doubt, in some sense closer to our own transcendental selves than to the Transcendental Objects, which can only generate appearances by acting upon us. The Cartesian belief that there is something indubitable about our own existence, and highly dubious about the existence of outer things, and the Berkeleian belief that outer things exist only as perceived by ourselves, are alike devoid of foundation.

Kant's Refutation of Idealism rests on his acceptance, in the First Analogy, of the need for something phenomenally permanent as representing the unknown and unknowable substrate of changeable states, as the logical subject of which all changeable predications must ultimately be made. This phenomenal permanent cannot, Kant argues, be found in ourselves as intuited in time, for our own mental states can only have a content and a character to the extent that they are oriented to objects other than themselves. They are, as Brentano would say, 'intentional', and can only secondarily be concerned with themselves, if there is something not themselves which has given a content to their primary concern. It follows that it is only if there is permanence in the objects, not ourselves, that we represent to ourselves, that there can also be permanence in ourselves, as again and again representing such permanent objects. This objective permanence, on which any subjective permanence depends, must accordingly be the phenomenal permanence of something that appears 'out there' in space, and not the secondary constancy of a series of mental representations directed to what is 'out there' in space. 'The perception of this permanent element is only possible', Kant says, 'through something outside of me, and not through the mere representation of a thing outside of me. It follows that the determination of my existence in time is only possible through the existence of *actual things* [my italics] that I perceive outside of me. Consciousness in time is, however, necessarily bound up with the consciousness of the possibility of such time-determination. It is therefore also necessarily bound up with the existence of things outside of me, as a condition of time-determination. Consciousness, i.e., of my own existence is therefore also an immediate consciousness of the existence of other things outside of me' (B. 275–6).

This argument is very momentous. Not only has Kant shown that it is only by minding something, not ourselves, that is lasting that our own minding selves can acquire any approach to such lastingness, but, further, that the lastingness that it minds must, in some cases at least, be a *real* lastingness, sensationally given and referred to what is beyond, and not one that is merely imagined or conceived. The principle that Kant is here building upon is the profound one that it is only because our subjective orientations sometimes fail of their target that we can ever be *aware* of them at all. It is only when I have judged 'That was an A', and have had to correct myself and say 'No, it wasn't really an A', that I also become aware of the mere being of an A for me, in which imagination or unfulfilled presentation consists. It is only because there are some incorrigible, sensational presentations of the real, to which other corrigible presentations can be opposed, that we can be aware of presentations at all, as being approaches which at times hit their target, and at other times miss it. Were *no* presentations of objects corrigible, we should only be aware of objects, and never of presentations. It is therefore, as put in Kant's first Note to the Refutation (B. 276–7), not correct to say that we only *infer* the uncertain existence of things external to our conscious approaches from the certain existence of those approaches. It is rather the case that we *infer* the existence of our conscious approaches from the certain existence in some cases – and non-existence or uncertainty in others – of objects external to those approaches; which neatly turns the table on Descartes. Kant adds a Note to this Note, in which he points out that we can only be aware of imagination as imagination in so far as we also have veridical perceptions with which imaginary encounters can be contrasted. As Kant puts the point: 'It is, however, clear that, in order ever to imagine something as being outside of us, and to present it in intuition to sense, we must already have an external sense, and so be able to contrast the mere receptivity of external intuition with the spontaneity which characterizes every imaginative act.' Imagination, in short, is parasitic upon on-target perception, and would not be possible if on-target perception did not at times exist. But, as Note 3 carefully points out, perception itself is occasionally off-target, and then verges towards imagination or includes imaginary elements. There is a Reproductive Imagination which at times counterfeits the Productive: only the latter is the absolute source of phenomenal objectivity. Special criteria will show when the imagination is departing from its primordial sources, but such criteria would, of course, not exist in the absence of those absolute sources.

To this line of proof, based on the parasitic relation of self-consciousness to the consciousness of external objectivity, Kant adds a second line of proof, also of great importance. This is stated in his second Note, and argues that 'not only can the determination of time only be undertaken through change in external relations (i.e. movements) relative to what is permanent in space, e.g. movements of the sun in relation to objects on earth, but we have nothing permanent which can be used as an intuition to found the concept of a substance, save only matter which is an *a priori* and necessary condition presupposed by all time-determination, and so also of the determination of our inner sense in regard to our own existence through the existence of external things' (B. 278). This argument is more fully developed in B. 291, where Kant says that 'in order to find something permanent in intuition to correspond to the concept of substance (and so to prove the objective reality of this concept) we require an intuition of matter in space, since space alone is determined as permanent, whereas time, and with it all that comes before inner sense, is always in flux. In order to exhibit change, as the intuition which corresponds to causality, we have to take movement, change in space, as our illustration, and it is only thus that we can bring changes to intuition, whose possibility no pure understanding can grasp. Change is the combination of contradictorily opposed determinations in the existence of one and the same thing . . . so, in order to make our own inner changes, and our successive existence in different states understandable in retrospect, we have figuratively to make time, the form of inner sense, graspable through the external intuition of a line, and inner change by the drawing of this line, i.e. by motion' (B. 291-2). In other words, spatial representation preserves earlier phases of time and keeps them together with later phases, as time itself does not, and for this reason space, though only a phenomenal representative of what is timeless, represents it better than time.

There would appear to be an obvious objection to this view; for surely, if *all* consciousness is in flux, our awareness of things in space is as much in flux as our awareness of our inner states in time. This difficulty Kant meets in his Note on B. xxxix–xl, where he distinguishes between the representation of something *as* permanent and a permanence of representation. The representation of something permanent in space, that is, matter, may be quite as changeable and fluctuating as any other representations, but it *refers* to something permanent which is different from all my representations, and which must be an external thing. Time cannot stand before me as permanent in this way, since vanishing supersession is of its essence. Kant's view does not of course exclude the existence of sensations, feelings, and moods which last unchanged in character for some time, and certainly not of dispositions and trends which persist throughout one's inner life. He only thinks that the retention of the past in the present is in some degree a logical and ontological mystery, which it indeed is, but which is mitigated by the projection of time on to a line, and ultimately by a recourse in thought to an order which is outside of time altogether, but which appears as in time.

One all-important question remains: Is Kant's Refutation of Idealism only valid within another, more embracing idealism, in which outer things in space and inner acts in time are alike there for the Transcendental Subject, and so without relation to anything beyond subjective experience? This is of course the line taken by a great deal of Neo-Kantian orthodoxy, barricading itself in the fortress of what Kant has said about the Transcendental Unity of Apperception, and only admitting the Thing-in-itself as a limiting concept within those high walls. To be clear, however, as to how Kant really understood his Transcendental Unity of Apperception, we must see that it represents no more than an empty, logical reference to something-or-other as active in all our intuitive and cogitative experience, and as having a deep nature which leads it to translate the impacts it receives from external sources into a set of space-time locations, in such a manner as also to satisfy certain requirements of intelligibility. The entity which has this nature is not given intuitively, and we cannot say in virtue of what intrinsic character it performs what it has to be taken to perform. It is, in fact, a Thing-in-itself, whose existence must be thought and posited, but whose intrinsic character and *modus operandi* are unknown. And while this unknowable transcendental self may, in Kant's view, have generated its own experience, and in its own style, yet it has not done so parthenogenetically: it has been fecundated by affections from other transcendental entities, and their differences and connections must, by an inner law of its being, have been translated into phenomenal differences and relations. Without the compulsive impact of other transcendental entities, the Transcendental Subject would certainly not, in Kant's view, have generated appearances, nor have appeared to itself and been thought by itself in the process. There is therefore the same demand for something outside of the subject to act on the subject in the case of transcendental self-consciousness, as in the case of empirical self-consciousness. Kant, we may therefore say, has, in the Refutation of Idealism, studiously used the terms 'outside' and 'external' in an ambiguous manner so as to cover *both* the phenomenal outsideness of bodies in space, and the met-empirical, transcendental outsideness of Things-in-themselves to that Thing-in-itself which is our own transcendental self.

ix

Chapter III of the Analytic of Principles is entitled 'On the Ground of the Distinction of all Objects in general into Phenomena and Noumena'. This is an interesting, but highly vacillating piece of writing, which should not be regarded as

summing up Kant's total reaction to the topics under consideration. In this Chapter, Kant constantly varies his attitude to
Noumena, that is, objects thought of as underlying appearances,
without any fulfilling intuition to back our references to them.
At times he suggests that, while they are unknowable, they
none the less can and must be thought, as part of all significant
reference to phenomenal objectivity. But at other times he
suggests that to indulge even in the thought of them is merely
to play with empty conceptions, to which no genuine content
or meaning can be given. It is not remarkable that, with so
varied an attitude to these matters, even in a short chapter,
Kant should have been so diversely interpreted.

Kant, in the first part of his treatment, is unwilling to concede that there *may* be significant references of such a sort
that, in some essential respect, they cannot be intuitively or
empirically illustrated; and that there need be no theoretical
defect, no lack of explanatory value or definiteness of structure,
because they are thus incapable of illustration. He concedes,
as we saw, the significance of references to unobservables,
for example, a pervasive magnetic matter, but only on the
assumption that, were our senses more acute, we should be
able to perceive them (A. 226). He has not realized, as modern
struggles with positivist sophistry have made us realize, how
the whole of experience and thought is honeycombed with
what is intrinsically unobservable: the foreign mind, the inaccessible past and future, transfinite aggregates, and so on.
The external Thing-in-itself, the thing as it would be in abstraction from all the ways in which it appears to sensuous or to
'pure' intuition, is the only case of the intrinsically unobservable that concerns Kant profoundly. He permits himself,
therefore, to make statements to the effect that concepts,
including our basic categorial concepts, only have a feasible
use in relation to possible experience, in a sense in which this
possibility does not itself range beyond what is empirically
feasible. He remarks in B. 298:

The transcendental use of a concept in any principle is this, that it can
be applied to things in general and in themselves, the empirical use is
its application merely to appearances, i.e. to objects of a possible experience. That only the latter application is feasible, becomes clear when
we realize that each concept, first of all, requires its logical form as a
concept, a thought, as such, and secondly, the possibility of finding an
object to which it can be referred. Without this latter it has no sense

(*Sinn*), and is completely void of content, however much it may have the logical function of framing a concept out of certain data . . . All concepts, therefore, and with them all principles, however much they have an *a priori* possibility, will none the less refer to empirical intuitions, i.e. data for a possible experience. Without this they have no validity, but are a mere play with imaginative or conceptual presentations.

The limitation to possible experience applies also to the categories, and it was for this reason that the various categories were not defined when first introduced in the Metaphysical Deduction: it would, Kant says, have been impossible to define them, even had he so wished (A. 242). Only in their schematized form, in relation to possible experiences of spatio-temporal appearance, did their elucidation become possible. Quantity is meaningless without the successive addition of unit to unit in sensuously occupied time; substance, if we ignore empirical permanences in time; causation, if we ignore regular succession in time; and the modal categories, if we regard them as more than extensions of experience (A. 242–4).

From all this it follows that, while the pure categories have a purely transcendental meaning, they can have no transcendental *use* (*Gebrauch*): they represent merely the pure form of the understanding in its employment on objects, and it can have no such employment except on the things of the senses, including the purified sensory things arrived at in mathematical constructions (A. 246–8).

Having thus categorically denied a meaningful use of the categories beyond sensuous, spatio-temporal experience, Kant weakens and qualifies this denial. In the First Edition he points out that the declaration that spatio-temporal experience can only give us objects as they appear, and not as they are, seems to imply that one could enjoy some sort of non-sensuous acquaintance with objects as they are; and it is true that we always refer appearances to a Transcendental Object, an X, of which we, however, know nothing, but which is none the less the objective correlate of the synthetic acts inseparable from thinking self-consciousness (A. 250). The Transcendental Object, thus conceived, can be called a Noumenon or thing of thought. But the reference to such a thing of thought does not, strictly speaking, *use* the categories, but is something like an empty synthetic gesture in which nothing objective is really put before us. A Noumenon thus conceived is, Kant says, a Noumenon in the *negative* sense: it is, that is, not an object in the sense in which intuitively giveable things are objects. Our reference to a Noumenon is, in a sense, not a reference to anything, since it can never be consummated in intuitive confrontation. To which Kant adds, somewhat inconsistently, that 'it is indeed the case that intelligible entities (*Verstandeswesen*) correspond to sensible entities, and there may also be intelligible entities to which our sensuous-intuitive faculty has no relation at all, but the concepts of our understanding, as mere thought-forms for our sensuous intuition, do not in the least extend to such entities. What we therefore call a Noumenon must only be understood to be such in a *negative* sense of the word' (B. 309).

Hardly has he said this, however, before he adds to this negative sense of the Noumenon a positive, but problematic sense, in which it is thought of as the object of an intuition other than the sensuous; a purely intellectual intuition, such as we certainly do not possess, and have not even the right to regard as possible. The concept of such an intellectual intuition is, however, without contradiction, and, in relation to such a merely possible possibility, we have the problematic right to entertain a positive concept of the Noumenon, as being the sort of object that this possibly possible faculty might reveal. This faculty would, that is, if it existed, reveal things as they intrinsically were, and not as they appeared to those endowed with a certain sort of receptivity. This problematically positive concept of the Noumenon has further, Kant holds, definite positive advantages. For it makes plain that there are *limits* to conception and knowledge, and that we cannot make valid assertions about things not giveable to our receptive sensuousness. It forbids us to try to venture into a field which for us will always remain closed, however much it may, in some unverifiable sense, be explorable by other sorts of intelligence (B. 311). Taken as a problematic, limiting conception, the notion of a Noumenon is therefore unavoidable (*unvermeidlich*). The understanding *has* to set limits to itself, and to think of certain objects as being things of which it can know nothing, and to which it cannot knowingly apply its categories (B. 312).

Kant's wrigglings in this Chapter are highly ingenious, but they cannot be regarded as successful. For if the concept of a Transcendental Object is empty, the concept of a mode of intuition that might apprehend it is equally empty, and brings us not a whit further. Both are pure thought-references for which no intuitive fulfilment is available. And if there is something wholly senseless in thought-excursions ranging beyond empirical limits, then there are in fact no useful limiting concepts which can set limits to what cannot be done: there are in fact no real limits, and hence no useful limiting concepts. There can at best be warnings which guard against certain conceptual muddles. The correct and truly Kantian solution to all these puzzlements is merely to admit that a concept which lacks intuitive fulfilment, and which, for intelligences such as ours, *necessarily* lacks intuitive fulfilment, may none the less play an important and an indispensable role in knowledge, if the latter be viewed as geared to intuitive fulfilment. The true import of Kantianism is to set bounds to the range, and also to the importance of such knowledge, by at the same time making it obligatory for us to range *in thought* beyond it, as is done in all Kant's transcendental discussions. For even the mere form of a judgement, for example, the thought of an X as being ϕ, is not, on Kant's submission (see B. 141-2), merely the thought of a subjective synthesis among different items, but the thought of their *objective* mutual belongingness. Even the geometrical certainties, which Kant bases on pure intuition, necessarily involve an excursion into infinities of extension and division, and into exactitudes of measure which transcend experience. So do all the apodictic judgements that Kant makes regarding sensibility, judgement, reason, and so on, and their manifold relations to one another, as well as their extension to other men equally with ourselves. That we dispose of *a priori* concepts and principles of various kinds; that their most fruitful use is in illuminating experience by seeing what it really can and does impart, and by at times viewing it in the light of what is more generally thinkable; and that we can, further, learn nothing from experience except by basing ourselves, explicitly or implicitly, on these wider thinkabilities, and so in a sense transcending experience: this, surely, is the true message of Kantianism, and not the exclusion of types of talk of which the whole of Kantian philosophy is full, and of which later positivisms have often been more full.

We may here simply quote what Kant says in a wise Note to B. 166:

My readers should not precipitately be offended by the detrimental consequences of this proposition (That there can be no *a priori* knowledge except of objects of possible experience). I must remind them that the categories are not limited by the conditions of sensuous intuition in thought, but have an unlimited field, and that only knowledge of what we think, the determination of its object, requires intuition. In the absence of the latter, the thought of an object can still have its true and useful consequences for the subject's use of his reason, which, in that it is not always concerned with the determination of the object, i.e. with knowledge, but with the subject and its volitions, cannot here be dealt with.

The extensions beyond sense-experience to which Kant here refers are, of course, mainly the postulational extensions which arise out of the exigencies of moral practice, and will concern us later. We shall, however, have abundant cause to show that they are also involved, on Kant's admission, in the whole of our *intellectual* practice. We have to transcend experience practically, even when that practice is cogitative, and not merely moral or religious, a lesson that will emerge from later discussions in the Transcendental Dialectic.

x

The Appendix to the Analytic of Principles deals with the Amphiboly, the Double-sidedness, of Concepts of Reflection, through the confusion of the empirical with the transcendental use of the understanding. It also deals, from the novel standpoint of the *Critique*, with what, in the *Dissertation*, were called problems of subreption, the invalid applications of principles valid for the pure understanding, which, in the *Dissertation*, was able to penetrate to noumenal realities, to sensible appearances in space and time; and, contrariwise, of principles valid for such appearances to the Noumena only accessible to the pure understanding. Here, in the Appendix, the antithesis is between phenomenal knowledge, tied down to sensible appearances, and intellectual approaches which try to ignore the data of intuition, and so propound principles which fail of application to what appears to sense. What is interesting in Kant's treatment is that he still really adheres to the *Dissertation* positions. He believes that, *if* what we have in intuitive experience were Things-in-themselves, then the pure laws of the understanding would apply to them. They are only *not* applicable because we are dealing with appearances, which need not conform to these laws, and are in fact proving their phenomenal character by not doing so. What Kant thereby affords us is an invaluable glimpse of his unchanged view of

Transcendental Objects. They are to be conceived as Leibniz and Wolff conceived them, and as Kant conceived them in his early days, that is, as dynamic, monadic simples underlying complex spatio-temporal appearances. But of these simples it is now impossible to have knowledge.

The Appendix on Amphiboly begins by dealing with the theme of transcendental reflection, by which Kant means the consideration of some matter in its relation to different sources of knowledge. Are we investigating something as presented to sensory intuition, or the same merely as thought by the pure understanding? The investigation may lead to a different solution as we relate our matter to one source or another. There are, however, *four* relations in regard to which questions of relegation are important: (a) questions of identity of kind (*Einerleiheit*), or difference of kind (*Verschiedenheit*); (b) questions of inner coherence (*Einstimmung*), or conflict (*Widerstreit*); (c) questions of internality, or externality; (d) questions of Matter, or Form. The first pair of questions sorts things into classes or kinds, and is connected with the categories of quantification. The second pair sorts things positively or negatively, and is connected with the categories of reality and negation. Kant does not connect the remaining sorts of questions with the two remaining groups of categories, but with his usual ingenuity could no doubt have done so.

As regards the first antithesis, that of identity and difference of kind, it is plain that the understanding cannot admit the possibility of two things which are exactly, in all respects, of the same kind, since it would have no means of distinguishing them. It adheres therefore to the Leibnizian axiom of the identity of indiscernibles: there cannot be two exactly similar things, differing only numerically. Our spatial, and also our temporal, intuitions, on the other hand, allow for the possibility of such merely numerical differences: things may be distinct, though there is no general property that distinguishes them. A repetitive cosmos, as in a wallpaper, is intuitively possible.

As regards the second antithesis, the understanding cannot admit the possibility of things which harbour internal conflicts or oppositions, since such conflict is destructive of possibility. Phenomena, on the other hand, are honeycombed with internal conflicts, for example, that of pleasure and pain in regard to the same object, which do not destroy their phenomenal possibility.

As regards the third antithesis, the understanding demands that everything must be something in and for itself; it must have an inner core-nature as a precondition of having relationships to other things. One's whole nature cannot consist in external relationships. Since a material body reveals itself to experience as no more than the centre of attractive and repulsive forces, the rationalistic understanding has to locate these in a centre in some ways analogous to the simple, monadic subjects responsible for our acts of thought. Empirical physics, on the other hand, is quite satisfied with bodies whose whole nature consists in their dynamic relations to other bodies, and contains nothing intrinsic.

As regards the fourth antithesis, the understanding demands that matter, or the constituent elements of something, should exist as a presupposition of their being organized in some relational manner. Leibniz therefore required the prior existence of elemental monadic unities, representative or non-representative, as the elements on whose interrelations all phenomenal relations in time and space depended. Our sensitive, intuitive faculty does not, however, require the prior existence of ultimate indivisibles in order that spatio-temporal structuring should be possible: spatio-temporal structuring itself renders all its own component parts possible, and demands nothing indivisible.

Kant then adjudicates upon the four amphibolic conflicts just set forth. The Leibnizian solution, he holds, would be correct if the objects of knowledge were Noumena in the positive sense, which could be given to the understanding as they intrinsically were. Leibniz, he says, took appearances to be Things-in-themselves, only confusedly apprehended, and correctly argued that there could not be two such things exactly similar in every respect. If they *were* Noumena, given as they are, even if confusedly, this would be an indisputably correct conclusion (A. 264, 281). In the same way, *if* we were apprehending noumenal Things-in-themselves, there could be no conflicts among their positive determinations: merely positive determinations, however combined, cannot effect a mutual suspension (A. 282). And *if* what appeared confusedly to our senses really were something that existed in and for itself, we should be entirely right in discerning in it something simple and monadic, with an intrinsic nature consisting merely of representations, or something like them, which did not take us beyond itself (A. 283). Finally, Leibniz's basing of spatio-temporal relations on the harmonization of the intrinsic states of monadic substances is how the matter would have to be — *so würde es auch in der Tat sein müssen* — if the pure under-standing were immediately related to its objects, and space and time somehow confusedly determined Things-in-themselves (A. 267). Since, however, the objects we have to deal with in order to give a concrete sense to our thought-categories, and to achieve reliable knowledge, are always objects as they in-tuitively appear to us in space and time, we have to accom-modate our conceptual demands to the intuitive material which alone fulfils them, and admit the possibility of phenomenal objects different *solo numero*, or as being able to reconcile conflicting properties, or as having no nature beyond their relations to other things, or as consisting of nothing that is absolutely elementary. This accommodation consists in refusing to press conditions of intelligibility on and on indefinitely, and being willing to call a halt somewhere.

If, however, we examine Kant's solution of the amphibolic situation, we shall see that it involves a perfectly definite view of the noumenal realm, which does not amount to knowledge only because it is emptily formal. There could be no other sort of noumenal realm than just this, and Leibniz had sketched it perfectly. If Things-in-themselves could be given to us just as they are, and not in a diremptive spatio-temporal perspective, they would be given as wholly simple units, each concentrating in its profound simplicity concentrated forms of all the char-acters which it regularly manifested together or successively, as well as concentrated forms of all the variable characters it showed forth either alone, or in concert with other things. The simplicity of the units would be all important from the know-ledge point of view, for it alone would explain the uniform coexistence and successions that we look for in phenomena. And there would, of course, have to be one crowning, neces-sarily existent simple on which all contingently existent simples were in some manner dependent. In this crowning simple all temporal and spatial relations would have their timeless, spaceless ground, and it would have to have some-thing like the omnipossibility and omnibeneficence with which Leibniz credited Deity. We may note that Kant, in limiting knowledge to phenomena, and denying it access to Things-in-themselves, in effect also demonstrated the phenomenal nature of all that we can know, through its failure to live up to the standards of what can be, and be understood. Only in a world in which all diversity became concentrated into partless unity, much as a wealth of sensuous detail can be crowded into one simple thought, and all partless unities became concentrated into a single crowning unity, could anything really be or be understood. Perhaps, however, we should be wrong to look in that partless unity for anything more than the sum total of the phenomenal possibilities that it concentrates, unifies, and explains.

Chapter VI

The Dialectic of the Soul and the World

i

We pass from the many badly overgrown, hazardous bunkers of the Transcendental Analytic to the comparatively smooth, green fairways of the Transcendental Dialectic, where there are far fewer hermeneutic problems. Here we study the manœuvres of a type of thought which is not content to use its concepts on empirical material, and to justify concepts by their empirical applicability, but which endeavours rather to ascend to certain highest conceptual Ideals — that of the absolute soul or subject, the absolute cosmos or sum total of reality, or the absolute divine source of all existence — and in so doing necessarily transcends possible experience. In studying such manœuvres, we have also to criticize the phenomenally empty judgements and reasonings to which they lead. The term 'Dialectic' is here used in an idiosyncratic manner by Kant, even if he thinks it stems from an ancient original (A. 61): his Dialectic examines both the thought-steps which lead us to frame and seek to apply the conceptual Ideals in question, and also seeks to expose their results as being epistemologically empty and nugatory. Dialectical thought-processes lead us to think that we have an actually known object before us when we have not, and therefore create transcendental illusion: dialectical criticism must therefore expose the transcendental illusion thus created (A. 61-2). In calling such concepts, judgements, and inferences 'illusory', Kant does not mean that what they set before us is transcendently unreal: they are only empty and unreal from the special standpoint of *experience* and *knowledge*. Kant never wavers in his view that there *are* simple thinking subjects confronting a complete world of objective simples manifest in the phenomena of nature, and all stemming from a transcendent, simple, real source called God. He never wavers in his belief that we are obliged, in virtue of grounds which stem from our moral and also from our theoretical practice, to think in terms of such transcendent sources, and to proceed as if they were real. He only rejects the view that we can ever *know* anything about them, or even refer to them as objects, in the sense in which knowledge and reference involve the possibility of intuitive fulfilment and phenomenal verification. The exposure is therefore much less momentous than it has seemed to many.

Kant uses the Platonic term 'Idea' of the concepts whose inner content is such that they necessarily transcend phenomenal illustration. Plato, he says, understood by an Idea a content not borrowed from sensuous sources, and also transcending the Aristotelian categories, which at least had some congruity with experience. Ideas were paradigms of things themselves, and not merely a key to their appearances. They were, according to Kant's account of Plato's view, outflows of the supreme reason, from which human reason derives, but from which it has declined, so that a difficult act of recollection is necessary before it can lay hold of such transcendent notions. Plato, he says, found eminent examples of his Ideas in the practical sphere of the virtues (though his application of them to nature also is important), and the *Republic* is an attempt to elaborate the Idea of an ideal constitution in which the complete freedom of each will accord with the complete freedom of all. Kant will himself later develop his own republic, the kingdom of ends, in his moral theory: at present his concern is with the three speculative Ideas of the soul, the cosmos, and God. Kant deplores the use of the term 'Idea' for any and every mental presentation, whether sensational, intuitive, or conceptual. It is best reserved for conceptions, which not only are not derived from experience, as, for example, the categories are not, but which also have no possible application to experience (A. 313–17). Such Ideas have none the less an important place in our thought-economy, greatly as they may be abused, and transcendental analysis and criticism must discover that place.

If understanding is the faculty which applies concepts to other concepts, and ultimately to intuitive material, and whose pure concepts, the categories, merely express the sort of unity common to all concepts, and to the judgements in which they function; reason is the faculty of the transcendental syllogism, which proceeds, by an infinite extension of inference, to the Transcendental Ideas. There is a certain artificiality in Kant's connection of the Ideas with syllogistic procedures, but it is part of his basing of his whole philosophy on the forms of the current logic. The syllogism had three established forms: categorical (All M is P, Socrates is M, therefore Socrates is P), hypothetical (If p then q, and p, therefore q), and disjunctive (Either p or q, but not p, therefore q); and, in the case of each, one can proceed *regressively* by inferring one's premises from premises of higher generality, or *progressively* by making the conclusions of one syllogism the premises of another. The progressive procedure merely derives more and more specific conclusions from given premises, and gives rise to no new notions, and to nothing that need transcend possible experience. The regressive procedure, on the other hand, tends to give rise to the notion of a limit, of a situation where we shall have arrived at premises of the highest generality and most unconditional validity, which cannot, and need not, be inferred from anything more general or more unconditional. Since premises of higher generality tell us *why* their specific or conditioned cases hold, it seems that we shall never know *why* anything is the case, unless we can regress to premises which bring in notions of the highest generality and most unconditioned application. Thus, in the case of the categorical syllogism, we regress to the notion of a simple substantial unit (or units) whose nature is exercised in whatever we predicate of it. The most salient instance of such a substantial unit is the simple subject within us (whatever it may be) to which we attribute our thoughts, feelings, inner states, and so on; but of course it has analogues in the external things around us (A. 66), whose inner self is as little known to us as the psychic self within us. The ultimate reason why anything is as it is, and does as it does, is that this is in some sense prefigured in what it is, in its concept or nature. For, as Leibniz says, the notion of an individual substance contains all that will ever be true of it. But such substantial units, and such comprehensive natures, certainly transcend possible experience, which only offers us particular phenomenal conjunctions. The reference of phenomena to subjects, and particularly to that very special subject we call our thinking selves, accordingly involves the emergence of a Transcendental Idea which transcends all experience, but which provides an ultimate reason for phenomena being as they are. In the same way, the reference of some phenomenal state of affairs to some antecedent which is its condition, and this to some further antecedent which is *its* conditions, readily gives rise to the notion of some absolutely first condition, which requires no condition upon which it follows; or, alternatively, to some absolute totality of conditions, perhaps following on one another in a finite or infinite sequence, of which a given state of affairs is the final consequence. When such a first condition, or such a totality of conditions, has been discovered, we shall, we feel, understand *why* things are as they are; and it seems that, without such a complete deductive base, things need not have been as they are, since something might always have interfered with any of such conditions. The regress movement from consequences to conditioning antecedents therefore introduces us to a second Transcendental Idea: that of a totally explained world in which everything has a sufficient set of conditions, which completely permits the deduction of whatever is the case. And, in the third place, the disjunctive placing of a state of affairs among other states of affairs, one of which is taken to be or not to be the case, and the regress of this to wider disjunctions in which further ranges of alternatives are taken into account, tends to a limit in which *all* possibilities will be summed up in a single comprehensive disjunction. Such a disjunction, according to the view taken by the Leibnizian-Wolffian metaphysic, adequately represents the nature of God, the being who cannot not be, since His existence and nature cover every possibility, and are therefore necessary. This is plainly a Transcendental Idea, which not only goes beyond all experience in the width of its range, but also in its modal notions, which are not those used in empirical contexts.

After considerable meditation one can thus see what Kant means by the very statement that 'Pure reason never relates directly to an object, but to the understanding's concepts of the same. It will likewise only become clear, in the course of a complete treatment, how reason, merely by the synthetic use of the same function it uses in categorical syllogisms, must necessarily arrive at the concept of the absolute unity of the thinking subject. In the same way, through logical procedures in hypothetical syllogisms, it will necessarily arrive at the concept of the absolutely unconditioned in *a single series* of given conditions, and the mere form, finally, of the disjunctive syllogism will necessarily entail the highest concept of reason, that of a being of all beings, a thought that, at the first blush, seems utterly paradoxical' (A. 335-6). That the use of the logical connective *or* will lead the soul to God, certainly seems bizarre, but Kant's whole argument is less wanton than it seems. It amounts to identifying reason with the deductive faculty which demands a completely sufficient grounding for whatever it believes. This demand leads to the formation of three concepts of such a completely sufficient grounding: the nature of a simple substance such as we conceive the ego to be, of a complete system of substances acting and reacting on one another, and of an all-harmonizing God, who compasses all that is possible, and adjusts the ways of everything to everything else. Syllogisms are only brought in because Transcendental Ideas involve transcendental inferences, which have to transcend possible experience.

It is at the same time important to note that, in using the term 'transcendental' on these inferences, he is linking the postulations in question with the whole structure of experience, and with the joint working of conception and intuition which this involves. The objects postulated may be transcendent, and we may not be able to achieve contact with them, but the act of postulating them is transcendental, part of the warp and woof of consciousness. Kant stresses that the *pure* use of reason, which generates the Transcendental Ideas, is a necessary extension of the *ordinary* or logical use, which merely serves to bring greater unity into empirical materials by importing principles of more general scope or less conditioned application. But this aim of reason can only be satisfied if the explanatory process can be brought to *completion*: we must find the unconditioned that corresponds to the conditioned knowledge of the understanding, so that the unity of the latter can be completed. This logical maxim, however, becomes a principle of pure reason when the assumption is made that, whenever the conditioned is given, the *whole series* of its conditions, each subordinated to a prior condition, is also in some manner objectively given, even though *we* cannot lay hold of it (A. 307). Kant also stresses the importance of the locution 'absolute', with its equivalent German adverb *schlechthinnig* — German seems to be the only modern language with an *ordinary* word for 'absolute' — a locution which, more than any other, gives expression to the central aspiration of reason; that is, to achieve 'absolute totality in the synthesis of conditions, which never ends except in what is absolutely (*schlechthinnig*) and in every relation unconditioned' (A. 326). This absolute use of 'absolute' must be contrasted with its merely relative use, when we consider some state of affairs in respect of its intrinsic content or in some special context. The absolute use of 'absolute' must be free of a relation to any context and must apply in all circumstances whatever. It would be very regrettable, Kant holds, if this absolute use of 'absolute' were lost (A. 325–6).

Our stretching out towards completions that can never be completed certainly involves illusion, but Kant stresses that such illusion is also irremovable:

Transcendental illusion does not vanish, even when it has been found out, and when its idleness has been seen as a result of transcendental criticism . . . The cause lies in the fact that there are basic rules and maxims of use inherent in our reason (considered subjectively as a human cognitive capacity), and that these quite have the appearance of being objective principles, which has the result that the subjective necessity of a certain conceptual combination, as an aid to understanding, is mistaken for an objective necessity in determining Things-in-themselves. An illusion which cannot be avoided, any more than we can avoid seeing the sea higher in the middle than on the shore, since we see the former through higher light-rays, or any more than the astronomer can prevent the rising moon from seeming enlarged, though this illusion does not deceive him (A. 297).

Kant, like Wittgenstein, admits that the notions of transcendent metaphysics have deep roots in our conceptual and linguistic apparatus, but he does not, like Wittgenstein, think that there is some sort of philosophical therapy which could exorcise them. Kant also retracts any suggestion that the Transcendental Ideas are idle and nugatory. Though they may determine no object, in the special sense in which objects must be capable of being sensuously given, they may still provide the understanding with a canon for its extended and consistent use, and enable it to know what it does know, better and more widely (A. 329).

ii

In the Paralogisms of Pure Reason Kant examines the transcendental inferences in which reason leaps from the synthesis of empirical predicates with empirical subjects to the transcendent synthesis of all such predicates in a subject which transcends everything empirical. It is an ultimate subject, association with which makes a synthesis of empirical predicates possible, and which, being an ultimate logical subject, is as such void of empirical predicates. The salient case of such a transcendent, empty subject is that of the conscious subject or 'I'. In all synthesis we attribute our thought-combinations to the single, thinking subject, 'I'; and all categories, as combinatory functions, have, whatever their objective aspects, a necessary relation to this conscious, thinking 'I'. The thinking 'I' is of course a Transcendental Object: having denuded it of all but its synthetic functions, it is merely the thing, whatever it is, that performs our conscious syntheses. As such an empty logical subject, the conscious self does not differ from the objective Things-in-themselves, whatever their nature or number, which are *also* taken to underlie the complex properties and modes of behaviour that we attribute to phenomenal things. According to Kant's view, in the Transcendental Deductions the reference to Transcendental Objects in fact goes hand in hand with the reference to a Transcendental Subject: they are two sides of the same act of reference, in both of which we reach out to what transcends experience. Error, however, arises, when such reachings are mistaken for an actual contact with something objective, and where we think that we can prove the real existence of the something in question. The reasonings by which such metempirical entities are established, are therefore, according to Kant's view, paralogisms. They apply forms of inference that would be appropriate in empirical contexts, in contexts which go wholly beyond experience. In what follows Kant only considers the paralogisms which establish the existence of Transcendental Subjects, though he might have equally framed paralogisms in the case of Transcendental Objects.

Kant is careful to distinguish the 'I' as Transcendental Subject from the 'I' which is genuinely an empirical object, and which is intuitively given to inner sense. The 'I' which is an empirical object is not merely given as thinking: it is perceived as perceiving empirical sensuous objects of various sorts, and as imagining them and thinking of them, and also as having various feelings, desires, and so on towards them. All such references to specific empirical objects, and all such varieties of answering attitudes, must be purged from our notion of our selves, if this is to be truly transcendental: what must be allowed to remain is merely the notion of an entity that can embrace unspecified objects in a single conscious survey, and be conscious of itself as doing so. Kant holds, very arguably, that it is an *inference* that brings such a majestic entity before us: we do not encounter our thinking selves as we encounter the laundryman in the street. Our awareness of what thinks in us springs from our realization of the differences between countless types of conscious act each directed to special empirical objects and goes beyond such objects and such references to something that is operative in them all. As Kant puts it: 'The expression "I", as a thinking being, stands for the object of a psychology which can be called a rational doctrine of the soul . . . Rational psychology is genuinely an undertaking of this sort, for, if the slightest empirical element in my thinking, any particular perception of my inner state, were mixed with the epistemic grounds of this science, it would cease to be a rational, and become an empirical psychology . . . *I think* is therefore the sole text of rational psychology from which it must develop all its wisdom' (A. 342-3). (The inferential element in the *I think* does not, however, mean that the entity which thinks need be a *different* entity from the one which senses, feels, and so on; it must rather be thought of as a different stratum of the same entity.)

The paralogisms to which the *I think* leads are, according to Kant, four in number, and are somewhat artificially connected, in a manner we need not go into, with Kant's four groups of categories. The First Paralogism is that of substantiality, and it proceeds to treat the self — of which Kant says, in a revealing passage, that it is 'I or he or it, the thing which thinks' and which is 'presented as no more than the Transcendental Subject of thoughts, $= X$, and which is only known through the thoughts which are its predicates and of which we have not the slightest conception in isolation' (A. 346) — it proceeds to treat this self as an ordinary substance, marked out by empirical permanences. The second paralogism is that of simplicity, which argues that the thinking 'I' can have absolutely no parts, and is therefore utterly simple. The third paralogism is that of personality, which argues for the permanence of the thinking self in time, while the fourth is that of ideality, which argues for the total unlikeness of the conscious self to divisible entities in space, and for the superior certainty of its existence. These are four transcendental arguments, since their conclusions wholly transcend experience. There would be analogous arguments establishing the existence of permanent, simple substances underlying appearances in space, and it is a pity that Kant has not developed them. We shall follow the First Edition in what follows: the Second Edition has not improved upon it.

In the First Paralogism the argument is purely that, in attributing all our thoughts to our thinking selves, we are attributing them to something which is not itself a predicate or an act of thinking, but rather something which *has* them: the thinking self therefore corresponds to the conception of a substance. Kant does not deny that the conception of a self is the conception of a substance (A. 350-1): he only denies that such a conception hits any definite target. For there is nothing intuitive about the postulated self: it is merely thought of as the unitary something or other in which all our thought-references come together, and are unified. All that is empirical about it are the unified thoughts and their definite objects, not the supposed pure thinker who unifies them all. We have indeed, Kant holds, to think of such a thinker − so much is involved in the structure of conscious awareness −, but a necessary thought does not constitute an act of knowing anything (A. 348-51). Kant's real objection here is to the dogmatic assumption that what underlies unified thoughts must be something essentially unitary and geared to thinking: it might be something hopelessly multiple and only subsidiarily geared to thought.

In the Second Paralogism the argument is apagogic. If the conscious self were composite, and if each constituent part of it cognized a distinct part or aspect of some complex object, for example cognized the distinct words or lines of a poem, there could be no synthetic consciousness of the object as a whole, any more than this exists when different persons each are aware of a different part or aspect. For a whole of parts to be cognized, there must be a *single* subject which cognizes them all, and brings them together in a *single* view. Such a single subject cannot accordingly consist of elements or parts, but must be absolutely simple. Kant does not deny that the unity of consciousness is a true unity: his whole epistemology rests upon it. He denies, however, that it can teach us anything regarding the noumenal substrates of our conscious acts. They may be many distinct Things-in-themselves, by some strange accident acting together, quite as readily as a single, simple thing: we can have absolutely no knowledge of the matter (A. 353). The unity of consciousness is a phenomenon which exists wherever consciousness exists, and so is hypothetically necessary: we cannot, however, pass from such a hypothetical necessity to the existence of something which generates such a unity. This critical argument is, Kant thinks, even clearer if we consider the case of *another* conscious person. If we conceive of *his* conscious states, as we indeed do conceive of them, as involving the same sort of reference to himself as subject as happens in our own case, we none the less feel that such a reference would be hazardous for him: it would not be plain that such a way of regarding his mental states need correspond to anything real (A. 354). This could only be the case if there were some empirical ground for supposing there to be such simple generative centres of conscious unity, as we have empirical grounds for believing in simple force-centres in matter. And so, Kant says, 'This celebrated psychological proof bases itself on the indivisible unity of a presentation, which merely governs a verb in its relation to a person. But it is clear that, in attaching our thoughts to an 'I' as the subject of their inherence, I am merely thinking of such an 'I' transcendentally, without discerning the least character in it, and without recognizing or knowing anything about it' (A. 355).

There are also, Kant argues, no interesting consequences to be derived from the simple character of the notion of an 'I'. We cannot, on the score of the 'I's' simplicity, hold it to be radically different from the external substances that appear around us in space. For we know as little of the substrates that underlie phenomenal bodies, as we do of those that underlie thinking activities. Phenomenally, bodies and states of mind are utterly different, and are given to different sorts of sense. Such phenomenal disparities need not, however, point to disparities of noumenal character. Bodily phenomena may be the outer expression of wholly simple substrates, while states of mind, though referred to some undivided, conscious unit, may be the expression of as many aggregated, interacting simple substances as bodily phenomena are commonly thought to be (A. 359). There is therefore no valid inference to any simple something-or-other which underlies our thoughts, and which is responsible for the unity of consciousness (A. 359).

This argument must not be given undue weight. Kant never questions the view that, in the noumenal order, what is complex must be composed out of wholly simple constituents, such as the thinking self is conceived to be. But Kant is expressing a profound doubt, ineliminable in the human condition, whether conscious unity, despite all its magisterial properties, may not be a casual by-product of blind interactions among the simples underlying phenomenal nature, rather than the expression of a single simple, geared to the production of conscious unity, and of all the high 'oughts', values, and rational demands that go with the latter. It is only, Kant holds, by appealing to those 'oughts', values, and rational demands that we can exorcise such doubts, and then only in a practical, not a theoretical manner. In Plato's view, we can escape in thought from the cave of the human condition, and so establish the reality of what, we hold, ought rationally to be; but, in Kant's view, there can be no such escape from the cave, within the limits of this life, and hence we can never be sure that what underlies conscious unity may not be in a position to bring it to nought at any moment. Rational faith can indeed counteract such a doubt, but rational faith is not knowledge.

The Third Paralogism tries to prove the self to be an enduring conscious substance, that is, a person, from the fact that, in memory and anticipation, it conceives of itself as the identical subject of many past, present, and future mental states. Kant says this only means that memories and anticipations, or their possibility, enter into the constitution of every unified conscious state, that we always embrace a past and a future in the same conscious unity as we do what is present, and accordingly regard them all as 'ours', and attribute them to a single conscious self. There need be nothing more to our persistent personal identity than the identifications involved in memory and anticipation: as far as their links go, and no further, we are one and the same conscious person. There is no additional intuitive content in our notion of our identity than just this: we are not acquainted with any entity that performs the linkage, and persists through it. It is in fact perfectly conceivable, to beings immersed in the human condition as we are, that what underlies our mental life is a *series* of different substrates, which communicate much of their gathered content from one to another, much as billiard-balls likewise communicate their motions (A. 363–4). We might have a continuous mental life without being a continuously existent substrate, and this would make no difference to our phenomenal identity, except, of course, that we could not be sure of the further continuance of such continuity. Kant also argues, somewhat doubtfully, that another person would not be as ready as I am to reason from my continuous self-identification to my persistent identity as a substrate (A. 363). We are quite ready to demote the mental life of our fellows into a mere flux of states which continue one another's pattern. Kant does not, however, forbid us to retain the conception of a persistent personal self responsible for all we remember to have done and thought, and whatever we anticipate. The postulation of such a self will, in fact, be shown to be unavoidable from a moral point of view. He will even go further than ordinary believers in themselves want to go, by attributing to the noumenal self timeless, intelligible acts which, at one go, determine the whole course of their conduct and experience. Any self thus posited is not, however, an object of knowledge (A. 356), and can never be freed from ultimate, existential doubts.

The Fourth Paralogism is the paralogism of ideality, which argues for the immediate certainty of the existence of the thinking self, and the merely problematic, inferential character of our belief in the existence of the bodies we see around us in space. This paralogism is barely represented in the Second Edition, where its place has been taken by the important Refutation of Idealism we previously considered. The paralogism argues with Descartes that, while we are wholly certain of our own existence as thinkers and experients, we can at best infer the existence of objects of the outer senses as being the causes of our sense-experiences. It is thinkable that the objects we see around us in space may be no more than a play of representations in ourselves, with no outer cause, or no cause that in any way resembles them (A. 365). Kant's reply to this Cartesian paralogism is simply that, considered as Things-in-themselves, whatever underlies our thinking is as unknown to us as whatever underlies external bodily phenomena: neither of these substrates can be certainly known to exist, and we are likewise ignorant of their intrinsic character, and can say nothing regarding their affinity or disparity. On the other hand, as phenomenally given, what exists externally in space is as much a phenomenal reality as what exists internally in ourselves. The outer sense which presents the former, and the inner sense which presents the latter, are quite in the same position. An object is phenomenally real if it really *does* appear in our sensory perception, or if it is connected with perception according to empirical laws; and in this sense bodies which appear in space may be fully real, that is, real as really and testably apparent, and not in any sense which bypasses the appearances (A. 375). And there will be no sense in which what goes on in ourselves has any superior certainty: it too is how we appear to ourselves, and not how we authentically are. Bodies outside of us have in fact a superior importance for knowledge than thoughts within us, in that bodily appearances involve such properties as extension, motion, impenetrability, and so on, which permit of great deductive elaboration, whereas this is not possible in regard to the vanishing data of inner sense (A. 381). (Kant, of course, is only very dimly conscious of the possibilities of depth-psychology.) Kant will later himself construct a whole *a priori* theory of the space-time world, while his study of the realm of mind goes no further than a discursive anthropology. Kant's disposal of the fourth paralogism therefore follows similar lines to the Second Edition's Refutation of Idealism. None of the critical arguments concerned with the fourth paralogism must be thought to involve real doubt as to the intrinsic difference between the Things-in-themselves manifest in states of consciousness and those manifest in unconscious material bodies. Only, we cannot be clear what this intrinsic difference is, and it may not be as great as we imagine it to be, or as suits our own self-importance, and we certainly cannot, in default of moral arguments, base any firm theory upon it.

Kant then applies his sceptical, phenomenalistic conclusions to a number of psycho-physical issues. He says that the problem of psycho-physical interaction is greatly lessened if we become fully aware of our complete ignorance of what really underlies exterior, and also interior, phenomena. Our unextended thought-acts, and the motions of extended bodies in space, *seem* deeply different, and not intelligibly capable of influencing one another, but what underlies them may have much more affinity than appearances suggest:

We must realize that bodies are not objects-in-themselves that are present to us, but mere appearances of who knows what unknown objects, and that motion is not the operation of these unknown causes, but merely the appearance of their influence on our senses: both, accordingly, are nothing external to ourselves, but merely representations in us, so that matter in motion does not arouse representations in us, but is itself a mere representation. The whole self-created problem therefore comes down to this: how and on what ground do the representations of our sensibility so cohere together, that those which we call outer intuition can be represented according to empirical laws as objects outside of us.

This question plainly does not involve the supposed difficulty of explaining the origin of our representations through completely alien causes operating quite outside of ourselves (A. 387).

Since we know nothing of the Things-in-themselves which underlie outer and inner appearances, we are at a loss to say what such Things-in-themselves can or cannot do (A. 392). We need not therefore attempt to decide among the three possible theories of the relations of minds to bodies: the commonsense theory of direct physical influence, and the more sophisticated doctrines of pre-established harmony or occasionalistic intervention. The two latter, in particular, spring from the effort to solve problems which need not arise (A. 390–1).

Problems concerning the existence of the thinking self, before and after its association with a body, likewise transcend all knowledge. We can *without contradiction* suppose that, before or after embodiment, we could be intuitively aware of the Things-in-themselves, that we now know only through their appearances to our senses, but such an absence of contradiction is not enough to generate a real possibility (B. 424–6). And, as regards the origin and demise of the thinking self, an unlimited number of hypotheses are possible: new souls may arise by fission, and be dissolved by coalescence, and the soul's end may be merely the limit of a steady languescence of its powers rather than a sudden annihilation (B. 413–17). Notwithstanding all these ingenious arguments, it would be wrong to think that Kant ever abandoned the Leibnizian-Wolffian view of souls as among the wholly simple, dynamic centres which, together with others whose dynamism is not revealed in thought-acts, underlie all the phenomena which make up the world, and which all derive from God's creative, integrative reason. He may talk as if he were seriously entertaining radically pluralistic foundations for our psychic life, comparable to those of Buddhism, but he certainly never makes use of such conceptions.

And that his use of the transcendental concept of the self is not merely practical and moralistic, is shown by what he says in A. 382–3, where he remarks that rational psychology has at least this great negative value: that it guards us from accepting a dogmatic materialism. It is not *necessary* to believe that the perishing of the body will end our existence as thinking beings: that it will not do so is an entertainable, though not a knowable, proposition. And it is also shown (A. 682–4) that the concept of self has important regulative functions. It encourages us to look for principles which systematically unify mental phenomena, and which connect as many of our mental powers as possible with a single basic power, the fit expression of a single, enduring being, distinct in nature from what appears corporeally in space. In such a passage Kant departs from his curious view of the life of the mind as an unprincipled flux of states in time, which derive whatever coherence and fixity they possess from the material realities they have to deal with. Plainly the empirical self has its own deep structures as well as the body, and the transcendental self will have to be thought of as the source of all these empirical depth-structures as much as of the object-oriented categories. It is because phenomena, psychic or physical, are not the independent, mutually external things they appear to be, but spring from what is deeply simple and single, that we have a right to deal with them rationally at all.

It remains to be asked why, in his treatment of the paralogisms, Kant has confined himself to proofs which regard the Transcendental *Subject*, and has not considered parallel proofs that would concern Transcendental *Objects*. For precisely the same arguments are possible in their case as in the case of the Transcendental Subject. Thus the coherent appearances which we attribute to a geranium or to a piece of wax can also be conceived as terminating in a substantial unit, or set of units, which are truly unitary, permanent, and more solidly real than the phenomenal manifestations we connect with them. Obviously, however, while we do always refer what appears before us in space to such simple, lasting, solidly real units, we are quite unclear as to their nature or number, and there is a prima-facie case for pluralism in regard to them. In the case of ourselves, contrariwise, there is a prima-facie case for monism. Our empirical self involves innumerable forms of close togetherness and synthesis, and our transcendental self is what we cannot help thinking of as active and revealed in them all. Of course, in Kant's view, we can never know this self; though, on a more acceptable view, there is nothing more to know of it than just the function of unity which shows up phenomenal externality and diremption as, by themselves, impossible. It is not, however, our task in this book to integrate appearances with their transcendental sources more closely than Kant has thought feasible.

It is interesting to note that Kant regards the proposition 'I think' as an empirical proposition (see Note to B. 422). He calls it such, since he does not think that anything we conceive of as thinking must necessarily exist: intuitive encounter is therefore necessary to assure us that a specific case of thinking exists. But intuitive encounter does not introduce us to the subject which is thought of as performing our thinking, though it is a necessity *a priori* that, *if* we think of anything, we should be *able* to refer our thought to such a subject. We are right, therefore, in holding that what transcends experience can, in a sense, that is, *qua* transcendent, be present *in* experience. Transcendental Objects are in this respect in the same case as the Transcendental Subject: their thought-of presence, and their phenomenal absence, is part of the phenomena. Kant, also says in the passage to which this Note is appended that the subject which uses the categories cannot use its use of the categories to gain knowledge of itself. For, in order to think of itself as using the categories, its pure self-consciousness must be presupposed (B. 422). In other words, Kant thinks that the subject must first use the categories, in order subsequently to connect that use with itself as subject, which subsequent thought will never amount to knowledge, since what it postulates lay beyond, and was not part of, its original use. The self has therefore to be divined through the vestiges that it leaves, rather than substantively seen. These insights should have made Kant more hesitant than he was in giving the Transcendental Unity of Apperception so central a place in his Deduction of the Categories. For it is only *after* we have used the categories to connect the manifestations of external things together, and have referred parcels of them to varying Transcendental Objects, that we can become aware of ourselves as the transcendent source of all the parcellings and the references in question.

iii

The Paralogisms have attempted to establish the existence, simplicity, persistence, and metempirical reality of a logical subject of predicates, of which the thinking self is the most natural example, since we must constantly refer our thoughts to it, though we need not, with like readiness, refer the contents of those thoughts to the substantial substrates of things outside of ourselves. The Antinomies, to which Kant turns in the Second

Book of the Dialectic, do not attempt to transcend experience in anything like the same extent or manner. They are concerned with the phenomenal world, but with the *totality* of this order in space and time, and their transcendence of experience lies in their attempting to conceive of this totality, which inevitably transcends experience, even if its particular contents do not. The trouble depends on the particular sort of syllogistic regression which reason here feels impelled to carry out, and on its deep incompatibility with what can be intuitively given in the two great media, space and time, in which our sensory experience is cast, and, more especially, on the refractory, piecemeal character of time.

The sort of syllogistic regression that reason tries to practise on phenomena is that of connecting one phenomenon Z with another phenomenon Y as its necessitating condition; judging, that is, that *since* Z exists, Y, on which it depends for its existence, must also exist; and then repeating the explanatory ascent to X, which is the necessitating condition of Y, W which is the necessitating condition of X, and so on indefinitely. The sort of logical procedure here followed is that of a sorites of hypothetical syllogisms. One syllogism argues that since Z is the case, and, since if and only if Y is the case, Z can be the case, therefore Y is the case; the next argues that, since Y is the case, and that since if and only if X is the case can Y be the case, X is the case, and so on. And, since the regression plainly aims at reducing contingency by making what can be otherwise depend upon and be decided by something *else*, it plainly is geared to the hope of finishing the syllogistic regress, either by gathering together *all* the conditions which are necessary and sufficient for everything else, or, better still, finding some single, *prime* condition which is necessary and sufficient for itself and for all else. This hope is, however, essentially out of key with the structure of space and time, in which everything that appears is conditioned by something *else* in several distinct respects, and in which prime conditions, or exhaustive totalities of conditions, are not to be found. And it is also especially out of key with the nature of time, which essentially presents phenomena piecemeal, and one after the other. Even if the sum total of things, whether finite or transfinite, could be arrayed before us in space, we should still have to run through it piecemeal in time, and this means that such a sum total could never be a sum total *for us*.

Its attempts to rise to a totality of conditions therefore leads reason in two directions, in each of which it experiences a different sort of frustration: in the one case it opts for a limited regress of conditions, terminating in a first condition for which no prior condition need be sought, and in the other case it opts for an unlimited, or open regress of conditions. And in the first case, it is frustrated because it feels that it should be able to progress further in the discovery of conditions, and, in the second case, because it cannot bring its regressive activities to a close. If it proceeds in the opposite direction, and merely considers the proliferating consequences of a set of conditions, it need not, Kant holds, experience similar frustrations. It would not care if its progressive arguments came to a close, and nothing, not included in them, followed from them. And it would not care if its progressive arguments could never come to a close, since it would feel no urge to pursue them indefinitely: it could simply go on as far as it wanted to. But, in the case of ascending arguments, it must be exposed to one deep frustration or another. It will be noted that Kant here thinks in terms of a notion of strict, logical priority: there are some states of affairs which come first, and are prior in the order of nature, even if what is thus prior could be inferred from what is posterior, as it in fact always must.

Kant also holds that, if we were dealing with Things-in-themselves, all our troubles would vanish. For, whether a series were finite in number, or exceeded all finite numbers, it could still be exhaustively presented to an intelligence that did not have to proceed piecemeal, from one time to another, but could comprehend them all in a single, timeless glance. The infinite only presents problems to intelligences that have to apprehend it successively. The fact that phenomena are unable to meet the demands of reason is, of course, the ultimate reason why they *are* phenomena. But for us, and for our knowledge, the frustrations in question are irremovable, and give rise to our Antinomies, which will now be studied.

The Antinomies are four Transcendental Conflicts, in each of which there are two members, one the Thesis, which argues, from seemingly self-evident premises, that the sum total of the necessary and sufficient conditions for something is *finite* in its membership, whether or not *we* are able to exhaust it; while the other, the antithesis, argues from just as seemingly self-evident premises, that the sum total in question is necessarily infinite in its membership, and cannot in consequence be exhausted by us. Both Thesis and Antithesis rest on transcendental arguments and involve transcendental difficulties: nothing empirical could ever resolve them. Their true resolution can only consist in showing how their conflict arises out of a common wish to transcend possible experience, and how something like an accommodation between them can be arranged, if only both will be satisfied with a finitude of conditions, which can, however, always be expanded and enlarged. At the same time, agreement can be reached in regard to transcendent situations, which, being quite metempirical, can only be conceived, never intuited or known.

The first two of Kant's Transcendental Conflicts are said to be mathematical, and are concerned solely with the quantitative nature of whatever is given in space and time. The second two are said to be dynamic, and are concerned with the necessitation of the contents of space and time by external causes, or with the absolute necessity, the ontological self-sufficiency, which might exempt something from external necessitation. The four Conflicts have obvious connections with the categories of quantity, of reality-unreality, of causation and modality, upon which Kant dwells (A. 411–15), but which we need not consider. The First Transcendental Conflict is concerned with the total range or amount of phenomena in space and time, the Thesis contending that this must be limited, and must in particular involve a *beginning* to the whole series of events in past time; the Antithesis that phenomena must stretch on without limit in every direction both in space and in time. The limiting, shifting focus of time is at the roots of this Antinomy, which would not arise were we dealing with Things-in-themselves.

The Second Transcendental Conflict is concerned with the continuum and its divisibility, the Thesis contending that there must be a limit to such divisibility and an arrival at simples; the Antithesis that there can be no such limit, and nothing simple in the phenomenal world. The Kantian solution is to keep his ultimate simples for the transcendent realm of Things-in-themselves, while boundless divisibility shows up phenomena for the phenomenal things that they are.

The Third Transcendental Conflict is concerned with causal necessitation, the Thesis contending that there are originative causes which in some fashion spontaneously choose their direction among more than one alternative, such choice of direction involving no determining factor other than the spontaneity of the originative cause in question. The Antithesis contends, contrariwise, that no such purely originative causation is conceivable, and that the alternative realized is always completely determined by conditions that precede it in time. Kant's solution to this Antinomy involves a difficult, Leibnizian harmonization of phenomenal determination, on the one hand, with noumenal spontaneity, on the other.

And, in the Fourth Transcendental Conflict, we have, on the one hand, a Thesis which argues for the presence in the world, whether as an element or a causative influence, of something whose existence is intrinsically necessary, and which is causally responsible for everything not itself, while not itself dependent on anything external: such an absolute will no doubt need some of the self-determining spontaneity posited in the Thesis of the Third Antinomy. The Antithesis rejects the possibility of any such all-determining, self-determined absolute in the phenomenal world, and leads to a solution in which such an absolute is placed securely beyond phenomenal bounds, and discussed solely in terms of pure concepts, which can never lead to so mundane a thing as knowledge. The transcendental treatment of the all-necessitating, necessary being is then relegated to the last Chapter of the Transcendental Dialectic. We shall now examine the arguments by which Kant seeks to provide a rational foundation for each side of his four Transcendental Conflicts. It is worth observing that they are all arguments which presuppose Kant's own views of the nature of space and time and of the categories, and that it is not profitable to criticize them from physical, mathematical, and metaphysical standpoints which are wholly unrelated to his own.

The Thesis of the First Antinomy argues that the phenomenal world must have had a beginning in time, on the ground that, were this not the case, every event, however remotely past, would have been preceded by a prior eternity of states, and that such a prior eternity could never be completely run through in a successive synthesis. Since everything phenomenal must be capable, at least ideally, of being successively run through, the phenomenal world cannot have had an infinite past history. It is easy to object to this argument that there is no problem in completing an infinite, successive series provided one has

never started upon it, but has always been progressing along
it: the man who completed the expansion of Π in reverse, and
sighed with relief as he uttered the last digits 95141.3, involves
no logical contradiction. It is only, one may argue, an infinite,
successive series that *has* a beginning that can never have an end,
but must always go on infinitely in the future. Such an objection would, however, in Kant's view, involve treating time as
a form for Things-in-themselves, as something stretching out
beyond the limited projections into the past and the future of
which we are only capable. Past time only means anything
phenomenally if we *could* ideally run through it all in the
present, and this is impossible for a being whose summarizations
are always successive, and so not capable of being consummated
in a final overview. In the case of the future, it need not be
possible for us to run through all of it in the present, since,
phenomenally speaking, it is always coming to be, and cannot
be comprehended in advance: only the timeless view of God
could envisage it totally. The impossibility of exhausting an
infinite series in time is then further used by Kant to prove
that if, *per impossible*, phenomena *in space* were infinitely
extensive, they could also never, in their totality, be phenomena
for us. Phenomena in space will therefore also necessarily have
limits. It must be noted that Kant has not, in his proof of
phenomenal finitude, identified magnitude with finite magnitude, nor its measure with the finite, inductive numbers, so
that an infinite magnitude would become analytically impossible (A. 430-2). He has anticipated the Cantorian insight
that a transfinite magnitude or number is not to be regarded
as one of the finite magnitudes or numbers that it includes
or surpasses, not even as their maximum, since they have no
maximum; but that it is rather a higher-order magnitude or
number which is the magnitude or number *of* them all. But
though the transfinite is thus freed from self-contradiction,
it is none the less, as Kant sees, not an object of possible experience, at least not for piecemeal journeymen like ourselves.

The Antithesis, on the other hand, argues for the infinitude
of the phenomenal world on the ground of the empirical
senselessness of the notion of empty space and time. If
phenomena in space and time did not go on indefinitely, we
should have to conceive of them as limited by empty space and
time, and so would be turning the mere forms of phenomena into
self-subsistent realities. Kant, we may note in passing — see

B. 461 — does not deny the significance of asserting the existence of unoccupied stretches of space and time *within* the web
of phenomena: he only rejects the possibility of empty space
and time *beyond* all phenomena. And he has already given
(A. 45) a queer reason for the impossibility of empty space
and time, by arguing that, even if we could not discern anything in a given region of space and time, we could never
exclude the possibility that something *would* be found in it:
only so could it be reckoned to be part of the phenomenal
world. Kant is therefore not arguing about pure space-time
as conceived substantially in modern physics, and he has,
of course, no notion of a quasi-spherical space that would
be finite but unbounded. He is arguing on the basis of his
own view of space and time as indefinitely, openly extending
structures that *we* bring to experience, but which also require
phenomenal occupants if they are to be anything at all. On
these assumptions a finite phenomenal world is certainly
excluded: if it seems to have limits, we must presume they
could be exceeded.

In the Second Antinomy the Thesis argues that composite
substances are complex wholes consisting of substantial parts
which, being substantial, can at least be thought of without
considering their relation to other substantial parts. It must
therefore be possible to ignore all the relations which substantial parts have to one another, and yet think of something
substantial. What is thus arrived at must be substantially simple
(though it may, of course, have a vast number of distinct
attributes), and so, whatever is substantially complex, must
ultimately be composed of simple, substantial parts. In default
of these it would not be composed of anything, and so would
not be a complex substance at all. There must accordingly
be indivisible, simple substances in the world, out of which
all other substances are compounded. This argument is, of
course, borrowed straight from Leibniz and Wolff: Kant calls
it the Dialectical Principle of Ontological Atomism or Monadology. There can be no doubt that Kant never abandoned this
agrument, or the view that follows from it: he only ceased
to believe that it had phenomenal validity.

The Antithesis accordingly states that no composite thing
in the phenomenal world is made up of simple parts: the sort
of mutual externality which composition involves is essentially
spatial, and in space there is nothing simple, space being

essentially made up of spaces, of which points, lines, and so on, are merely the limits. If the phenomenal world consisted of simples, they would have to be simples that consisted of parts that consisted of further parts, and so on, which is self-contradictory. To this argument Kant adds the more ingenious argument that, even if we were unable to discover parts in some spatially located object, we could not thereby prove that it did not have further parts that *could* be discovered: absolute simplicity, therefore, eludes possible experience (A. 437). And, if we turn from external to inner phenomena, their lack of extension forbids us to attribute composition to them: our thoughts and so on, whatever their basis, do not exist outside of one another as do bodies in space. But neither will this absence of composition enable us to attribute simplicity to inner phenomena, since, with the vanishing of space, composition and simplicity vanish together (A. 443). As a Thing-in-itself, the thinking subject *may* be simple, but such simplicity is not a matter of possible experience.

Kant none the less points out, importantly, that this rejection of phenomenal simplicity does not mean that the *articulation* of phenomena can be carried on indefinitely: only their space is indefinitely divisible. Kant is rejecting Leibniz's doctrine of the infinite *emboîtement* of one articulated system in another, so that the machines of nature are machines in their minutest parts, and so that each portion of matter is like a garden full of plants, or a pond full of fishes, and so also that each branch of each plant, each member of each animal, and each drop of its water, is a similar garden or pond (see *Monadology*, §§64, 67). How far organization goes in an organized body, only experience can show, and Kant does not think that it can be carried on indefinitely. An indefinitely divisible body may therefore involve only a finite number of organized units (A. 527–8), and these, presumably, will spring from a finite number of noumenal units.

In Kant's Third Transcendental Conflict his Thesis is to the effect that, if everything that happens is determined by a prior cause in time, there will at no point be a complete set of conditions for anything that happens, and hence no *sufficient* determination of it: phenomenally, at least, we shall never achieve the exhaustiveness and the finality of determination that reason demands. We must accordingly posit the existence of causes which, with absolute spontaneity, can initiate a *new* series of causal determinations, that is, without being determined to do so by prior causes. Kant gives, as a thinkable case of such spontaneity, my free decision to rise from my chair, a decision which indeed follows upon many prior conditions, but which is not necessitated by any of them (A. 451). Subsequent treatments (e.g. A. 554–5) show that such free spontaneity has always a *disjunctive* aspect: if I tell a malicious lie in certain circumstances, it is absolutely the case that I *could* have refrained from telling it. What it is important to note is, that from the point of view of the Thesis, spontaneity and freedom are not taken to be *violations* of causality, as they must be to all who have been bemused by Hume: they are rather a *specific form* of causality, and one *necessary* to the completeness of causal explanation. Some causes, that is, must be such that they can either produce or not produce a given outcome, and, whichever occurs, it is perfectly explained by the sort of causality here exercised. The Antithesis, however, turns the crank of reason in the opposite direction: it simply argues that there *must* be some prior factor which incites the so-called spontaneous agent to exert its spontaneity at a given instant, or in a given direction. In default of this, there can be no complete conditioning of what it does and hence no genuine causality. Absolute spontaneity would therefore be a violation, and not a species of causation, and there can accordingly be no causal determining of happenings beyond their complete necessitation by prior events according to fixed laws. And Kant adds that the supposed species of spontaneous causation would render all unity of experience impossible (A. 447, 551); an extreme view, since all who have believed in such spontaneity have always held that it operated within strict limits, and that some exercises of it were highly improbable.

In the Fourth Transcendental Conflict the Thesis argues somewhat obscurely for the presence *in* the phenomenal field of something which exists of necessity, whether this be simply nature itself, in its total history of phases, as in the Spinozistic *Natura naturata*, or some privileged, non-natural element which persists throughout nature's history and is operative in it all (A. 456). This vaguely sketched concept is then rejected by the Antithesis. The necessary existent cannot be nature itself in its serial totality, since all the alterations in nature are necessitated by prior alterations, and are never independently necessary. But a series none of whose members is independently necessary cannot be necessary as a whole. If, on the other hand, the necessary element is a non-natural element operative in all nature's operations, it must be active in nature's time, and so must begin to act at a definite point in time, and so cannot be non-natural, but must be part of the natural order. What has transpired is therefore that, if anything non-natural is necessarily operative in all nature's transformations, its operations must be as timelessly transcendental and non-natural as the postulated element itself. A necessary being cannot therefore be discoverably active in the phenomenal order.

iv

Having stated his four Transcendental Conflicts of Theses and Antitheses, Kant devotes six lengthy Sections (iii–viii, A. 462–515) to discussing in general terms how they should be dealt with. This is followed by a long Ninth Section (A. 515–67) in which they are disposed of. Reason, Kant argues in Section iii, has powerful interests which make it come down on one side of the Antinomies rather than the other. The Theses of our four Antinomies have an interest for dogmatism, which term for Kant covers moral and religious concern. Morally and religiously, it would be acceptable that the world, as a created and finite thing, should have a beginning in time, that the thinking self should be a simple and indestructible substance, that a voluntary agent should be free in some of his decisions, that the contingencies in the world should derive, not merely from other contingencies, but from a primordially necessary being (A. 466). The Theses also satisfy reason by finalizing enquiry, and not pushing it back indefinitely; and such finalization, to minds not prepared for endless hard thinking, is also highly popular (A. 467, 472–3). The Antitheses have none of these advantages, but, in return, they satisfy our empirical demands, since the understanding stays always on its own ground, and does not try to ascend to principles which certainly transcend experience and knowledge. Free causes, necessary beings, simple entities, and so on can never be experienced, and ought not to be treated as anything of which we could have knowledge. The effect of the Antinomies, backed by the conflicting interests of reason, would thus lead towards a constant vacillation which cannot be accepted by reason, but which demands a resolution. Reason cannot,

Kant holds, refuse to resolve such conflicts as transcending its powers, since the problems in question are cosmological, and concern the world as a sum total of phenomena, and not as a set of transcendental substrates of which knowledge would be impossible (Λ. 479). Kant presumes, as we have previously noted, that, since the question as to what appears or can appear is a domestic question, it can therefore be made a clear question (A. 480-1). We shall not here attempt to argue that domestic questions are among the most recalcitrant of all, and that, because a difficulty exists only 'in our thoughts', it is not therefore easy to find out exactly where it lies and how it may be resolved. We have, Kant thinks, merely to relate empirical appearances to our Transcendental Idea of the unconditioned, to see where the dialectical shoe pinches: we need not attempt to relate them to unknowable Things-in-themselves.

In the next four Sections (v–viii), Kant sketches the general pattern of a critical treatment which will enable us to transcend the conflicts of antinomic, cosmic principles, rather than opt for one against the other. He points out first (Section v), that the Theses of the Four Antinomies are always too *small* for the understanding. They posit a beginning to time, an end to division, or an original, unconditioned type of causality or species of existence, and then leave us gasping at the further question: But what conditions this? The Antitheses, on the other hand, are much too *large* for the understanding, since no regression to further and further conditions can ever exhaust an infinite totality. This explanation says much the same, though with another emphasis, as what Kant said in a previous passage (A. 422): that a regress adequate to reason is too large for the understanding, whereas a regress adequate to the understanding is always too narrow for reason. In the previous passage the understanding was thought of in its boundlessly expansive tendency, whereas in the present one it is seen in the perpetual finitude of its actual achievement.

In Section vi Kant seeks the solution of his difficulties in the transcendental idealism which teaches that the objects of which we can have knowledge are never Things-in-themselves, but only things *as* apparent to us. Treated in their relation to appearance, the realities which are not as yet apparent, are merely realities that *would* or *could* be apparent if an empirical regress or progress were pursued further. Thus it may be the case that there are people on the moon, though no one has seen them — Kant forgets that they must have seen one another — but what this means is that, in a suitable empirical advance, compatible with the laws of nature, we may yet encounter them. For anything can be called 'real' if it can be connected with some perception by the laws of empirical advance (A. 493). A similar account can be given of the realities of past time: they would have presented themselves to possible perceptions conceived in the light of history, or in the light of causal inferences based on what we now perceive (A. 495). Kant is here considering issues that the verificationists and the positivists have worked over much more thoroughly in our own time.

Section vii then makes the important pronouncement that the regress of conditions required by conditioned empirical situations is only given to us as an *Aufgabe*, that is, a task. It is not, strictly speaking, *gegeben*, given, only *aufgegeben*, prescribed as a task. If how things appear coincided with what they in themselves are, the totality of their conditions would be given with them, would really provide their supportive background. But, since appearances do not coincide with things as they really are, their supportive backgrounds are there only in the sense that one *can* or *could* advance towards them. In arguing from a conditioned phenomenon to its unconditioned totality of conditions, we are therefore exploiting a verbal ambiguity: we are treating a feature of Things-in-themselves as holding also of a set of their appearances. A regress of advances among Things-in-themselves must either be finite or infinite, by the law of excluded middle, but this law does not entitle us to say that such definite finitude or infinity must characterize things as they appear to us: they may appear as neither finite nor infinite, but merely as a set of appearances that *can* always be further expanded. They involve, as Section viii makes clear, not a progression into the infinite, but a progression into the indefinite: they are essentially *open* progressions (A. 511). It is important to note, among the side-implications of this passage, that Things-in-themselves, like Leibnizian monads, are thought of by Kant as timelessly *containing* all that is ever spelled out in their temporal history: dispositions, readinesses, potencies, and so on, are the translations into phenomenal time-diction of the timeless containment of detail by absolutely simple unities. To be acquainted with Things-in-themselves would be to be acquainted with such simple, all-containing unities, to see in one flash all that they ever were, are, or will be, together with other possibilities that they freely chose not to realize. Since this is impossible, endless phenomenal routes of empirical advance have to do duty in their place. And it is because we have to think in terms of such deep unities as the substrates of empirical sequences that empirical advances can have for us the substitutionary value that they do have. Remove the deep unities in thought, and we should have to cease to expect anything whatever.

Section ix now applies the principle of the indefinite, but open regress, as opposed to that of the infinite regress, to the four Antinomies. As regards Antinomy I, it is clear that there can be no imaginable or thinkable limit to events in past time, or to objects as occupying space, since the notion of an empty time or space beyond those limits has no empirical meaning. On the other hand, the notion of a fully actual, phenomenally given, but also infinite past or infinite occupancy of space, is likewise inadmissible: all that can be admitted is that appearances always *could* be extended further, and that also, as a rule for ourselves, they always *should* be extended further (A. 517–23). Kant does not here attempt to spell out any thinkable conclusion regarding Things-in-themselves, but it is plain that both alternatives would then become open. Remove the piecemeal character of temporal apprehension, and the infinite could as readily present itself, whole and complete, and be recognized as such, as the finite, since Kant certainly sees no self-contradiction in it. And, remove the endless divisibility of space, and there might prove to be only a finite number of simple agents and acts manifesting themselves in the endless divisions of space.

As regards Antinomy II, Kant involves himself in a subtlety which is not very intelligible. Because a finite bodily phenomenon is given whole and entire in intuition, all the infinite divisions and parts which could be discovered in it, are also, he says, given together with it, and we have therefore to say, not that it is indefinitely, but that it is *infinitely* divided. Since, however, such division can never be carried to a final limit, we are not entitled to say that we have infinitely many parts before us, but only that what we have before us is infinitely divisible. Body, Kant thinks, is therefore divisible to infinity, without consisting of infinitely many parts (A. 525). There would appear to be confusions in Kant's argument, which it is not worth unravelling further. If divisions can always be carried further, then divisions too, like the parts they isolate, can never be actually infinite; but if, *qua* mere possibilities, they are actually infinite, then so too, *qua* possibilities, are the parts that they isolate. Phenomenally speaking, however, the transfinite certainly eludes temporal apprehension, and Kant should simply have followed Aristotle and have held phenomenal bodies to be indefinitely, not infinitely, divisible. Kant points out, however, as we have already indicated, that the indefinite divisibility of bodies does not mean that they contain organized parts within parts indefinitely: there may be natural units which are only geometrically, but not dynamically, divisible (A. 526). These may very well correspond to the simple substances which the understanding requires, but which the phenomena themselves poorly illustrate.

As regards Antinomy III, Kant argues that a compromise between Thesis and Antithesis may very well be open to us. There may be nothing but deterministic causality in the phenomenal order, while there is also undetermined, spontaneous causality, able to decide freely among alternatives, in the noumenal order. As Kant puts the point:

We need the principle of causation among appearances in order to be able to look for, and cite, natural conditions for natural situations, i.e. phenomenal causes for them. When this is understood, and not weakened by exceptions, the understanding, which sees nothing but nature in all happenings, and is entitled to do so, has all that it can ask for, and physical explanations can proceed unchecked. It does not affect this in the least if one assumes, perhaps quite gratuitously, that there are also, among natural causes, some that have a purely intelligible capacity to be determined to action, not by empirical conditions, but by reasons for the understanding, and in such a way that the action which manifests this cause, accords with all the laws of empirical causality. In this fashion, the active subject, *qua* phenomenal cause, will be found in utter dependence on nature in all its actions, and only the noumenal side of the subject (with all its phenomenal causality) would contain certain conditions which, if one rose from the empirical to the Transcendental Object, would have to be regarded as merely intelligible (A. 544-5).

By an intelligible condition Kant here means one's motivation by a mere reason, of which the concept of obligation, *sollen*, is the supreme example. 'No matter how many natural grounds or sensuous incitements act on my will', Kant writes, 'they can never generate an obligation, only a by no means necessary, always conditioned volition, against which the obligation that reason enunciates can set boundaries and goals, and can disapprove and approve' (A. 548). The free decision to *fail* to do what one ought is, however, *also* an alternative, defective expression of one's noumenal causality, since it can be blamed quite as much as one's decision to do what one ought is praised. Kant so far forgets himself over the issue of noumenal causality that he even speaks incautiously of our *knowing* ourselves (A. 548) in our intelligible capacity. We shall not, however, hold this statement against him. What he ought to have said is that we cannot but *think* of ourselves as exercising such spontaneous, noumenal causality even if we cannot ever know anything of it.

But even the thought of such noumenal freedom is only possible because Kant locates freedom quite out of time. A transcendental self must choose the whole course of its actions in time, its improvements and deteriorations, its changes of heart, and its adherences to old ways, not successively, as situations develop, but in one single, metempirical package. Only so can its choices be harmonized with all the choices made by other selves, and with the circumstances and influences which act upon it, and by which what it does is necessitated according to natural laws. The Transcendental Subject must choose its whole life, much as the souls in Platonic eschatology choose their whole lives, with all their crimes and glories, before descending into incarnation: only so can God really be blameless. Or, to use another analogy, they must freely choose the parts that they are to play in the cosmic drama: once they have chosen, they cannot improvise or alter their lines, nor will they want to do so, since they are then only *executing* what, in depth, they have determined to be and do. The shadow of the Leibnizian pre-established harmony is here, as elsewhere, in evidence. That Kant really does believe in this difficult, but in the last resort arguable, theory is clear, not only from later treatments in *Religion within the Bounds of Mere Reason*, but also from the example given at this point, where a malicious lie, led up to by innumerable corrupting circumstances, some of which have nothing to do with the agent, is none the less such that the agent was *wholly* responsible for it, and could have chosen and acted *otherwise* (A. 554-5). Some of the difficulties of Kant's theory spring from the rigour of his belief in deterministic causality. For if spontaneity, and the power to realize alternatives, represents a genuine causal concept, this might have been accorded an interstitial place in the phenomenal order, as well as among the great noumenal orderings that take place in eternity. The former may in fact be the phenomenal expression of the latter, without destroying the systematic coherence of the whole. A system, it may be argued, *can*, and perhaps *must*, be loose at some of its joints in order to give meaning to the fact that it is rigid at others. We shall not, however, attempt to improve upon Kant's basic opinions, except, perhaps, in a brief chapter at the end of this work.

As regards Antinomy IV, Kant sees a way to reconcile the Thesis with the Antithesis by making the necessary being, on whom the whole series of conditioned states depends, a being belonging to a different order, a noumenal source on which the concatenated states of the existent world all depend (A. 560-1). Thus the thoroughgoing contingency of all natural existences, taken together with all their empirical conditions, is quite reconcilable with the optional assumption of a necessary but purely intelligible existence, which is a sufficient condition of everything. This notion may be intrinsically impossible and self-contradictory, but, since it transcends empirical existence, nothing in the empirical order can prove it to be so (A. 513). We have therefore to go on from transcendental cosmology, which does not attempt to go beyond the phenomenal order of things in space and time, to transcendental theology, which attempts, in a problematic, analogical fashion, to do so.

Chapter VII

The Dialectic of Divinity

i

We shall now examine Kant's critique of transcendental theology, perhaps the most shatteringly influential and also the most seriously misunderstood of all sides of his philosophy. In it he has tried to show that the Leibnizian-Wolffian conception of God as a being who embraces all possibility, and whose existence is therefore unconditionally necessary, and who conditions the existence of all that is contingent, is a conception without empirical content, and therefore incapable of being shown to correspond to anything real, whether by a pure manipulation of concepts, or from the experience of what is phenomenally real. We may make transcendental leaps from the contingent to the necessarily existent, we may forge conceptual bridges from the ontologically perfect to the ontologically necessary, and vice versa, we may seek to confirm our immense inferences by citing numerous orderly and purposive phenomena which they alone can render intelligible: all this does not affect the fact that our reasonings never achieve the cogency of some cases of arithmetical and geometrical proof, and not even the cogency of some experimental proofs in natural science. There is also an element of illusion, of transcendental subreption, in the arguments we are to examine: what is possibly, necessarily, or actually the case in some purely notional, hypothetical, and unillustrated manner, is confused with what is possible, necessary, or actual in the sense that it is actually illustrated in experience, and that it is capable of being empirically refuted as well as emptily confirmed. There is, further, and must always be, an element of transcendental doubt, as well as an element of transcendental belief, in our attitude towards the supreme grounds of rational explanation. Things-in-themselves may, for all we know, by their sheer plurality, be a source of disunion and disorder as well as of union and order, and may at the last gasp let us down, rather than provide a supportive background for our confident procedures. The transcendental self is not a free improviser, and could (we may emptily conceive) be unable in some juncture to make sense of the impacts pouring in upon it, in which case experience, knowledge, and rational practice would alike become impossible. We can indeed make no empirical sense of such a breakdown, but equally little can we conceive of anything, not emptily hypothetical, that would exclude it. The possibility of experience and rational practice never have anything categorical about them.

All this might seem to give the quietus to transcendental theologies, except perhaps for one that continues to demand support for its moral goals and procedures through irrational postulations. It is clear, however, that the impact of Kant's treatment is not solely to discredit transcendental theology in favour of solidly based, empirical knowledge: it is just as much to demote solidly based empirical knowledge in favour of transcendental theology, or perhaps in favour of a highly rationalized version of the latter. For what Kant's arguments show is that, while the ideal of comprehensive, rational explanation which underlies transcendental theology, and which in fact coincides with the latter, is simply not realizable through the piecemeal, purblind procedures of empirical knowledge, it none the less provides a point of orientation and a goal for those piecemeal, purblind procedures, and one without which they could not be carried on at all. It is indeed only *as if* all that we experience sprang from a unifying, ordering source behind the phenomenal mirror − (see A. 644–5) − and we can certainly never, in this life at least, venture beyond that mirror's surface − but the reference of phenomena to such a source is not only indispensable to all our theoretical practice, but seems also to be the characteristic way in which intelligences like our own must approach the unknowable, real source of all that appears to them. The principle of unity and order is not therefore proved to be illusory as certain appearances are proved to be illusory by their failure to survive empirical tests. Their failure to be confirmed empirically rather shows up the limited, purely phenomenal character of all such confirmable realities.

Kant sees a peculiar inaccessibility in the object intended by the concept of the necessarily existent source of all possible contingencies of existence, in that it has both to be conceived in a purely categorial manner, without the help of empirical or phenomenal predicates, yet must none the less refer to something uniquely *individual* (A. 568), which is not merely the sum total of the predicates used in referring to it. God, or the Ideal of Pure Reason, as Kant now prefers to call his supreme Transcendental Object, must be more than a supremely beautiful, well-formed intellectual construction, since it must concretely embody and realize the latter, but there must nevertheless be nothing beyond such a purely intellectual construction in terms of which it can be pinned down or given flesh and blood. It must not even have the in-built reference to thoughts which limits the Idea of the Transcendental Subject, nor the remote reference to phenomena in space and time which limits the Idea of the total cosmos or world.

The Ideal of Pure Reason must, according to Kant's Leibnizian view, be constructed solely on the basis of the logical law of excluded middle operating on the total range of possible, positive predicates. It must be constructed by selecting the positive member of every thinkable disjunction of a positive property and its negation and rejecting the negative member, and by conjoining all the positive members thus selected. It is assumed that we can be really, and not merely conventionally, clear as to whether a predicate is positive or negative, the latter being wholly derivative from the former, and expressing nothing beyond its absence or lack or defect. It must not involve some alternative, positive predication, which is perhaps incompatible with the positive predicate in question, or perhaps combines with it in an uneasy relation of conflict or of mutual cancellation. Kant has elsewhere argued that there is such a thing as real negation in the phenomenal world, and perhaps even in the world of Things-in-themselves, and that such a real negation sometimes permits the positive and the negative to be *combined* in the same individual (A. 273–4). In the present context, however, negation is merely negative, and the profile of every individual can be constructed simply by asking whether it is characterized by a given positive property or not so characterized, it being taken to be impossible that it should be both positively and negatively characterized, or that it should be characterized in neither manner. In such a construction the Leibnizian principle of the identity of indiscernibles also plays its part, for this, Kant holds, certainly applies to Things-in-themselves if not to pure appearances (see A. 271–2). It therefore ensures that there can be one and only one individual characterized by any selection among the total list of positive properties, and by the accompanying negations of other positive properties. The notion then inevitably arises of a limiting individual characterized by *every* positive property in the list, and by *none* of the corresponding negations. It will have every positive qualification, and none that amounts to the lack or defect of anything positive. It will be an *ens realissimum*, since all that gives anything a positive or real character will be in it, and it will also cover all *possibilities* of characterization, since negative characterizations merely mean that something exemplifies *less* than all of the properties that characterize it, has simply failed to be characterized by *some* of them, and not that it is positively characterized in some manner in which the *ens realissimum* is not characterized. In other words, the projected *ens realissimum et omnipossibile* will represent a sort of storehouse of positive characteristics on which everything else can draw for its positive characterization (A. 575-6), and so, indirectly, in virtue of the limited selectivity of everything other than the *ens realissimum*, for its negative characterization also. The *ens realissimum* will, in fact, resemble the infinite, total extent of space, in which all figures arise merely by limiting that sum total (A. 578), and it will also resemble that same total space in that, by the identity of indiscernibles, it will be one and unique. There can be one and only one individual characterized by every positive character, from which, by some mode of derivation, everything else can be conceived as possessing whatever characters it has and which make it what it is.

The conception of an omnipossible, omnireal being here introduced will, of course, not square with ordinary notions of negation, and with Kant's own special views on the matter. For, according to these views, many positive characteristics are such that one entails the negation of the others — for example, colours, pitches, shapes, sizes, and so on, and many other determinate values of the same determinable — and in such cases there could be nothing that realized the conjunction of the positive predicates in question. It would, however, be a possible ploy to argue that such incompatibilities among positives are the result of the manifestation of positive properties in space and time. It is, on this view, only space and time that rend certain positive properties from one another in their expression, and make it necessary for them to appear *outside* of one another in space, or *after* one another in time. It is only if they are to be shown forth in the *same* place or the same time that they cancel one another, and cannot be jointly present. But in other media, for example, the medium of pure thought or the medium of dynamic latency, such incompatibilities vanish. Even in the phenomenal order it is possible to combine incompatible positives in thought, as when we observe their contrast or their incompatibility — Aristotle makes this point in the *De Anima* — and even in the phenomenal realm things are often credited with forces tending in contrary directions. The *ens realissmum* could therefore combine all positive characters in the manner of an all-thinking thought or an all-powerful dynamic agency. It is pure sensualism to think that sensible instantiation represents a more positive, fulfilled condition for a property than its presence in and for an understanding, or in a dynamic drift. The mutual exclusion of positive characters in finite, sensible instances can then be taken to be a consequence of their defective, merely phenomenal character. It points to some weakness in the phenomenal, spatio-temporal instance that it cannot conjoin certain positive characters after the fashion of what is noumenal. Spatio-temporality, the disease of mutual exclusion, is, in fact, precisely the name of this defect.

Two other points must also be made at this juncture. The first is that, while the *ens realissimum* bases itself on a comprehensive *disjunction* of all the possible cases of being, it itself represents a supreme *conjunction* in which all these disjoined possibilities are brought together. The second is that we shall indeed have to revise the working of the categories when we come to consider the most real of all beings. For it is highly arguable that the *antitheses* of general character and instance, of position and negation, of cause and consequence, of possible and actual, and so on, all owe their dirempted form to the dualisms of our conceptual-intuitive constitution, and must vanish into some sort of a higher unity when we advance to the absolutely real being itself. It will have to be not so much a unique, individual case of perfection as a self-subsistent perfection itself; not so much a synthesis of all positive properties as a negation of the exclusiveness which, for ordinary thought, is the very mark of the positive; not so much an all-inclusive possibility as an actuality which relegates the possible to its one-sided expressions. We shall not, however, develop these thoughts in the present context, but reserve them for a final excursus on the noumenal world. It is here sufficient to argue that Kant's notion of an all-real being, though replete with difficulty, probably permits of a consistent, illuminating working-out.

Kant, however, having introduced his all-real individual being as a mere concept, has to raise the question as to whether there really is, or can be, anything that satisfies its difficult requirements. It is natural and easy, Kant tells us in the Note to A. 583, to hypostatize or personalize this mere concept, and to conceive of it as a subsistent sum total of all that is, or as an understanding or intelligence that covers this all in its thought; but is such a proceeding at all legitimate? Is it not a case of the transcendental subreption condemned in the *Dissertation*, the turning of an empty thought-reference into something concretely fulfilled? Kant holds, however, that there is a special motive that reinforces our tendency to such subreption, if indeed this is present in this case. This motive is none other than the aspiration of reason to pass from cases where one thing is conditioned by others, seemingly without end, to a first condition, or to a totality of conditions, which requires no condition beyond itself. What occurs is a curious interplay between this special motive and the motive which leads us to frame the notion of a logically comprehensive *ens realissimum*. We are in quest of a necessary being to explain the existence of finite, contingent things, and it appears that an all-real, all-possible being will precisely do this trick. For, possessing all the properties that finite, contingent things can exemplify, it is a fit candidate to explain their prime origin, and hence the necessity which that origin implies. At the same time, the mere concept of such an all-real being suggests that we credit it with some sort of a nisus to realize all the distinct, if limited, possibilities of being that its comprehensive reality covers, and with a spontaneity that can make an orderly selection among them, so that the all-real being readily figures as the necessary being on which regressive reason seeks to hang its syllogisms. Ontological necessity therefore accords with ontological perfection, and ontological perfection with ontological necessity, so that the passage from one transcendental conception to another, and their consequent notional marriage, becomes hard to avoid. In neither direction is the passage, however, inevitable. What is ontologically imperfect could, without self-contradiction, be treated as the ontologically necessary source of all (A. 586), and what is ontologically perfect, in default of a special argument, could be ontologically contingent. It is, however, in some deep sense natural to align the two notions with one another, and wanton to conceive of them as disjoined. What compasses all in its essence is naturally the necessary and the necessitating source of all, and what necessitates all is naturally what compasses all in its essence.

Human reason therefore naturally constructs arguments which link the two notions with one another: (1) an ontological argument which reasons from the notion of all-inclusive ontological perfection to the real existence of what seems entailed by such inclusiveness; (2) a cosmological argument which argues from the absence of necessity in finite existences to the existence of an all-inclusive, necessary positivity on which it must depend; and (3) a physico-theological argument which dwells on particular cases of positive order present in the contingent, phenomenal world to reinforce the marriage between a necessary and a transcendentally inclusive source. Kant believes that these three are the only basic types of argument that reason can employ (A. 590–1). But he is also to argue that all three treat as a real object what transcends possible experience, and which cannot be more than a point or orientation for investigative thought, and never anything of which we can have knowledge.

ii

Kant conceives that the natural order of the three transcendental proofs is to start with the physico-theological proof, which reasons from specifically constituted phenomena, exemplifying beauty, order, unity, and so on, to an all-perfect source of them all; then to go on to the cosmological proof, which argues from *any* contingency whatever to an all-perfect, necessarily existent source; and then, finally, to ascend to the ontological proof, in which the existence of such a supreme source is simply seen as part of its essential perfection. Kant proposes, however, to deal with the three proofs in a reverse order, beginning with the ontological proof, progressing to the cosmological proof, and ending up with the physico-theological proof. He does so because he thinks that the existence of a necessary being is not really entailed by any contingent existence, but that a belief in its possibility, and in its capacity to explain contingencies, lurks in the background of all arguments that start with contingent experience, and that it is then introduced to provide explanation for the latter: it is the ontological all-inclusiveness of the *ens realissimum*, its coverage of every possibility, and hence its dependence on nothing beyond itself, that explain why it is thus appealed to. The ontological proof is therefore the fundamental theological argument, and must be considered before all others: their strengthening of it is, in a manner, redundant, since they all secretly build upon it (A. 590–1). And if it is fundamentally questioned, their cogency will also presumably fall apart.

Kant does not, in his criticism of the ontological proof, dwell on the very serious difficulties involved in the possession of *all* possible positive properties, but rather on the difficulties involved in the concept of necessary existence. It is easy to give a verbal circumscription of this concept, as connoting the status of something whose non-existence is impossible or unthinkable, but this affords no clarity as to what this status is (A. 592–3). The trouble is that the standard uses of necessity are mainly conditional and hypothetical: they are, in the main, necessities that, *if* something of a certain sort exists, or *if* certain conditions are realized, something else will also exist. They are seldom or never necessities connected with the simple existence of things, or, if they seem to be so, they are not without a covert reference to hypothetically presumed existences or circumstances. In the *a priori* mathematical field this hypothetical species of necessity is prominent. Platonists may argue that the Triangle Itself exists, and must have angles equal to two right angles, but the ordinary man is content to hold that, *if* there are triangles anywhere in the world, then they must have angles equal to two right angles. The case of the triangle, however, tempts reason to imagine that, if it makes real existence, or the necessity of real existence, part and parcel of the content of a concept, it will in some manner be able to evade the introduction of a restrictive hypothetical clause. It will then be able to say, simply, that something of a certain sort must exist, since existence is part of its concept. We need not, as in the case of the triangle, say that, *if* it exists, then something else will be the case in regard to it, but will be able simply to say of it the something or other in question, which in this case is simply the affirmation of its real existence. Now, the *ens realissimum* seems to be precisely in this position, for it is conceived as endowed with every positive determination, and with none that connotes privation or defect. Real existence, whatever it may involve or connote, is plainly a positive determination, and the *ens realissimum* seems to be in the enviable position of being able to ensure *that* it is, solely in virtue of being *what* it is (A. 495-5).

Kant points out, however, as Aquinas did before him, that the *if*-clause cannot be eliminated by the mere fact that the concept of what it concerns includes real existence, or necessary existence, in its scope or sense. For, the real existence, or necessary existence, that something will enjoy *if* there is such a something, is not at all the same as a real existence, or a necessary existence, that a thing *does* enjoy. Nor is there, Kant holds, any contradiction in holding that something which, *if* it existed, would exist necessarily, nevertheless does not and cannot exist. The very fact that, if it existed, it would have to have such a strange ontological property, might in fact be a sufficient reason for holding that it does not and cannot exist. There is no contradiction in denying the possession of any predicate of a subject of which one has denied the existence. Though being omnipotent is part of the concept of God, it cannot be said that God is omnipotent if there is no such being as God (A. 595), and to be omnireal is in no different case from being omnipotent.

Kant, however, goes further and argues that there is a latent *contradiction* in making existence part of the conceptual content of a thing that we are considering merely conceptually, merely as a possibility (A. 597). For it suggests that 'An X exists' can in some cases be a purely analytic judgement, whereas, if all such judgements are synthetic, no such addition of existence to the content of a concept is in fact possible. Being, Kant argues, is not a genuine, but a spurious predicate: it can add nothing to the purely conceptual content of any concept to which it is added (A. 598-9). The concept of a hundred real dollars is exactly the same as the concept of a hundred dollars. Real existence can add nothing to this concept, it merely realizes it or exemplifies it, which, in the case of beings like ourselves, means that it connects it with intuitively given objects in space and time. The perceptual intuition through which we realize or illustrate a concept is not itself a concept, though we can no doubt form a concept of it: it is the something more which mere conception never can include. Hence, for us any judgement of existence is limited to the realm of appearance, of the sensuously given instance, and the conception of an omnireal, necessary being cannot be illustrated there. God Himself, in being in some manner self-aware, may *ipso facto* be aware of His own existence and necessary existence, but this sort of self-authenticating concept, which is one with an intuition, is certainly not for us. Stated as Kant has stated it, the argument that we *cannot* significantly make real existence or necessary existence part of the concept of something is certainly false. Conception is an essentially free matter, and we can, however real existence be conceived, conceive of any conceptual content as being realized in existence, or of such realization as having a realization in existence, and so on *ad infinitum*. Kant is, however, correct in holding that such piling of merely conceptual being upon merely conceptual being remains redundant and unenriching. The modal moment, as Meinong would put it, is always lacking: we are always operating within conceptual brackets. To argue, however, that there is a latent *contradiction* in treating real being as being part of the essence of something proves too much. For it would imply that there absolutely *could* not be anything that existed of necessity, nothing which is such that it would be impossible for it not to exist. If this were to be held to be the case, we should be in the curious, but not self-contradictory position, of affirming a necessity of contingency: that the existence of anything cannot be other than contingent, that for whatever there is, it would be possible for it not to be. This position is curious, since it appears to be self-contradictory: we seem to be saying of the same matter of fact that it is both necessary and contingent. This appearance is, however, specious, since the necessity is a *higher-order* necessity attaching to the contingency of something, and it is a necessity of something's being the case, and not of something's existing. And the proposition that all modal attributions, whether of possibility, or necessity, or contingency, or whatever, are necessarily necessary is of course a widely accepted, though not incontrovertible, axiom of modal logic.

That this, that is, the necessary contingency of all facts of existence, and hence the impossibility of the existence of an object that necessarily exists, is the real message of Kant's argument, would be acceptable to some, and I myself thought it was Kant's message when I wrote my *Mind* article, 'Can God's

Existence be Disproved?', in 1948. For what I there argued might be stated in the syllogism: A God is a being who cannot be thought of as existing contingently. But everything that exists can only be thought of as existing contingently. It is therefore impossible, not merely indemonstrable, that a God should exist. Kant does not, however, hold that a necessity of existence is not part of the concept of a God, since the function of a God is precisely to provide a supreme, unconditioned condition for everything contingent. And Kant also does not hold that there is anything self-contradictory in the conception of an omnipossible, necessarily existent God. He argues in fact, in A. 641, that the Idea of an omnireal, necessary being is an ideal *without any internal conceptual flaw*. The latent self-contradiction, which he therefore detects in a concept involving necessary and real existence, must be a contradiction which only arises for beings like ourselves, for whom the exemplification of a concept in an existent case always involves its embodiment in a sensuous instance. And it is not merely not the case, but impossible that it should be the case — *pace* the Incarnation — that the omnireal and omnipossible should be incontrovertibly, that is, not merely for the eye of faith, present in a conditioned, sensuous instance. Kant does not reject, and in fact fully believes, in the non-phenomenal, metempirical existence of such a supreme reality, and, in acknowledging the flawlessness of its concept, he has in effect acknowledged its reality. For, the concept of an omnipossible being has at least this logical peculiarity: that the real existence of its object is entailed by its own internal consistency and logical thinkability. One cannot be an *all*-possible being if there are any circumstances in which it would be possible for one not to be. The ontological proof is in fact incontrovertible for all who accept the possibility of the existence of its object, as Leibniz long ago realized and stated.

The only condition, therefore, on which the *non*-existence of an *ens realissimum* is in any way entertainable, is that its concept should be found, after a long weighing of its content and consequences, to be itself a self-contradictory or non-entertainable concept, one for which realization in existence does not represent an option. The *ens realissimum* either exists necessarily or impossibly: no middle option can be possible in its case. It is, however, hard to resolve such a disjunction on premisses such as Kant's. For, obviously, the antithetical use of the categories possible when we can plainly distinguish existence, *qua* sensuous embodiment in an instance, from non-existence, as the defect of such embodiment, quite fails us when we are conceiving of a being in whose case it may not be even possible to draw the distinction between *what* it is, and *that* it is, that we can so readily draw in the case of a sensible instance. And it is plain, further, that, as long as we can frame alternative theological characterizations of the necessary being, we can draw no certain conclusions regarding the reality or possibility of any of them, since the essential nature of an all-real, necessary being can permit of no alternatives. It is therefore not possible for intelligences structured like ours to pronounce, positively or negatively, even on the possibility of something that exists of necessity, and Kant must therefore merely be expressing his own deep rational faith in holding it to represent a flawless, rational ideal. And this means further, though Kant does not stress it, that the fact that for him the existence of the all-real being is only a matter for transcendental faith, also implies that for him its existence must always remain a matter for transcendental doubt. That existence should always be contingent, and at best necessitated by prior contingencies, cannot be excluded as a principle holding for Things-in-themselves as it does for their appearances. Kant's viewing of the conception of the all-real being as a flawless rational ideal therefore amounts to his making a practical decision for transcendental faith as against doubt. The ontological proof is therefore for him not so much misguided in making the inner consistency of its concept and the possibility of its object an unquestioned premiss, as in failing to see that the sort of existence it would hope to establish would not be at all like the sort of contingent existence that made sense at the phenomenal level. He therefore leaves the all-real being in a stronger position *noumenally* than his own principles actually warrant. This, however, is as rational an outcome as the contrary decision would yield, and will be reinforced by what he subsequently says about the regulative value of the concept in question.

From the ontological proof Kant passes to the cosmological proof, which does not reason from the concept of the highest reality, and from the sum total of possibility that it embraces, to the necessity of its existence, as in the ontological proof; but reverses the reasoning and argues from the necessary existence of something or other, which will serve as the ultimate, un-conditioned condition of everything contingent, to an identi-fication of this something or other with something having an unlimited, perfect reality and a total coverage of possibilities (A. 604). It argues that if anything exists conditionally, as, for example, I myself do, then there must be something that exists unconditionally, and provides the final ground for a contingent existence like mine, a ground that will put an end to all further quest for grounds. This part of the argument certainly invokes a new principle, which is not present in the ontological argument. But obviously the argument cannot rest by invoking the unconditioned existence of something or other, since many things, for example, my tea-cosy (example not used by Kant), are not the sort of thing that could exist unconditionally. We therefore have to excogitate some sort of thing that could arguably have the blessed property of necessary existence; and here, Kant suggests, we at once have recourse to the notion of an omnireal being in whom all positive possibilities are vested, and which being is therefore fit to be the ultimate unconditioned condition of myself, and my tea-cosy, and of everything else phenomenal. Hence, an omni-real being exists as the only suitable candidate for the all-explanatory task that the cosmological argument imposes upon something or other. Kant then argues that the argument is covertly parasitic on the ontological argument, whose in-validity has been sufficiently exposed. It argues from the existence of the contingent world to a necessarily existent source, and this is indeed a new and important step; but, in its next step, it assumes that only an all-real, all-possible being can possibly be necessarily existent, and this accepts the in-ference from omnireality to necessary existence which has been set forth in the ontological argument, and which Kant has tried to expose as wrong (A. 606-8). The new argument was only propounded because there was tacitly thought to be a candidate waiting in the wings for the unconditioned, necessary existence which the argument required: in default of such a candidate, one would simply have had to give up the cosmological line of argumentation. The new argument has, therefore, tacitly built upon the possibility of an un-conditioned, ultimate explanation of contingencies which the all-real being alone is in a position to provide: it has ad-vertised a position, because it thought it had a suitable candidate for it. But if there is no such candidate, and this cannot be proved cosmologically, the new argument fails, or must base itself, in default of intellectual intuition, on arguments like the ontological. The new argument has in effect only made the implication between omnireality and necessary existence two-sided, instead of letting it hold in one direction alone. The piece of reasoning here under examination is one of Kant's most brilliant and subtle, and conclusively shows that unless we opt for, or have insight into, the inner consistency and possibility of the concepts here under examination, there is nothing in the sort of reality and conditioned necessity possessed by phenomenal things that will enable us to give value to them, or even to use them. But whether this shows up a defect in them, or in phenomenal things, may be left unanswered.

Kant further argues (A. 609–10): (1) that causal arguments from a contingent existence to its cause can only have validity, that is, can only count as knowledge, in the sensible world; (2) that the inference to a first cause is illegitimate in the world of experience and must be more so in the transcendental realm of noumenal causes — presumably Kant means that we cannot *know* how causality will be transformed in their case; (3) reason is emptily satisfied with a conclusion to which it can give no intuitive fulfilment: it cannot imagine what its unconditioned source would be like; (4) it confuses the internally coherent and non-self-contradictory with the real. These four arguments only prove the unillustrability of the Idea of an unconditioned prime condition: they do not show that the thought of it may not be fully consistent, and that we cannot think that it is somehow, we know not quite how, given fulfilment.

Kant concedes (A. 612) that we may legitimately *postulate* the existence of an all-sufficient something as the cause of all possible effects, only denies that such a postulation can give rise to an apodictic certainty. The Idea of a necessary, omnireal being is, therefore, Kant says, nothing that can be realized in the phenomenal world: it can at best inspire us to reason about nature *as if* it had a first, necessary ground beyond the contingent grounds we can discover. Matter, he notes, was often treated as a necessary absolute by the ancient philosophers, and space has also been regarded as the ineliminable foundation of all contingent being. It is, however, obvious that there is nothing necessary in the existence of the extended, impenetrable objects that occupy space, nor in space itself, which is merely a contingent condition of appearance (A. 618–19). What Kant might have noted is how practically all philosophers, even such as have sought to reject absolutes, have held to their own, ineliminable, foundational existents — thought, the subject, the universal, the particulars, sensibilia, logical space, language-performances, and so forth — and have aspired towards an omnipossible absolute that does justice to them all. Even theories given to looseness, disparity, and plurality adopt absolutes of a sort, and absolute-theory, of which theology is only one variant, will obviously always be a thriving thought-industry. The fact, further, that an absolute's existence may for us be merely postulated or regulative does not mean that it may not be constitutive in and for itself. The cosmological proof may therefore be held to strive towards true conclusions, even if not by epistemologically justified steps.

Kant finally passes in Section vi to the physico-theological proof, which argues from the beauty and order in the world to a divine source. This proof, Kant says, is the oldest, clearest, and most in accord with the common reason of mankind. It is hard to survey the multitudinous marvels of existence, and their many signs of purposive adaptation, without supposing that all these marvels flow from a sublime and wise cause, working not blindly, but intelligently. The unity of this cause follows from the unified, integrated nature of the cosmos (A. 625–6), and we have to suppose that, behind natural mechanisms, there is always supernatural art. Such a line of argument would, however, only point to the existence of a world-architect, not of a creator responsible for his materials as well as their form. And it would at best only enable us to reason to the existence of an artificer of limited powers and perfection, since omnipossibility cannot be illustrated by a limited phenomenal range, however extensive (A. 627–8). It is as vain, therefore, to attempt to rise to the certain affirmation of an all-possible, all-real being from the marvels of experience as from necessary connections among concepts (A. 639). The Ideal of Pure Reason remains, however, an ideal without flaw, and one that completes and crowns the whole of human knowledge. And it permanently excludes such atheistic, deistic, anthropomorphic, and naturalistic absolutes as involve admixture with contingent, empirical contents. The Ideal of Pure Reason must be constructed in terms of pure universality, pure possibility, and pure necessity, without empirical admixture. As such, it diminishes the merely analytic or merely empirical arguments that are unable to reach it, rather than suffers diminution from their incapacity.

iii

In the Appendix to the Transcendental Dialectic (A. 642–704) Kant deals with what he calls the 'regulative' use of his Transcendental Ideas. They do not serve to introduce us to noumenal realities, nor to constitute these for us as objects of knowledge, and, when they tempt us to think that they can do so, they become the sources of a dangerous and almost irresistible illusion. They have, however, like the mechanisms of cognition, a very good use, provided only that they remain *within* the domain of possible experience, and do not attempt to stray beyond it. Reason, Kant says, is not capable of creating valid concepts of objects, but only of ordering and unifying those that the understanding has excogitated. It must attempt to systematize the conceptual work of the understanding, just as the latter must unify and systematize the intuitively given features of objects. But, though the Ideas of Reason do not introduce us to definite objects, they cause us to look in definite directions, and to aspire towards definite goals. There is an imaginary focus from which the concepts of the understanding seem to proceed, even though there is nothing knowable at that focus, just as, in a mirror, there seems to be a point behind the mirror from which the rays reflected by the mirror seem to proceed, even though there is nothing, or nothing relevant, at that point. Kant here makes use of a most interesting comparison. Previously, in A. 297, transcendental illusion was compared to the apparent enlargement of the moon on the horizon, or the apparent upward slope of the level sea before us: now it is compared to the apparent source of mirror-appearances in an object behind the mirror. In this case the comparison has a further relevance, in that Kant's words (A. 673) suggest that, just as the mirror-appearances have a real source, not where we see it, but behind our backs, so the unity of appearances must have a real source, not in appearances, but beyond them, a source that we can conceive but never know. And this source is not merely the transcendental self, as a neo-Kantian might like to think, but the grand sum total of Transcendental Subjects and Objects acting in concert under the direction of one transcendental orchestrator and choirmaster. This Leibnizian picture is arguably always within the background of Kant's thought, and the true role of the Transcendental Ideas is to impel us to search for such a systematic unity among concepts and intuitions as they would possess if they indeed sprang from a single, unconditioned source.

Kant then distinguishes *three* directions in which the regulative power of the Transcendental Ideas may lead our thought to progress. It may lead us, first, in the direction of ever higher generality, that is, to look for ever wider and deeper homogeneity of character and behaviour. It may, in the second place, lead us in the direction of ever increasing specification and differentiation of kinds, to search for ever more distinct species of things. And it may, in the third place, lead us in the direction of ever more finely graded transitions from one sort of thing to another, so that there are continuous affinities, and an absence of gaps or leaps, among specific forms. Kant illustrates investigative movement in the first direction by attempts to lessen the number of independent conscious faculties, and to find them all to be differentiations of a very few, or preferably of one single, basic, conscious power (A. 649). He also illustrates it by the efforts of chemists to reduce the different kinds of earths to three, the salts to acids and alkalis, and to hope that all chemical substances will ultimately turn out to be variously compounded out of particles of the same general sort (A. 653). The maxim of this first thought-tendency is the so-called Razor of Occam: Never multiply entities any more than you need. But the maxim of the second, equally important, tendency might be expressed as *Entium varietates non temere esse minuendas*, that is, Don't be too quick in reducing the varieties of entities. Kant gives few concrete examples of this second tendency, but cites the assumption of those who attribute special inborn capacities to men belonging to different races and so on. The third tendency has as its presiding maxim *Non datur vacuum formarum* or *Datur continuum formarum*, that is, There is no gap among forms, or There is a continuum of forms. Kant illustrates this tendency by our conceptual approach to the paths of the planets and comets, passing from circles to ellipses, and from ellipses to parabolas, and thence finally to hyperbolas (A. 662–3). But Kant points out that only experience can fill in what the

Transcendental Ideas lead us to look for, and that experience cannot be expected to satisfy them completely. There is not an infinity of specific forms in nature, nor are there infinitely gradual distinctions among the distinct species of a genus. All Kant's treatments here stress the role of affinity, close resemblance, in the notion of a rule or a concept: would that modern logical treatments of induction had realized that, in default of a use of the notion of *closeness* or affinity, no theory of inductive procedure makes sense at all.

In the ensuing, final section of the Dialectic (A. 669–704) Kant applies the regulative principles more specifically to his three Transcendental Ideas. He explains the difference between having an object absolutely (*schlechthin*), and having it only in Idea (A. 670). In the former case, an object is actually determined by a concept, that is, our concept hits a target, actually pinpoints something. In the latter case, it only suffices to bring systematic unity into *other* conscious materials, which must be *as if* they derived from a certain hypothetical source. In psychology it is legitimate to view our inner life *as if* it were the expression of a single, unitary, enduring substance which binds all its states and faculties together; in cosmology we must pursue our enquiries *as if* we were dealing with a total, indefinitely extensible world, having no source that lies beyond itself; while in theology we must view everything *as if* ordained by a self-subsistent, creative reason (A. 672). In the case of the psychological and theological Ideas we can go further, and *hypostatize* their hypothetical objects — the Antinomies forbid us to do so in the case of the cosmological Idea — but such hypostatization is only allowable if we realize that it in no sense extends knowledge. God and the soul are postulated only as Ideas, and the positing is only inspirational and directive, not constitutive and existential. These objects are in fact not posited absolutely, but only relatively, that is, for the sake of the harmony and unity that they inspire us to look for in the empirical world (A. 677–9).

Kant then reapplies these considerations to the soul (A. 682–4), to the cosmos (A. 684–5), and finally to the Idea of God; and goes on to say, in relation to the last-named Idea, that its most important use is to make us look for *purposes or ends* in natural phenomena. The treatment of this sort of regulation is carried further in the *Critique of Teleological Judgement*, which will concern us in the next chapter. Kant also makes a number of weighty assertions, which tend in opposing directions, and create a somewhat confusing impression. He asserts (1) that there *undoubtedly* is a transcendental ground, distinct from the world, for such order as is to be found in the world, and for the world's internal coherence (*Zusammenhang*) according to universal laws. For the world is a sum of appearances for which there has to be a transcendental ground, thinkable only by the pure understanding (A. 696). This is one of the many passages where not only the 'manifold', but the *Zusammenhang* among them, is attributed to something beyond our conscious syntheses. He also asserts (2) that, since this ground is outside the world, it cannot be an object of possible experience, and so cannot meaningfully be said to exist, or to be a substance, or to be necessary, or to be a cause and so on, at least not in the senses in which these categorial expressions have a use in empirical contexts (A. 677, 696). The categories will certainly have to suffer a systematic transformation in the new contexts, and we cannot perfectly understand what this might be. But he maintains (3) that, since the maximum possible use of my reason indispensably requires the Idea of a systematically complete unity that can never be illustrated in experience, 'I am not only entitled (*befugt*) but also obliged (*genötigt*) to realize this Idea, i.e. posit it as an actual object, though only as something in general, that I do not at all know in itself, and to which, as a ground of such systematic unity, and in relation to the latter, I can attribute properties analogous to the concepts of the understanding in their empirical use' (A. 677–8, see also 696–7). (4) It is legitimate in such uses to personalize the actual object thus obligatorily postulated, and to introduce certain subtle anthropomorphisms into our conception of it. It can be thought of as having substantiality, causality, necessity, and so on, in their most perfect form; and, since it is postulated by reason, as being a self-subsistent reason, which is the cause of the whole world on principles of harmony and unity (A. 678, 697–8).

In these statements and elsewhere Kant seems to vacillate between positions which make the Transcendental Ideas meaningful notions, though unfulfillable intuitively, and positions which make them non-significant, and useful only for what they inspire us to look for. According to the latter view, the Transcendental Ideas ought not to be indispensable: we could exploit their pragmatic charisma without straining ourselves to conceive them. They could in fact be replaced by heuristic maxims, for example, Look always for maximal unity, integration, and purposive accommodation in objects. Some of the things Kant says towards the end of this Section suggest that he really favours this pragmatic, heuristic approach. For he says that the analogical Idea of an ordering intelligence behind nature has its entire basis in the use of *our* reason upon the world: '*Diese Idee ist also respektiv auf den Weltgebrauch unserer Vernunft ganz gegründet*' (A. 698). And he also says that it ought to be a matter of entire indifference, when we perceive unity in nature, whether we say that God has wisely willed it so, or that nature has ordered it thus (A. 699). He even suggests that philosophers have shown becoming modesty in preferring naturalistic to theological assertions in their accounts of natural arrangements (A. 701).

Yet, at the same time, Kant never wavers in his view that the postulation of really existent, transcendent unities is not a dispensable option, but a necessity of thought. That it never amounts to knowledge is a limitation for knowledge, not for the transcendental unities in question. Phenomena would in fact fall wholly apart if there were no Transcendental Subjects sustaining unified views of the world, Transcendental Objects revealing themselves in affinities, regular concomitances, and interactions in that world, and a transcendental, supra-reason co-ordinating them all. For us it may only be *as if* these things are there, but the *as if* has no connotations of the contra-factual, only of the imperfectly certifiable. We discern these objects only through their manifestations, not in some supra-intuitive or supra-conceptual manner which transcends these. We may, in this connection, admire the rigorous rationality of Kant's conception of God. He is without a trace of Judaic arbitrariness, concerned only to guarantee the possibility of the rational enterprises, and to express Himself in a world where scientific discovery and rational, practical love will be possible. To love scientific thought and rational, practical love is to love God, and vice versa: surely the perfection of the deep but enlightened piety characteristic of the eighteenth century.

Chapter VIII

Kant's Metaphysic of Nature

i

We shall, in the present chapter, deal with a very perplexing stratum of Kant's teaching: his philosophy of the natural world and of our knowledge of it. There are some works, for example, the *Anthropology*, in which Kant treats of natural phenomena in a wholly unproblematic manner: he applies his *a priori* categories and principles to empirical data, and takes no step whatever in the direction of the Transcendental Object, the Noumenon, or the Thing-in-itself. But there are other works, such as *The Metaphysical Foundations of Natural Science*, and his fragmentary last work on the Transition from Critical Philosophy to Physics, in which a distinction is drawn between *secondary* phenomena, or phenomena *of* phenomena — which are merely the coloured, sounding, tangible, odorous phenomena of the outer world, together with the sensible, cogitative, desiderative, and affective phenomena of our inner life — and *primary* phenomena, which represent a deeper phenomenal layer, full of mysterious moving forces which operate in a space and time stripped of sense-qualities and feeling-qualities, and which in some manner come closer to the underlying structures of Things-in-themselves, and of the transcendental thinking subject, than do the piebald phenomena of ordinary experience. What is also remarkable is the predominantly materialistic character of this primary phenomenal stratum: it is a spatio-temporal world stripped of the secondary qualities, which in fact spring from the brain-motions which are the internal reactions to external actions impinging on the senses. The life of the empirical psyche is, at this level, as much an epiphenomenon of these moving forces as is the structure and character of the externally perceived world. Only the reluctant admission, in the *Opus Postumum*, of the possibility of there being teleological as well as mechanistic moving forces working at this level would rescue it from complete subservience to bodily mechanism. Kant's strange doctrine of phenomena and epiphenomena is, of course, of long standing: in a well-known passage in the First *Critique* (A. 45), he contrasts the rainbow a variable appearance dependent on the reflections of light from raindrops, with the reflected light and the raindrops which, relatively to the rainbow, play the part of underlying Things-in-themselves. He also stresses that they in no sense represent authentic Things-in-themselves, since their spatio-temporality stamps them as pure appearances. Here, however, in these later writings, we are introduced to a level of primary phenomena from which all the secondary qualities, due to psycho-physical interaction, are removed, and only spatio-temporality and moving forces remain. And yet we are not, at this plainly non-empirical level, dealing with Things-in-themselves. What sort of phenomena are these non-empirical phenomena which Kant locates somewhere in a *Zwischenraum* between empirical phenomena and things as they are in themselves? In the treatment of this difficult question we shall not merely consider the treatise on the *Metaphysical Foundations of Natural Science*, but also the *Opus Postumum*, which tries to bridge the gulf between the latter and empirical physics. This last is of course a set of fragments, hard to interpret, but in most cases stamped with Kant's uniquely penetrative genius, and certainly necessary to the full understanding of even his earlier views on physics. The possibility of making use of this last source depends, further, on the exegetic genius of Erich Adickes, whose volume on the *Opus Postumum*, and whose later work (1929) on *Kant's Doctrine of the Double Affection of our Self*, has brought light and intelligibility into almost impenetrable darkness. On the work of Erich Adickes I have throughout relied: my treatment is an epi-phenomenon of the way things appeared to him.

The notion of appearances of appearances gives rise to many questions. Are the primary appearances beneath the secondary appearances, with which they are said to affect us, perhaps no more than conceptual constructs brought in to explain the appearances of ordinary experience? In other words, are the primary appearances really those of ordinary experience, whereas the so-called primary appearances of natural science are merely the secondary appearances to con-ceptual thought? If we did not have the *Opus Postumum* before us, but merely the *Critiques* and the *Metaphysical Foundations of Natural Science*, this would perhaps be the natural view to take, but it is clear that Kant did in some manner believe in a double, even manifold, affection of the empirical self, remotely by Things-in-themselves in concert with its own transcendental subjectivity, less remotely by the spatio-temporal dynamisms postulated by physics, and most directly by the coloured, resonant, fragrant, tangible sense-objects that we observe around us and by the vanishing thoughts and feelings that they excite in us. If Things-in-themselves are, in virtue of their independence of our subjective approaches, the ultimate paradigms of objectivity, while their affection of ourselves is likewise the ultimate paradigm of causal action, it may none the less be the case that something of this objectivity, and of this causal action, communicates itself to us through a whole series of phenomenal representatives: through a basic level of spatio-temporal dynamism, through a level of ordinary, external phenomena, through a level of inner sense which presents our inner responses to these, and also through a level of constructive conception which presents our interpretative thought regarding all these previous levels. According to this view, the basic level of spatio-temporal dynamism represents a phenomenal level, not for the empirical self which is consequent upon it, but for the Transcendental Subject itself: this sees the world as a stripped spatio-temporal stage on which the only actors are moving forces, but its vision gives rise to a secondary phenomenal level at which phenomenal objects confront the empirical self; the transcendental self and its attendant prime phenomena remaining active behind the empirical self and *its* secondary phenomena, and being in fact the same self and the same objects in a double overlaid condition. And many of Kant's utterances suggest that the deeper phenomenal levels not only underlie the more superficial ones, but also seep through into them qualitatively. Thus the pure intuition we are said to have of the whole of space and time (see, e.g., A. 25), and the synthesis we are said to practise on its innumerable parts in order to achieve this intuition (see, e.g., A. 99–100), are certainly not given in ordinary, secondary experience, but perhaps in some manner dimly seep through into the latter: we feel such things as the infinity of space and time 'in our bones', and it is (in our bones) likewise that we must recollect the synthetic activities that went to the making of these infinite synthetic outcomes. Strange as they may seem, these certainly are the sort of doctrines that

Kant in his own depth-persuasions espouses: they will not make much sense to his idealist and phenomenalist simplifiers. There would seem to be for Kant not merely one phenomenal veil behind which transcendental objectivity lies hidden, but a whole series of veils, each of which only makes it possible for us to think, but not to know, the next, less veiled appearance, but which, from the standpoint of more thickly veiled appearances, can be treated as introducing us to things as they are in themselves. We must, however, see how these suggestions develop in a more detailed study of the *Metaphysical Foundations of Natural Science*, and of the *Opus Postumum*, in which Kant tries to relate the *Foundations* to empirical physics.

ii

The metaphysics of nature is, according to the Kantian view, of necessity mathematical (*MFNS*, 470–1), since mathematics is the science of the spatial and the temporal as such, and since material bodies and thinking beings are essentially given as occupying space and time. A metaphysic of nature will attempt to determine whatever can be asserted *a priori* of such occupants, abstracting from all their further, detailed qualifications which can only be given empirically, or *a posteriori*. Most of the detailed content of chemistry, of biology, of anthropology, and psychology will therefore, in Kant's view, fall outside the metaphysic of nature, since such content involves much that is not merely spatio-temporal, and that does not admit of purely mathematical treatment. (In their contemporary form, the sciences mentioned by Kant will of course go far towards satisfying his requirements for a metaphysical treatment.) Kant further demands that his metaphysic of nature should be founded four-square on his table of categories (474). It must therefore have a section which determines the quantity of the occupation of space and time, such quantity being understood as some form of extensive magnitude capable of being measured by denumerable units. It must also have a section concerned with the quality of spatio-temporal occupation, with the intensive degree to which space and time can be occupied. And it must further have a section concerned with the permanent and the variable aspects of occupation, and with the relation of its variable aspects to one another, a section which will apply to spatio-temporal occupation the three relational categories of substantial permanence, of cause and effect, and of reciprocal interaction, of which so much has been said in the Analogies of Experience. And it must finally contain a section concerned with the conditions necessary, or possible, or impossible for an experience of spatio-temporal occupancy, it being assumed that nothing is metaphysically allowable of which an empirical test is impossible. The headings dealing with these categorially predetermined sections are Phoronomy, or the pure theory of motion, Dynamics, or the pure theory of the fixed occupancy of space and time, Mechanics, or the pure theory of the interplay of motions and moving bodies, and Phenomenology, or the theory of the necessary relations of spatio-temporal occupancy to the possibility or impossibility of experience. It cannot be held that Kant's table of categories has much to do with the categorizations here arrived at.

In the Metaphysical Foundations of Phoronomy Kant defines matter as the movable in space (480): as such it serves as the necessary substrate of the secondary qualities given to the senses, Kant taking it for granted that, without motions extending from sense-object to sensitive organ, there could be no sense-experience. He thereby excludes any form of telegnosis that would dispense with such motion; and, certainly, a direct sensitivity to what was spatially or temporally remote would, in a sense, do away with space and time altogether, and would be more suitable to a noumenal than a phenomenal world. Kant further remarks that the movable in space can always be taken to be a point (480), or, as later remarks bring out, a set of points moving in concert. This stress on points as the ultimate elements of mobile matter must not be taken to be an arbitrarily abstract way of looking at things: it is a residuum deliberately retained from the Leibnizian monadology, in which what is composite always presupposes the existence of the simple, a view which Kant affirms to be the only correct way to think of the unknowable world of Things-in-themselves (507). Obviously, however, these point-like elements will have a phenomenal ambiance that extends more widely: so much is implied by the discussions that follow. And, thirdly, we may note that bodies carry about with them relative spaces in which they can be regarded as either at rest or in motion, and such relative spaces can themselves be regarded as moving in relation to some more embracing relative space. The whole series of relative spaces boxed within wider relative spaces tends, however, towards a limiting or absolute space, which Kant regards as no more than a Transcendental Idea, unrealizable in appearance or experience. 'Absolute space', Kant writes, 'is in itself nothing, and is no object at all, but signifies merely every other relative space, that I can at any time think of outside a given space, and that I can extend beyond each given space to infinity, as being such a space as includes this given' (481). It is difficult to reconcile such statements with the doctrine of the Aesthetic, which makes all spaces in the plural mere limitations of a single, all-inclusive space. And it is odd that a thinker who has no difficulty in believing in mobile, relative spaces, which are certainly not given in experience, should make a pother about an ultimate, absolute space.

The movement of a bodily centre, or of an aggregate of such centres, is said to lie in the change of its external relations to a given relative space, which latter, presumably, is the space of an aggregate of similar centres all mutually at rest (482–3). In all such movement, velocity and direction are the necessary descriptive moments: these, when uniform, determine a uniform movement, when variable, a movement which changes in velocity, or direction, or both. Circular movement is a peculiar movement in which direction is continuously changing, though we misleadingly speak of it as invariantly circular (483). Kant here recognizes the strange prerogative of the straight line, so essential, despite all relativistic complications, to the understanding of space. He also stresses the conceptual mystery of the difference between movement towards the left and movement towards the right: that they are opposite and different, and can be *seen* as such, is all that we can say about them (484). Rest, as opposed to motion, is a *perdurable* presence in the same part of a given relative space: a momentary presence at such a place, as in the case of a tossed ball at the top of its flight, will not count as rest, but merely as an infinitesimally reduced, limiting state of movement (485–6). In all such movement, it is open to us to view a body as being in motion in relation to a space which is at rest, or as at rest in relation to a space which is moving in an opposite direction with the same velocity. (Such alternativity in viewing is not, however, permissible when non-rectilinear movements are in question, as here empirical dynamic effects arise, which are not, however, relevant to pure phoronomy (488, 561–2).) A number of movements can further be compounded, in which case the relative space in which a body is moving is itself conceived as moving, with another velocity and direction, in a more embracing relative space, which, for the purposes of the exercise, counts as absolutely at rest. There are three manners in which such movements may be combined: according as the direction is the same, but the two velocities differ; or according as the direction is opposite, but the velocities differ, or are the same; or according, finally, as the directions are inclined to one another at some angle, while the two velocities differ, or are the same (489–90). The additions, subtractions, and angular accommodations which follow need not be considered, but are plainly the analytic consequences of the conceptual constructions involved. Kant points out, however, that, only if there are moving forces, will such compounded motions become realities, and such moving forces are not a mere matter of phoronomy (494–5).

From the metaphysics which considers the quantitative aspects of bodily motion we pass to the metaphysics which considers its *qualitative* presuppositions. To move in space implies that one is able to *fill* space, and can resist the penetration of that space by other mobile occupants. Such occupancy stands opposed to the negation of being totally unoccupied, and is accordingly, in terms of the then current logical usage, a qualitative matter. The filling of space, involves, however, not the mere presence of matter in it, but the existence of a special moving force which keeps *other* matter out of an occupied region. Metaphysical structure at the physical level seems, in fact, to be little beyond the existence of variously located centres of force, all concerned to keep other force-centres out of their territory. Hardness and solidity, Kant points out, do not by themselves prevent external penetration: they only do so as the manifest forms of repulsive moving forces. Matter fills space, we are informed (499), by the repulsive forces of all its parts: these have, however, a definite degree, so that expansion to infinity is not possible. Matter can, however, be indefinitely compressed by external moving forces, though such compression can never amount to the total penetration of its space. At a later point in his theorizing, Kant does entertain the possibility of a sort of total penetration, which is, however, rather a case of *interpenetration* than of the reduction of one bodily unit's extension to nothing. Heat-matter and magnetic matter may, he supposes, penetrate other matter in this pervasive, non-compressive fashion (532). But where spatial occupancy is compressed, its expansive force will also be intensified: this will become manifest in the elastic expansion of a compressed body when the compressing force is removed (501).

Kant now passes to the somewhat surprising theorem that matter is divisible to infinity (503). It might have been thought that space could have been completely filled by the mutual repulsion of a *finite* number of ultimate force-centres. This is, however, rejected because Kant holds that the continuously present repulsive forces entail that every geometrically distinct part of a material substance could be physically separated from every other, and that therefore, since the geometrically distinct parts of every body are infinite in number, so are the dynamic units which repel one another in it. This leads Kant on to a half-hearted rejection of the monadism which his theory really presupposes. Monadism, he says, would allow the repulsive forces of one centre to operate in places where they are not resisted by other countering repulsions, and this has just been proved to be impossible. All that Kant's argument proves is that the number of monadic centres is infinite, a view quite orthodox from a Leibnizian standpoint, though difficult from his own. Kant, however, achieves an accommodation of his geometrical and Leibnizian persuasions by appealing to the distinction between phenomena and noumena. Phenomena may offer us an infinity of extended units, each embraced in the extensions of others, but noumena can and must be thought of as meeting the Leibnizian requirements. 'The ground of this aberration', that is, the belief in a limited number of force-centres, lies, Kant says, 'in a badly understood monadology, which does not at all belong to the explication of natural appearances, but is a Platonic concept of the world carried out by Leibniz. This concept is correct in itself in so far as the world is regarded, not as an object of the senses, but as a Thing-in-itself, i.e. as merely an object of the understanding, which none the less lies at the basis of the appearances of the senses. Now the composite of Things-in-themselves must certainly consist of the simple, for the parts must here be given before all composition. But the composite in the appearance does not consist of the simple, because in the appearance, which can never be given otherwise than as composite (extended), the parts can be given only through division, and thus not before the composite, but only in it' (507–8). In other words, space is not analysable into a set of mutually exclusive, discrete, simple units, but is none the less the appearance of a set of discrete, mutually exclusive, monadically simple and essentially unknowable units, which have to be conceived in a non-sensuous, that is, Platonic, fashion. It cannot be said that Kant's treatment here achieves lucidity, and it is impossible to see why the *dynamic* division of phenomenal matter into zones dominated each by a single force-centre should at all correspond to its indefinitely various *geometric* divisions, if that is indeed what he is contending.

The repulsive moving forces which keep bodily units out of each other's territories, require, however, to be supplemented by attractive moving forces which draw them towards one another. Without such attractive forces, matter would be dispersed to infinity: there could in fact be no such thing as matter at all. Nor would the mere compression of other re-pulsive units suffice to prevent such dispersion, for this would only work if there were an attractive moving force which drew the mutually repulsive units together, and so enabled them to exert compression on one another. Such attractive moving forces must, however, be as much dependent on re-pulsive forces as the latter depend on the former. For if, in the absence of attractive moving forces, all matter would vanish in indefinite dispersion, attractive forces, in the absence of repulsive moving forces, would concentrate all matter into a mathematical point, and so cause it to vanish in another manner (511). But, though these moving forces are thus mutually dependent, repulsive forces, as manifest in hardness, pressure, and impenetrability, they are far more obvious than attractive forces, which latter act at a distance, and are only inferred from the movements of bodies. Hence also the perpetual tendency to reduce or explain attractive forces by means of unobserved pressures. Attractive forces are, however, as ultimate and inexplicable as are the forces of repulsion, and it is only the presence of surface contact in the latter which gives it greater obviousness. The tendencies of bodily centres to fly apart, or to come together, are equally irreducible, and are also, in virtue of the point-like character of dynamic centres, as much cases of *actio in distans*. Newton was right in refusing to make hypotheses explanatory of gravitation; he was only wrong in refusing to regard it as an essential property of matter.

Repulsion, however, operates at a distance only through intermediate units, whereas attraction ignores intermediate units
in its operation, and is therefore more completely an *actio in
distans*. Attraction, therefore, holds the remotest parts of the
universe together in unity, and would do so even across empty
tracts of space, the possibility of which Kant refuses to reject,
though it cannot derive the slightest support from experience
(535). Through the balance between attraction and repulsion,
the existence of matter is accordingly made possible, and
Kant observes with satisfaction that he has also given fresh
employment to his three categories: of reality (the impenetrable
solidity due to repulsion); negation (the attractive force which
would cause all matter to coalesce in unity); and limitation (the
compromise between repulsion and attraction which makes
spatial occupancy possible). Such a falsely tidy result should
not blind us to the originality of Kant's theory of matter, and
of his reconstruction of the Leibnizian monadology.

The third chapter of the *Metaphysical Foundations* deals
with the foundations of mechanics, where matter is always
considered in its dynamic causal relations, as imparting its
motion to other matter. Here the relational categories of
permanence, causality, and reciprocal action are given due
employment. Since matter is always divisible to infinity, its
quantity can never be established by considering the number
of its parts: only the quantity of its *motion* measures its true
quantity (538). This leads to the formulation of three laws of
mechanics, which are Kant's restatement of Newton's three
laws of motion. The first law is that of material or mobile
permanence: there must always be the same amount of matter,
or, what is the same, the same amount of motion in the universe
(541-2). Matter has a guarantee of substantial permanence,
which is lacking in the case of the thinking ego or psyche, an
old persuasion of Kant's, which is here once again aired. The
second law (543) is that all changes in matter, that is, in the
velocity or direction of its motion, must be due to the action
of an external cause, in the absence of which a body will
continue indefinitely in its state of rest or uniform rectilinear
motion. And the third law is that, in all communication of
motion, action and reaction are equal and opposite (544),
a theorem which simply follows from Kant's relativistic conception of motion, and involves no mysterious transference of
motion from body to body (550). Kant has tried to make

philosophical sense of these basic mechanical theorems, but what he says is too frosted over with the rime of antiquity to be worth considering further.

The last chapter of the *Foundations* gives employment to the modal categories of the possible, the actual, and the necessary, all of which concern the manners in which the spatio-temporal continuum with its moving forces will *appear* to the cognizing subject. It accordingly bears the title of the Metaphysical Foundations of Phenomenology, the consideration of the movable as an object of possible experience. Here three principles are stated. The first tells us that rectilinear motion in relation to *no* given set of external bodily units is a mere possibility, and, if thought of as absolute, is impossible. The second is that circular motion is always actual, and not merely possible, since it has specific empirical consequences. And the third is simply that if one body moves relatively to another, the second body will move in an equal and opposite manner relatively to the first.

It cannot be held that Kant's working out of his metaphysical physics is either completely clear or completely cogent. It contrives throughout to convey an impression of rather funny oddity. It also leaves us with the problem which faced us at the beginning of this chapter: does Kant mean his space and time, peopled only with moving forces, to be merely a construct necessary for the explanation of ordinary phenomenal experience, or does it represent some deeper phenomenal level, which the Transcendental Subject constructs in concert with the Transcendental Objects which affect it? And is the ordinary empirical world a secondary product in which the Transcendental Subject is further affected by its original vision, and becomes an empirical subject facing a world full of empirical, secondary qualities? There can be little doubt that it is this second, bizarre doctrine of 'double affection' which Kant really accepts. The world of moving forces in space and time is the primal phenomenal world which, backed, of course, by the force of the Transcendental Objects behind it, again affects the subject which has constructed it, and leads to the construction of a secondary phenomenal world. This leads to the question: is a world consisting only of space, time, and moving forces really imaginable and conceivable? It is perhaps arguable that it is, and that this primal sort of imagination seeps through to the clear and definite level of our secondary imagination of the things around us. We are at all times aware, in a dim way, of the great media of space and time extending indefinitely around us, and of vague forces hindering movements in certain directions and facilitating them in others. Pure kinaesthesis, which, as a sensation, is almost devoid of sensuous quality, is perhaps what represents the primary phenomenal level at the secondary phenomenal level. The world revealed by primal experience would then be, as it were, a purely kinaesthetic world, with its phenomena sharpened to a degree of exactness unknown in our confused, secondary perceptions. This is perhaps the world that Kant is talking of in the *Metaphysical Foundations of Natural Science*. This suggestion will make the work even more of a painful puzzle to Kant's idealistic and positivistic interpreters than it now is.

iii

We shall now comment on some of the main points in Professor Erich Adickes's work entitled *Kants Opus Postumum dargestellt und beurteilt*, which was published in 1920 as a Supplementary Volume to No. 50 of the journal *Kant-Studien*. This exhaustive, 855-page work has to a large extent made it unnecessary for anyone to try to decode the cryptic messages contained in the twelve Convolutes of loose pages of Notes, which are now assembled in the Academy Edition of Kant's works. The present writer is not a Detailforscher capable of executing such an appalling task. And Adickes is so careful to distinguish exposition from interpretation, and to cite relevant passages in full, that one is always quite able to evaluate *his* opinions, and to distinguish them from Kant's. It will therefore be through Adickes that we shall, in the next two sections, approach these last views of Kant. Adickes's work falls into four parts, each with several sections and chapters. The first part deals with the interesting history of the *Opus Postumum*, the second with the problematic dating of the various strata of its material between 1795 and 1798, the third with the predominantly natural-scientific material contained in Convolutes II–VI and VIII–XII, while the fourth deals with the very significant metaphysical and epistemological material to be found in Convolutes VII and I. This last material has also been dealt with by Vaihinger in his *Philosophie des Als Ob*, though Adickes has rejected his interpretation.

As regards the history of Kant's posthumous work, we learn

from a letter of Kiesewetter to Kant in 1795 that Kant had for
some years planned to produce 'some pages' which would
provide a transition between the *Metaphysical Foundations of
Natural Science* and empirical physics. This led to Kant's
actual absorption in the preliminaries of the new work, which
in his case took the form of a vast number of scribbled notes
covering vastly more than 'some pages', and which created in
him, we learn from a letter written in 1798, 'the anguish of
Tantalus, in which despair and hope constantly alternated'
(Adickes, pp. 1–2). After Kant's death in 1804 the manuscript
passed through the hands of a series of nearer and remoter
relatives, till it was handed over to one R. Reicke in 1865,
who published an inadequate account of its contents, and
later nine of its Convolutes, inadequately amended, in the
Altpreussische Monatsschrift between 1882 and 1884. In
1884 the manuscript was purchased by Albert Krause, an
enthusiastic cleric from Hamburg, who published popular
expositions of Kant — *Gesetze des menschlichen Herzens*
(1876) and *Populäre Darstellung von Kants Kritik der reinen
Vernunft* (1881) — and who believed the *Opus Postumum*
to be Kant's greatest work, and expounded it in semi-popular
fashion in 1882 and 1902. The excessive enthusiasm of this
admirer was confronted by the cold deprecation of Professor
Kuno Fischer in 1884, who defended his idealistic simplifications of Kantian teaching with all the arrogance then expected
of an eminent Heidelberg professor. Kuno Fischer failed to
see anything in the new Kantian material that did not accord
with his own hermeneutic stances, which had for him, and for
many others, become an unassailable orthodoxy. And he
cast the same stigma of senility on the contents of the *Opus
Postumum* that Zeller had likewise tried to throw over Plato's
late, but deeply interesting, reduction of Ideas to Numbers.
Vaihinger, the greatest of all Kantian commentators, had
likewise recognized, in 1884, the importance of the doctrine
of 'double affection' taught in the *Opus Postumum*, and of
its necessity for the interpretation of the Refutation of Idealism.
And, though he failed to find coherent sense in the physico-
philosophical sections of the work, he discovered a remarkable
fictionalist approach in its metaphysical-epistemological sections.
The history of Adickes necessarily stops at 1920, but he produced two subsequent studies on the same material, *Kant und
das Ding an Sich*, in 1924, and *Kants Lehre von der doppelten*

Affection unseres Ich, in 1929. Since Adickes's death in 1929, important work has been done on the *Opus Postumum*: we need here only mention Burkhard Tuschling's *Metaphysiche und Transzendentale Dynamik in Kants Opus Postumum* (1971). The Academy Edition of Kant's works now of course includes a complete version of the manuscript material, which it can be no pleasure for anyone to read.

Kant, when he wrote the *Metaphysical Foundations of Natural Science* in 1786, seems to have believed that it exhausted the *a priori* or pure part of the investigation. From that point on, everything was empirical application, and no *a priori* guidelines could be hazarded. Towards the middle of the 1790s, he came, however, to believe that some sort of a *transition* must be constructed between the *a priori*, essentially mathematical doctrine of the *Metaphysical Foundations* and the empirical detail of physics. Adickes remarks (p. 162) that 'to the establishment of these necessities, and thus to the proof that the new transitional science made an indispensable contribution to transcendental philosophy, Kant devoted much time and labour, but also wasted it, since the end he was striving for was a mere *Fata morgana*.' A vain effort it certainly was if Kant thought that one can so smooth the passage from general principles to brute facts that there is absolutely no jar or jolt in it: obviously, at a certain point, as Plato says in the *Philebus*, one must desist from eidetic specification, and descend into the indefinite variety of individual detail. But Kant may have felt that the necessary point of transition should be wisely and carefully judged, not stupidly anticipated or presumed, and that the *Metaphysical Foundations* had not judged the transition-point quite rightly.

If one turns, however, to the numerous notes treating of moving forces and the basic properties of matter examined by Adickes in Section II of his work on Kant's *Opus Postumum*, it is hard to see that they represent much of an advance beyond the general principles of the *Metaphysical Foundations*, or that they arrive at any uniform and coherent conclusions. The fourfold scheme of the categories is again put to work, and one is offered various fourfold lists of moving forces and material properties which have little beyond the vaguest plausibility to recommend them. Sometimes the stress is on the various possibilities permitted by movement as such, sometimes on subjective possibilities of experience, but nothing clicks, or makes it worth while to devote much time to the headings listed. An innovation arises in the negative place left for the aether in each of the divisions, otherwise there is little to excite enquiry. We meet with grandiose programmatic statements such as:

> To arrive at physics as a system of empirical natural science, we must first develop, as far as their form goes, a set of *a priori* principles of the synthetic unity of the moving forces in natural science: this must be done completely in the transition to natural science. No aggregate of fragments can contain this totality of the possibility of physics, since, being a totality which is given *a priori*, it must necessarily be a system, to which nothing can be added and from which nothing can be taken away. It must consist of regulative principles that are at the same time constitutive (Adickes, p. 169).

After these stringent demands it is a little disappointing to be informed that the moving forces of corporeal nature must be divided in respect of (1) origin, (2) direction, (3) place, and (4) filling of space, and that, as so divided, they are either (1) intrinsic (*congenitae*) or imparted (*impressae*), (2) repulsive or attractive, (3) progressive or oscillatory, and (4) compressible (coercible) or incompressible. A considerable number of slightly differing lists follow, some including the distinction between 'living', that is, active forces, and 'dead', that is, cancelled or potential ones. A typical list opposes the ponderable to the imponderable, the compressible to the incompressible, the cohesible to the incohesible and the exhaustible to the in-exhaustible: the mysterious aether is characterized by all the negations (p. 194). Obviously, a theory that is so unfruitful in mechanics will be even more helpless in dealing with the complexities of magnetism, electricity, and chemical interaction. And particularly vexatious is the constant dragging in of the table of categories, which are quite unable to throw light on anything. It is interesting to note, however, that, in this primal forest of moving forces, organic, teleological forces are in a number of passages given a distinct role. These work towards goals, operate according to Ideas and an immaterial principle, and operate from the whole to the parts, and not vice versa (p. 219). It is possible, Kant holds, that 'in the inner ground of nature, which is unknowable to us, physico-mechanical and purposive connections among the same things are joined together in a single principle' (p. 221), a view which he had also put forward in the Critique of Teleological Judgement. But it is also maintained (p. 222) that 'the multiplicity whose unified connection depends on the Idea of a purposively (artificially) operative subject, cannot spring from the moving forces of nature, in which this unity of principle is lacking.'

In the Third Section of his examination of the natural-scientific part of Kant's *Opus Postumum* Adickes deals with the 'new Transcendental Deduction' expounded in the Tenth and Eleventh Convolutes of the Manuscript, which Kant needs to cover the new *a priori* material brought in by his 'Transition' to Physics. An exhaustive, *a priori* account has to be given and justified of the moving forces which affect our senses and arouse perceptual reactions in us, as well as an account of those moving forces as primary phenomena, that is, as posited by the transcendental self in its first responses to Transcendental Objects, but as yet unqualified by any secondary, sensuous enrichments. As Adickes points out, this new Transcendental Deduction must deduce not merely the *existence* of the power-centres which are the primal occupants of space and time, but also their *Sosein* or qualitative character (p. 238). These occupants are, for metaphysics, appearances, but, for physics, Things-in-themselves which affect our senses (p. 239). Our self is accordingly doubly affected, both by Things-in-themselves, and by its own primal phenomenal rendering of these things, and these secondary affections will give rise to the secondary appearances, or appearances of appearances, of which mention was made at the beginning of this chapter. The old Transcendental Deduction, Adickes points out, merely dealt with the synthetic unification of sense-data which, in the new Deduction, spring from the reactions of the brain and nerves to the moving forces of external objects in space. And the new Transcendental Deduction will then also have to deal with the metaphysically *prior* projections of moving forces into time and space, in response to the interactions with Things-in-themselves. We must determine what such projections will have to be like if experience is to be possible (p. 240). Adickes points out that it is really a *Geschmackssache*, a matter of taste, whether we attribute all these systematic constructions to a transcendental self, or to a phenomenal self which emerges in the course of such constructions: the latter is in fact the same as the former, only *qua* apparent to itself (pp. 243-4). And equally, of course, it is a *Geschmackssache*, though Adickes does not stress it, whether we choose to stress the role of Things-in-themselves *qua* primally affecting us, or *qua* underlying our secondary affection by what we thus make of our primary affection, or *qua* underlying our tertiary affection by what we have thus secondarily made of this, and so on, so that Things-in-themselves are also, at all stages, involved in the systematic of consciousness. Adickes says (footnote to p. 246) that:

in so far as our self-in-itself, by way of its *a priori* sense-forms and synthetic functions, reconstructs the purely internal, timeless and spaceless relationships among Things-in-themselves (in virtue of its affection by the same) into the form of law-governed spatio-temporal relationships, it imposes on the world of force-complexes that thus emerges all the unity, order, systematic connection, affinity, regularity and legality of coexistence and succession that our empirical self can afterwards extract from its phenomenal world as the result of its affection by the moving forces of matter.

What this statement leaves unstressed (though Adickes elsewhere stresses it) is that Things-in-themselves are *likewise* involved in the emergence of all the unity, order, affinity, and so on which can thus be empirically excogitated, since it is *their* unknowable systematic unity which lies at the root of the systematic unity which appears in consciousness, the latter being no more than a translation of the former into the special diction of space and time.

Kant makes great use of the notion of self-affection in his account of the development of secondary out of primary appearances. 'The act', he says, 'through which the subject affects itself in perception, contains the principle of the possibility of experience. Experience cannot be given, but has to be made, and its principle of unity in the subject makes it possible that even empirical data, as materials through which the subject affects itself, can enter into the system of experience, and be counted and classified as moving forces in the system of nature' (pp. 248-9). In other words, our own sensory affections by the force-complexes which we ourselves have projected into space and time can provoke secondary constructions of the phenomenal world as we ordinarily know it, and these secondary constructions can then themselves be regarded as resting upon, or identical with, movements in the set of force-complexes that we call the material brain. 'The moving powers of matter', Kant says (p. 256), 'affect the subject, the man and his organs, since the former is a bodily thing. The inner changes produced in him are, with consciousness, perceptions: the reaction to matter and its external movement is a movement.' In other words, sense-perception is a sort of inner aspect to reactive movements, and the same external impact which produces the latter also produces the former, and renders it accessible to inner sense (p. 261). On the precise nature of the reaction which underlies sense-perception we have further information: it consists of some sort of chemical alteration in the water which tenants the hollows of the brain (p. 267), a hypothesis no sillier than contemporary theories. That sense-perception is not the passive undergoing of sensory impacts, but involves an active response to the latter, is of course a valuable insight. And Kant of course believes in a self-affection covering the acts of synthetic elaboration occurring in our various empirical judgements: though the transcendental self may be the ultimate framer of these judgements, it also sets itself before itself as their empirical framer, and so undergoes further affections at its own hands (p. 280, N. 1). Kant further sees in the self-affection accompanying the self's active response to external pressures, and its own active modifications of brain-stuff and muscles, the paradigm for those moving forces which it projects everywhere into the physical world. He here furnishes another proof of the monadological substructure of all his transcendental theorizing. And, as we have said, together with the concept of self-affection goes a rich use of the concept of second-order appearance, or appearance of appearance. Adickes distinguishes (§§129 a–f, pp. 292–304) six quite different uses of this concept, according as Things-in-themselves, or the Transcendental Subject (or the acts of either), or moving forces, or sense-data, or empirical objects, or the empirical subject, are chosen as starting-points. There is no fundamental obscurity in all these Protean changes of standpoint, but there would be no point in discussing them in more detail. Kant was after all writing notes for a projected work, not coherently composing one.

Adickes comments unfavourably on the success of Kant's new and enlarged Transcendental Deduction. Its use of the table of categories in establishing fundamental moving forces is quite without rigour, and it ignores the role of the Thing-in-itself in determining what varieties of fundamental force will be given in experience. He says (p. 352):

Kant often speaks of the affection by Things-in-themselves and of the givenness of the matter of appearances through such affection. But, in relation to such a givenness, the self-in-itself cannot act with complete autonomy, and, on the basis only of its own inner laws, determine the most general properties and species of moving forces, since in these latter the inner differences of the *content* of Things-in-themselves come to light in the form of appearances . . . The self-in-itself does not preside autocratically over Things-in-themselves and cannot one-sidedly determine how they will appear to it. Not only the self's own nature, but also their own nature, must fully come out in it.

Adickes also objects to Kant's attempts to connect his moving forces with various types of sensation: attraction, for example, is not uniformly presented by a peculiar sensation (p. 347), and there are moving forces such as the magnetic which are merely inferred from certain sensible effects and not sensibly given (p. 350). He also argues that Kant will have to posit a pre-established harmony between moving forces and types of sensation of a sort that he elsewhere repudiates. All this is very true, but leaves one with the feeling that Kant was very right in seeking to move beyond the many sharp antitheses of his critical theory. He only erred in pushing this smoothing effort too far, in directions, in fact, which anticipate the nature-philosophy of a Schelling.

Such Schellingian excursions are to be found in Kant's treatments of the aether, and in its use in explaining the phenomena of heat, light, magnetism, electricity, crystallization, fusion, friction, and lustre. A few illustrations will suffice to show the directions in which his mind was moving, and the way in which he tackled his problems in the last phase of his philosophical effort. The aether, Kant holds, exists of necessity, if experience is to be possible: transcendental proofs of this proposition abound in the *Opus Postumum*. The *Metaphysical Foundations* had allowed the mere possibility of empty space, though held it not to be an object of possible experience. The mere absence of an experience of something could plainly never amount to an experience of that thing's absence. But, in the *Opus Postumum*, this impossibility of having an experience of empty space has been changed into the illegitimacy of postulating its existence: it is not the sort of thing to which dynamic, material realities could stand in any real relation, or to which their dynamism could afford a positive inference. It is in fact not an existent object at all, but a mere form in which existent objects can be intuited, and which presents nothing at all when emptied of sensuous content (p. 364). Nor can it be saved by peopling it with material atoms, that is, indivisibles, since whatever occupies space must, like space, be indefinitely divisible. Space therefore must, in order to be an object of possible experience, and to have reality for us, be occupied throughout by an all-pervasive, all-penetrating world-stuff which is practically the same as space itself hypostatically conceived, as Kant candidly tells us (p. 365); a stuff which is the seat of its own moving forces, which will connect, and also separate, the moving forces of particular bodies:

We can acquire no information as to what is near us, or far from us, without presupposing the occupation of the space between both points, whether we have a sensation of it or not [p. 366] . . . In an occupied space there can be no change in position, only internal movement in the same spot. But experience none the less constantly shows us movements of bodies involving change of place. Body-building matter can therefore not be the stuff that fills space continuously. There must be, in addition to bodies endowed with locomotive power, and which consist of ordinary ponderable matter, separated by spaces void of such matter, a further sort of matter which fills space continuously, and is in perpetual agitation, to be a medium for the progression of bodies. It is not something hypothetically invented, but a real stuff shown through its powers, and providing a ground for the movements of bodies, whose existence is known *a priori*, since without it not the slightest motion could be given to us . . . The mere possibility of experience is quite sufficient, even by itself, to assure us of the reality of this stuff which pervades all space (p. 369).

But not only is this universal aether necessary to space: it is also necessary, in virtue of its perpetual agitation, to provide the pervasive filling of time. Kant says:

The mobile is mechanically moved in so far as it only moves on account of something-else's motion, but, in so far as it originates movement through its own power, it is dynamically moved. Mechanically caused motion is not originative, and moved matter requires other moving matter to incite it. Since, however, matter could only originate motion if we credited it with a spontaneity at variance with the notion of the moving powers of matter, and since to derive movement from prior movement would involve an infinite regress, dynamic principles can only lead to motion if they postulate a matter endlessly and beginninglessly moved and moving, which, endlessly divided, keeps all matter in motion (pp. 370–1).

The aether is thus postulated for Aristotelian reasons, as an eternal source of movement which makes temporal succession possible: it is, however, at once a mobile and a movent, and points to no unmoved first movent. We are therefore assured of the existence of 'an absolute, self-existent sum total of matter which, moved and moving by an intrinsic and original attraction and repulsion, is independent of mechanical moving forces, and must in consequence be thought of as the imponderable, incompressible, incohesible, inexhaustible, and all-penetrating basis of the elemental system of all dynamically moving forces. This, whether called thermal matter or aether, is no hypothetical stuff, used to explain phenomena, and therefore empirically grounded and not given *a priori*' (p. 372). There are also passages where Kant attempts to establish the *analytic* character of the postulation of the aether as involved in the very notion of moving matter. For, movement is self-contradictory in empty space, and is even impossible in occupied space, if there is not in the latter some perennially agitated and agitating matter.

Adickes comments critically on the resemblance of Kant's arguments for the aether to the cosmological and ontological arguments for the existence of God, which an earlier Kant had subjected to such drastic criticism. For the aether is not merely a regulative, but a constitutive conception, and its object not merely generic, but concrete and individual.

There is a certain resemblance: [Adickes says (p. 390)] between the aether-proofs and the cosmological and teleological theistic arguments that Kant attacked so energetically and victoriously, inasmuch as there is an inference from the general fact of motion as such, to a first mover (the aether), or from a qualitatively determinate fact (of the one, unified experience) to its external cause: the aether as a transsubjective stuff existing outside of the consciousness of the empirical self. But there are not a few twists in the aether-proofs which remind one of the ontological God-proof, especially when Kant operates with the law of identity and the principle of an *omnimoda determinatio*. In such places there is also an attempt in the aether-proof to build a bridge from pure thought to being, to deduce the necessary existence of an actual thing from pure concepts. And in the ontological as in the aether-proof, the things demonstrated are unique of their kind, the relevant concepts individual.

The resemblances may be acknowledged, but they do not involve so devastating an exposure as Adickes thinks. For God, or the *ens omnipossibile*, remains for Kant something that we have to conceive and believe in, even if we cannot, in Kant's special, technical sense, have *knowledge* of it. We may in fact say that the transcendental self, the system of Transcendental Objects, God, and the aether are alike in transcending what it has pleased Kant to call 'knowledge', yet are all alike necessary to the theory of the latter. The transcendental self no more guarantees the indefinite continuance of an ordered phenomenal world than do God, or the system of Things-in-themselves, or the aether, since all transcend ordinary, empirical discovery.

The aether is perhaps in a weaker position than the others, since it is little beyond an hypostatization of the possibility of motion in space, and the arguments for its existence are in many ways feeble. Had Kant been able to frame the modern physical conception of a non-homogeneous space-time, he would perhaps not have needed it.

But, though it very much resembles a purely regulative, Transcendental Idea, Kant certainly uses his aether to explain many empirical properties and performances of matter. He imagines that it eases the problems of gravitational attraction (p. 417). He connects it closely with the transmission of heat, and with the expansive and liquefying force of the latter (p. 453): aether and thermal matter (*Wärmestoff*) are in many passages not distinguished. It is also closely connected with the transmission of light, in regard to which Kant hovers between the wave-theory of Euler and the emission-theory of Newton (p. 464). The aether also does routine duty in respect to both electricity and magnetism, as it did for Schelling, whose ideas seem to have influenced Kant at the turn of the century, through the work of the physicist J. W. Ritter (p. 471). The table of categories is once more brought out to do duty in explaining 'the elemental system of the moving forces of matter': this amounts merely to the consideration of those forces from the four standpoints of quantity, quality, relation, and modality. As regards quantity, Kant tries to show that the variable ponderability of ordinary matter is throughout made possible by the invariant imponderability of the aether (p. 482). As regards quality, matter divides into the fluid and the solid, the former opposing no resistance to an internal shift in its parts, whereas the latter opposes an internal and a superficial shift (p. 484). The ever agitated, wholly fluid aether manages to promote the agitation and fluidity of one set of bodies, while, in the case of others, it isolates a hard core that resists such agitation. The spherical shape of drops of liquid, and the rise of fluids in capillary tubes, are unconvincingly explained by the action of the aether, and crystallization and freezing are likewise attributed to aetheric agitation. On all this theorizing Adickes remarks: 'From whatever side one may consider the matter, the result is the same. We have, under the heading of quality, to deal with matters that belong entirely to the region of natural science, to which the philosopher has nothing of his own to add, whether in concepts or deductions or methods' (p. 518). There was abundant empirical discussion of these matters in the time of Kant to which he seems to have been unfitted to make the smallest contribution. And, under the heading of relation, Kant considers cohesion, friction, and lustre, the last with some irrelevant beauty. But, under the heading of modality, he covers nothing significant apart from the perpetuity of the aether, and the absolute universality of its agitating activity.

iv

We pass finally to the consideration of the latest stratum of the *Opus Postumum*, the metaphysical-epistemological material to be found in the Seventh and the First Convolutes. Though it is not strictly a part of the philosophy of nature, which is the concern of this chapter, it is of immense importance as revealing Kant's final opinions regarding his three 'Transcendentals': the Transcendental Subject or percipient, thinking self, the Transcendental Object or Thing-in-itself, and the Transcendental Ideal of Pure Reason, the God in whom all objectivity and all subjectivity must be thought of as grounded. These Transcendentals assume a new importance in the final phase of his thought, but they are not so much considered as metaphysical realities of which we can know nothing, though Kant never changes his views on this aspect of them, but rather as necessary parts of the economy of self-conscious subjectivity, things in whose ambience we necessarily live, and move, and have our being. (This scriptural phrase is several times repeated by Kant.) In the Notes strung together in the First Convolute, the last ones jotted down by Kant after 1800, there is even a project of passing from the transitional science, on which he had up to that point been working, to a new, comprehensive version of transcendental philosophy, in which the Ideas of the subject, of the ordered world of Transcendental Objects, and of the supreme, necessary, all-grounding God would be given pride of place.

In Kant's last treatments of the transcendental self much use is made of Fichte's term 'positing' (*setzen*). The self is said to posit itself, and also to posit the not-self as set over against it. This term brings out the *active* role of the subject, its making of its objects, if not absolutely, then at least as being objects for itself, and also in the process, making itself its own object. These notions are not original to Fichte, but were garnered by him from many passages in Kant's critical writings. Kant was willing to take back his own concept of an essentially active 'putting there' of objects in the new clothing of the Fichtean term *setzen*, even if he was not willing to devote much time to the whole 'pack' of writings that Fichte had sent him, and which he had left half-read on the floor of his *Vorstube* (p. 606, N. 2). Kant takes the line, present in the Transcendental Deductions, where he had stressed that the thought of the 'I think' must be capable of accompanying all our presentations, that all awareness of anything, whether sensuous or conceptual, elemental or synthetic, must also be capable of mediating an awareness of the self which is the subject of such awareness. This self can itself be posited as an object, can be made its own object (pp. 629–30). This awareness is, as also taught in the first Critique, not to be regarded as the empirical discovery of some novel object, but as a unique transformation of the act of awareness itself: to be aware of anything implies that one can be aware of being aware of it. 'The presentative faculty', Kant puts it, 'proceeds from the consciousness of self (*apperceptio*), and this act is merely logical, an act of thinking by which no object is actually *given* to me. In the proposition "I am thinking" we have merely a non-progressive identity, not a synthetic judgement: it is a tautology, and the would-be syllogism "I think, therefore I am" is no syllogism at all' (pp. 631–2).

Kant goes on (Adickes points out) to distinguish four distinct ways in which the self can be conscious of itself as the owner and author (*Inhaber und Urheber*) of its own presentations: (1) it can be aware of itself in a purely logical manner, in that it posits a subject wherever it posits an object; (2) it can be aware of itself in its purely formal role (2a) of being the source of the intuitive forms of space and time, or (2b) as being the source of the various categorial forms of synthesis; (3) it can be aware of itself as positing (3a) all the distinct contents of sense-experience or (3b) as positing these contents systematically unified into empirical objects; (4) it can be aware of itself as positing a whole, ordered, empirical world (p. 633). We may here interject that it is more than odd that, in this enumeration of cases, neither Kant nor Adickes stress the activity which is most truly and absolutely subjective, the activity which is in an obvious sense personal and arbitrary, as when I group a number of arbitrarily selected items and consider them together, or as when the manner in which things connect with other things depends on my personal interest, attitude, habits, predilections, and so forth. These subjective linkages do not merely come before us as passive observers, are not mere data of inner sense: they are given as most essentially active, and as the most essentially *ours* of all our experiences. It is in Kant's blindness to the central importance of our sense of *this* sort of subjectivity that, as we have seen, his two Transcendental Deductions are largely a failure. For while self-consciousness accompanies the use of the categories, it equally accompanies the failure to use them or the abuse of them, and the transcendental self is as much implicated in *either* case as is the empirical self.

Adickes illustrates all these forms of self-consciousness with a variety of quotations, from which a few will suffice for our purposes. Most of them are very strange, and all suggest that the self-conscious subject has been thoroughly indoctrinated with Kantian transcendentalism, and that it sees itself as the transcendental source of spatio-temporal order, of categorial synthesis, and so on. The undoctrinated, ordinary subject would certainly not describe itself as positing spatio-temporal order, categorial connection, and so on, but rather as acknowledging and accepting them. Thus we read that 'space and time are primitive intuitions through which the subject affects itself *qua* appearance.' 'The subject which makes for itself the sensuous presentation of space and time becomes an object to itself in this act, is self-intuitive' (p. 635). 'The subject posits itself in pure space-relations and time-relations as pure (non-empirical) intuition' (p. 638). 'The subject posits itself through synthetic propositions *a priori*, through space and time, the forms of sensuous intuition, inasmuch as it exercises powers which affect itself and conditions itself to appearances' (p. 645). 'Space as an object is not intuited, but is the synthesis of the manifold in the presenting subject itself. In this sort of representation the subject constitutes itself' (p. 647). 'The receptivity of intuition in respect of its form, i.e. in appearance, and the spontaneity of the consciousness of synthesis in a concept (apprehension), are the acts of the synthetic *a priori* propositions of transcendental philosophy, through which the subject is given to itself as an appearance *a priori*, while the object (= X) is the Thing-in-itself.' The correlate of the thing in appearance is the Thing-in-itself, i.e. the subject, which I turn into an object' (p. 652). (The many unintelligibilities in the above passage are not the result of mistranslation.) 'The object-in-itself (the Noumenon) is a mere thing of thought, in whole presentation the subject posits itself' (p. 654). In all these remarkable passages, there is a sort of identification of the transcendental self with its work in setting objects before itself, and of intuiting and understanding them. In being aware of unified objects and a unified world and of an object beneath or beyond that world, it is, after a fashion, aware of itself as unifier. This doctrine is also, as we have seen, the much-lauded 'message' of the Transcendental Deductions. And it is not a message to be wholly rejected, provided we remember that the Transcendental Subject has other fish to fry *besides* recognizing objective connections — it may, for example, select and combine its materials in an entirely personal, arbitrary manner — and also that the subjection to rule which characterizes knowledge is as much the outcome of the humble, background operation of Things-in-themselves as of the act of the magisterial, synthesizing ego. *Both* factors render experience and knowledge possible, and were their co-operation to cease, which is not an entertainable supposition, experience and knowledge would alike lapse into the impossible.

The Thing-in-itself is then, in the Seventh Convolute, treated from a transcendental rather than a metaphysical point of view, as something that *we* posit as the ultimate background of appearances, rather than as something indubitably real and thinkable, though also quite unknowable. This transcendental, fictive point of view probably represents the influence of Fichte in the last phase of Kant's thought. In this phase the Thing-in-itself becomes a mere alias for the synthetic unity of apprehension: it amounts to the *form* of objective unity without any content to fill it, and is accordingly a mere *ens rationis*, rather than a genuine object. Kant says: 'The distinction between the so-called object-in-itself, as opposed to the object-in-appearance (*phaenomenon adversus noumenon*) does not mean an actual thing which stands over against the object of the senses, but is, as = X, nothing beyond the principle, that the determining ground of the possibility of experience is contained in nothing empirical' (p. 670). Or again: 'Not empirical intuition with perceptual consciousness, but the pure intuition of the formal side of the synthesis according to a principle or rule, is the Thing-in-itself, an *ens rationis*, which precedes everything material in the object, and is subjectively the ground of its appearance. The object, = X, the *dabile*, presupposes the unity of the synthesis of the manifold in respect of its form (the *cogitabile*), as the formal principle of the phenomenal object that it underlies. The Thing-in-itself is an *ens rationis'* (pp. 671–2).

The tendency of these jottings, and of countless like them, is not obscure. They emphasize, as Adickes says (pp. 676–7), that 'the Thing-in-itself must declare its bankruptcy in this purely epistemological problem from which everything transcendent has to be excluded. Its place is taken by its epistemological surrogate or *Döppelgänger*, the Transcendental Object, which does not, however, come into question as a transcendent reality, but can only fill the role of a thought, and must immediately hand over its synthetic functions to the Transcendental Unity of Apperception . . . The X of the Transcendental Object only points out that the ground of unity of the possibility of experience must be sought in nothing empirical, but, for the rest, the transcendent must be wholly replaced by the transcendental.' Adickes, however, refuses to accept the idealistic trend of the passages we have quoted, and attributes them to the *epistemological* orientation of Kant's writings at this period: 'For the theory of knowledge . . . Things-in-themselves are necessarily mere things of thought, regarding which it is wholly unclear whether any real existence-in-itself corresponds to them. And, especially in discussion of the transcendental presuppositions of experience, their function passes over entirely to the unity of pure apperception. But all such concessions leave the *man* Kant quite untouched, with his firm belief in the real being of a plurality of Things-in-themselves affecting us' (p. 679). It must, however, be conceded that the idealistic slide from the unknowable to the merely supposititious has always been an Achilles' heel in Kantianism, and it is undoubtedly possible that, in the decline of his originality, and in the face of the innovations of Fichte, it may have made itself felt. Yet, it must be remembered that, even in these last slides, Kant never doubts the reality of the unknowable subject which affects itself through a variety of outer and inner appearances. This unknowable subject is itself a Thing-in-itself, and to be prepared to posit it, is also to be prepared to posit all the other Things-in-themselves which, by their unknowable affinity, render phenomena associable, and enable the subject-in-itself, and its phenomenal representative, to conduct their synthetic activities. Kant himself sums up his view at this time in the sentence: 'The Thing-in-itself which corresponds to a thing-in-appearance is a mere thing of thought, but not for that reason a nonentity (*Unding*)' (p. 693).

Adickes dwells at some length on the glee with which the idealists A. Drews and H. Vaihinger greeted the discovery of these Fichtean declensions in the latest work of Kant. Drews interpreted the spontaneity of the subject as responsible for everything in experience, including its sensory content: nothing can come to the subject from without, but all must emerge from its interior depths. And Hans Vaihinger, the greatest of Kantian commentators, who had done so much to stress the problematic realism of Kantianism, came, in his later interpretations, to see Kant's last utterances as an anticipation of the fictionalism or as-if philosophy into which he had himself advanced or declined: 'The division into appearances and Things-in-themselves is a mere standpoint, or point of view, merely subjective, ideal, scientific — only therefore an heuristic fiction for purposes of treatment. The Thing-in-itself is clearly and unambiguously recognized and acknowledged by Kant to be a fiction, a useful and necessary way of treating things by our reason, a product of consciously fictitious abstraction' (p. 710). These statements are all plainly exaggerated. The Thing-in-itself *can* be seen as a heuristic fiction, it *does* correspond to the search for an objective source of the unity the mind seeks in experience, but nothing makes it in any way credible that Kant departed from his belief in a real source for the unity and affinity of appearances in the transcendent Thing-in-itself, as also in the transcendent subject whose essential nature it is to go in quest of such unity, and to find it wherever it is to be found. Nor need we deal with other fictionalistic interpretations of the Thing-in-itself that are to be found, for example, in the later phenomenology of Husserl, or in the writings of those Anglo-Saxon interpreters of Kant who have identified his special use of the terms 'meaning' and 'sense', which does not reject the reality of what lacks such sense or meaning, with the limited verificationistic and criteriological uses of the same terms.

In the First Convolute, which there is reason to hold contains the very last set of Kantian jottings, all produced after 1800, there are few additions to the treatment of self-positing and object-positing in the Seventh Convolute. What is novel is the stress on a new transcendental science, concerned mainly with the relations of God and the world, and with man and his freedom as the connecting link between them. There is also great stress on the conclusions of the moral theology, which will concern us in the next chapter. The three Transcendental Ideas are not to be treated as transcendental illusions, as they were in the Transcendental Dialectic, but as necessarily posited by the thinking and willing subject, and posited as a systematic whole. 'God above me, the world outside me, and the free will in me, presented in one system' is the programme of C. 341 (p. 725). Many titles were devised for the new systematic work in which the Transition to Physics was to be absorbed, for example, *Die reine Philosophie in der Vollständigkeit ihres Systems dargestellt*, and *System der reinen Philosophie in dem Ganzen ihrer Prinzipien aufgestellt*. One projected title even brought in the name of Zoroaster, which a work of Anquetil du Perron, translated by J. F. Kleuker, had made popular: *Zoroaster or Philosophy in the Sum Total of its Content unified under a single Principle* (p. 728). But, though God, the world, and the free individual person are to be treated as necessary structures in the new transcendental system, they are to be treated as structures necessary *for* the human spirit, and not in any sense in and for themselves. Transcendental philosophy, in fact, must concern itself solely with the human spirit (p. 743). Thus Kant tells us (p. 761) that 'Ideas are prime images (intuitions) created by reason which, as purely subjective things of thought, precede our knowledge of things and the elements of the latter: they are the prototypes according to which Spinoza thought that all things must be seen in God.' And again: 'The sum total of all beings (the universe) is God and the world. Neither are objects of possible experience, but are Ideas, self-created *a priori* things of thought (*entia rationis*), and include principles of the systematic unity of the thought of objects. We see all objects (according to Spinoza) in God: we can just as well say that, as regards their reality, they must be encountered in the world' (p. 761). The attribution of these transcendental notions to Spinoza is sometimes varied by an attribution to Malebranche: together with Zoroaster, they occupy a central place in the gathering mysticism of this last period in Kant's thought. Lichtenberg, a Professor of Physics at Göttingen, who embraced many Spinozistic and Kantian opinions, is also often cited. And the humanistic emphasis is sometimes varied by a theistic emphasis: it is not merely the subject that constitutes itself in the system of Transcendental Ideas, but God, the most basic of those Ideas, that gets constituted in them. God is declared to constitute Himself *a priori* and as a person, to be the supreme being, supreme intelligence, and supreme good, and even interestingly, to be incomprehensible to Himself (p. 766). Man, in these perspectives, is seen predominantly in moral terms, in the free personality which makes him a moral agent. But God, in relation to man, becomes practically the same as the moral law within man: to recognize the moral imperatives and to affirm the divine existence are, transcendentally speaking, the same thing (p. 779). 'There is', Kant says, 'only one practically sufficient argument for belief in one God, which is theoretically insufficient: the knowledge of all human duties as if they were divine commands' (p. 780). Adickes rightly points out, however, that while, transcendentally speaking, belief in the divine existence does not differ from unconditional deference to the moral law, this does not affect the fact that there *is* such a transcendent existence, and that we cannot treat it as a mere fiction designed to give extra strength to the demands of morality (p. 782). Kant was a very subtle thinker, not unable to reconcile a transcendental as if with a transcendent being the case, which, being transcendent, also transcends knowledge. It is in fact only as if God were speaking to us in the moral law, because He does exist, and is actually speaking to us. Adickes further points out how, for Kant, the removal of God's existence beyond the pale of verifiable knowledge, represents a purification of morality. His existence is not the sort of thing that can be proved by any intuition stemming from without, but solely through the action of a will moving us from within.

We may, in conclusion, say that, while many of the utterances of the *Opus Postumum* suggest some scepticism as to the reality of objects which transcend possible experience, and have seemed to justify some sort of conscious fictionalism, the main drift of even this latest work does not differ from that of Kant's earlier writings. We can only understand the possibility of theoretical knowledge and moral experience by postulating the existence of entities which transcend the possibility of knowledge and experience. We do not err in such postulations: we only err if we think them to be cases of knowledge.

v

Our treatment of Kant's philosophy of nature requires to be filled out by a consideration of his doctrine of organic teleology, a theme dealt with in the second part of the *Critique of Judgement*. In this work organic teleology is treated from the standpoint of a peculiar sort of judgement, the judgement of reflection. This is distinguished from the more ordinary judgement, which definitely *determines* an object by ranging it under a concept which it plainly satisfies. A determining judgement can be a case of knowledge or error according as some spatio-temporal intuition or sensuous experience verifies or refutes it, but a judgement of reflection can be neither: it is a way of looking at objects, of finding a concept which problematically makes sense of them, without excluding alternative ways of regarding them. It is nothing that can be verified or refuted by a pure or empirical intuition, but which requires a quite different, more subjective sort of justification. Kant also sees a field for such reflective judgements in the realm of aesthetics, where it is as if some sensuously presented object had been specially constructed to make our apprehension of its structure easy and delightful: the judgement of taste sees an object as fitting our cognitive faculties, and everyone's cognitive faculties, in this manner, without thereby claiming to know how this is so. We shall study Kant's doctrine regarding this sort of reflective judgement in a later chapter. The reflective judgement of teleology, a whit more objective in its orientation, sees an object as filling not our own cognitive purposes in apprehending it, but a set of purposes of *its* own, which in some fashion make it what it is, and behave as it does behave. Both kinds of reflective judgement are, however, quite without knowledge-status: the sort of connection which they predicate can at best find a place in the supersensible foundations of experience and knowledge.

Judgement, Kant says, in a particularly involved passage (*CrJ*, IV (Introduction))

is the capacity to think of the particular as contained under the universal. If the universal (the rule, the principle, the law) is given, then the power of judgement which subsumes the particular under it, is a determining one . . . But, if only the particular is given, for which a universal is to be found, the power of judgement is purely reflective. Determining judgement under universal, transcendental laws given by the understanding, is merely subsumptive. The law is prescribed to it *a priori* and it does not have to think out a law by itself, in order to subordinate what is particular in nature under what is universal. But there are many natural forms, many modifications, as it were, of universal, transcendental nature-concepts that are left undetermined by the laws which the pure understanding gives us *a priori*, since these laws only concern the general possibility of nature as an object of the senses. There must therefore also be laws which, though, *qua* empirical, they must seem contingent to the understanding's insight, must yet, being laws that the concept of nature demands, be seen as deriving their necessity from some principle of the unity of the manifold of which we have no knowledge.

In other words, while objects in nature necessarily obey such principles as the permanence of substance and the subordination to causal law, which our understanding *cannot* question, they must also obey principles of a more specific character, that our understanding can indeed question, but which it must none the less follow if it is to be able to find its way through the rich variety of experience. Experience must, in short, be taken to be accommodated to the degree of complex interdependence that our understanding finds tolerable, and 'the particular empirical laws, in respect of what in them is left undetermined by universal laws, must be regarded as conforming to such a unity as an understanding (not of course our own) could have given them so as to meet the needs of our cognitive faculties, and to make an empirical system, governed by specific natural laws, possible for the latter' (IV). We must accordingly accept a transcendental, teleological principle of the accommodation of natural variety to our degree of intelligence (V), a principle irremediably vague, and lacking in *a priori* warrant, but which may none the less be backed up by experience in varying degrees. Under this general principle many subordinate principles will be ranged, among which that of organic teleology will be one.

Kant points out, further, that every discovered accommodation of empirical variety to the requirements of our understanding must be accompanied by pleasure, the more so since there is felt to be something gratuitous, contingent about such an accommodation (VI). This occurs when the accommodation is merely aesthetic, when something given in sense-experience only *seems* to be well adjusted to our cognitive powers, though there may actually be no definite concept to which it is thus well adjusted (VII). It also occurs when teleology is attributed to some object or arrangement in nature, when various parts or functions of an object are conceived as adjusted to one another, precisely as if their mutual adjustment had been designed or planned by some intelligence, of which, however, there is no direct sign (VI). Kant points out, further, how the reflective judgement, with its tentative employment of ordering principles that are only imperfectly illustrated in experience, in a way mediates between the understanding, which confidently applies principles without which experience would be impossible, and the pure reason whose Ideas necessarily transcend experience. The understanding can frame no determinate concepts of the noumenal realities which transcend experience; pure reason can only respond to them practically; but the reflective judgement can grope towards them by looking for empirical harmonies and simplicities that seem to betray their unifying presence. As Kant puts it: 'Understanding establishes, through the possibility of its *a priori* legislation for nature, that nature is only known to us as an appearance, pointing, however, to a supersensible substrate, which it leaves wholly *indeterminate*. The faculty of judgement, through the *a priori* principles by which it judges nature in terms of possible particular laws, gives to nature's supersensible substrate, whether outside of us or within us, a certain *determinability through our intellectual capacities*' (IX). This passage is interesting as showing the confidence with which Kant is willing to apply concepts to the 'supersensible substrate' of phenomena, whether within us or without us, even if he does not allow that such application can ever amount to knowledge.

In his subsequent, more detailed treatments of teleology (§§61–91), Kant leads up to true, organic teleology by a number of cases that only foreshadow it. There is, he holds, a curious, quasi-teleology in a constructive discipline like geometry, where there seems to be a surprising fertility and felicity in a constructive concept such as that of the circle, which has a vast number of surprising properties, and which permits a vast number of remarkable inferences (§62). But this adjustment of the circle to our intuitive and intellectual faculties is not a true case of teleology, since the nature of our intuition of space renders it wholly necessary, and removes all surprise. There is likewise in nature a case of relative teleology which is a mere case of causality: we treat a consequence of certain natural conditions as if it were a goal towards which they were tending. Thus, it is natural to treat the deposit of silt by rivers as directed to the vegetable growth that it favours, and the latter as directed towards the nourishment of animals, that in their turn nourish further animals, and ultimately man. This sort of naïve anthropocentricism is not, however, in default of some metaphysical or transcendental proof of man's teleological centrality, a true case of teleology. It is merely an arbitrary, human way of looking at things.

A true case of teleology is only present when the organization of some object does not seem possible, at least prima facie, in terms of the working of ordinary causal rules, and so impels us to think in terms of a rational, goal-directed will, or in terms of something which bears some analogy to the latter. The former would be the case if we found a neatly outlined geometrical figure on the sands of a seemingly unpeopled island, but the latter arises in the case of living objects, for example, a growing tree. Such living objects seem to obey other than ordinary causal rules in three remarkable respects. It seems true, in their case, that they are in a manner self-caused, since they spring from individuals of precisely the same specific form as they are. 'A tree begets another tree according to a well-known law of nature. But the tree that it begets is of the same kind, and so it begets itself, generically speaking, in that it is continually being brought forth as effect from itself as cause, and so preserves itself generically' (§64). But a tree is also always re-creating itself individually, a proceeding we call growing, but which differs entirely from any other form of increase in size, since the same total pattern is preserved in the increase. And a tree is, thirdly, such that the preservation of any one of its parts depends on the preservation of all the others. 'I shall only refer in passing', Kant says, 'to the self-help of nature when such creatures are maimed, when the lack of a part necessary to the preservation of neighbouring parts is made up for by the others, and also to the abortions and malformations in growth due to defects and hindrances, which lead certain parts to form themselves in quite new ways, so as to preserve what is there, and (not) give rise to anomalous results: these are, however, among the most wonderful properties of organized creatures' (§64). Kant points out that, in such organic phenomena, there is also a curious reciprocity of cause and effect: the effect, a final outcome, is in a sense the cause of the whole development; the parts, which by their interaction produce the whole, are also in a sense produced and sustained by that whole; and each part is in a sense both the cause and the effect of every other (§65). This last property yields, in fact, a good definition of an organized product of nature: it is one in which everything is both end, and also means, to everything else (§66).

This defining concept, Kant points out, sharply differentiates organic structures from mechanically constituted things: they have to be thought of as springing from a single organizing principle, to which ordinary causation is subservient. But, Kant argues, to admit such a unifying principle into the interpretation of nature leads to the demand that it should apply *universally*, and not piecemeal. For there is no way of introducing piecemeal intrusions of teleology into a mechanical system of causation:

This teleological concept leads reason to quite a different ordering of things from a mere mechanism of nature, which will no longer satisfy us. An Idea must underlie the possibility of a nature-product. But this involves the absolute unity of a presentation, while matter is a plurality of things, which will not provide us with a determinate unity for their coming together. If this unity of Idea is to serve as an *a priori* ground of determination for the causality of such a form of coming together, nature's teleology must extend to *everything* that she produces. For once we refer such a total effect to a supersensuous determining ground, beyond the blind mechanisms of nature, we must judge of all of them according to this principle. There is no occasion to make the form of such a thing only partially depend on such a principle, for the mixture of unlike principles would then leave us with no certain rules of judgement (§66).

In other words, Kant is arguing that, if mechanism is ever subordinated to teleology, then it cannot be a chance matter that it is so subordinated, but that there must be a basic law which determines when, where, and how mechanical causation yields to teleological determination. To hold this is to subordinate the *whole* realm of mechanical causation to the higher realm of teleological causation, since a teleological system that was wholly subordinate to mechanical causation would not really be teleological at all. We therefore pass to the universal teleological maxim: 'Everything in the world is good for something, and nothing in the world occurs vainly: the example which nature gives us in her organic products justifies us, in fact compels us, to expect nothing of her, and of her laws, but what is in its totality purposive' (§67).

The astonishing extension of teleology from organic products to the whole of the natural world, leads, however, to a basic antinomy, which Kant deals with in the second, 'dialectical' section of the Critique of Teleological Judgement (§§69–78). Here there is a first maxim, which asserts that all production of material things must be judged possible according to purely mechanical laws, which is opposed by a second maxim, which asserts that some products of material nature cannot be judged possible according to purely mechanical laws: their possibility seems to require quite another law of causality, that of final causes (§70). If these maxims are turned into objective, constitutive principles, their conflict becomes even more crass. And, as we have seen, Kant holds that we cannot hold *some* natural products to be subject to teleological causation, without holding this to be true of *all* natural products, which makes the conflict yet more extreme. Kant resolves his antinomy by pointing out that a principle for reflective judgement is not a principle for constitutive, determining judgement:

If I say that I must judge of the possibility of all events in material nature, and so of all forms which are their product, according to purely mechanical laws, I am not thereby saying that it is only on this basis, and exclusive of other forms of causality, that they are possible, but only that I must always *reflect* on such forms according to a principle of pure mechanism in nature, and investigate nature on this principle, as far as I can, since without it there can be no genuine natural knowledge. This does not hinder my occasional use of the second maxim in the case of certain natural forms (and, on their suggestion, in regard to the whole of Nature), and my investigating them, and reflecting on them, according to a principle which differs entirely from explanation through natural mechanisms, the principle namely of final causes (§70).

This purely pragmatic solution is not, however, one that Kant is, in the end, able to stomach, and he feels forced to accept a noumenal basis for the teleological view of the world, while giving the mechanical view universal application in the realm of phenomena. The same system of things which, in themselves, are teleologically ordered, and would be given as such to an intuitive intelligence, may also, *qua* appearances, be subject to a rigorous regime of mechanical causation. We can always discover the mechanical linkages which bind phenomenal things to one another, but we cannot see, or divine, except in a few, privileged cases, the purposes which lie behind them. It may, from our phenomenally bound, yet noumenally thinking standpoint, Kant holds, 'be left undecided, whether physical mechanism and teleological connection may not throughout inhere in the same things according to a single principle in the unknown inner ground of nature, even if our understanding cannot unite them under such a principle, and our power of judgement, acting reflectively and subjectively, and not in obedience to an objective principle of ontological possibility, must accordingly employ a principle other than that of natural mechanism in explaining the possibility of certain natural forms' (§70). It seems plain that, if occasionalistic interference is to be avoided, a teleological system can only be harmonized with a system of rigorous mechanism, if either the former is a mere appearance or epiphenomenon of the latter, a possibility which Kant does not seriously consider, or if the latter is a mere ephiphenomenon or appearance of the former. But thoroughgoing teleology will have to operate out of time, or, metaphorically, before all time, if it is to be able to use mechanism in time for the fulfilment of its purposes. It must, in short, have devised the whole mechanistic scenario, into which its special acts are cast, and so have no need to disarrange anything. We have, that is, all freely chosen roles in a drama whose developments are at all points predictable. But, that the world fails to reveal the sustaining purpose behind it will be yet another, conclusive proof of its purely phenomenal character.

The Dialectic of Teleological Judgement is followed by a long, wordy, and very repetitive Appendix (§§79-91), which explores the metaphysical, ethical, and theological consequences of envisaging natural teleology. The possibility of uniting teleology with mechanism, cannot be achieved at the phenomenal level: we have to think in terms of the supersensuous substrate of nature, where the same phenomena, superficially ordered by a system of mechanical laws, are also the expression of a deeper system of organizing purposes. Such a system of purposes must be woven around a single, unifying purpose, and no such unifying purpose is to be found in phenomenal nature, even though countless organized things make use of other organized things in the fulfilment of their purposes. It is here, however, that practical reason, with its unconditioned moral imperatives (that we shall consider in the next chapter) rescues us from the impasse: man as subject to the moral law has an unconditioned, absolute end in the fulfilment of that law; and it is, as directed to such fulfilment, that, not only all human existence and conduct, but also all natural existences and developments must be thought of by us. Such explanation necessarily takes us beyond everything phenomenal: it is at the moral perfection of *homo noumenon* that everything in the natural world must be thought of as aiming. As Kant puts it (§84):

We have only one sort of beings in the world whose causality must be thought of as teleological, i.e. as directed to ends, and which are such that the laws by which they have to fix their ends, are thought of as determined unconditionally by themselves, and independently of all natural conditions, intrinsically and yet necessarily. A being of this sort is man, treated, however, as a Noumenon, the only being in nature in which we can recognize, as part of its intrinsic character, the supersensuous faculty of freedom, and, together with this, the law of a causality, i.e. freedom, and the object which that causality is able to set before itself as its highest aim, and the highest good in the world.

Man's moral willing is *his* supreme, necessary aim, but it is also the aim of the whole of the rest of creation, which exists only, through varying means, to make such moral willing possible. It is a judgement which the meanest understanding cannot avoid, when it reflects on the existence of the things in the world, and on the existence of the world itself: that all its manifold creatures, however artfully put together, and with whatever multifarious, purposively interrelated contrivances, and even the whole which consists of so many sub-systems, which are wrongly called 'worlds', would exist to no purpose if it did not contain men (that is, rational beings as such). Without men the whole creation would be a mere desert, existing in vain and without a final goal. And to moral willing as the supreme goal of creation must be added the happiness or blessedness which men only deserve as a result of such moral willing.

The possibility of achieving this morality, and this blessedness, depends, however, on the existence of a being who at once exemplifies the perfection of moral willing, which we imperfectly exemplify, and which has also the power to ensure that both blessedness and moral progress are possible; the latter of course involving the indefinitely continued existence of the rational person, through many worlds and states of being, until full perfection is achieved. We cannot of course know anything about the transcendent objects in which the absolute teleology of morality make us believe, and we cannot even form opinions (*Meinungen*) regarding them, in the ordinary sense of 'opinions'. We can only have faith or belief (*Glaube*) regarding them, this being the moral mode of thought, which accepts as true what is inaccessible to theoretical knowledge. These passages make it very plain that Kant believes in a thought and a faith that are necessary to our understanding of the teleological aspects of the world, both in their moral and non-moral aspects, but which entirely transcend the possibility of this-world experience.

We may, in conclusion, note that Kant's theory of teleology is to some extent more transcendental than it need be. For he assumes that teleology must stem from a Transcendental Subject, and must exemplify the transcendental concept of freedom. In our own times, however, teleology and teleonomy have been given meanings that are purely phenomenalistic and naturalistic: we can define the teleological behaviour of rats in terms of varied effort till a given outcome is realized, of persistence in lines of behaviour that result in such an outcome, and abandonment of lines of behaviour that fail to achieve it, and so on. And such phenomenalistic teleology evinces itself in the inner life of the mind as well as in external behaviour. The integration of such teleology with mechanistic causation will, however, necessarily raise problems, and we shall arguably have to choose between making teleology a mere epiphenomenon of certain complex cases of mechanism, or follow Kant in making all mechanism something merely instrumental in the working out of teleology. Kant is further right in holding that a thoroughgoing teleology will involve something like a Leibnizian pre-established harmony, the pre-establishment being placed out of time altogether. A providential world-order — and this necessity applies to impersonal, oriental doctrines of Dharma and Karma, as much as to the personalistic theism of the Judaeo-Christian-Islamic tradition — can only be comprehensive if it is imposed out of time altogether upon all the events that take place successively in time. A world in which time is fully real, is also necessarily a world in which external interference, the essence of the unpurposeful, is always possible. Only in a world whose deepest roots are timeless, can everything have a perfect teleological adjustment to everything else.

Chapter IX

Kant's Metaphysic of Morals and Religion

i

We now approach what is perhaps the most important part of Kant's thought from the standpoint of transcendental objectivity: his doctrine of practical reason, with its three postulates of freedom, God, and immortality, all of which absolutely assure us of the real existence of objects which transcend possible experience, and of which the first is even said, in a number of passages, to provide us with actual knowledge of such existence. It is in fact arguable that, in his doctrine of the will, Kant has moved some way towards the doctrine afterwards taught by Schopenhauer: that in the experience of volition we, as it were, break through the crust of phenomenal knowledge, and achieve some sort of a direct contact with noumenal activity, even though such a deliverance cannot be incorporated in the fabric of phenomenal knowledge. And it is further arguable that, in the direct experience of volitional spontaneity, and of the passive affection by objects that provides its necessary foil, we have the primeval experiences of causality for which regularity of succession is only the surrogate. The necessary being of God and the imperishable being of the soul, are, however, never taken by Kant to be cases of knowledge, only of conception and practical belief. And, at an even less perspicuous level, we have the experience of the beautiful, where our distinterested joy in some appearance to the senses, is reflectively judged, though not necessarily believed, to stem from some transcendent adaptation of objectivity to our cognitive faculties. We shall, in the present chapter and the next, consider the knowledge, the belief, and the reflective judgement which are the necessary expression of the volitional and affective side of our nature; the deep dynamism of that nature seems in a position to throw more light on the other deep sources of phenomena than is available to purely speculative reason.

The works in which these problematic extensions of phenomenal knowledge are introduced by Kant are, in the first place, the much studied in isolation, and so much misunderstood, *Foundations of the Metaphysic of Morals* (*Grundlegung zur Metaphysik der Sitten*) of 1785; the lengthier and wordier, but much less penetrating *Critique of Practical Reason* of 1788; and the little considered *Metaphysic of Morals* of 1797, which shows us how Kant actually applied his principles to the detail of practice, an application in regard to which many commentators have preferred to use their own imaginations. To these works must be added the *Religion within the Bounds of Mere Reason* of 1792–3, which is all-important in its emphasis on the elective side of the will, which enables it to deviate from, as well as to obey, its own intrinsic moral laws. This aspect of the will is certainly presupposed in the earlier writings, but not half so clearly brought out. The treatment of beauty, and the as-if judgements it involves, were of course worked out in the *Critique of Judgement* of 1790, whose second part, the treatment of the as-if judgements of organic teleology, were a theme of our last chapter.

Kant's *Foundations* (*Grundlegung*) *of the Metaphysic of Morals* (henceforth simply called *Grundlegung*) starts by arguing for the unconditioned goodness of good willing; all other forms of goodness, of which Kant admits many, having the good will as their necessary precondition. Goodness of will is, however, a concept greatly in need of elucidation, and this requires that we should study the Kantian concept of the will, which the *Grundlegung* rather presupposes than circumscribes, and which has to be pieced together from what he says in many places. Perhaps Kant's most carefully comprehensive attempt to articulate the factors which enter into the constitution of a will is to be found in the Introduction to the *Metaphysic of Morals* of 1797, where Kant places the will in relation to desire, feeling, inclination, motive, law, maxim, obligation, and so on, and also points to various important aspects or functions that can be distinguished in it. What he says in this work is much clearer than what he has said in earlier writings, but, once grasped, its distinctions can be readily seen to be at work in his earlier writings also.

Will, for Kant, is a very special case of desire (*Begierde, Begehren*) and desire is, *qua* faculty, defined as the power to be the cause of the object of a presentation (*Vorstellung*) through that very presentation (*Metaphysic of Morals*, 1797, p. 211). Desire is therefore bound up both with consciousness and with causal efficacy: we are aware of what we desire, and our awareness is in some manner an exercise of an efficacy or a productivity, which *can* result in the realization of what we desire, though of course it does not always do so. It seems plain that Kant — though he does not spell the matter out — does not wish the actively causal aspect of desire to be the mere outcome of experienced regularity, of phenomenal succession *à la* Hume, though of course experience will reinforce it. And just as our primitive sense of being passively 'affected' by unknown things beyond ourselves is not, for Kant, based on experiences or inferences; so our sense of ourselves actively bringing something about, or at least trying to do so, is something not based on experiences or on inferences, but is simply a character distinguishing conscious states which involve desire from such as are, by contrast, purely cognitive. Desire can, however, be of two sorts, according as it is, on the one hand, an effect aroused by the purely contingent pleasure or displeasure which originally attends or attended upon some presentation of sense; or according, on the other hand, as it springs purely from some concept, without any source in a contingent, sensuous pleasure, though it might very well, if satisfied, give rise to a pure pleasure of its own. Desires of these two sorts are by Kant called sensible or pathological (on the one hand), and non-sensible (*sinnenfreie*) or rational (on the other); while the same terms may also be applied to the corresponding habitual trends of consciousness, the *Neigungen* or inclinations, and the interests in which those *Neigungen* have been made subject to a general rule. There are then sensuous, pathological desires, inclinations, and interests, and non-sensuous, non-pathological, rational desires, inclinations, and interests; the former having their origin in what, when presented to sense, we *happen* to find pleasing or the reverse; while the latter have their origin in pure concepts or notions, whose satisfaction or dissatisfaction may of course occasion pleasure or displeasure.

From desire or interest we proceed to the will, a form of rational desire characterized both by an elective or executive aspect, to which Kant applies the term *Willkür*, and a legislative aspect, to which the general term *Wille* is appropriate. The term *Willkür* is prominent in Kant's later ethical writings, and is clearly distinguished from the legislative *Wille*, but parallel distinctions are certainly to be found in earlier writings. The distinction is, briefly, that between the general principles or policies involved in voluntary causation, which are the preserve of the *general*, legislative *Wille*, and the ability to decide either to implement, or not to implement, these in practice, which are the field of the elective, executive *Willkür*. Rationality, in practice as much as in theory, is a faculty of operating according to rules: if we determine the natures of substances or the regularities of their interactions according to rules, so do we likewise determine what we shall do or not do in terms of rules. These rules may, in the practical case, be purely subjective and personal, and may depend on the desires, inclinations, and interests of the individual person: they may be compared to the purely empirical rules of the natural scientist which adjust categories and analogies of experience to empirical material. Such personal, subjective rules are called by Kant 'maxims', an unfelicitous term in English with its many suggestions of *belles lettres*. Thus a man's rational choices may be governed by the maxim that one should always break a promise if its keeping would damage one's own long-term interests. But, just as empirical laws are only particular applications of *a priori* principles, such as the permanence of substance, to the actual detail of experience, so our maxims should be subordinated to *a priori* moral laws which apply whatever the special interests of the agents and patients involved, and which it is the business of the moral philosopher to excogitate.

Kant emphasizes that these moral laws, analogously to their speculative counterparts, must have detailed application to the facts of the case and to the particularities of human interest: the metaphysic of morals is mainly concerned with such applications. He also stresses that these moral laws must have a more general application to the empirical nature of man, without any detraction from their *a priori* purity:

Just as, in a metaphysic of nature, there must be principles for the application of the supreme principles of a nature in general to the objects of experience, so a metaphysic of morals cannot omit such principles, and we shall often have to take as our object the particular nature of man that is only known through experience, to show in its case the consequences of universal moral principles, without thereby taking away from the purity of the latter, or casting doubt on their *a priori* origin. This means to say that, while a metaphysic of morals cannot be founded on an anthropology, it can very well be applied to the latter (pp. 216–17).

The *a priori* laws of practical reason therefore govern the actions and choices of *all* rational beings, whatever their natures, however much it may be *our* task to apply them to the specificities and individualities of *human* nature and interest. It is important, also, to stress at this point that practical reason *is* practical: it is not some sort of a theoretical faculty which determines by transcendental reflection what a purely rational being must will. Such a transcendental determination of the *a priori* direction of volition is the prerogative of the moral philosopher, not of the moral agent. Practical reason is prescriptive, not theoretically axiomatic or deductive: its utterances are framed in the imperative, and not in the declarative mood. It is, in fact, *identical* with the legislative will (see, for example, p. 213) and not with any intellectual discovery of the principles which actuate and govern it.

The will has, however, another aspect beside the legislative: it is also elective, capable of *Willkür* or *arbitrium*, capable, that is, of particularizing its essential laws so as to fit the detail of fact and interest. This *Willkür* or *arbitrium* is for Kant of two fundamental sorts. It may, on the one hand, be such that nothing external to itself determines it to act in a manner which in any way deviates from its fundamental legislative norms: it may, no doubt, particularize these creatively in various permitted directions, but it can have no tendency to transgress them. Such a *Willkür*, which remains absolutely within the bounds of its own basic legislation, is the elective side of an entirely pure or holy will, such as God's will presumably is. But there is also, plainly, a second sort of *Willkür*, which we regretfully recognize as our own, which is subject to driving desires (*Triebfeder*), which impel it in directions falling outside of its own legislative principles; and it may, unlike entities in nature, fail to implement its own inherent laws, a situation that we cannot understand, but of which we have abundant empirical evidence, both in ourselves and others. Only the deepest penetration into the noumenal foundations of action could, in fact, show how such a deviation is possible; the decision, for example, to tell a malicious lie on a certain occasion in time, must have been taken out of time altogether (see, e.g., *CPR*, A. 554). Kant is, however, unwilling to let us *define* the elective aspect of the will by its capacity to act indifferently for or against its own law, since *not* to implement that law is an incapacity (*Unvermögen*), rather than a capacity (*Met. of Morals*, p. 227). But calling it an incapacity does not mean that it is not a genuine, if defective, expression of our

Willkür or *arbitrium*; if it were not, and we were simply *unable* to follow the law, there would be no *Zurechnung* or imputability in our disobedience, and no consequent blame or demerit. Our capacity to deviate from our own *a priori* laws is, however, the foundation for a profound difference between *our* relation to those laws and the relation to them of a pure and undeviating will. For us these laws often present an aspect of quasi-external necessitation or compulsion, which is what we know as obligation (*Verbindlichkeit*) or duty (*Pflicht*): we are capable, when our contingent inclinations are involved, of kicking against the pricks of the law. For a holy will no such possibility obtains: the containment of its *Willkür* is necessary in another, non-practical sense (p. 223). The holy will necessarily implements the law, and is not constrained by duty to implement it.

The distinction between the legislative and elective aspects of the will has a further relevance for Kant's concept of freedom. For the legislative aspect of the will, freedom is its essential immunity from any contingent, *a posteriori* interest. For the elective aspect, it is its essential power, not always for some mysterious reason exercised, to implement *a priori* laws in practice. The two senses of freedom obviously have the deepest mutual coherence, and represent the same basic power in two different contexts — in one case unaffected by external impulsions, in the other case, able to triumph over all such impulsions — and are therefore rightly referred to by a single word. The terms 'legislative freedom' and 'elective freedom' would, however, have helped to stress what distinguishes them.

The remarkable Introduction to the *Metaphysic of Morals* (1797) contains a wealth of further distinctions and determinations, which we can here only indicate. There are distinctions betweens laws which prescribe, laws which prohibit, and laws which merely permit: that one *may* exercise one's *Willkür* in certain directions is as much part of our *a priori* moral legislation as that we *must* exercise it in others. There is a distinction between laws of right (*Recht*), on the one hand, which prescribe definite external actions, and which can be externally enforced, and whose violation involves demerit; and on the other hand, laws of virtue, which prescribe inner attitudes as well as actions, which cannot be externally enforced, and whose fulfilment involves merit (pp. 219–28). There is an interesting treatment of the so-called conflict of duties, which Kant regards as a misnomer: he opts for a conflict of imperfect grounds of obligation (p. 224). These last are practically the same as Ross's prima facie duties. All in all, the treatment is far from being the narrowly rigorous moralism with which Kant is ordinarily credited. We return, however, to the principles of morality as set forth in the *Grundlegung* of 1785 and in the *Critique of Practical Reason* of 1788.

ii

Kant's *Foundations of the Metaphysic of Morals* (*Grundlegung*) has no theme other than the investigation of the supreme *principle* of morality: all treatments of particular moral duties are only brought in as illustrations. It falls into three Sections; the first of which effects a transition from the reasoned moral knowledge (*sittliche Vernunfterkenntnis*) at the level of common life to the philosophical world-wisdom achievable at that level; the second passes from such popular, ethical world-wisdom to the philosophical metaphysic of morals; while the third, unique in its audacious originality, attempts to deduce the whole content of morality from the single, emptily universal concept of self-determining spontaneity or freedom.

The *Grundlegung* makes basic to morality, as commonly understood, the possession of something called goodness of will, which is not only unconditionally and absolutely good, but is also a necessary condition of every other case or form of goodness. Kant does not deny that there are countless other cases of goodness besides that of the good will. He cites the goodness of intellectual powers, of understanding, wit, and good judgement; of traits of temperament such as courage, determination, and persistence; of gifts of fortune such as power, wealth, and honour; as well as the blanket goodness of *Glückseligkeit* or happiness. But without goodness of will, which alone can render us *worthy* of all these other cases of goodness, they would not, Kant holds, in the slightest degree deserve to be thought good at all. The same applies to various adjuncts to goodness of will, such as moderation of the passions, self-control, and sober deliberation: they can be very bad indeed if not accompanied by goodness of will. And, finally, goodness of will remains absolutely good in the total absence of all such auxiliary excellences, and even in situations where execution of what is willed is impossible. The good will, Kant holds, does not need them, and will continue to shine with its own light, even if quite impotent or unrewarded. It is not hard to see that Kant in these utterances is somewhat exaggerating the axiology of the common man, who might very well see something tragically wasted, not sublime, in a good will that failed wholly of its purpose or its fruits. And Kant himself sees the point of such an ordinary view in his subsequent doctrine of the *summum bonum*, in which happiness is to be apportioned relatively to goodness of will. And the ordinary man would also see goodness of will as an empty concept unless there were other forms of good that such goodness could pursue or could apportion, and which might be worth having even in cases where something so exalted as goodness of will was not achievable at all, for example, in the case of the happiness of infants and animals. None the less Kant is right in discerning something very remarkable, and challengingly transcendental, in the transcendence of a man's particularity of interest, which is part of what we understand by his moral goodness or goodness of will, and in the seemingly unmotived ascription to it of a value that surpasses all others.

Having argued for the view that goodness of will is the supreme case of goodness, and the necessary condition for the realization of any other case of goodness, Kant goes on, in the First Section of the *Grundlegung*, to establish a number of propositions whose sense will be clearer to us now that we have studied some of his later pronouncements on these matters. The first is to the effect that goodness of will depends, not on the extent to which an action *accords* with duty or is *pflicht-mässig*, but to the extent that it is done *from duty* or *aus Pflicht* (*Grund.*, p. 398). This proposition means that the legislative will, the source of all duty, must itself be a sufficient causal condition of the action in question, and must not require the assistance of some other desire or interest, which may of course be quite legitimately present. Thus if I spread joy around me merely because such diffusion pleases me, my desire, spring-ing from a contingent personal *pathos*, may have goodness, but not the specific goodness of the good will. The latter it can only have if it springs directly from the will's own legislative dynamism expressing itself in an elective choice. (Kant points up the issue by contrasting cases in which one or the other form of causal conditioning obtains *alone*: there is of course no reason why *both* should not be present.) The second pro-position is that the goodness of an act of will does not derive from the specific intention (*Absicht*) that it involves, that is, from the specific goal towards which it is directed, and certainly not from its success in realizing that goal, but solely from the maxim or general policy which underlies this intention, and which, in Kant's view, is part of its causal explanatoriness. And the third proposition simply brings the first two propositions together: that dutiful, morally good willing is simply willing in which the legislative will is sufficient to move us to action without aid from contingent, pathological inclinations, which spring from personal pleasure or displeasure. In dutiful willing, in short, the determining maxim of the will will in fact *coincide* with its general, legislative direction. It is not clear that Kant's three propositions say anything importantly different, though the third adds that good willing may, without detraction from its goodness, be motivated by a respect (*Achtung*) for the laws of the pure will. The nature of such respect will be considered more fully in the *Critique of Practical Reason*: here the point is only made (footnote to p. 401) that such a respect is not the pathological source of good willing, but an *effect* produced on the pathological inclinations, which it overcomes and subordinates to itself. The legislative will must, in short, be able to *scare* the pathological inclinations into conformity with itself, and is thus by itself a sufficient determinant of the action willed.

In the Second Section of the *Grundlegung* Kant first argues for the wholly *a priori* character of the moral law. The will, or legislative reason, must bring such a law to the determination of its choices: it cannot garner it inductively from an experience of its own or other men's actions or choices, whose determination by given maxims is in fact always open to question (p. 407). And we must also be able to see how such legislation necessarily flows from the will's strictly rational character, and must therefore hold for *all* rational beings, whatever their generic or specific make-up, and whatever their individual inclinations and circumstances. It cannot be derived from examples of any sort, even from such as purport to be divine, since divinity can only be inferred from the fulfilment of the *a priori* Idea of the morally perfect will (pp. 408–9). What sort of a law can then be formulated for a being or beings not bound to any particular, empirical make-up, nor with specific or individual interests and circumstances?

Kant first dismisses as irrelevant to strictly moral legislation a set of laws which indeed hold for all rational beings, but only on the hypothesis that they are interested in the realization of certain objectives. Such laws are of the general form 'If p is to be realized, do q', and are called by Kant 'hypothetical imperatives'. They are, in most cases, of little interest, for they depend for their applicability, not only on the contingent fact that someone wishes or wills the realization of p, but also on the fact that the doing of q will actually lead to the realization of p, a truth established empirically, and with no *a priori* warrant. These common-or-garden hypothetical imperatives are called by Kant rules of skill or *Geschicklichkeit*: they are morally irrelevant, since they are obviously as much ancillary to immorality as to morality. There is, however, *one* class of hypothetical imperatives which Kant specially distinguishes, as involving an end that all rational being *must* have, and these are what he calls counsels of prudence (*Ratschläge der Klugheit*, p. 416). These tell us what must be done by someone if his own greatest well-being or happiness is to be secured. Kant does not deny that such counsels involve necessity, since every man must wish to pursue what he thinks will conduce to his own happiness; but he dismisses them, since they only hold under subjective and contingent conditions, that is, the conditions that a man reckons as part of his happiness (p. 416), which obviously vary indefinitely from person to person. Kant despairs of any rational determination of the sources and means to the satisfaction of human wants: the very circumstance that it is so difficult a task, and that we have no instinct which tells us where to look, points in fact to the possibility that the aim of our existence may be something higher than happiness (pp. 395–6). Kant, we may note, *identifies* happiness with the gratification of all our inclinations: 'we have', he says, 'the most powerful and intimate inclination to happiness, since in this Idea all inclinations are unified in one sum' (p. 399). Of such a vague sum total there can only be an indefinite, empirical concept. 'It is unfortunate', Kant writes, 'that the concept of happiness is so indefinite that, though every man wishes to achieve it, he can never definitely and consistently say what he really wishes and wants. The cause is that the elements belonging to the concept of happiness are all empirical . . . it is, however, impossible that even the most penetrating and universally endowed finite being should frame a definite concept of what he really wishes' (p. 418).

The counsels of prudence having thus been dismissed, together with the rules of skill, as being merely hypothetical imperatives, and so unfit to rank as *a priori* laws of the rational legislative will, we shall now have to look in another direction for rational laws framed only in terms of categorical, not of hypothetical imperatives. These categorical imperatives are, Kant holds, the laws of pure morality, and to these he now turns his attention. Kant must not, however, be misunderstood as denying that we have a duty to pursue the happiness of others, and also under certain conditions, our own happiness. He will, in fact, try to *deduce* the existence of such hedonistic duties, and also to make happiness a part of the highest good, and a complement to goodness of the will. What he is holding is that such a place for happiness, as both object and also complement of the good will, is essentially a *consequence* of the unconditional, un-hypothetical moral law which is the direct expression of our legislative will.

Before we proceed to examine Kant's three famous and fascinating formulations of the categorical demands of morality, we must first vastly regret that, though he had knowledge of practically all the eighteenth-century British moralists, he had never encountered the *Sermons* of Bishop Butler, possibly, together with his own, the greatest of all works in moral philosophy. (This widespread ignorance of Butler's ethical master-piece has, for some strange reason, persisted up to the present day in Germany.) Bishop Butler, in the *Sermons*, draws an invaluable distinction between men's particular passions, all disinterestedly directed to specific objects, and the self-love which co-ordinates them all, and which takes thought for the over-all satisfaction of the man rather than for the satisfaction of some single, narrow want, or for the realization of its object. Kant does not in fact see that all our basic wants are disinterested, that they aim at specific objects, and not at the satisfaction that such objects will yield. And he does not see that having what one wants, and what will most satisfy one on the whole, is quite a different object of endeavour from having food, or sex, or flattering attentions on a given occasion, or even from having them repeatedly, and over the whole of one's life. It is essentially a higher-order end, which is not to be identified with the sum total of particular things, or states, or acts that will in fact satisfy one, and it has the same open universality, the same transcendence of empirical content, that Kant attributes to the imperatives of morality. To rise from the demands for definite, empirical objects to a comprehensive demand for what will most satisfy or please one is also pre-eminently an exercise of practical reason, of a universal, legislative will.

This is even clearer when we pass from the interest in a man's *own* happiness, the only sort of happiness that Kant generally considers, to the benevolent interest in the happiness of anyone and everyone, the desire that everyone should, as far as is consistent with the happiness of others and his own happiness over the whole of life, and also the imperatives of morality, have as much of what he wants, and of what gives him satisfaction, as possible. Such universal benevolence is eminently an attitude involving rational co-ordination, and the substitution of generic form for empirical content. If self-love and benevolence are alike subordinated to Butler's conscience, which is the equivalent of Kant's legislative will, they none the less have much of the higher-order, co-ordinating character and the open universality of that conscience, and that will: they are not to be identified with a mere rabble of particular passions and interests. It is also obviously the case that, just as we do not always obey the *a priori* dictates of morality, we just as often, under the pressure of passion, fail to pursue our own general happiness: the same contrast between what we ought to do, and what we in fact do, obtains in the one case as in the other. And it is of course even more plain that we often fail to choose what we know will really benefit others, in our desire to grant them some immediate gratification. And rational self-love and benevolence can, of course, be further extended to cover, not merely the satisfaction of contingent personal interests, but also the satisfaction of universal, rational interests other than those of morality, the interest, for example, in truth or in beauty, which Kant likewise recognizes. Obviously there is rational legislation at a large number of levels, and not only at the supreme level which Butler makes a function of conscience, and Kant of his categorical, legislative will.

iii

We now pass to the consideration of the three distinct formulae in which Kant seeks to give expression to the single, ultimate, unconditional imperative of morality. He argues, first of all, that the *mere conception* of a law that will apply regardless of pathological inclinations and interests will of itself suffice to give content to its apparent emptiness (p. 420). It will be a law to the effect that we should only act on a maxim or practical rule that we can also will to be a general law (p. 421). This formula seems to have performed the improbable task of conjuring something out of nothing, a definite principle of action out of the mere requirement that one should have *some* such principle. An examination of Kant's formula, and of the four famous examples which he uses to illustrate it, will show, however, that it is not as vacuous as it at first seems. For it does not license us to set up *anything* as a law that is free from internal self-contradiction: it will not license us to prescribe the enslavement of any dark-haired by any fair-haired person, nor the assiduous chewing up of paper by anyone and everyone. What it does license us to set up as a law is something that we ourselves, having whatever general nature we do have, and whatever specific wants we also have, have some interest in willing (not what it is analytically possible for us to will); and it licenses us to do this on condition that also we simultaneously will that *everyone*, whatever his general nature and specific interests, should have a licence to will just as we will, and whatever the effect of such willing on ourselves or on anyone else. The formula gains content because it is a formula for *agents* who are also possible *patients*, whose actions have effects that can be suffered by others who are also possible agents; and it also gains content because it presupposes widely shared generic, and stable, individual natures in those agents and patients, which are, in all *practically* relevant cases, common human types of interest, or individual variants of these. The formula is not based on the peculiarities of human nature (p. 425), but would apply to fairies, or Houyhnhnms, or any sort of rational creature whatever; but it does apply to beings who have interests and inclinations of some sort, and, in regard to all such, it legislates that they should will what they are prepared that everyone should will, whether or not they themselves are, or were, the agents or patients of such willing. It thus has the same higher-order, co-ordinating character as the self-love, benevolence, and conscience of Butler; and what it co-ordinates are contingent, personal inclinations and interests, whether of men or other rational beings, while it itself, in its higher-order role, is wholly free from anything contingent and pathological. Like the categories and principles of the understanding, it systematizes a contingent, empirical manifold: this manifold consists, however, not of data that affect us intuitively, but of the contingent impulses and interests that they call forth, which are as essential to action as intuitive data are to knowledge. The moral imperatives of Kant have, therefore, as essential a relation to contingent, empirical material as his categorial principles. It is also important to note, in this connection, that Kant's imperatives are really laws of permission, rather than of prescription or prohibition. They *allow* us to will anything whatever, provided we are also willing to make whatever we will a possibility for everyone in relation to everyone, including ourselves. As such, they presuppose generically human, as well as individually personal, inclinations and interests, without which they would be without any application.

A careful consideration of Kant's four famous illustrations will confirm this analysis. The first illustration is that of a man contemplating suicide when reduced to despair by a series of disasters. Is it not possible for him, impelled by self-love, to accept as a maxim that life should be shortened whenever its prolongation promises more misery than pleasure? No: for there is an inner contradiction in willing that a principle of self-love, which has the function (*Bestimmung*) of tending towards the improvement (*Beförderung*) of life, should be instrumental in destroying that life. As the example is phrased, we might imagine that it is some merely logical contradiction that is here being invoked, which is of course not the case. There is no contradiction in a system of nature where, in given circumstances, an inbuilt impulse towards X is cancelled by another, conflicting impulse, or is itself diverted towards the prevention of X. The real point of the objection is that life is not merely the necessary condition for the many contingent, pathological satisfactions in which our body plays some part, but also for the many desirable, rational, and, in some cases, obligatory activities sometimes connected with the happiness of others, which involve much more than merely personal satisfactions and freedom from dissatisfactions. Life is not merely a source of satisfaction and dissatisfaction: it is the necessary basis for many rational and moral activities, and must share the respect that we accord to the latter. We are not free to dispense with it merely because it has ceased to provide entertainment. It can, of course, be objected, that, since Kant believes men to be immortal, a man need not imagine that, by committing bodily suicide, he is terminating all his rational and moral activities, or even his personal satisfactions. But he does not, in Kant's view, have certain *knowledge* that he will be able to continue the life of reason and pleasure in some other form of life, and he certainly has no reason to expect this if he has lacked respect for the only sort of life of which he has knowledge, and for the activities and satisfactions it has provided. We are incarnate, not discarnate intelligences, and as such we cannot but set store by the activities and satisfactions of which we have knowledge, and by the bodily life which is their precondition. It is in some such way that we must interpret Kant's first illustration: it will not work without a consideration of the special facts of the human condition, and the special interests which this engenders. Were we freely floating, Swedenborgian spirits, perhaps plunging in and out of bodies at will, we might very well have decided differently and perhaps legitimately.

Kant's next example is, however, much easier of interpretation. Plainly a man who borrows money from someone, secretly intending not to repay it, would not desire to be treated by others as he is now treating someone, and would also not desire the destruction of the whole system of mutual credit of which he is now availing himself. But equally plainly, though Kant does not spell it out, if we were beings so circumstanced or constituted as not to need the institutions of borrowing or lending in the realization of our purposes, as can readily be imagined, we might preach and practise a doctrine of universal self-help, or of gratuitous aid, or of the communism of the means of production, and so forth. As men, we are not, however, thus circumstanced or constituted, and stand in need of the financial assistance of others, to which concrete need Kant's general imperative has applied itself. And Kant's third example resembles his first. We are tempted, in our own case, to avoid the labour and annoyance of cultivating our various talents, but are not prepared to will that their non-cultivation should be general, since both the products and performances which evince talent involve rational activities which are satisfactory to us as rational beings. If we were brutes or gods, having no talents or only fully developed ones, the demand would not arise. Kant's fourth example also resembles his first: though we are tempted to deny others the support and sympathy that their distressed state calls for, we cannot will

that such non-support and lack of sympathy should be universal.
For we are not Epicurean gods, but men geared into society
for our happiness and our survival. To beings so geared sympathy and support are essential, and must be freely given,
even if we ourselves may not be so much in need of them as
others. And, obviously, to exploit them, and yet not to reciprocate them, would involve a graver departure from duty
than neither to exploit nor reciprocate them. Kant's four
examples therefore all involve natural or rational interests
common to men, which provide the necessary material which
his principle organizes. But perhaps Kant has not sufficiently
stressed that our interest in life, in mutual trust, in the cultivation of talent, and in mutual support are not merely pathological
affections that we as men happen to feel. They have in some
sense arguably as *a priori* a character as the moral law which
builds itself upon them, and organizes them. A deduction of
rationally approvable ends is as necessary as a deduction of
moral imperatives.

Kant passes, however, from his first, somewhat inadequate
formulation of the moral law to a more satisfactory formulation
in which the disinterestedly legislative will, and the beings who
are capable of exercising it legislatively and obeying it electively,
are themselves the end of their own legislation. The will must
direct itself to sustaining the existence and the unimpeded
activity of such legislators and moral subjects. As Kant puts it:

> Supposing there were something whose existence has in itself an absolute
> value, which, as an end in itself, could be the source of definite laws, then
> we should have in such a thing, and in it alone, the ground of a possible
> categorical imperative of practical law. I assert now that man, and any
> rational being at all, exists as an end in itself, and is not merely a means
> to be freely used by this or that will, but must in all actions, whether
> directed upon itself or upon other rational beings, always also be treated
> as an end. All the objects of inclination have only a conditional value. If
> they are non-rational beings, they have only a relative, instrumental value,
> and are therefore known as *things*. Rational beings, on the other hand,
> are called *persons*, since their nature distinguishes them as *ends in them-
> selves* (p. 428).

It is therefore a practical law that we should never use anyone's
humanity (with its power to legislate rationally) as a mere
means to anything else, but also as a supreme end. We must
respect legislative reason whether in ourselves or anyone else.
It is not altogether clear whether Kant means us to take this
principle as a mere restatement of the previous one, but plainly

it involves something more. For it extends the awe which surrounds the moral law to the subject which promulgates it. But, though thus extending the sense of the previous principle, it also does so inevitably, since disinterested willing is inseparable from the disinterested subject that wills it.

Kant's four examples work better under the new formula than under the old one, which shows that there has been a genuine deepening of sense. Suicide is illegitimate, since it involves treating oneself, a moral legislator, as a mere means to the avoidance of certain vanishing pains. Defaulting on debt-repayment is illegitimate, since it involves manipulating a moral legislator in what cannot be to his pathological or moral benefit. Failing to cultivate one's talents is illegitimate, since it involves disrespect for all the rational capacities which necessarily cluster around that of rational legislation. And failure to help others in distress is illegitimate, since it represents a failure to accept the contingent needs of those others, which is plainly involved in accepting them, *qua* rational legislators, as ends in themselves (pp. 429–30). The nimbus of a legislator must shed its light on his non-legislative aspects, since the same rational person is involved in both.

From his two formulae of legislative generality and respect for legislators, Kant turns to his third formula, which we may call that of legislative consensus. Practical beings, for Kant, *qua* rational, necessarily constitute a system in which all prescribe the same general rules to all: since the rules are the same, everyone legislates as much for himself as for others, and is always autonomous, subject to his own rules, never heteronomous, subject to rules which are *not* his own. And all the autonomous moral legislators accord to one another the same unconditional deference that they accord to the moral law: all treat all as ends in themselves, and never as mere means. The rational legislators may of course differ in the elective implementation of their common legislation: without differing in their deference to it, the one may have interests that lead him to implement it in a given manner, while the other implements it quite differently. There are thus possibilities of *non*-accord among legislators, *qua* elective, which are not in any sense cases of *dis*cord. There will, however, also be cases of elective discord among legislators when, *qua* elective, they yield to pathological inclinations, and fail to implement the moral law in some respect. When this happens they will no doubt be as much condemned by themselves *qua* legislators, as they are also condemned by others. Despite all these possibilities of disharmony, the rational legislators, who are also the subjects, sometimes dissident, of their own common legislation, will all constitute a single legislative system, the constitution of which will be pre-eminently preserved in an inner core of holy wills, who have no temptation to deviate from the laws which they all alike prescribe to all alike. And this inner core will have its centre, though Kant does not mention him at this point, in a supremely holy moral legislator, whose existence is not contingent, and who has created all the other moral legislators who exist contingently. The holy members of the system do not, however, impose the moral law on the other, less holy members, for each member of the system, however deviant electively, is a sovereign, autonomous moral legislator. 'Thus arises', Kant tells us, 'a systematic combination of rational beings through common, objective laws, i.e. a kingdom, no more than an ideal, which, since these laws aim at the relations of these beings, as means and ends, to one another, may be called a kingdom of ends. A reasonable being belongs to this kingdom of ends as a member if it is itself subject to these laws, which it also lays down as legislator. It belongs to this kingdom as sovereign, since in its legislation it is not subject to the will of another' (p. 433).

iv

The Third Section of the *Grundlegung* attempts the difficult task of showing that the three formulae that he has given are in fact the ways in which the rational, legislative will must declare itself. That it will thus declare itself is not analytically evident: it is not, Kant holds, part of the concept of an unconditionally good will that it must necessarily will universally, that it must have infinite respect for its own legislative functions, and that it must always achieve a harmonious consensus among all the individual wills in which it is embodied. There must, he holds, be some property of the unconditionally good will from which these maxims follow analytically as absolute laws, but it is not easy to see what such a property can be. Kant then makes the audacious assertion that it is simply in the concept or Idea of freedom (if indeed we have, or can have such a concept or Idea) that the notion which links goodness of will to his three formulations of the moral law is to be found.

If there can be a will, a positive source of causal determination, which is also *self-determined* or *autonomous*, and so free from definite determination by external inclinations and interests (though it can of course associate itself with and endorse the latter), and which is also *rational*, in that it necessarily guides itself by general rules or principles of action, unless diverted from the latter by particular, momentary impulses (as it can of course be diverted); then it can be shown, Kant thinks, that such a will necessarily will guide itself by the three principles in question, and that what we call its goodness will consist in following such principles, whereas its weakness or badness will consist in its neglect to follow them. As we have seen, the Kantian notion of freedom is Janus-faced, according as we consider it in relation to the legislative or elective aspect of the will. The will is free in its legislation according as it follows its own necessary line of absolute generality, undeterred by the pulls of particular pathological interests; but it is free, in its elective aspect, according as it follows, or, by defect, fails to follow, its own legislative programme in this particular case, and in a context of particular solicitations.

It seems plain that *both* these notions enter into the complex notion of freedom which is now in question: the will, as a *rational* power, must of necessity prescribe general principles which set it above the particularities of person and impulse, and which will enable it to co-ordinate them all, and it must also have the *ability* to implement its principles (or, by defect, not to implement them) in the particular case, whatever the impulses that tell for or against this. And, on examining the various strands in the Kantian conception of freedom, it is highly arguable that they *do* entail something like the three formulae he has put forward, and that it *is* reasonable to claim that what we ordinarily call moral goodness consists in conforming to such principles, while moral defect or badness consists in the failure to conform to them. For there is nothing *rational* in a principle which aligns itself with one person, or one set of contingent interests, rather than with another person, or another set of interests, even if that person happens to be oneself, and the interests one's own. And there is an obvious rationality in an interest in rationality as such, and in an interest in the elimination of irrationality. Interests are as such self-endorsing and self-approving, and rationality in interest is not exempt from this principle, so that rational agents will respect rational agency whether in themselves or anyone else. And rationality of interest, being without fear or favour towards persons or interests, will necessarily work towards a consensus in which all demand the same of all and for all. And it is also not in doubt that Kant's three formulae cover much that is fundamental in morals, certainly what he himself called duties of right, which are the same for all, and from which it would be *wrong* to depart, even if they do not so well cover what he called duties of virtue, which differ from person to person, and which are meritorious rather than obligatory.

Kant has, however, defined freedom purely in negative terms: it is a form of causality in which there is *no* prior inclination which precisely determines what is done or chosen, or determines whether there is an endorsement of a given inclination, or a contrary decision to abide by the moral law. To use such a notion in explanation demands, however, that we should give it a positive meaning, and this, in the sense of being able to illustrate it intuitively, is something that we *cannot* do. Logically, the notion of a condition which entails either of two outcomes, and which requires no added determinant to decide which is realized, is perhaps emptily entertainable: it amounts to our being perfectly satisfied with the explanatory value of such a ground or cause. But, in intuitive illustration, we have nothing beyond the *absence* of an extra determining factor to go on, and this hardly suffices to establish the existence of the sort of positive causal determination in question. Kant in fact refuses to offer more than a *practical* reason for believing in such a sort of causality. Freedom is not an ordinary concept of which plain illustrations can be given: it is rather a Transcendental Idea whose possible cases transcend illustration. If we ask why we should believe that we possess such an extraordinary power, whether in its necessary or its facultative aspect, Kant gives the remarkable answer that 'we must necessarily credit every rational being possessed of will with the Idea of freedom, under which alone it can act', and also that 'every being that cannot act otherwise than *under the Idea of freedom*, is therefore, from a practical point of view, really free' (p. 448). In other words, to legislate to the effect that we *shall* comport ourselves in certain ways is to presume that we *can* comport ourselves in those ways, no matter what the force of opposing inclinations may be. To this Kant adds, in a footnote, that he has argued in this manner in order to avoid the necessity of *proving in a theoretical manner* that there really is or can be such a thing as freedom. For, even if this *cannot* be proved, the same laws will hold for the practice of beings that cannot act except under an Idea of their own freedom, as would govern them if they were actually free. Beings endowed with a will therefore necessarily think of themselves as free, and take themselves to be free, and this is so even if the Idea of freedom has nothing corresponding to it in intuition, and in fact transcends all possible experience. But, of course, that we must think in this manner, or must proceed as if such thinking were valid, gives a definite fillip to such thinking: it gives to a transcendent power a definite place in the phenomenal order, even if only in the thought of rational agents. To be obligatorily thinkable seems, in fact, to be the characteristic manner in which the transcendently real insinuates itself into phenomenal experience.

Kant comments on the strange circle, which obliges us to believe in our freedom, that is, our non-pathological self-determination, in order to understand the possibility and the necessity of moral laws; but which also obliges us to accept the possibility and necessity of unconditional moral laws in order to understand the possibility and necessity of such freedom (p. 450). The two concepts are in fact equivalent: a will free to determine its direction without the pressures of particular interests must necessarily follow laws of the purest generality — it cannot dispense with *all* laws since it is a rational power — and a will governed by laws of the purest generality must necessarily be able to resist determination by particular interests. Both these concepts are, however, products of pure reason rather than understanding. They are not thoughts which serve to bring sensuous presentations under rules, as the concepts of the understanding always are: they are rather thoughts springing from the spontaneity of the pure subject, in which it posits the existence of a supersensible order to which it intrinsically belongs. 'As a reasonable being, belonging as such to the intelligible world', Kant tells us, 'a man can only think of the causality of his own will under the Idea of freedom. For independence of the determining causes of the sense-world, which reason always has to attribute to itself, is freedom. And with the Idea of freedom the concept of *autonomy* is indissolubly bound up, and with this the general principle of morality, which in Idea underlies all the actions of *rational*

beings, just as natural law underlies all appearances' (pp. 452-3).
A being, in short, which transcends empirical particularity, as
the rational self always does and must, cannot escape from the
highest-order generalities of morality. To this we may add that
the sort of unity which is not drawn out in phenomenal phases
outside of one another in space, or coming after one another in
time, necessarily has all its laws, and all its implementations
(or non-implementations) of such laws, concentrated in its
own, single being, and has nothing that can depend on what
is external.

The concluding paragraphs of the *Grundlegung* do much to
show how vivid is Kant's belief in the transcendent world of
the understanding, which we can spontaneously think but not
know, but to which we none the less, as rational agents, in-
defeasibly belong. It is said to be the ground of the sense-world,
and hence also of the *laws* of the latter (p. 453). This sentence
proves that the *connections* in the sense-world, and not merely
the *elements* of the latter, reflect deeper, transcendental connections, involving teleological and moral, as well as causal
links; and that the linkage of phenomenal causality is in some
sense an inadequate *translation*, into a passively intuitive,
spatio-temporal idiom, of these deeper interconnections and
relations. The phenomenal order is a systematic rendering of
the noumenal order (even though it may leave many features
out): it is not, as many have thought, a free fabrication from
disjoined impressions with which the noumenal order affects
us. In what manner, or on what principles, the rendering proceeds, or how precisely the richer noumenal order is cut down
to its reduced, phenomenal surrogate, we are of course wholly
ignorant. But in the practical consciousness, Kant tells us, of
even the commonest and most errant man, we have, in the
form of an 'ought', the awareness of patterns in the noumenal
order that transcend all that he can, in the order of phenomenal
causes, achieve. He is able to transcend himself in thought, and
to take up the standpoint of a member of a non-phenomenal,
rational order, to become in his thought a better person than
he phenomenally is (p. 455). In that noumenal order, in fact,
deviant, phenomenal man is represented only by acts of lenience
or self-indulgence (*Nachsicht*), in which he freely gives way to
influences and impulses *external* to his own intrinsic legislation
(p. 458). Such *Nachsicht* no doubt is as marginal in the
noumenal order as acts of moral heroism are marginal down

here. (The whole problem of *Nachsicht*, or the declension from morality, will concern us when we consider Kant's treatise on *Religion within the Bounds of Mere Reason*.) Kant does not, however, attempt to project the structure of one order from that of the other, nor suggest any principles on which such a projection might proceed. Where intuition ceases, systematic projection also ceases. He affirms, however, his general faith in the monadology which he inherited from Leibniz: 'The concept of a world of the understanding is therefore only a *standpoint* which reason feels itself impelled to take up beyond phenomena, in order *to think of itself as practical*. But this thought definitely involves the Idea of an order, and a legislation, other than that of the nature-mechanism which applies to the sense-world, and makes the concept of an intelligible world, i.e. of the totality of rational beings as Things-in-themselves, a necessary one' (p. 458). There will, of course, also have to be a place for dynamic agents which are *not* rational agents in such a transcendent world.

v

The *Critique of Practical Reason*, professedly the central treatment of morality in the critical philosophy, is less central than its name would lead us to imagine. For, the whole first part, the Analytic of Pure Practical Reason, is in the main merely a more elaborate setting forth of the points already made in the *Grundlegung*, while for richness of detailed application one has still to proceed to the 1797 *Metaphysic of Morals*. There are, however, a few points made in the Analytic which merit special attention; while the Dialectic of Pure Practical Reason extends the account of the kingdom of ends given in the *Grundlegung* by considering the nature and content of the three postulates of freedom, God, and immortality, which are necessitated by the relation of that kingdom to the kingdom of nature. The nature of such postulates, which have only a cogitative and a practical, but not an epistemological use, is of course highly relevant to our central theme of Kant's notion of transcendental objectivity.

The most significant of the new points raised in the Analytic of Pure Practical Reason is the nature of the *Achtung*, the respect which enters into the intrinsic dynamism of the moral law (see pp. 126–59). It is plain, Kant holds, 'that what is essential in all moral worth, is *that the moral law should directly determine the will*. Should the determination of the will be *in accord with* the moral law, but only by way of a feeling, no matter of what sort, that has to be presupposed so that the law can become sufficient to condition the will, this determination is *not for the law's sake*, and an action may have legality, but not morality' (pp. 126–7). The operation of the moral law is therefore to this extent negative: its determination of the will must be wholly *unassisted* by pre-existent, affective motives, and it must in fact dismiss (*abweisen*) all such motives as forces that can work against itself. This negative thwarting of all pre-existent feelings must, however, *itself* generate a feeling, which can only be one of pain: our particular, contingent interests are not to be satisfied. And not only that, but it also must strike down that lower form of self-interest (*Selbstsucht*) which endorses our personal interests simply because they are ours, and which is called *Eigendünkel*, arrogant self-complacency, rather than rational self-love. In striking down this affect, the moral law engenders a sense of humiliation (*Demütigung*) in the self-complacent, pathological self, and so removes a resistance to itself, and makes its own fulfilment easier. This sense of humiliation is indeed an affect *distinct* from the moral law, but, since it is a product of the legislative will, we are moved by nothing but the dynamism of the moral law itself, which is the source of the affect in question. The genesis of this affect is, moreover, no discovery of the empirical psychologist: though not an analytic truth, it can be foreseen *a priori*. The legislative aspect *must* thus affect its pathological aspect. Kant comments on the remarkable character of this insight: it indeed represents an anticipation of the *a priori*, synthetic phenomenology of Husserl.

Another important point in the Analytic is its unequivocal endorsement of the use of the category of causation beyond the limits of possible experience. There are so many passages in the epistemologically oriented *Critique of Pure Reason* where such a transcendent use is condemned, or even said to lack meaning, that many have taken this to be the authoritative stand of Kant, from which all deviations are to be regarded as slips or errors. In the Analytic, however, he makes plain that, while phenomenally evident, causal connection is only possible through the regular, phenomenal successions which alone set objective time before us, and while we cannot extend such a method of knowing beyond the limits of experience; we can, none the less, make good, *non-epistemic* uses of the category of causation beyond empirical limits, in the case, for example, of free, voluntary decisions:

> How will it be in regard to an application (*Anwendung*) of this category of causation (and of all the other categories necessary to the knowledge of existence) to things which are not objects of possible experience, but lie beyond the bounds of such? For I have only been able to deduce the objective reality of these concepts in relation to the objects of possible experience. But by this very fact, that I have rescued them (for knowledge) only in this case, that I have shown that they allow us to think objects, but not to determine them *a priori*: this is the fact that gives them a place in the pure understanding which can then refer them to objects in general, whether sensible or non-sensible. If any condition is lacking for the application of these categories (e.g. causality) to objects, it is the lack of intuition which renders an application to the object *qua* Noumenon impossible for the *purposes of theoretical knowledge* . . . For that this concept involves no impossibility in relation to an object, is proved by the fact that it has an assured place in the pure understanding in all references to sensible objects. And if it is thereafter immediately referred to Things-in-themselves which cannot be objects of experience, and is in this use incapable of any determinate presentation of an object for the purposes of theoretical knowledge, it may none the less be capable, perhaps for other practical purposes, of a determinate application, which would not be the case if, as Hume thought, causality were a concept incapable of being thought at all (pp. 94–5).

What these syntactically deplorable sentences seem to be saying is that categories must permit of a wider cogitative application, where a narrower epistemic application is impossible, and that, if they were not capable of the former, they could not be capable of the latter. (Or, what is the same, if they are capable of the latter, they must be capable of the former.)

And what they further seem to be saying is that what we may call the agent-sense of causality is more fundamental than the phenomenally dependent, knowledge-sense, and that the Humean causality, which depends on phenomenal antecedents, is an inadequate substitute for the former sense. That this is what Kant thinks is shown by a passage in which he says that 'in the concept of a will the concept of causality is already contained, and thus in the concept of a pure will the concept of a causality of freedom is contained, i.e. of a causality not determinable through natural laws, and so incapable of empirical intuition as a proof of its reality. This causality fully justifies its objective reality *a priori* in the pure practical law, not indeed for the purposes of the theoretical use of reason, but for the purposes of its practical use' (pp. 96-7). And in a subsequent passage he also says: 'And so it happens that, since all the prescriptions of pure practical reason only concern the determinations of the will, not the natural conditions for the practical execution of its intentions, practical concepts *a priori* immediately become, in relation to the supreme principle of freedom, matters of knowledge (*Erkenntnisse*), and do not need to wait for intuitions to acquire meaning. This is so on account of the remarkable fact that they themselves engender the actuality of the voluntary intention at which they are directed, and which is not the case in regard to theoretical conceptions' (p. 116). In other words, our own free action involves the same category of causality or agency that we apply in the knowledge of the phenomenally given, only in *its* case we can dispense with the empirical criteria necessary in the case of the latter. Hume's empirical criteria for causation are thus criteria that we only apply when we are unable to probe beneath the phenomenal surface. But volition is a mode of causation which requires no verifying intuition. It seems not far, we may say, from the intellectual intuition that God possesses.

Another concept interestingly developed in the Analytic is that of the *summum bonum* or complete good. There Kant reluctantly recognizes that there can be something rational in the pursuit of happiness or *Glückseligkeit*, of our own personal weal or woe (*Wohl oder Übel*), even if he identifies the latter with the definite feelings which various objects or actions occasion. He acknowledges that our weal or woe is very important in the judgements of practical reason, and that our 'happiness' is what concerns our nature as sensuous beings, provided that this happiness is judged, not in terms of vanishing sensations, but in terms of the influence such things have on our whole existence, and on our satisfaction with the same (p. 107). But he also suggests that the rationality of such a pursuit is merely instrumental, since the end it seeks, that is, enjoyment, is not an *a priori*, rational good, but a *wohl*, a merely sensuous, personal good, the only thing rational about which is our deliberation as to how to obtain it (p. 110). And since Kant, ignorant of the arguments of Butler, fails to see that the pursuit of one's own over-all welfare is as independent of the concrete needs and satisfactions that it covers, and hence as truly rational, as the moral law itself, and that it is as often as hard to pursue as that law, he necessarily excludes it from the unconditional, *supreme* good, which consists in virtue (*Tugend*) or the good will alone. But, in the Dialectic of Pure Practical Reason, Kant assents to the proposition that virtue or the good will makes a man worthy of happiness, and worthy of a degree of happiness proportioned to his virtue, and that virtue without its proportionate complement of happiness will therefore necessarily be an incomplete good, and one not to be desired for, or by, a rational being. 'Virtue', Kant says, 'is not the whole or perfect good as the object of desire for finite rational beings. For that, happiness is also demanded, and that not only in the partial eyes of the person who makes himself his end, but even in the judgement of an impartial reason, which treats such a person as an end in himself. For to have need of happiness, and be worthy of it, yet not to share in it, is not consistent with the will of an all-perfect rational being, if we allow ourselves to conceive of the latter for the sake of argument' (pp. 198–9).

The connection of virtue with happiness is not, however, analytic, and Kant therefore requires a Transcendental Deduction for it. We have therefore to ask *why* a reasonable will should not simply be satisfied to conform to the moral law, but should further desire that such conformity should be rewarded with happiness. If this has to be shown, Kant has not succeeded in showing it. He has not even tried to show that it is rational to pursue happiness as well as virtue, but has only conceived of transcendental arrangements that might make the achievement of both possible. To show that happiness is a fitting complement to virtue, we must be able to show that it is an independently rational goal when not definitely coupled with immorality; which is not the same as saying that it has to be a mere accompaniment to morality. Happy children and animals should be so, even if they are incapable of goodness of will. And *positive* goodness of will is not involved in the enjoyment of beauty, the love of persons, or the extension of knowledge; which are all goods that Kant acknowledges, even if moral badness may be capable of devaluing all of them. These issues have, however, often been raised, and it is not profitable to dwell on the exaggerated moralism of Kant.

vi

We now turn to the three postulates of freedom, immortality, and God, which Kant connects with the moral law as enlarged by the codicil of the *summum bonum*. The case for freedom has been argued for at the end of the Analytic, and repeats some of the contentions raised in the resolution of the Third Antinomy. The will must be unbiased by pre-existent inclinations and other causative factors, both in its general legislation and its elective implementation. The moral law requires such freedom for its possibility, just as freedom requires the moral law for its characteristic expression (p. 168). Such freedom from determining factors is, however, incompatible with the universal determination of our volitions, like everything else, by prior conditions in time, without which their objectivity for knowledge would be eroded. But what has happened, or has been done in the past, is no longer in our power, and cannot leave us with untrammelled freedom to conform to the moral law (p. 169). It is a vain subterfuge, Kant says, to say that the factors which trammel us are in ourselves, and so do not affect our freedom, for the freedom required is the transcendental freedom to do our duty, not merely to please ourselves (pp. 171–2). Kant's epistemological rigour has, however, made it impossible for him to inject a limited quantum of spontaneity, though admitted to be a form of causality, into the phenomenal fabric. His only recourse, therefore, is to a purely *noumenal* injection of such spontaneity, placed beyond the range of experience, and entirely out of time. As the souls in the Platonic myths freely choose their *whole lives* before descending into incarnation, so our noumenal selves must have decided on their *whole course of action*, including its pettiest details, in passing out of eternity into time. The very same subject, Kant argues, who sees himself as a long-lived historical agent in time, and whose acts at one point of time are not revocable at another later date, is also, *qua* moral, conscious of himself as an agent that exists out of time; and 'in this his existence', he says, 'nothing precedes the determination of the will, but rather every action and every changing determination given to inner sense, and even the whole course of his existence *qua* sensuous being, is, in the consciousness of his intelligible reality, seen only as an effect of his noumenal causation, and never as a ground which determines the latter' (p. 175). There can be little doubt that

Kant is here describing a profound, widespread, and quasi-mystical experience, in which we feel ourselves to have chosen to be the sort of person we are, and to have chosen to meet every contingency or circumstance in the way that we did in fact meet it, and also perhaps to have chosen to change our life-style in the remarkable, unpredictable way that we did at some points change it, absolutely from all eternity. (To quote Brünnhilde: *Ach Siegfried, dein war ich von je.*) And if we accept Kant's view that the many antinomic absurdities of time compel us to supplement it with something, not fully imaginable, which transcends time, preserving perhaps its ordinal but not its supersessive properties, then there is nothing unacceptable in Kant's doctrine that, as timeless beings, we have always made ourselves, or are always making ourselves (tense does not apply) eternally. Kant argues further that even our creation, by a necessarily existent, supremely real God, need not remove this transcendental freedom. For God may have given us some measure of the transcendental freedom that He Himself possesses (pp. 183-4).

From the postulate of freedom we pass to the postulate of immortality. The moral law, the expression of our own rational spontaneity, demands the *complete* conformity (*völlige Angemessenheit*) of our, in part, deviant nature to its basic prescriptions: it demands in short, that our wills should become *holy*. The rational demand for morally deserved beatitude also involves the same requirement. It is, however, impossible for a will capable of defecting from its own, intrinsic legislation to achieve this sort of sanctification and beatification in a finite time: it can at best approach it asymptotically. This means that the phenomenal aspect of our existence as conscious subjects must necessarily present itself as an infinite temporal progression: the psyche, *qua* phenomenal, must accordingly be immortal (pp. 219-20). But, from the standpoint of an infinite divine being, endowed with an intellectual intuition which transcends time, this whole endless approximation to the goal of holiness will be seen as the actual achievement of the goal in question (p. 221). That our psychic life should go on for ever is a speculative proposition, and as such incapable of demonstration: practically, however, Kant holds, we must rely unconditionally on its truth. Yet, he discourages theosophic dreams of any final *achievement* of holiness, with its attendant experience of beatitude, but it is not clear that he is arguing cogently. If phenomenal, temporal being necessarily presupposes a style of being that is not temporal, then it is not incredible that it should have a last stage, in which it has no anticlimactic future, but only something like the still glory of the painted saints on the illuminated windows of Gothic cathedrals. Such a blessed eschatology has been argued for, with careful consistency, by McTaggart, as well as by other great philosophers of like tendency.

Kant's third postulate is that of the existence of his comprehensively possible *ens realissimum*, from the thought of which epistemic reason can at best derive regulative inspiration, but of which it can never achieve proof or knowledge. Kant makes great appeal to the synthetic connection of happiness with morality in the *summum bonum*: there must be a self-existent, non-natural cause of contingent, natural existences which will absolutely assure us of this connection, which is both demanded and acted upon by our rational will, though lacking an analytic or an empirical warrant (pp. 224–6). This stress on happiness suggests that the all-real being is not required for any other purpose, and that we could very well approach holiness, and deserve happiness, without his assistance. This is not, however, Kant's view, since, plainly, our contingent existence is taken by him to depend *completely* on the non-contingent existence of the all-real being. Otherwise there could be no certainty that we, and our moral endeavours, could continue into the future, or that the perfection demanded by the moral law could in fact be approached indefinitely. It is clear, too, that morality would become void through inapplicability if we had none of those great communities and affinities of natural interest which make it possible for us to compare one man's case with another's, and to construct maxims that apply to them all. Such communities and affinities must have been engendered by a co-ordinating supreme reason, much as similar communities and affinities must have been engineered by it in phenomenal nature, if knowledge and science were to be possible. A self-existent, sanctified centre is in fact necessary for the whole constitution of the realm of ends which underlies phenomenal experience, whether outer or inner, cognitive or volitional, and not merely for the fitting of virtue to desert, on which Kant, in typical eighteenth-century fashion, lays so much stress.

And that Kant does not in fact think of God in this merely

paymaster-fashion is shown in such a passage as the Note on pp. 229–30; where he contrasts the heroic self-sufficiency of the Stoics, who recognize no temptation in themselves sufficient to make them violate the moral law, with the Christian sense of a complete inadequacy to measure up to the unyielding requirements of morality, accompanied with the hope that, if one has done the best one could, one will receive help from a superior source that will enable one to do better. It would appear from this passage that the all-real, necessarily existent agent responsible for the existence of contingent, finite agents also has the power to reinforce their faltering moral performance, provided they make the first efforts in this direction. There is no heteronomy in such a doctrine, since the supreme legislator, who has created the kingdom of ends, has not prescribed the moral law to its citizens, but has merely strengthened them in obedience to a legislation that is intrinsic and common to them all.

God, in Kant's scheme, is therefore the necessarily existent agent responsible for the existence of the kingdom of ends, for the continued existence of its various self-legislating members, as well as for the possibility of their achieving their various contingent, but innocent ends, in which they have placed their happiness, and the higher, rational ends which are also a necessary part of this. Strangely unmentioned in this context are the use of the categories and the Transcendental Ideas in knowledge, and the use of judgements of taste in the enjoyment of beauty. God is certainly, for Kant, not a person in the sense in which we are persons, but rather a pervasive, underlying agency such as Christians have conceived the Holy Spirit to be, which speaks *through* persons, rather than *is* one among them. God is above all the living and perpetual guarantee of the possibility and continuance of the rational enterprises, and as such must be postulated as existent by those who take part in them.

The nature of such postulation is discussed in the last chapters of the Dialectic of Practical Reason, and it is clear from these that Kant does not mean by a postulate an assertion whose sense is obscure, and whose truth is doubtful, and which we have merely to *pretend* has sense and truth, in order in some manner to add a fillip to our rational endeavours. The existence of a self-determining form of causality called freedom, of a simple, psychic substance whose existence is everlasting, and of a necessarily existent ground of all contingent existences:

these are assertions having a clear, if emptily formal meaning, and have to be accepted as true by such as have experienced the unconditional ought of morals. They are, in fact, theoretical, and not practical, assertions, though our reason for asserting them is practical, and not theoretical. As Kant puts the point:

Thus through the practical law which commands the existence of the highest good possible in a world, the possibility of the objects of pure speculative reason is postulated, the reality of which speculative reason could not ensure. By this, the theoretical knowledge of pure reason certainly acquires an addition . . . But this addition *to* speculative reason is not an addition *of* speculation . . . For since nothing further is hereby achieved by practical reason, but that these concepts are real, and really have their (possible) objects, and since no intuitions are given to us in regard to them, or can be demanded, no synthetic proposition becomes possible through granting their reality . . . There is therefore no extension of the knowledge of *given supersensible objects*, but yet an extension of theoretical knowledge in relation to the supersensible in general, in so far as it is compelled to grant *that there are such objects*, without however determining them further (*CPrR*, Pt. I, Bk. II, ch. vii).

Or again:

In every use of reason in respect of an object, pure concepts of the understanding are required, without which no object can be thought . . . But here we have Ideas of reason, which cannot be given in any experience, that have to be thought through categories in order to achieve knowledge. Only we are not here concerned with the theoretical knowledge of the objects of these Ideas, but only in the fact that they have objects at all. This reality pure practical reason provides, and hence theoretical reason has nothing further to do, but merely to think those objects through categories, which, as we have clearly shown, can quite well happen without intuition, whether sensuous or supersensuous, since categories have their seat and source in the pure understanding independently of and prior to all intuition, solely from a capacity to think, and since they always mean (*bedeuten*) an object, in whatever manner it may be given to us (ibid.).

These citations make the position perfectly clear: practical reason ensures that objects satisfying certain transcendent thoughts, whether categories or Ideas, certainly exist. In this sense theoretical knowledge is extended, but, since such objects lack the support of a fulfilling intuition, we have no Idea *what* they are, or what they are like, and so cannot be said to have knowledge *of* them. If an obscurity still attaches to the notion of a moral impulsion to *do* something, which none the less enables us to know of the existence of this something, this obscurity is perhaps removed when we remember the passages

in which the active character of volition is said not to require
any further intuition of the agency underlying it: we are somehow sure of its reality in simply exercising it. Perhaps, as we
have suggested, the intellectual intuition of God is simply
such an exercise of free causality, which is indistinguishable
from the knowledge of itself.

vii

There are two further postulates which are important for
Kant's doctrine of transcendental objectivity: both have connections with his deeply implanted Christian pietism. The first
postulates an original Fall from holiness, differing from the
orthodox, Christian Fall in that it occurs out of time: the
second a revolutionary repentance, which can restore the subject to holiness, or which, seen in the perspective of time,
can set him back on the road towards it. Both are altogether
incomprehensible: we cannot understand why a will should
elect to depart from its own self-imposed legislation, or how,
having thus departed, it should again wish to return to its
original path, and to enlist superior assistance in this endeavour.
These doctrines obviously explore deep, antinomic strains
in human nature, and are to be found, together with a great
deal of discussion of the desirable and corrupt forms of religious
practice, in Kant's *Religion within the Bounds of Mere Reason*
of 1793.

The evil into which we men have fallen from all eternity,
and which we carry with us into time, is radical, moral evil,
or evil of the rational will. It is not the evil of our merely
animal nature, our tendencies to exceed in eating and drinking,
in sexual indulgence, or in general disorder; nor the evil of
our undisciplined, self-concerned, rational nature as shown
in tendencies to envy, jealousy, vainglory, ingratitude, *Schaden-
freude*, and so on. It is rather an evil which attacks our allegiance
to the moral law itself, and our will to carry out its mandates
(*Religion*, pp. 26-7). Nor is the ground of this evil to be found
in our sensuous inclinations, for which our will is not at all
responsible, nor in the will's own legislative aspect, since this
is rational, essential to the will, and as such incorruptible.
Sensuous inclination could only make man bad in an animal
sense, while the inner corruption of the legislative will would
render him devilish. As Kant puts it: 'As providing a ground
for what is morally evil in man, sensuality provides too little,

since, by taking away the impulses which spring from freedom, it turns man into a merely animal being. Reason, on the other hand, liberated from the moral law, and as it were evil-minded (an absolutely evil will) contains too much, since it would make opposition to the law itself a motive (for without all motive the will cannot be determined), and so turn the subject into a diabolical being' (pp. 34–5).

Kant further decides that moral badness cannot be due to the mere adoption by practical reason of the goals set by natural, sensuous inclination, and their enshrinement in maxims. There is no immorality in deciding to eat, drink, and be merry, or in making this, in given circumstances, the maxim of my action. Such action may be entirely legal and moral, as might also be an action based on a contrary maxim. Immorality, in Kant's view, only arises if the contingent, natural maxim is given a place above that of the moral law, if the moral law is subordinated to it:

Man, even the best, is only for this reason evil, that he inverts the moral order of his motives in his adoption of the same. He adopts the moral law along with (*neben*) the laws of self-love into his maxims, but, becoming clear that one cannot exist alongside the other, since one has to be subordinated to the other as its ultimate condition, he makes the motive of self-love, and its inclinations, into a condition for following the moral law, while the latter should rather be taken up into the general maxims of the elective will as the supreme condition of the former, and the only motive for satisfying it (p. 36).

Such immoral inversion occurs even if what the man chooses to do is quite in accord with the moral law, and so legal, but if the man would not have done what he did do out of reverence for the moral law alone, but needed to be pushed on by sensuous inclinations, then such a man is acting immorally, and is, for the time being at least, a morally evil man. There is, for Kant, no position of moral indifference in this field: either one is a good man, who *would* subordinate all other maxims to the moral law, even though this may not, in fact, be necessary, or one is an evil man who would not do so (see the Note to pp. 22–3). Kant is not, however, going as far as the Stoics in holding all deviations from morality to be equally evil, nor is he denying that there are actions indifferent in the sense that *either* their performance or their omission would accord with the moral law.

The tendency, however, to subordinate the moral law to

sense-based maxim in one's choices must, Kant holds, be *original* in man: it cannot have its origin in any external cause operative in time, nor in the timeless decision of a divine superior; for, in neither case, could the tendency or its expression be imputed to man. Man must freely have elected to be immoral in certain circumstances, and he must have elected to do so from all eternity. The biblical story of Adam's primal Fall merely expresses this necessity in the language of parable (p. 43). Kant, however, finds Man's capacity for deviating from his own legislation profoundly unintelligible and inscrutable (*unerforschlich*): he even refuses to use the same word for it as he uses for the good tendencies in human nature. We have *Anlagen*, good predispositions, in the case of our tendencies towards self-preservation, propagation of the species, desire to be esteemed, and so on, but we have only a *Hang*, or leaning, in the case of our tendency to deviate immorally. Kant defines such a *Hang* as the subjective ground of the possibility of an inclination, in so far as this ground is *contingent*, which differentiates it from an *Anlage*, or *necessary* predisposition of human nature. Such a *Hang* may be inborn, but, being a tendency of the *self*-determining will, *need* not have been activated: if at all, it must, however, have been timelessly activated.

The concept that Kant here delineates is indeed somewhat inscrutable, but, carefully considered, it appears less mysterious than he thinks it is. For, the Kantian will, as we have indicated, always has two sides: it has a legislative side which, in its pure form, promulgates the moral law, and it also has an elective or executive side (*Willkür*), which, in men, is never committed to following the moral law, but can deviate from it in favour of sensuous inclinations. It is surely not hard to see how a being having a self which does not, like God's, cover all possibilities, should have tendencies that stem from its finitude, and which can come into conflict with the unbounded universality which God necessarily embodies and pursues. Combining, as men do, a godlike freedom from external compulsion, as well as a solicitation peculiar to their limited and contingent state, they are necessarily able, by defect or non-resistance, to deviate from their freely espoused morality, as an infinite and necessary being can have no *Hang* to do. What Kant does not note is that his doctrine of a supratemporal Fall introduces supratemporal temptations which induce it: there must be analogues of sensuous allurement even in that Eden which lies out of time.

The solution would seem to be that our noumenal state covers *everything* in our temporal existence, together with *all* its sensuous content: our noumenal life must, after a non-temporal, non-spatial fashion compass all that we appear to do in time and space, together with all that we authentically and timelessly are. A pure thought can plainly effect just this. In such a noumenal rehearsal, the ordinal arrangements of time will all be present, even if its slow progression is not. Seeing all our life-possibilities thus arrayed, we may elect, in certain life-passages, to kick over the traces of morality: like the souls in Plotinus, who experience a certain audacity (τόλμα) and a desire to be on their own (τό βούλεσθαι ἐαυτῶν εἶναι: *Enneads*, IV. viii. 3), our timeless selves may timelessly have opted for certain episodic or persistent delinquencies. Such a pre-destination is, at least, less offensive to reason and morality than that of Calvin.

But if finite rational selves have an inborn *Hang* or propensity towards departures from morality in the timeless roots of their being, they must also have a timeless *Anlage*, or predisposition, to return to conformity with the legislation which is, after all, their own. The laws written into their wills tell them that they *ought* to act in accord with certain principles, and, since they ought to do so, they also *can* do so, no matter what enormities of deviation they may have fallen into (pp. 44–5). That a good tree should bear bad fruit is an inscrutable mystery, and it is equally a mystery that a bad tree should return to bearing good fruit. Both mysteries are, however, practical certainties: the very structure of the at once legislative and elective will ensures that this must be so. This is, however, where religion enters the picture, and with religion Kant is concerned in the rest of the treatise. Such religion must, however, for Kant, be consistent with the autonomy of the moral subject. He must, sunken in deviations, first do whatever he *can* to restore himself to the morality for which he has an essential *Anlage* or pre-disposition, and, by so doing, deserve and receive the co-operation of a holy will which is incapable of such deviation. It is not essential, Kant says, for any man to know what God is doing or has done for his salvation, but only what *he himself must do*, to be worthy of such support (p. 52). The infinite corruptions of religion, whether dogmatic, superstitious, thaumaturgic, mystical, and so on, are all seen as springing from a neglect of religion's necessary roots in free moral endeavour.

viii

Kant's theory of religion is both deeply religious, and also deeply moralistic and rational: he regards religious doctrines as more or less figurative, mythic expressions of metaphysical and moral truths. Thus the doctrine of the incarnation is for him merely the personification of a basic moral Idea: that of 'a human person who not only himself tries to perform all human duties, but also tries to spread goodness around him, through teaching and example, in as wide a circle as possible, and who also, though subjected to the strongest temptations, is willing to endure every sort of suffering, and even the most infamous of deaths, for the best state of the world and even for his enemies' (p. 61). But, Kant says, 'we require no example from experience, in order to frame for ourselves the ideal of a man morally well-pleasing to God, since this is already present in our reason. And we do not genuinely embellish such an Idea of reason by crediting the historical figure who embodies it for us, with an unnatural kind of birth, and with many other miraculous occurrences. To demand miracles in order to believe in an *a priori* Idea of practical reason is to give absolute proof of one's own total unbelief' (p. 63). The statements of Jesus as to his own sinlessness and closeness to God only express his embodiment and acceptance of the moral law within him, in virtue of which he, a man, can set an example to all men: doctrinal embellishments that credit him with a metaphysical subsistence from all eternity diminish, rather than increase, the force of such an example (pp. 64-5). The effect of his life is to give us hope that we too, with the help of a strengthening, comforting Spirit, which radiates from the prime source of goodness and reason, should be able to come ever closer to its absolute holiness (pp. 70-1); and that the anguish of our resolve to lead a new, difficult, and wholly different life may suffice to atone for our previous wrongdoing (p. 74). It will be seen how authentically Kant reproduces the moral and religious convictions of his early pietism, and yet how wonderfully he integrates it with his own, equally profound eighteenth-century Enlightenment. Plainly, we feel, these two very different growths must have a common root.

In much the same way he constructs the notion of an ethico-civil commonwealth which is also a Church Universal, devoted to the cultivation of all those duties of virtue which cannot be enforced by sanctions, and which supplements the political right-state, which must enforce only the duties which are enforceable. We are in duty bound, as moral beings, to strive for the realization of an ethical commonwealth which will embrace the members of all nations, each enjoying freedom to the extent that they will grant this to others, without being clear whether such an ideal is fully realizable. Such a commonwealth, treated as an Idea of reason which transcends possible experience, is the Church invisible: the visible Church is the actual body of men who strive to realize that ideal, and who pray continually for the coming of the divine kingdom, and that the divine will should be done. Such a Church satisfies the table of categories: it is *universal* in respect of its invariant moral essentials; it is qualitatively *pure* from motivation by non-moral superstition and false enthusiasm; it is *free* or liberal in the relation of its members to one another, and to external authority; and it is *unchangeable* in its modality, despite all surface modifications of constitution (pp. 101–2).

This Universal Church always teaches one and the same metaphysically ethical religion, but it is none the less divided into many styles of faith (*Arten des Glaubens*), such as the Jewish, the Mohammedan, the Catholic, and the Lutheran, each venerating their own historical founders, scriptures, ceremonies, usages, devotions, and so on, and employing their own body of ecclesiastical officials. It is part of the regrettable pathology of such styles of faith that they each tend to proclaim themselves as the one Church Universal, castigating all who are not their members, and some who are, as infidel, unorthodox, heretical, schismatic, and so on. To such spurious Catholicisms many Protestantisms rise in opposition, but Kant wryly remarks that there are quite as many catholicizing Protestants as there are protesting Catholics (pp. 107–9). What is to be hoped for, and worked towards, is that 'religion should ultimately and gradually be freed from all empirical grounds of determination, from all statutes based on history, which have unified men provisionally for the advance of the good through ecclesiastical belief. So at last the pure religion of reason will reign over everyone, in order that God may be all in all' (p. 121). This eschatology may, for us, savour not a little of positivism and Marxism, but it has profound ethico-spiritual roots which are not to be found in such creeds. Asked what time is the best in the whole history of the Church, Kant does not hesitate to answer: the present.

'For in the present age', he says, 'moral and spiritual considerations have been largely freed from the dogmatic arbitrariness of the interpreters of so-called revelation, and have been
made subsidiary to the moral improvement which alone can
be well-pleasing to God' (pp. 131–4). The kingdom of heaven
is within us, says Kant, mistranslating the New Testament
in the usual manner.

The treatment of his ethico-metaphysical religion is then
rounded off by a long treatment of *Pfaffenthum* or clericalism,
a perversion in which the officials of the visible Church, instead
of working towards the elimination of historical, statutory
elements in their cult, treat such elimination as damnable, and
make adherence to historical, statutory elements alone needed
for salvation. *Pfaffenthum* holds that, in addition to the duties
prescribed by the moral law, we have special duties to the
divine lawgiver, many courtly services (*Hofdienste*) that we
must pay to Him, and that we can make good for a deficiency
in our ordinary duties by being specially zealous in such services.
But there are, Kant holds, no special duties to God in the
universal religion, since God can receive nothing from us, and
we can neither act upon Him nor for Him (Note, p. 154). The
universal, natural religion may, however, be brought to men
in an adventitious, external manner, and may indeed be *revealed*
to men by a particular person at a particular time; although,
once revealed, it can be found, on reflection, to coincide
with universal, rational principles written into men's minds
and hearts. Kant believes that this was in fact the case with
the religion proclaimed by Jesus, which demanded no outward,
ecclesiastical observances, but only a purely inward and moral
turn of the heart (p. 159). This contingently revealed religion
had, however, a historical and statutory side which still requires
learning for its exposition and interpretation: its exponents
must be able to cut down to the rationally necessary core
hidden beneath the contingent, revealed husks, and must know
how to *subordinate* the latter to the former. A false cult,
however, subordinates the core to the husk, and creates a
religious *Wahn* or delusion in which men seek to placate the
divine lawgiver in ceremonial ways that have nothing to do
with morality. Kant lays it down as an axiom that everything
apart from a good way of life is religiously delusive, and a case
of misworship (*Afterdienst*). Such misworship, being radically
delusive, can assume infinitely many senseless forms, reinforced

by all manner of superstitions and enthusiasms (pp. 174-5). It is inevitably exploited by a body of self-arrogating, clerical authorities, who proclaim themselves the spokesmen of an invisible revealer and legislator.

To counter the danger of such clerical imposition Kant holds that a large measure of scepticism can operate as a purifying factor in religion: we should not be afraid to confess our sincere unbelief in what fails to convince us, or is not a part of what is morally relevant or certain. Kant considers that prayer, church-going, and participation in ceremonies are to be practised only as ways to strengthen moral endeavour: they are not mandatory for everyone. If Kant, in these utterances, seems to have little understanding and regard for the deep joys and other mystical elements in religion, such an appearance is perhaps itself delusive. Though he was infinitely fearful of opening the doors to any sort of *Schwärmerei*, there can be little doubt that there were many mystical notes in Kant's own feeling for the moral law, to which the passage, for example, about the starry heavens above and the moral law within bears eloquent witness.

ix

We shall conclude this chapter with a brief reference to the wonderful wealth of ethical material, all sensitively treated, in Kant's *Metaphysic of Morals* of 1797. Here we have a carefully drawn distinction between duties of right, which can be enforced by the state, and duties of virtue, which have to be left to man's free decisions. Duties of right govern the acquisition and ownership of property, the making and execution of understandings, promises, and contracts; the relations which spring from sexual intercourse, marriage, and the begetting and rearing of children; from loans, gifts, inheritances, punishments, military service, international treaties, and so forth. Kant's views on all these subjects are austere, but also in many respects advanced and liberal. Duties of virtue, on the other hand, fall for him into the two great classes of those which concern one's own moral perfection, and those which concern the happiness of others. One has no duty to pursue one's own happiness, for its own sake, since Kant, failing to distinguish between our motivation by self-love and our motivation by particular passions, thinks that we always *do* pursue our own happiness: one may, however, he holds, have a special duty to pursue one's own happiness for special moral reasons. In the case of others, it would be impertinent to try to pursue *their* moral perfection, since this must spring from the exercise of *their* freedom. It is not, however, clear why Kant thinks that we may not be of help to others in clearing up the obscurities of their consciences, and so assisting the functioning of their own legislative and elective wills. In considering our duties towards ourselves Kant deals interestingly with such things as suicide and self-mutilation, with masturbation, and with intemperate eating and drinking, and so on. In the case of duties towards others he writes instructively regarding meanness and sycophancy on the one hand, and also regarding beneficence, gratitude, sympathy, respect, friendship, fidelity, and the avoidance of pride, scorn, and slander on the other hand. In all these cases he uses the criterion of respect for persons much more than the more abstrct criterion of universalizability. Kant appears, in fact, to be no mean moral counsellor, and the fact that his discussions say much even to our own contemporary susceptibilities bears witness to the timeless validity of his moral theory.

Chapter X

Kant's Metaphysic of Beauty

i

Our task in the present chapter is to deal with Kant's transcendental doctrine of the aesthetic judgement or judgement of taste, in which transcendental objectivity plays a fascinatingly obscure but all-important part, which helps to gather together Kant's whole thought regarding the relation of the phenomenal to the noumenal. Kant's treatment of the aesthetic judgement forms the first part of the *Critique of Judgement*, whose second part, the Critique of Teleological Judgement, has been discussed in our treatment of Kant's metaphysic of nature. Judgement for Kant, as we saw, has a reflective as well as a determining role: in the latter capacity, it brings phenomenally given instances under appropriate general concepts which they plainly exemplify; in the former, it brings such instances under notions which it is only more or less *as if* they exemplified, and which perhaps, as notions, involve such obscurities, that it is not quite clear whether they deserve to be treated as concepts at all. In our teleological judgements we treat certain organized natural structures as if some will had sought to embody certain concepts in them as their indwelling ends, without necessarily believing in such a directive will, and without envisaging what it might be like. In our aesthetic judgements we see certain objectively given structures as in some manner having been adjusted or harmoniously proportioned to the build of our cognitive faculties, and so affording us a pleasure which is not only ours, but is also shareable by all beings who share such a build of cognitive faculties, that is, all beings who have the same sort of sense, imagination, thought, reason, and so on, as we have, and so can pass as men. But what exactly the cognitive structures thus functioning may be, and how they must have been harmonized or proportioned so as to give rise to the pleasures in question, and what role the transcendent things thus given phenomenally must play in the necessary genesis of such pleasures: all these matters are not anything of which we can have knowledge, but in regard to which we must be content with a set of somethings and somehows which are in sum responsible for a given outcome, which we judge to have been realized, without knowing how it came about or even what it is. The sense or feeling of beauty is, however, the centre and core of such an outcome, and in this sense or feeling we divine all the transcendental acts and processes that were involved in its making, and which would be necessary for its full understanding. The sense or feeling of beauty is therefore a simple result that calls for an immense amount of transcendental analysis and explanation, and which at certain points eludes all clarification.

Kant's treatment of the harmonization of the cognitive faculties presupposed by the judgement of taste throws great light on his view of those faculties, and advances far beyond the views expressed in former writings. There we have simply had intuition, pure and sensuous, the latter of which has been metempirically produced and arranged by the Productive Imagination, upon which the Reproductive Imagination follows in somewhat hidebound fashion, innovating in a few directions, but in the main only extending the lines which its productive sister has laid down. Over against both intuition and imagination stands the understanding, whose pure concepts have governed the work of the Productive Imagination, and whose empirical concepts derive from what has been intuitively set before it. And beyond the understanding stands reason, with its Transcendental Ideas ranging infinitely far beyond intuitive fulfilment, but which none the less manages to guide and direct the work of the understanding. All these faculties have, in the previous writings, had a dispositional fringe as well as a clearly lighted focus: we have, for example, an obscure, half-formed intuition of the whole of space; our imaginative schemata are in the nature of rules that *can* be applied to indefinitely many cases; and our conceptions, particularly our Ideas, have much in them that eludes all circumscription. Now, however, in the aesthetic sphere, this dispositional fringe becomes emphatic, and our various faculties reveal their presence and interaction through various unclear feelings and sensations, rather than through clear-cut, objective achievements. And a new sort of Productive Imagination hovers over the whole phenomenal stage, not, like the old Productive Imagination, arranging the stage and its properties *before* the curtain rises, but now presiding over the whole stage-action, and regularly adding suggestive effects and lightings to the solid things and actions which it has put upon the stage.

This new sort of Productive Imagination, in fact, represents everything personal, arbitrary, creative, and spontaneous in our experience, as opposed to the impersonal, objective order represented by the categories, the analogies, and the laws of morality, which are only spontaneously projected in the sense of representing disciplines to which we, as rational beings, must freely subject ourselves, and in relation to which our more intimate, often rebellious subjectivity acquires all the sense and the zest that it has. This new sort of imagination gives life to our sense-bound intuitions by making them suggestive of an infinity of contents which are not, in strictness, given; and also gives life to our concepts by extending their range beyond everything definite and clear, and by making us feel that we are conceiving something when we are not, in the sense relevant to the determinative judgement, really conceiving anything at all. The aesthetic judgement is, in fact, a new sort of cognitive activity which is only a judgement by courtesy; our groping towards a predicate in terms of which a given object can be characterized is in it treated as if it were a predicate of that object. The judgement of taste, Kant further teaches us, is always singular in its reference, however much it may demand universality of participation: it predicates beauty of *this* object, as given *here* and *now* to *me*; and says that, in virtue of what is universal in men, everyone who had before him an object such as I here and now have before me and see it as being, would agree in finding it beautiful. This singularity of reference involves a groping towards the infinitely rich essences which, in a Leibnizian view, are those of individual things. These, in the aesthetic judgement, are *as it were* laid bare to our conception and intuition: we enjoy, in imagination, the intuitive intelligence of a God, for whom Things-in-themselves simply *are* as He chooses to think them. But we also, *as it were*, enjoy in such a judgement a sense of how *everyone* must feel regarding such an object, in so far as he advances towards the same deep vision towards which we also are moving. The judgement of taste is thus doubly transcendental: it moves towards objects as given in their infinite individuality, and it moves towards a subjectivity in which infinitely many subjects can participate. It is therefore unintelligible apart from our transcendent thought of Things-in-themselves, whether in ourselves, and in other selves, and in God Himself, or in the objects we have before us in common. And Kant stresses this connection of beauty with what is thus transcendent in his final view of it as a symbol of morality (Cr. of Aesth. J., §59). It represents the same sort of transcendence of the immediate perspective of personal presentation and impulse as does morality. We must, however, attempt to follow out these thoughts, in the complex windings of Kant's actual expositions.

ii

Kant divides his treatment of the judgement of taste into four 'moments', which correspond to the four divisions of the categories into those of quality, quantity, relation, and modality. Quality is treated before quantity because the qualitative character of the aesthetic judgement is the prime condition of its being aesthetic. This quality has little or nothing in common with the quality, positive or negative, of determinative judgements: it consists simply in the essential *subjectivity* of the aesthetic judgement. In it we are saying how an object affects us, but in a manner that cannot be referred to an object, as being part of what it intrinsically is, not even, Kant holds, to that object which is ourselves. It is, it would appear, essentially a relational phenomenon, which arises in the commerce of objects with subjects, rather than in either alone, though more definitely attributable to the subject than the object. Beauty, for Kant, is *between* the beholder and what he beholds, rather than *in* either, even phenomenally. In this respect, the manner in which we are affected by beauty differs from the manner in which we are affected by the objects of sensation, though the *word* 'sensation' is often used in both cases. As Kant puts the point:

When a determination of the feeling of pleasure or displeasure is called a sensation, this expression means something quite different from what it means when I call the presentation of a thing (through the senses, as a receptivity belonging to the knowledge-faculty) a sensation. For, in the latter case, the presentation is referred to the object, in the former case solely to the subject, and contributes to no knowledge, not even to that through which the subject knows itself . . . The green colour of meadows pertains to sensation in the *objective* sense, as a perception of a sense-object, but its pleasantness pertains to sensation in the *subjective* sense, through which no object is presented (§3, p. 206).

Meinong, in his interesting doctrine of emotional presentation, has of course queried Kant's radical distinction between the pleasantness of meadows and their green colour (see *Über emotionale Präsentation*, §4, p. 33): both, he holds, are seen 'out there' in the phenomenal thing. But Kant's view has seemed acceptable to many, and the intermediate status he gives to hedonic quality further enables him to make the feeling of pleasure something that *can* be attributed, in a relational manner, to the object, as being a property that it has in relation to some subject. The judgement of taste, Kant holds, does precisely this.

Kant holds, however, that the quality of the pleasure thus attributed to the object in relation to the subject (or vice versa) involves further important peculiarities. It must be distinguished from the sort of pleasure which at once arouses a desire that the object should go on existing, and affecting the subject, just as it is now doing. Pleasure in the beautiful may indeed lead to such an inclination, but, in so far as it does so, we are not simply rejoicing in an object's beauty, but rather having a want directed to it, just *because* it mediates such enjoyment. Pleasure in an object's beauty is not pleasure in what an object does to us or does for us, but in what the object itself is, in the character that it presents to us. It is, in a very important and special sense, a disinterested pleasure, in that our own satisfaction does not form part of what satisfies us, as it does indeed form part of what satisfies us in the case of most ordinary pleasures, where we not merely find things pleasant, but also like them *because* they occasion pleasure. The element of objective judgement hardly enters into the assessment of the merely agreeable: we are not so much concerned with what pleases us, as with the mere fact that it *does* please us (p. 207). But the disinterested quality of the aesthetic judgement also distinguishes it from judgements of goodness or value, whether these be restricted to the pre-eminent case of the morally good, or are broadened to include such objects of rational pursuit as health, over-all happiness, or whatever is useful towards such ends. Such judgements are always, Kant holds, connected with judgements of existence: what we judge to be personally or impersonally good we also want *to be*, to continue in existence, to be freed from obstructions or menaces to its being, and so on. The aesthetically pleasing is, however, untouched by such existential concerns: we take delight in seeing the aesthetic object, in imagining or conceiving it, not in actually judging it to be really existent (see pp. 205, 209). This doctrine of the existential, judgemental concern of valuation, as opposed to aesthetic appreciation, has been greatly stressed in the value-theory of Meinong, which builds on the intentional psychology of Brentano: valuation is existence-concern or being-concern, or judgementally oriented concern, whereas aesthetic appreciation is merely so-being-concern, or concern with character. For aesthetic estimation it is sufficient that something should *seem* to be of a certain sort, whether to sense or imagination: it is not necessary that it should actually be so, or be judged to be so, nor that we should practically exert ourselves to make it be so, or keep it so. And, aesthetic delight is delight *in* contemplating a sensed or imagined or conceived object, without being concerned with its reality or unreality, nor even with the reality of our delight in it. The conception of the judgement of taste as being disinterested in its quality is therefore somewhat complex, and does not involve, as will be seen later, that what we judge beautiful may not afterwards come to interest us, both existentially and practically, just because it has been adjudged beautiful.

Having thus defined taste and its object in the disinterested, purely contemplative, character-oriented quality of our liking, Kant, in the second moment of the judgement of taste, describes it in terms of (1) the absence of a concept as the definite ground of our delight, (2) our procedure *as if* we were guided by a definite concept, which could be understood by, and communicated to everyone. As Kant puts his extraordinary point:

This elucidation (*Erklärung*) of the beautiful follows from our previous definition of it as an object of delight apart from all interest. For a man who recognizes his pleasure in something to be free from all interest, cannot but judge that it must afford a ground for the pleasure of everyone. For, since it is not based on any inclination of the subject (nor on any other reflectively developed interest), but leaves the judging person quite free to bestow his pleasure on the object, he can discover no private condition, dependent only on his own subjectivity, for the satisfaction he feels, and must therefore believe it grounded in what can be presupposed in everyone else. He therefore thinks that he is entitled to expect a similar satisfaction in everyone . . . He will therefore speak of beauty as if it were a property of the object, and his judgement of it a logical one, yielding knowledge of the object through concepts. It is, however, purely aesthetic, and merely involves a relation of a presentation to the subject, even if it resembles a logical judgement in being presupposed valid for everyone. This universality cannot, however, spring from concepts. For we cannot pass from concepts to feelings of pleasure and displeasure (§6, p. 211).

Kant must not, of course, be interpreted as holding that concepts play no part at all in the aesthetic judgement: obviously, the objects that we judge beautiful must in many cases, though not in all, be more or less clearly conceived as being of a certain sort, having certain qualities and relations, and so on. Rosalind in *As You Like It* must certainly be conceived as a young woman, and as a very specific sort of young woman, and not as a free pattern of sensed or imagined items of which no conceptual characterization is possible. What Kant is rejecting is any view which *identifies* the evaluative epithet of beauty, which is intimately bound up with feeling, with any assemblage of non-evaluative features, even psychological ones, which have no such intimate connection: he is, in short, forbidding us to commit the naturalistic fallacy, or, in a different style of diction, to confound emotive with cognitive meaning. We cannot, that is, simply say that *because* Rosalind is presented as a young woman and a certain definite sort of young woman, *therefore* she is a beautiful and poetic object of contemplation: to pass to this further characterization we must find Rosalind pleasing in that unique, contemplative, disinterested manner which we call 'aesthetic', and which, being disinterested, can be expected of everyone, whatever his personal interests. Kant, in short, is holding that, while there may be many rules exemplified in the structures of aesthetic objects, their specific aesthetic character cannot be reduced to rules, or made to depend on rules. We cannot identify beauty with any objective description, and not even make it rigorously dependent on any objective description. There is no way of arguing: This *must* be beautiful, since it is ABCD, where ABCD are a set of determinations, even psychological ones, that can be taken account of in cold blood, without the arousal of the specifically aesthetic response of disinterested, contemplative pleasure.

The position is highly paradoxical, and *seems* to involve that the aesthetic reaction must be purely individual, both in its subject and its object, and can only be universal in the quite nugatory sense that, *if* anyone were able to react to the object X just as a disinterestedly delighted subject Y reacts to it, then he would be right in judging it as Y judges it. Kant in fact says that, in respect of their logical quantity, 'all judgements of taste are singular in that, since I must immediately submit an object to my feeling of pleasure and displeasure, without the help of concepts, they cannot have the quantity of universally and objectively valid judgements' (§8, p. 215). And he adds that 'when one judges objects merely conceptually, any notion of beauty disappears. There can therefore be no rules which could compel someone to acknowledge something as beautiful. That a dress, a house, or a flower is beautiful is what no one will allow himself to be talked into supposing, on grounds of principles; one asks to have the object before one's own eyes, just as if one's pleasure depended on sensation' (p. 216). This would seem to involve that one could only assert problematically that Beethoven's Fifth Symphony would be aesthetically pleasing to everyone, and that the basic aesthetic judgements would be tied to the individuality of the subject as well as to that of the object. It is, however, arguable that Kant is here simply recognizing that one has to take account of the *way* someone sees something, a way that would involve much of his personal, historical, and cultural background, in order to penetrate to the valid universality of the aesthetic judgement behind his immediate aesthetic reaction. Only a man, for example, who understood all that a certain Gothic window in Venice meant to Ruskin, all that a certain view of Sirmio meant to Catullus, with his many personal memories and so on, would see that the aesthetic judgement in question was something into which everyone could and must enter. An object is, after all, only what a subject makes of it, and this is above all true of an aesthetic object. What we do in most appreciations of the aesthetic judgements of others is merely to come nearer to the object as given to them, and to them as apprehending that object, in a manner that defies exact analysis, and whose felt validity could only become clear to an intuitive intelligence that could see something infinitely complex in a single, summary glance. Kant is not forbidding us to formulate aesthetic judgements which ignore the infinite complexity of the subject, the object, and the occasion: he is only arguing that such judgements have not the assured validity of their bases. Thus he says that 'the judgement which arises through a comparison of many singular judgements, e.g. Roses are in general beautiful, is no longer pronounced as a purely aesthetic judgement, but as a logical judgement founded upon an aesthetic one' (p. 215). That Venice is a beautiful city is thus, as it were, a somewhat unreliable, composite judgement, founded upon the countless individual Venices that are felt as beautiful by a wide consensus of individuals on many occasions of contemplating it. All of which makes the aesthetic judgement point to a certain sort of consummation which is certainly not achievable in actual human experience.

Kant then attempts in §9 to elucidate the sort of interaction among the various cognitive faculties out of which aesthetic pleasure must arise. It is not an interaction in which a definite concept has been found to fit a given manifold of intuitive data which have been unified by the imagination. To recognize a given object as a chair may, to the weary or others, give satisfaction, but it is not an aesthetic judgement. We should, however, have an aesthetic judgement if the object before us seemed in some manner to bring before us, and to make wonderfully vivid, the authentic particularity of a given chair seen on a given occasion, as in the case of the archetypal chair seen and painted by Van Gogh in a peasant kitchen. The beautiful object does not plainly and obviously embody a concept, and that is why geometrically exact circles, cubes, and so on, contrary to the view of Plato, are not properly to be regarded as beautiful (p. 241). What gives aesthetic pleasure is a certain titillation of our conceptual faculty by a given imaginative synthesis, so that it becomes *as if* a luminous concept was about to emerge and to cover the whole synthesis, though in fact no such concept does emerge. There is conceptual foreplay, but no conceptual consummation.

As Kant puts the point:

If the determining ground of our judgement as to the universal communicability of the presentation is to be thought of as merely subjective, i.e. without the concept of an object, it can only consist in the state of mind which we find in the relation of the presentative powers to one another, in so far as they relate a given presentation to knowledge as such. The cognitive powers brought into play by this presentation are in this case in free play, since no definite concept restricts them to a particular cognitive rule . . . To a presentation by which an object is given, and which can therefore yield knowledge, imagination is necessary for the synthesis of the manifold of intuition, and understanding for the unity of the concept which unites the presentations. This state of free play among the cognitive faculties . . . must be capable of general communication, since knowledge, as the determination of the object in which given presentations must accord (in any subject) is the only mode of presentation that is valid for everyone (p. 217).

The free play of imagination and conception do not there-fore, in the aesthetic judgement, actually yield knowledge, only, as it were, promise to yield it. We feel as we would if we knew something, though such knowledge is beyond human capacity. (It is, we may note, not wholly clear why such unclear intimations of a knowledge not actually attainable might not differ from person to person.) The free play in question is further characterized as harmonious: the faculties involved feel well-adjusted to one another. 'The arousal of both faculties, the imagination and the understanding to indefinite activity, but also, as stirred by the given presentation, to activity which is harmonious (*einhellig*), the activity in short that pertains to knowledge in general, is the sensation whose universal communicability is postulated by the judgement of taste' (p. 219). The sensation peculiar to knowledge is therefore communicable even where knowledge is not achieved. And the harmony that we feel is often described by Kant in quasi-mathematical terms as being one of proportion (pp. 83, 318). Such a description must be analogical: the imagination is felt to stand up to the understanding in a relation that is felt to be right for knowledge, the same sort of relation, in short, in which one number stands to another when they stand in some definite ratio to one another.

iii

The third moment of the judgement of taste is a relational one, and consists of a seeming purposiveness or teleology (*Zweck-mässigkeit*). Teleology exists wherever some will has actively made some object satisfy or exemplify a certain concept, but we can judge an object to be teleologically structured, even if we do not seriously believe it to have had a concept imposed upon it by some will. 'Purposiveness can therefore exist without a pur-pose, in so far as we do not locate the causes of its form in a will, but can none the less make the explanation of its possibility intelligible by deriving it from a will' (p. 220). We here have another case of the as-if, reflective judgement, which involves no conviction, and which is really only an *Annahme*, an entertain-ment, in the technical sense of Meinong. Such an *Annahme* naturally associates itself with the pleasurable interplay of the cognitive faculties: it is as if the object were designed to promote such interplay. Kant even *identifies* the aesthetic judgement of finality with the pleasure that goes with it. He says:

the consciousness of the merely formal purposiveness in the play of the subject's cognitive powers in the presentation of some object, is the pleasure itself, since it contains the determining ground of the subject's activation of his cognitive powers, an inner, purposive causality with a direction to knowledge as such, without being limited to a determinate item of knowledge . . . This pleasure has an inherent causality, i.e. to maintain our presentative state and its cognitive concern without further motive. We *linger* in the consideration of beauty, since such a consideration reinforces and reproduces itself (p. 222).

In this passage the judgement of taste is not only identified with a felt pleasure, but also with a causality directed to preserving our contemplative state. Kant thus sees pleasure, judgement, and causality as so closely connected together that they count as mere aspects of a single conscious attitude.

The as-if teleology which is thus variously experienced is not, however, confined to the relation of the object to our cognitive faculties: it also extends to the object's intrinsic *form*, the *manner* in which its various constituents are put together to constitute it. This form or manner must give the object its unity, and so make it easy and delightful to apprehend. But the connection of beauty with form seems to involve that nothing that is quite unstructured can be beautiful, a consequence that gives Kant some trouble, since many simple colours and tones please us aesthetically. Kant suggests that Euler may be correct in supposing that our awareness of colours, tones, and so on involves some obscure awareness of the regular vibrations which underlie them, and which constitute their form; but, if this is not the case, their purity, their freedom from admixture, is, in its way, a negative case of form. Kant is, however, resolute in rejecting mere stimulus (*Reiz*), or mere excitement (*Rührung*) as aesthetically relevant. Our conscious intelligence is essentially synthetic, and it is therefore only when it can put items together and be conscious of their emergent form, that it can experience the peculiar titillation that we call 'aesthetic' (pp. 66-8). Such an enjoyment of emergent form defers to no extraneous concept of standard or good form in a thing of a given sort, for example, an article of use. Our judgement, Kant says, 'is aesthetic precisely because its determining ground is no concept, but rather the feeling (for inner sense) of a harmony in the play of our cognitive powers in so far as this can only be sensed' (p. 228). Thus I may find beauty in a little grass plot neatly surrounded by trees in a forest, without considering it as good for some banal, social purpose (p. 227).

Kant inquires, at a later stage, whether the judgement of taste involves only the as-if assumption of a merely *subjective* teleology, or also that of an *objective* teleology. Must we think of the beauties of flowers, crystals, and so on as if *objectively* structured to fit in with our cognitive powers, and to promote their attunement, or is it sufficient to be aware of the merely subjective attunement, which is also only given in an as-if manner? Kant, after some hesitation, decides for the latter alternative. There is so much evident mechanism underlying the beauties of inorganic and organic nature that it is gratuitous to have recourse to the conceived presence of an objective teleology, problematic and obscure as such a conception must in any case be (§58, pp. 346–51). It may be justifiable to use as-if, teleological explanations in the case of certain natural structures, but Kant is unwilling to counsel even a semi-serious recourse to such explanation in the mere case of natural beauties. Flowers must have the form and colour they have in order to attract insects, not to delight aesthetes. It is not, however, clear, since for Kant all teleology is only a matter of as-if, reflective judgement, with perhaps a transcendental root, why the adaptation of nature to our aesthetic enjoyment should be treated less respectfully than her adaptation to purely biological ends. Kant's third moment of the judgement of taste therefore informs us that beauty is the teleological form of an object, in so far as this is perceived in the object without the presentation of any definite end (end of §17, p. 236).

iv

The fourth moment in the judgement of taste is that of modality. In the judgement of beauty, pleasure is felt to be *necessarily* present, necessity being the strongest of modal qualifications. This necessity is not, however, that of an *a priori* analytic, or *a priori* synthetic judgement, such as might recommend itself to the understanding, nor is it an *a priori* practical necessity, expressive of an obligation imposed on itself by practical reason, the unconditional, legislative will. It is, says Kant, an 'exemplary' necessity, that is, a necessity of the agreement of all to a judgement regarded as an example of a universal rule which cannot be stated. Since an aesthetic judgement is not an objective knowledge-judgement, it cannot be deduced from definite concepts, and is therefore not apodictic. Much less can it be inferred from universal experience, that is, from the thoroughgoing agreement of judgements regarding the beauty of a given object (§18, p. 237). In other words, it is not a necessity that can be established as actually obtaining, and for that reason imposed on everyone: it is at best a necessity that can be *claimed* to hold for everyone, in virtue of some common internal ground. The typical language in which such a claim utters itself is that everyone *ought* to approve of a given object and declare it beautiful (§19). And, provided a liking for the object really is necessitated by some inner ground common to all men, we are justified in our claim; but the justification is conditional on the presence of such a common, inner ground, and this we can only presume and not know.

Such a postulated common ground may best, Kant holds, be denominated a sense, since it operates not through concepts, but through feelings: it is not, however, a sense such as the ordinary bodily senses, since these have no necessary connection with pleasure or displeasure, nor yet a sense such as the common sense of ordinary parlance, since this certainly employs concepts, even if highly obscure ones. It must be a capacity for inner experience, arising out of the internal interplay of understanding and imagination, and from their mutual adaptation, and this experience, in virtue of the universality of the cognitive functions in question, must be something that all men may share and can presume in one another. As Kant puts the point:

Acts of knowing and judging must, together with the conviction that accompanies them, admit of universal communication, for otherwise they would have no agreement with their object, but would amount only to a mere subjective interplay of cognitive powers, just as scepticism says they do. But, if acts of knowledge are generally communicable, so also must be the state of mind, i.e. the accord of the cognitive faculties, suitable for knowledge as such, and in the proportion suited to a presentation which sets an object before us, in order to constitute knowledge. For without such an accord, as the subjective condition of knowledge, knowledge would never arise as an outcome . . . But this accord of the cognitive powers involves a differing proportion which corresponds to the differences in the objects presented. There must, none the less, be one proportion in which the inner relations of the cognitive faculties achieve an optimum of mutual stimulation for the sake of knowing a given object. This accord can only be determined by feeling, and not by concepts. But since this accord must be universally communicable, so must, in the case of a given object, be the feeling of such an accord. But universal communicability of a feeling presupposes a common sense, and this can therefore be assumed with good ground, without appeal to psychological observations (§21, pp. 238-9).

Kant's arguments on this head are not very convincing, and involve quantifying the wholly obscure joint operations of the imagination and the understanding, and of the obscure feelings which these operations entail. They are rather like the quantifications of belief, which are held, by some moderns, to underlie our judgements of probability. And that Kant is not satisfied by such obscure arguments is shown by his attempt, at a later stage of the work, to give a Transcendental Deduction of the judgement of taste, and to resolve an antinomy which he thinks arises in regard to them. The Transcendental Deduction (§38), however, makes no advance on the arguments previously offered. Though held to be astonishingly easy, since it is spared the trouble of justifying the objective reality of the concept of beauty — the judgement of taste not being a judgement that can yield knowledge — it fails to prove that there must be universally shared feelings which correspond to Kant's posited accord of the cognitive faculties. At best it provides an argument for the *possibility* of such feelings, as an explanation of the extraordinary claims made by the judgement of taste. And, in the resolution of the antinomy of taste, Kant freely takes refuge in Things-in-themselves, and in their unknowable, thinkable accommodations to the subject, the necessary background, as we have argued, for all his philosophizing.

The Antinomy of Taste (§56) is to the effect: Thesis: that the judgement of taste *cannot* be based upon concepts, since, if it were, it would admit of demonstration and refutation; but, Antithesis: that the judgement of taste *must* be based upon concepts, since, if it were not, it would not admit of any argument for and against, and any claim upon the agreement of others. The solution to the antinomy consists in holding that aesthetic disputants, while not basing their attempts at persuasion on any agreed set of conceptual norms, but only on an arousal of feelings, none the less make gestures, by way of such feelings, to certain supersensible relations of accord which they *think* are evinced by such feelings, though they can, of course, have no knowledge of this matter. There are, indeed, peculiar aesthetic concepts, but they must for us remain eternally empty, since they concern an accord among transcendental

faculties which necessarily transcends experience and knowledge, while only its outcome, certain feelings and claims,
can be phenomenally given. We know that we experience
certain normative feelings, and place them in reflective aesthetic
judgements, and we have to posit transcendental arrangements
to account for such feelings and for their normativity, arrangements of which we can have not the faintest approach to
knowledge.

As Kant puts the point:

Now the judgement of taste refers to objects of the senses, without determining a concept of the same for the understanding, since it is not a
judgement of knowledge. It is therefore only a private judgement, an
individual, intuitive presentation of a feeling of pleasure, whose validity
is restricted to the judging individual . . . The object is an object of pleasure
to me, to others it may be otherwise — each has his own taste. But none
the less there is, in the judgement of taste, a wider reference of our presentation of the object (and also of the subject) which enables us to
enlarge the necessity of this sort of judgement to everyone. A concept
must necessarily underlie this extension, but a concept which cannot
be pinned down intuitively, which does not enable us to know anything,
nor to adduce a proof of the judgement of taste. Such a concept is the
purely rational concept of the supersensible, which underlies the sensuously given object (and also the judging subject) which are its appearances. For without accepting such a reference, the claim of the judgement
of taste to universal validity could not be rescued . . . All contradiction
is, however, dissipated if I say: the judgement of taste bases itself upon a
concept (of a ground of the subjective teleology of nature for our judgement) through which nothing can be known or proved in regard to the
object, since it is not determinable by, nor amenable to knowledge.
Through this concept it however acquires validity for everyone (i.e.
for every singular judgement which immediately accompanies intuition),
since the determining ground of this concept is perhaps to be found
in the concept of what can be regarded as the supersensible substrate
of humanity (§57, pp. 339–40).

In other words, our own transcendental subjectivity finds
the translation of the message affecting it from transcendental
objectivity a smooth and easy matter: what we imagine seems
to accord with the demands of our understanding, though not
in too obvious a manner, and this supersensible accord generates
the delight which, since it has its roots in a common transcendence, can be judged to be communicable to all men. Since
we all can have the same sort of mutual adjustment whether
as subjects or objects — objects, like subjects, are in a sense
part of the same transcendental We — and this mutual adjustment has to be thought of in transcendent, noumenal terms, we

can understand the shareable pleasure which attends the good working of our common faculties. The judgement of taste involves, in fact, a deeper penetration beyond the phenomenal veil than the imperatives of morality or the regulative Ideas which inspire science. For it conceives of something which can only reveal itself in interior feelings, the most intimate of all revelations. We, like Dante, in his report on the Beatific Vision (in *Paradiso*, xxxiii, ll. 91-3) know that we are seeing or have seen something simply because we are so surpassingly overjoyed:

> La forma universal di questo nodo
> credo ch'io vidi, perchè più di largo
> dicendo questo, mi sento ch'io godo.

v

The thought-reference to something which transcends possible experience becomes even more emphatic in Kant's treatment of the sublime (§§23-9). Kant, like his predecessor Burke, distinguishes the sublime from the less exalted beauty which is the predicate of our more ordinary aesthetic judgements. If the more ordinary aesthetic judgement acts as if it were applying a concept to some object, where this concept is merely the empty notion of an unknowable harmony among our cognitive faculties, the judgement of the sublime acts as if it were applying a Transcendental Idea, which in its very content transcends possible experience, to some object presented before us. The harmonious proportionment of our cognitive faculties is, at least, very much closer to what could be intuitively given than, for example, the simplicity, the fully real infinity, and the necessity of existence postulated in a Transcendental Idea. As Kant puts the point:

Beauty in nature concerns the form of the object which consists in limitation. But the sublime can be found also in a formless object, in so far as limitlessness is presented or suggested by it, a limitlessness to which totality is none the less added, so that the beautiful seems to count as the presentation of an indefinite concept of the understanding, the sublime as an indefinite concept of reason. The pleasure in the former case is accordingly bound up with a presentation of quality, in the latter case of quantity. Our pleasure in the latter case also differs in quality from that in the former case, in that the beautiful directly imparts a feeling of fostering life, and can therefore be combined with allurements (*Reizen*) and imaginative play, whereas the feeling of the sublime is a pleasure which only arises indirectly, in so far as it is generated by the feeling of a momentary inhibition of the vital powers, and an immediately consequent reinforcement of the same. As an emotion, it appears to be serious, not playful, in its use of the imagination. And since it cannot be combined with allurements, the mind being not merely attracted but also repelled by the object, the pleasure in the sublime, does not so much involve positive pleasure, as astonishment and respect. It deserves, that is, to be called a negative pleasure (§23, 244-5).

Kant goes on to say that, whereas the narrowly beautiful seems and is felt to be teleologically adapted to our conceptual and imaginative faculties, the sublime, on the other hand, seems and is felt to be at odds with these faculties, and to do violence to the imagination, while yet seeming to be all the more sublime for doing so. In the sublime, moreover, the aesthetic quality of sublimity seems, Kant holds, not to attach so closely to the object as is the case with ordinary beauty, but rather to hover above it, or beyond it, or to have its location in ourselves. Kant denies that the stormy ocean can *itself* come before us as sublime. It is itself *grässlich*, horrible (p. 245) but it arouses in us an awe, which is not felt towards nature and its performances, but towards something beyond nature and resident in ourselves. It is doubtful whether Kant is here doing more than registering his own, characteristically ambivalent, eighteenth-century aesthetic reactions: to the Byronic aesthete of a slightly later date the infinite, stormy ocean was *itself* sublime. It is also doubtful whether the sublime stands in antithesis to every other form of aesthetic appreciation as something which overrules, rather than promotes, the harmony of the cognitive faculties. Plainly there are a vast number of distinct species of the aesthetic, all disinterestedly contemplative according to the Kantian recipe; some involving abstraction and isolation, others rich involvement in the concrete; some deliberately stylized and one-sided, others deliberately balanced and normal; some 'aesthetic' in some exclusive, exquisite sense, others hospitable to all ordinary interests and impulses, and so forth. The interest in the sublime is but one note in the aesthetic repertoire to which Kant has given undue importance on account of its relation to his Transcendental Ideas.

Kant divides the sublime into the mathematically and the dynamically sublime. The mathematically sublime is what frustrates the efforts of the imagination in seeming to be great beyond estimation, so great that everything else seems small in comparison with it (p. 97). The dynamically sublime is merely a seeming case of superlative greatness in might or power, of a force (*Gewalt*) that can overcome all resistances and obstructions (p. 109). The mathematically sublime humiliates only the faculty of cognition, whereas the dynamically sublime also humiliates the faculty of desire, the former defying our endeavours to comprehend it imaginatively or conceptually, the latter our endeavours to do anything against it practically (p. 94). In all these cases the absolutely great is great only for imaginative comprehension, for a grasp that can run through many parts successively apprehended in time, but which none the less aspires to apprehend all such parts *together*. If one is content to go on grasping the parts piecemeal, as one's eye might follow the stones of the Pyramids, or the beauties of St. Peter's, one after the other, and without seeking to see them together, sublimity will not arise; nor will it arise if the object, for example, the Pyramid, is seen so distantly, or so confusedly that its complex structure remains unapparent (pp. 99–100). It is plain, in fact, that any sublime object must be seemingly, that is, aesthetically speaking, infinite, of a size or power which transcends any size or power we can lucidly imagine, no matter whether or not it is actually infinite: it may, in fact, measured by suitable standards, be quite small. All comprehension of magnitude, according to Kant, involves both the successive apprehension of parts, and also a certain supersession of such succession, when the whole is seen *as* a whole: when we are faced by infinite magnitudes, or by magnitudes that are, aesthetically speaking, infinite, we experience this sense of the sublime. (Kant does not here consider that infinity may not be seen as sublime, but as tedious, as in the Hegelian reactions to the 'bad infinite'.)

As Kant puts the point:

Measurement of space (as an apprehension) is also a description of that space, and so an objective movement and progression. But the comprehension of the manifold in unity, not in thought but in intuition, and of whatever was successively apprehended in one instant, is, on the other hand, a regress, which again supersedes the progress of the imagination, and renders coexistence intuitive. Such measurement is accordingly a subjective movement of the imagination which does violence to inner sense, succession in time being a condition of inner sense and intuition. This violence must be more notable the greater the quantum which the imagination comprehends in a single intuition. The endeavour, therefore, to take the measure of quantities, which have taken a noticeable time to apprehend, within a single intuition, is a sort of presentation which, considered subjectively, is counterpurposive, but which, being necessary to the estimate of magnitudes, is purposive, so that the same violence which the subject undergoes imaginatively is adjudged purposive for the whole determination of his mind. The *quality* of the feeling for the sublime is that of displeasure directed to our aesthetic power to assess an object, which displeasure is at the same time seen as purposive. This is possible because one's own incapacity brings out the consciousness of an unlimited capacity in the same subject: the mind can only assess the latter aesthetically by way of the former (§27, p. 259).

In other words, one's own inability to complete a synthesis, which is for human purposes infinite, in the manner satisfactory to the imagination operating under the aegis of the understanding, helps us to feel in a dim manner what such an infinite synthesis would be like: the sort of synthesis possible for an intelligence that has overcome the supersessive character of time, and by which an infinite aggregate can be seen 'all together', just as a finite aggregate can. God presumably can see all the finite cardinals exemplified in some comprehensive aggregate before Him, without running through them one *after* the other, much as a shepherd can at a glance see the finite cardinal number of his flock: that *His* flock are infinitely numerous will be immediately perspicuous to the divine shepherd. In our case, however, the reaching out to a transfinite summation yields only a feeling of the sublime, a feeling intelligible in the light of its divine archetype.

Kant, with his strong preference for the Transcendental Subject above the Transcendental Objects which affect it and which play in with it, naturally sees the roots of the sublime in *our own subjectively* felt transcendence over everything finite and sensible. Thus he says that 'the feeling for the sublime in nature is a respect for our own vocation that, through a certain subreption, substitutes respect for a natural object for respect for the Idea of humanity in our own subjectivity. Such an object, as it were, shows us intuitively the superiority of the rational determination of our knowledge-faculty over the greatest power of sensibility' (§27 p. 257). And he further assimilates our feeling for the aesthetically sublime to our respect for the moral law within us, which respect certainly confers sublimity on its object. As Kant puts the point:

We therefore at once see that unconditional, absolute greatness is wholly absent from nature in space and time, a greatness that is none the less demanded by the meanest understanding. And we are thereby reminded that we have only to deal with nature as a phenomenon, and that this must be regarded as the mere presentation of a nature-in-itself, which reason grasps in an Idea. This Idea of the supersensible that we cannot further determine, and do not *know* but can only *think* of as presented in nature, is aroused in us by an object whose aesthetic estimation taxes our imagination to the limit, whether of mathematical enlargement or dynamic power over our minds, since it rests on a feeling, the moral feeling, of a vocation in ourselves which entirely transcends nature, and in relation to which the presentation of the object is judged to be subjectively purposive. One can in fact not well conceive of a feeling for the sublime in nature, without connecting it with a mood of the mind which is akin to the moral (p. 268).

One must necessarily respect Kant's emphasis upon the subjective and moral resonances of the judgement of the sublime, and of aesthetic judgements generally. One may, however, make the suggestion that there is also something of the sublime in the *disregard* for everything subjective and even moral shown by certain great natural existences and forces. They are magnificent in their total unawareness of what they are, and of what they are doing, in their contentment, as it were, simply to be what they are, and to function as they do function. And God likewise, as many good theologians have taught us, may only be said to know or will anything, not as some extraneous subjective exercise, but solely by *being* the comprehensive reality that He is. There certainly is a sublimity of being which transcends the restless sublimity of thought and consciousness. We may note further that the felt infinity which Kant connects with the mathematically and dynamically sublime is rightly held by him to occur also in many cases of the simply beautiful. An aesthetic Idea, Kant says is 'an imaginative presentation which accompanies a given concept, and which is bound up with such a multitude of partial presentations in free imaginative use, that no expression meaning a definite concept can be found for it, and that therefore permits us to add to a concept much that cannot be named, whose feeling excites the cognitive faculty, and adds *Geist* [we may translate this by "mental aliveness"] to the mere letter of speech' (p. 316). Kant is here acknowledging the importance for the judgement of taste of those vague *Bewusstseinslagen*, nutshell states of consciousness (to borrow a term from the Würzburg School of psychologists), states which condense in themselves an indefinite amount of detail, which can be teased out by questioning, but which is present in an undivided conscious stance or mood. Such a *Bewusstseinslage* is often seen as resting on an illusion or a fallacy by lovers of the sensuous, for example, Hume, Titchener, or the Wittgenstein of the *Blue Book* and the *Philosophical Investigations*, but it is upheld by Kant in his talk about syntheses and feelings of this or that, and it is very arguably the most fundamental of all mental concepts. For, to condense and bring to partless unity what is dispersed and mutually external, is arguably the characteristic achievement or *Leistung* of the mind. The doctrine also fits in with the Leibnizian conception of the monad with its reduction of infinite complexity to simplicity and unity. For the Leibnizian monad, unfathomably one and simple, also harbours unfathomable complexities in what it represents: it is arguable that the Kantian Transcendental Subject and Transcendental Object must be similarly conceived. And the aesthetic judgement is precisely the territory where we feel and enjoy the presence of a unity and a simplicity too absolute to be spelled out either imaginatively or conceptually, but which is combined with a richness of inner content which also defies intuitive or conceptual spelling out.

There are a great number of other vividly made points in the remainder of Kant's Critique of Aesthetic Judgement, of which we can only briefly take note. There is the rather strange view that all our aesthetic pleasure in what seems a beauty of nature will evaporate if it is proved to be a beauty of art. If we discover that flowers, birdsong, and so on are not naturally produced, but artificially contrived, they will at once lose all their beauty (p. 299). This judgement seems to rest on the late eighteenth-century idolization of the natural, which we, as moderns, do not share: the contrivances of the stage can for us be as lovely; though differently lovely from the devices of nature. There is further a romantic stress on the essential irregularity of genius and its creations. Genius is for Kant 'a talent for producing something for which no rule can be given: it is not a readiness for a skill that can be learnt by any rule, so that *originality* is its prime property' (§46, pp. 307-8). Kant, with his period background, does not think that beauty can at times be as regular as it is at other times irregular, and that the originality of genius may at times consist in being as regular as Racine or Boileau. If obedience to a tradition manages to bring out some significant aspect of the ultimate unity-in-difference, which Kant has described in terms of imagination and conception, and can do so with perspicuity and poignancy, then such obedience is aesthetically legitimate. Nor has Kant, with his love of antinomy, stressed the antinomy that confronts us in every field of the sublime and beautiful: that which is aesthetically arresting can be sought in the most incompatible directions.

Kant has further classified and compared the Arts in an interesting fashion, and has given an amusing characterization of the comic in terms of an expectation or tension which is suddenly reduced to nothing (p. 332). And he has argued that beauty is a symbol of the morally good (§59), which ignores the radical disparity between aesthetic and moral disinterest — the one caring for nothing but the impartial presentation of what things are, and the latter for nothing but the practical realization of what everyone can, with full existential earnestness, seek to realize for everyone. He ignores the possibility that clashes between these two forms of disinterest may arise, in which morality no doubt may claim to have the last word, but in which it will still have to respect a kind of impartiality radically different from its own. By and large, however, Kant's treatment of aesthetics is as superior in depth and originality to all others as his treatment of morality is similarly superior. And his aesthetics perhaps throws a more revealing light on his ultimate noumenal conceptions than other parts of his philosophy, since, as we have said, it is perhaps in our obscure 'feelings' for the beautiful and the sublime that we enjoy a better intimation of what a purely intellectual intuition would be like, and what its objects are 'in themselves', than in any other exercise of our speculative or our practical reason.

Chapter XI

Last Comparisons and Assessments

i

We wish, in the present chapter, to gather together the threads of our interpretation of Kantian transcendentalism, seeing what it amounts to, and how it compares with other related types of doctrine, especially to such as came after it and built upon it. We must also consider to what extent it should be accepted or amended, laying our wonted stress on the Transcendental Object, which, in our view, plays an essential, if highly problematic role in Kantian theory. We have to inquire into the feasibility of a view which sees the world of our common experience as throughout dependent on objects and relationships, including those of the subject, which can and must be thought, in quite empty, formal fashion, if the world of our common experience is to be understood, and if we are to find empirical surrogates for what ultimately underlies it.

It may, in the present context, be profitable to compare Kant's account of our phenomenal predicament, forced to make do with appearances and relations among appearances — though such a 'making do' involves the conception of a 'doing without' all that such a 'making do' represents — with Plato's myth of the life of men in the cave of the instantial and the phenomenal, with which it has a large number of analogies. There is, in fact, much in Kant that is profoundly Platonic, since his Things-in-themselves, like Leibniz's monads, are practically the same as their uniquely specified essences, which all depend upon a single supreme Thing-in-itself which is simply the united sum total of all positive predicates. The Platonic cave-dwellers, like the Kantian ones, are unable to see the objects that cast the variously shaped and arranged shadows on their cave-wall, and have to be content with noting how they accompany or follow one another, and with projecting such regularities into the imagined future, finding their substitute for substantial things and causal relations in the systematic interrelations of the shadows, whether actual or possible.

But the Platonic cave-dwellers have the advantage, in that a turning of the head and the gaze from the ectype to the prototype is not an impossible, though a difficult operation. And it is also not impossible, after suitable dialectical training of their limbs, to walk out of the phenomenal cave altogether, and to explore eidetic relations of various degrees of loftiness, with all the resources of a luminous, intuitive vision. The Kantian cave-dwellers enjoy no such privilege, at least not in this life, and the concepts they form of the real sources of their appearances, and of their relations to one another, are merely abstract structures of variables, quite devoid of intuitive content. The Platonic cave-dwellers are also acquainted with one another, and can bandy conjectures as to the course of the shadows on the walls of their common prison: the shadows also are as much a common show as are the cave walls. The Kantian cave-dwellers, on the other hand, live each confined in his private cave-cell, and may not be seeing exactly similar shows on exactly the same sort of walls, though there is some sort of vague rumour which establishes connection among them, and a rational presumption that they all see much the same. The Platonic cave-dwellers can, further, certainly see themselves and take notice of their fettered state, whereas the Kantian cave-dwellers have their heads and eyes so fixed that they cannot directly see themselves at all. They can at best distinguish certain persistent shadows from the general mass of the shadows, and identify them as their own. And of themselves as subjects conscious of the whole phenomenal scene they have only a floating, Transcendental Idea, which never acquires any definite phenomenal content. Obviously the Kantian cave-dwellers are much disadvantaged in comparison with the Platonic ones, and their intimations of a being-in-itself which transcends the vanishing and the bounded, and which is necessary rather than contingent, are much dimmer than those of the Platonic troglodytes. And their intimations of a moral law which transcends impulse, and of a freedom which promulgates and can carry out that law, and of a secret teleology responsible for the beauty and order they see in appearances, are likewise much vaguer and more problematic than those of the Platonic prisoners.

None the less, both accounts describe the human condition, with its immersion in circumscribed, vanishing, fortuitous details, which by themselves do not hang together intelligibly, and in practical and emotional problems which require, but cannot reach to an axiology in terms of which they can be faced and dealt with. Certainly we feel ourselves to be the inhabitants of such a cave, with its flickering shows never capable of one, simple, unambiguous interpretation, and with its many dark and terrible shadows contrasting with all that is bright and clear and alluring. But the *totally* imprisoned character of our ordinary condition also encourages some to induce in themselves a deliberate sort of cave-happiness, which takes comfort in the thought that we are not really prisoners at all, and that the in-itself of things may consist merely in the systematic parade of their external and internal shows. Kant, in the exquisite balance of his thought, has encouraged much cave-happiness in others, particularly in more recent times, though there is also a neglected side of his thought, which we have tried to bring out, which tells against such an accommodation. This would appear to have gained strength in very recent times, in view of the vanishing firework displays in which the parade-view of things seems to have ended.

ii

The great objection to Kant's placing of the roots of things beyond possible experience and knowledge is, of course, that it is thought to import a hopeless surd, a mere Lockean something-we-know-not-what, into discourse, concerning which nothing significant can be said. This conception is what mainly encourages cave-acquiescence. It rests, however, on a misunderstanding, since Kant does not hold that we cannot form significant conceptions, even quite specific ones, concerning what transcends possible experience and knowledge, nor even that we in some cases have to do so. What he denies is only that it is possible to *know* something by such means, a wholly empty statement, since knowledge has been technically defined as what arises when concepts are correctly applied to what is intuitively given.

The amphiboly passages we have cited (*CPR*, A. 263–6), and others, make plain that Kant never departed from the Leibnizian view that the noumenal substrates of appearance must be incomposite unities having inner natures peculiar to themselves, on which all their outer relationships are founded; that they cannot have parts external to one another in space or in time; and that they cannot be conceived except either as thinking selves, or as something analogous to thinking selves, whose concern with objects is intrinsic to themselves, and impairs neither their unity nor their simplicity. Noumena in this sense certainly transcend experience and knowledge; since they are not in space and time, the universal forms (respectively) of outer and inner sense, on which experience and knowledge base themselves; and since even their most intimate and personal instance, the self which performs all our thinking and imaginative syntheses, is itself supersensible, and beyond experience and knowledge. And, if our own conscious selves are beyond experience and knowledge, how much more will this be so, in the case of the noumenal substrates of external bodies, which we can only credit with something remotely *analogous* to thought and imagination? Kant does not try to extend his thought and his diction in Whiteheadian fantasies as to how Things-in-themselves 'prehend' one another, or have 'objective immortality' in one another, or experience various remarkable 'feelings' towards one another. (Not that Whitehead's speculative fantasies are not in many ways enlightening.) It is plain also that, since Kant's physical monads are not credited with the spontaneity which modern physics attributes to its electrons, their analogue of consciousness will be wholly receptive and passive; it will perhaps offer no more than a screen on which other entities will be, in some quasi-spatial and temporal manner, mapped, and to which its own dynamic responses will be purely mechanical. And how much more obscure will be the non-sensuous, non-spatial, and non-temporal analogue of conscious thought and will which will have to be attributed to the *ens realissimum* or monad of monads, in whom all positive realities and possibilities are summed up, and whose creative thoughts are self-realizing and indistinguishable from their objects? But, though all these noumenal substrates transcend knowledge and experience, they still do not transcend the criteria which give them their meaning: they are conceived at least as simple unities summing up multiplicity in themselves, in a manner *analogous* to thinking beings; and as having a root-being which is neither sensuous, nor spatially extended, nor temporally piecemeal; and as manifest or quasi-manifest to one another in a manner which *is* sensuous and spatial and temporal, or which bears some analogy to the sensuous, the spatial, and the temporal.

The world of Things-in-themselves is therefore, as in Leibniz, a higher order of points of view, which runs parallel to the qualitatively variegated spatio-temporal order given in experience, but which is not itself spatial or temporal or sensuously variegated: something of its nature has perhaps been sketched by Bertrand Russell in his Lowell Lectures entitled *Our Knowledge of the External World*. Obviously the system formed by many systematically varying fields of spatio-temporal phenomena, will not itself be spatio-temporal, nor at all like its members, since its members will be phenomenal systems, and itself a system of such systems. There will, however, be isomorphisms in the two types of order, and the one will be capable of being fitted into the other rather as, in modern physical theory, the multiplicity of local times fits into one encompassing, higher-order space-time. One must not, of course, press such suggestions too far, nor venture into territories where Kant *could* not venture.

It may also be pointed out that, though the Kantian system of Things-in-themselves thus transcends experience and knowledge, Kant does discover, in experience and knowledge, many special features which point to what is noumenal. Our ordinary experience may be said to be taken by Kant to be always trying to transcend the limitations of time, space, and the sensuous. Thus our retention of the immediate past, in what Kant calls a synthesis of apprehension, certainly does violence to the supersessive character of time: the whole of a small span of time, without loss of its order, achieves the joint presence that all temporal phases would have for an intuitive, timeless intelligence. In the same way we have many experiences that abolish the mutual externality of spatial regions: since we are never aware of anything absolutely punctual, *all* our experience may be taken to do so. And there are innumerable states of mind in which sensuous illustration lapses or is reduced to a vestige, and in which, as Kant points out, we experience complex readinesses that could be intuitively realized in a vast variety of ways, but are not actually in any. And Kant, in his treatment of the imagination and its art, does not, like Hume, Titchener, Wittgenstein, or Ryle, think that a disposition for sensuous experience cannot itself be an *actual* higher-order experience, in which an infinity of detail is perspicuously summed up. In the words of a poem innumerable meanings may be concentrated, and *experienced* as concentrated, that it would require pages of dull explication and protocolization to sum up. And, in the thought of an intuitive intelligence, *all* experience must be *wholly* of this sort; it is only our dependence on affections from without that make this impossible in our case. We therefore have a considerable inkling, on Kant's admission, as to the nature of a non-temporal, non-spatial, and non-sensuous experience which none the less embraces everything that is laboriously spelled out for us by sensibility in the media of space and time. And, in our experiences of moral obligation, and of the delights of taste, we certainly, as Kant says, achieve an understanding of a conceived end which is intrinsically capable of self-realization, and of an ideal simplicity which is also indefinitely complex, both of which possibilities are not fully given in what is before us. Kant is not, therefore, offering us a mere assortment of blank surds in speaking of realities which transcend experience and knowledge: those he brings in are approachable in various ways as well as being necessary for the understanding of appearances.

iii

We may now, somewhat impertinently, seek to illuminate what we may call Kant's metaphysic of experience, or his fundamental ontology, by likening it to a circle, with sensuous, spatio-temporal phenomena at its periphery, and with radii that run back to the centre, and that end in a point of unity. On the periphery everything involves the supersessive order of time, which gives to each nuance of being its separated status, however much it may pass over into other nuances, while the togetherness of all these nuances will appear in the external togetherness, real or imagined, of spatial co-existence. (The supersessive order of time has, in Kant's view and in actual fact, to be projected on to a line.) Space and time need not then be treated, though Kant does in fact so treat them, as the merely contingent forms of our subjectivity, since they, or something like them, are plainly necessary to give apartness and definiteness to all the distinct facets of whatever exists, as well as embodying the continuous togetherness which integrates them into a world. And sensibility, or something analogous to sensibility, will necessarily arise in so far as the various nuances of being affect one another, or are in some manner present to one another, thus giving an indefeasible proof of their derivation from a common centre. Something *like* the sensuous presence of one thing to another must characterize the sleeping, mechanistic monads as much as the wakeful, spontaneous ones: if we like to be fanciful, we can imagine their phenomenal field to have something like kinaesthesis and organic sensation at its centre, as it is at the centre of ours.

At the centre of the circle, which more and more resembles some Tibetan Mandala, is the common root of all phenomena, the *ens realissimum* which embraces all possibilities and therefore exists of necessity, and which must also be credited with a spontaneity, in virtue of which it pushes some of these possibilities into actuality. But it must embrace them all nonsensuously or in a purely thinking manner, in which alone conflict among positive possibilities, acknowledged by Kant, can be ruled out; and it must therefore embrace the infinitely spatial and temporal without needing to run through them in the piecemeal fashion necessary at the periphery. We have, as Kant allows, many feelings and apprehensions of the infinite totality of time and space. This central *ens realissimum* is, by Kant, analogically conceived in the language of Judaeo-Christian personalism, but it could equally well have been conceived after other analogies, for example, in the impersonal language of Plato or Plotinus, or in the purged diction of Aquinas or of many Oriental theologians. We could, in fact, follow the least metaphorical of religious traditions, and see in it simply the uncluttered emptiness and unruffled repose which is always to be found at the centre of the Whirling Wheel of Being, and which, by some strange magnetism, draws all things to itself. But, however we may choose to conceive of it, it will have to be as essentially related to phenomena as they are to it: it is the possibility of all phenomena and they are merely defective excerpts from its riches, spelled out in spatio-temporal separateness, and with the sharp outlines of the sensibly affective.

There will, however, have to be countless lines running from the periphery to the centre, as also in the reverse direction, and it will be along those lines that we shall have to place all the phenomena of our inner, subjective life, with their imperfect overcoming of the sensuous, the temporal, and the spatial, and, may we add, though Kant does not, of the distance from the other person. And where the lines draw near to the centre, they will, in a special, rational set of cases, become full of Transcendental Ideas of the subject, the object, and the *ens realissimum*, Ideas which will transcend peripheral experience and knowledge, though they cast infinite light on the latter. And the higher phenomena of the ethical and the aesthetic life will also emerge close to that centre: the rational lines will become gathered together into a kingdom of ends in which all will legislate impartially for all, and into an aesthetic confraternity in which all will rejoice in the presentation of anything at all, provided only that it is presented with a perspicuity and poignancy which make us feel it was specially constructed to suit the needs of our cognitive faculties. The Mandala we have sketched is plainly an impertinence, horrible indeed to all analytic thinkers; Kant may have toyed, in his latter years, with the mysteries of the Zend-Avesta, but he was certainly ignorant of the mysteries of the Mahayana. We have, however, sketched it in, since we wished to bring out the thinkable continuity between the phenomenal and the noumenal, and the necessity of the latter to the understanding of the former, which is implicit in all Kantianism, and which certainly makes of its various transcendentals more than the mere surds they are commonly taken to be.

iv

We shall, in the remaining sections of this chapter, give an account, schematic to the last degree, of the relation of Kantianism to various important philosophical movements that came after it. We have sketched the origins of Kantianism in Hellenic, Scholastic, Leibnizian, and Wolffian sources: we now wish to see how its influence worked in the two centuries that came after it. This influence was predominantly one in which the Transcendental Object or Thing-in-itself was looked upon as a confusing surd in Kantian theory, and one inconsistent with basic Kantian principles. Since there could, according to Kant's view, be no knowledge of things as they are in themselves, he should not have talked about them so abundantly. The imputed inconsistency was, however, not there, since Kant throughout distinguished between what we must think, and can therefore talk about, and what we can know, giving to the word 'know' a very special, restricted connotation. But the misinterpretation led to the abandonment of the transcendent Thing-in-itself from a reconstructed Kantianism, and a transformation of the latter into a constructivism in which knowlege became some sort of an unassisted *making* of its objects. It is to do something towards demolishing this view, which not only distorts Kant, but also the very notion of knowledge, and which is thereby infinitely productive of intellectual and even practical hubris, that this book has been written.

The three monumental idealists who immediately succeeded Kant, that is, Fichte (1762–1814), Schelling (1775–1854), and Hegel (1770–1831), were all highly critical of the Kantian concept of the Thing-in-itself. Fichte is, however, the only one of the three whose idealism can unreservedly be called constructive, since he makes all objectivity, including the subject's own making of itself into an object, into an active thought-performance (*Tathandlung*) in which something is simply posited (*gesetzt*) or *put* there by thought. The subject or ego puts itself there, by taking itself to be there, and it puts what is not itself there, by a precisely similar act of positing. The process of positing objects, and itself as subject, is, however, more complex than the previous sentence suggests, since it is only by contrast with what is not itself, but a mere object, that the subject can posit itself as a subject. The two acts of positing itself as subject, and of something not itself as object, therefore go hand in hand, and are interdependent, though Fichte takes many complicated steps before reaching this conclusion. The doctrine which is here presented draws its inspiration from the Kantian Refutation of Idealism and from the Analogies of Experience, where objective permanences and regularities depend, roughly speaking, for their recognition on a contrast with subjective impermanence and irregularity of approach.

For the content of what is objective Fichte depends on the activities of the Productive Imagination, now totally emancipated from the impacts of anything external and independently active. There is, however, what Fichte calls an objective activity of the subject which, by some strange misconception, seems to the subject to proceed from some objective source wholly beyond itself. In reality this objective activity is a part of the infinite positing activity of the subject, which has, as it were, gone forth from itself centrifugally, and now returns to itself centripetally, just *as if* it had been reflected back from some obstacle or resistance (*Anstoss*) beyond the subject, though there is not, and cannot be, any such thing. The reflected activity meets the outgoing activity of the subject, just as a disturbance in a pond meets its own returning current from the pond's edges, and, at the point of confluence of the two opposed currents, the Productive Imagination gets to work, generating a whole set of phenomenal shows on which the subject's understanding imposes categories and concepts. What Fichte is describing is precisely Kant's account of the work of the Productive Imagination, without the disciplining presence of the ordered system of Things-in-themselves which require to be phenomenally and subjectively translated. But the subject thus surrounded by an objective, sensuous world of its own construction, still retains a residue of its outgoing activity, and this it pours forth in its absolute or practical activity, in virtue of which it seeks to modify the imagined objectivity which it has built around itself, and which it seeks to make more absolutely consonant with itself. The moral law is, as in Kant, the intrinsic legislation of this absolute or practical activity, and to give this its appropriate sense and content, it must put or posit itself into a large number of diverse impersonations, into finite selves, for all of whom, and in relation to all of whom, it can proclaim its universal moral legislation. It is in the reality of the moral struggle, the eternal combat of itself, *qua* infinite subject, with the imagined obstacles with which it has surrounded itself, and with the varied impersonations into which it has projected itself, and which often come into conflict with one another, that it is able fully to posit itself *as* the infinite subject that it is, and to achieve a complete spiritual self-consciousness. In its finite impersonations it will, however, see its own infinite subjectivity as a goal of moral perfection that it can only approach asymptotically, and which it attributes to an imaginary moral legislator or moral world-order infinitely beyond itself, and which it also identifies with a Thing-in-itself beyond phenomena and the transcendent source of the latter.

Nothing can exceed the brilliance of the Fichtean construction, of which we have here given only the most inadequate of sketches. It is a metaphysical and ontological exercise of the profoundest sort which, while it may have liquidated any objectivity not itself subjective, has none the less gone infinitely beyond surface appearances to a subjectivity and to transcendental acts that are certainly not given to experience or knowledge. In this sense it has *not* liquidated transcendental objectivity, since the positings that it posits are in some sense prior to phenomenal experience. What we may object to in

Fichte is his deficient respect for the humbler objects of nature, which must in some obscure manner be there for themselves and not merely for us, and to whose ontological simplicity and integrity we cannot help turning with infinite relief: they are so free from any of our intellectual theorizing and our moral posturing. And the device of making the natural world common to us all simply because we are all merely the impersonations of one and the same absolute subject surely fails to do justice to the infinite gulf between one conscious subject and another, and the gulf between all of them and the integrating transcendence which cannot be opposed as a subject to an object, or as one subject to another. All this, we may say, is less obscured by Kant.

Turning from Fichte to the early transcendental idealism of Schelling (1800), we have an exposition in which the positions of Fichte are carefully copied, but which, in a series of later works on the philosophy of nature and the philosophy of identity, admits of a curious dual reading. We can indeed, following Fichte, let all forms of objectivity be constituted by transcendental subjectivity, but we can equally well reverse the interpretative perspective, and see the forms of subjectivity as arising out of and constituted by the unthinking objectivity of nature. The same forms and categories that exist in a fully conscious form in the subject, can then also exist, in an unconscious or 'petrified' form in nature, and there is no absolute priority of the one over the other. What we thus advance to is an absolute of Spinozistic two-sidedness, which preserves its absolute identity alike in the unconscious phenomena of nature and in the conscious phenomena of thought and feeling, and which has its supreme expression in the union of these two aspects in the creations and enjoyments of art and beauty. Kant also has thought in terms of an unknown, common root between various conscious activities, and of an unknown analogy and affinity between our transcendental selves and their objects, and some of his later philosophy of nature is likewise very Schellingian.

And, turning from Fichte to Hegel, we are introduced first to an absolute principle called the *Idea* which, in a threefold expression, is at once a Platonically subsistent system of abstract logical categories, which transcend the distinction of the subjective and the objective; then to an objectively natural embodiment consisting of sensuous forms of existence in space and time; and, finally, to a subjective or spiritual order which emerges out of nature, and which re-enacts in itself all the forms spelled out in the abstract logical Idea and in external nature, and in itself as summing up and transcending both. And the whole series of logical, physical, and spiritual 'shapes' are further ordered by a famous dialectic, vaguely prefigured in the various triadic tables of Kant, in which one-sided, often opposed, forms of thought and being are taken up into more comprehensive forms of thought and being, which overcome their seeming isolation and opposition, and transform them into inseparable aspects of themselves. This dialectic certainly does not proceed *analytically* from one notion or ontological stage to another, which enters into the explicit content or meaning of the former, nor is it, in Kant's sense, a case of the *a priori* synthetic, which is held to be necessary for the intuitive-conceptual structure of experience and knowledge. It rather depends on a basic notion of conceptual and ontological *completeness*, a notion obviously derived from Kant's Transcendental Ideas of pure reason. For these all proceed from the conditioned and incomplete to the unconditioned and complete. Only, for Hegel, these ontologically complete and completely intelligible termini of the dialectic do not proceed *beyond* experience and knowledge, but are rather its final consummations. They are to be found in the three forms of absolute spirit, which are art, religion, and philosophy. Hegel is therefore infinitely far from Kant, in not seeing the meaning of beauty, of ontological and moral perfection, and of the higher aspirations of metaphysical thought as reaching out to what is beyond the empirical, phenomenal realm.

Hegel may be held to be essentially a this-world thinker, who seeks to transfigure the cave of human experience with all the transcendental lights and perspectives which other types of thought put entirely beyond it, and whose dialectic gives him the immense respect for time and history which is only faintly present in Kant. And, if, contrary to Schelling, he gives a priority to the subjective over the objective, it is not a priority which regards the subjective as the constructive, originative source of its objects, and particularly of phenomenal nature. The natural world, with its mutually external, phenomenal entities in space, and the succession of their states in time, represents for Hegel not a projection of the conscious subject, which is existentially posterior to it, but an externalization of the absolute Idea, the Platonically conceived blueprint of the absolutely thinkable and the absolutely good. The phenomenal, sensuous character of the space-time, natural world is explicated in terms of its defective, alienated expression of the absolute Idea rather than in terms of its dependence on an intuiting subject. The Productive Imagination, and its pre-conscious manœuvres has therefore absolutely no role to play in the Hegelian transformation of Kantian transcendentalism. 'The things themselves', he tells us, 'are in reality spatial and temporal: that double form of mutual outsideness is not merely put on them one-sidedly by our intuition, but is provided for them from the very beginning by the infinite spirit which is in itself, by the creative, eternal Idea' (*Encyclopaedia*, §448, *Zusatz*, final paragraph). The 'infinite spirit' here mentioned is only the Platonically real *category* of spirit, not its actual carrying out in existence.

Out of the self-externalization of the Idea in nature conscious subjectivity painfully develops itself, shedding its naturalistic integuments as it proceeds, and creating a social and political order which develops in history, and ultimately rising to an absolutely spiritual order of the aesthetic, the religious, and the philosophical, in which the absolute Idea, which was always 'in itself' or implicit, in all stages of the dialectical process, becomes 'for itself', fully explicit, and realizes its inner potential by *seeing* itself to be the inner potential and 'truth' of all being. Hegelianism was, in the later years of the nineteenth century, particularly in Britain, interpreted in a much more one-sidedly subjective, constructivist manner than was warranted, and was assimilated to a Kant interpreted in a similar manner, which left transcendental objectivity without a significant role. It is, however, clear that, if Hegel is to be reckoned an idealist, he is so in a teleological and not an epistemological sense, and that his thought involves powerful injections of a dynamic Platonism and a realistic naturalism. The absolute spirit into which everything is by him finally taken up is the complete expression and goal of everything notional and natural, rather than something which is existentially prior to these orders, and which in some sense makes them through its thought and action. Hegel, we may say, is a Kant in whom a reconceived noumenal order completely transfigures the phenomenal order, and governs all its developments: in it all transcendences are superseded and bracketed. It is, however, arguable that something very important is lost, both for thought and action, in such a thoroughgoing immanence.

It is not feasible for us to attempt to sketch the indefinitely proliferating nineteenth-century and twentieth-century scene in its further relation to the thought of Kant. Nearer to Kant than any of the three major idealists we have mentioned is, of course, the thought of Schopenhauer, with its Thing-in-itself which he identifies with an infinitely unsatisfied, striving will, active behind all natural phenomena; and for whom the Transcendental Ideas of beauty and morality point, as in Kant, to a consummation in which this will loses itself in an ultimate Nirvanic quiescence. The coming of these Asian metaphysical conceptions to Europe is, of course, of vast cultural and historical importance, but not for the understanding of Kant. In the later neo-Kantianism of Cohen, Natorp, and many others, we have a Kantianism in which the Thing-in-itself becomes purely vestigial, a limiting concept without ontological significance: if anything transcendently objective remains, it does so in the thinking subject, which is, however, rather more of a presupposition than an object of knowledge. In the thought of British thinkers like Caird and Green a similar subjectivistic constructivism prevails, though thinkers like Bradley and Bosanquet enriched this constructivism with many Spinozistic and Hegelian additions. The constructivist view of knowledge met, however, with devastating criticism in the thought of Cook-Wilson; and in Prichard's very important work entitled *Kant's Theory of Knowledge*, published in 1911, which lays bare the many shifts and confusions in Kant's Transcendental Deductions, and stresses the basic point that knowing is not making, on which we in this book have likewise insisted. Kant, however, was not the sort of pure constructivist that Prichard believed him to be, since the Productive Imagination is not, as we have argued, rightly interpreted as a creative improviser, but as a translator of noumenal interrelations into a set of sensuously schematized, spatio-temporal arrangements according to some unknown but inherent law of its own, and is dependent, for the continued success of its efforts, on the continued feed-in of an appropriate pabulum by what is transcendently objective. The Transcendental Subject is only one of these transcendently objective sources, though the major one for us.

V

We may conclude this chapter by dwelling in the next three sections on the relation to Kant of three major thinkers nearer our time: many others clamour for honourable mention, but these three are for us the most important. They are Husserl, Wittgenstein, and Strawson. Each has produced, in his own way, a complete re-working of basic Kantian principles in terms of conceptions and ideas which have become prominent since the time of Kant. Edmund Husserl (1859–1938), whom we shall deal with first, was the creator of a new, infinitely rich philosophy of mind to which he gave the name of phenomenology; a name not closely related in meaning to the phenomenology which occurs in the title of Hegel's early masterpiece, the *Phenomenology of Spirit* of 1807, which only contemplates the various shapes or forms assumed by consciousness until it achieves absolute knowledge, a form in which it sees everything in itself and itself in everything. Husserl's phenomenology is a much elaborated form of the psychognosy or abstract mind-theory of Franz Brentano (1838–1917), who, in his *Psychology from the Empirical Standpoint* of 1876, saw the essential property of psychic (i.e. mental) as opposed to physical phenomena in the necessary direction of a psychic phenomenon to an object, which is, in the paradigm case, wholly other than and beyond itself. To this direction to objects the scholastic name of 'intentionality' was given. All psychic states were said to intend objects; though they might intend such objects in a variety of ways, the basic types of intention being three: first, the mere presentation or *Vorstellung*, which only sets an object before consciousness, whether sensuously or noetically, without taking any further attitude towards it; then, second, the judgement or *Urteil*, which brings in positive or negative conviction in relation to its object, either taking it to exist or be the case, or, contrariwise, rejecting it as non-existent or as not the case; and, thirdly, the love-hate pair of attitudes, which either, on the one hand, accept their object as pleasing or desirable, or, on the other hand, reject it as undesirable and unpleasant. It is plain that this trichotomous division of conscious attitudes has much in common with Kant's presentations, whether intuitive or conceptual; with his judgements which always impart conviction, and a sense of the real; and with the feelings, desires, and acts of will dealt with in his aesthetic and moral theory. But it is clearer than Kant ever is, in making all normal, conscious references *self-transcendent*: the object I intend is, for Brentano, not part of my interior psychic life, but exists, if it does exist, utterly beyond it. There are, however, in the intentionalist theory, reflexive intentions which correspond to Kant's inner sense, in which I *do* direct myself, in secondary fashion, to my own primary direction to objects. Brentano's theory of such inner perception is, however, difficult, and involves both the presence of a primary direction *and* a secondary, reflexive direction within one and the same conscious intention; a complication which Husserl is unable to accept, holding, as against Brentano, that an inner perception of an inner state is as essentially self-transcendent as any outer physical perception.

Brentano also holds to the important position that, while the object to which my thought or perception is directed *may* exist independently of my thought, and may be conceived precisely as it is, and may even, in the privileged case, be *evidently seen* to be just what it is, it may also not exist at all, or may lack many of the features which our judgements attribute to it. The objects of our intentions can be *said* to have intentional inexistence in those intentions, but it is important to realize that, for Brentano, such 'inexistence' involves a dangerous metaphor: there need not *be* any entity, whether within or beyond the subject's intentional experience, which actually *is* what he is intending, or is *as* he is intending it. The grammar of intentional verbs is said by Brentano to be *relation-like (Relativliches)* rather than relational: one cannot infer from the fact that A is conceiving or even perceiving a B that there is a B which A is conceiving or perceiving (see Appendix I to *Psychology from the Empirical Standpoint*). We can only assert that a B is essential to the description of the perception or conception in question, though not as anything actually contained in the latter. These elementary truisms, which it is not presumptuous or dogmatic to claim enter into the absolute definition of reality, truth, and knowledge, are throughout implicit in the doctrine of Kant, who does not hesitate to hold that there are empty conceptions which aim at objective targets which simply are not there at all, and that all our sensory perceptions, whether exterior or interior, perceive their objects not as they are in themselves, but only as they seem to us to be. Kant has not, however, any perfectly clear and consistent grasp of the logic of the conception of intentional objectivity, and sometimes nonsensically conceives of a thought-object as being some sort of a real interior structure or modification in the conceiving mind itself.

Husserl, however, in his phenomenology, develops the theory of intentionality in a fascinatingly intricate manner, distinguishing a vast number of intentional orientations, and aspects of intentional orientations, which Brentano did not distinguish, and also distinguishing a vast number of different sort of objects, of lower or higher order, to which intentional attitudes may be directed. In addition to *real* objects, or real aspects of such objects, which either are, or might be, present in the really existent natural world, which we at all times posit as surrounding us in space and in time; we can also set before ourselves irreal or ideal objects, such as classes, numbers, properties, relations, and states of affairs, of various types and variously related to one another, all of which only have an *ideal* being, which does not lend them a definite position in space or in time. Plainly this conception of ideal objectivity represents an advance on the views of Kant, who does not always distinguish between the psychic processes which lead us to form conceptions of such abstract objects, and the various abstract objects themselves. All this is a doctrine first worked out by Husserl in his *Logical Investigations* of 1899–1900, and more elaborately in later works. It was even more elaborately and carefully worked out by Alexius Meinong (1853–1920), Husserl's great contemporary, and also a distinguished pupil of Brentano. Husserl further makes a distinction, closely parallel to that of Kant, between intentional acts which are *empty* or partially empty; or which are, in other words, merely notional and symbolic, and other intentional acts which are *erfüllt* or fulfilled, which have their objects before them *leibhaft* or in bodily form, an arresting metaphor, or which, as Kant would also say, involve *Anschauung* or intuition. And Husserl, very much like Kant, holds that knowledge is consummated when an empty intention is fulfilled by a matching intuition, when its object is not merely *meant* or referred to, but is 'present in person', or intuitively given. The whole Sixth Investigation of Husserl's *Logical Investigations* is concerned with the problems of such fulfilment. Thus, if I only know what it would be like to be cubical or pleased, without seeing or imagining an actual case of this, then I am living through an empty, conceptual intention to what is cubical or pleased, whereas if I *see* or imagine a cubical structure, or actually experience pleasure in myself, then I have *knowledge* of something's cubic structure, or of an actual state of pleasure in something. (The doctrine is considerably more complex than I have suggested.) And there are also fulfilled and unfulfilled intentions in the ideal realm: there are, Husserl holds, 'categorial intuitions' which set ideal structures before us as they actually are, and as they actually stand related to one another. These would resemble the performances of an intuitive intelligence in the theory of Kant, though for Husserl there is nothing transcendent about them. All these notions involve the development and use of a vocabulary which Kant would have found very useful. He seems, for the most part, to be groping his way towards phenomenological distinctions which no one before Husserl, or Meinong, had drawn satisfactorily.

Husserl is, however, much more of a subjective constructivist than Kant, since he does not wish to conceive of any sort of ontological independence in the natural objects given as in space and time, or even in their substrates: they are in all respects dependent upon, and 'constituted' by, our intentionality. Natural objects and states of affairs do indeed *transcend* the intentions which constitute them, in that they are not real parts or constituents of the latter, but they only transcend our intentional, conscious life in that they are throughout posited, or believed in, as transcending it, a kind of positing which Husserl comprehensively sums up as the 'natural attitude'. Husserl repudiates Berkeleian positions, but he is completely and absolutely Berkeleian in his teaching that it is only as a *given* transcendence, in and for our conscious references, whether empty or fulfilled, that natural objects have any ontological status at all (see, e.g., *Ideas Towards a Pure Phenomenology*, §§53-4). And he reaches this quasi-Berkeleian position by what one can only regard as a sleight of words, or a confidence trick. For he starts by persuading us, quite legitimately, that we must practise a method of the suspension or withholding (ἐποχή) of our confidence in natural realities, in order to become aware of the omnipresent psychic intentions which constitute them as objects for us; and then turns this purely methodological withholding into a paralytic stance, so that it is held to be utterly meaningless to conceive of such reality as existing otherwise than as our complexly constituted intentional object. This sleight of words is deftly carried out in

§§47–55 of Husserl's *Ideas towards a Pure Phenomenology and Phenomenological Philosophy* of 1913; which magnificent work need not be judged by the sections in question, which do not, in any case, point to some sort of mental dishonesty, but only to a deep confusion to which all language renders us subject.

According to the new, phenomenological view, objects in nature are inseparable from the infinite sensuous perspectives (*Abschattungen*) in which they are intuitively given to us, and the Thing-in-itself, for which Husserl does not hesitate to use the Kantian symbol X (see *Ideas*, §131), is simply the unreachable, sum total of all the possible views of it. Husserl does not, however, use a similar, subjectivistic, constitution-approach, in regard to the acts of the intending subject or ego, and to that subject or ego itself. The subject and its acts are not given by way of one-sided perspectives, but in a wholly direct and adequate manner: we therefore have intuitive, evident knowledge of our inner cogitations and of the thinking self which is their inner pole. There can, of course, hardly be a wider gulf between Husserl and Kant than is to be found in these subjectivistic doctrines. Husserl, further, does not regard his intuited ego-pole as something universal and eidetic, of which there could be many distinct instances: it is essentially one's *own* ego-pole, which means that the ego-poles of others require the same sort of subjectivistic 'constitution' as do the objects of material nature. Husserl, on his death, left three vast volumes of written material on the problems of inter-subjectivity, which were also treated in the *Cartesian Meditations* of 1930. These posthumous studies are of immense value and profundity, as are also his writings on phenomeno-logical time, a more essentially Kantian problem. But his treatment of intersubjectivity remains covertly solipsistic: the other subjects are merely constituted by the one and only subjectivity which is my own. It is arguable that all consistent forms of epistemological idealism or subjectivism are necessarily solipsistic, for, if an absolute ontological status can be given to other minds, why not to matter? All these idealistic defects do not diminish the immense richness and depth of Husserl's phenomenological analyses, and it is indeed only in the light of a full study of them that Kant can be fully understood and evaluated. A great number of these analyses, in fact, merely carry Kantian thoughts a little further. Heidegger's interpretations of Kant are also of interest, particularly in what he says about the role of the Productive Imagination. It is, of course, impossible to provide a fully documented justification of all the controversial statements made in the present section.

vi

Turning from Husserl to Wittgenstein (1889–1951), we encounter a philosopher whose thought was in certain respects deeply Kantian, both in its earlier and its later phases: this Kantian influence probably sprang in the main from an early reading of Schopenhauer. Wittgenstein, it may be observed, combined an original philosophical genius of the highest order with a narrowness of philosophical scholarship which in some cases amounted to illiteracy: he probably knew little more than the names of Husserl's works and of his system of phenomenology; and he certainly knew little or nothing of the important psychological school founded by Oswald Külpe (1862–1917) at Würzburg, which was deeply influenced by Husserlian intentionalism, and which discovered imageless elements in experience in the psychological laboratory, both in the phenomena of thought and in those of volition. (That Wittgenstein knew little or nothing about this work, despite its relevance, even as a subject of criticism, to the conclusions of his own later work, was to me evident from many conversations.) Wittgenstein's species of Kantianism was not, however, concerned with intentional thought-acts, which he held to be products of a systematic misunderstanding of the language of so-called inner experience, but with the use of words to refer to ordinary mundane objects and to make statements about them, or to serve many other infinitely varied, picturesquely described, purposes, for example, counting, naming, describing, narrating, ordering, and so on. If Kant was, in the main, a philosopher who tried to set bounds to the thought-acts that contribute to knowledge, and to place many of our important thought-concerns in metaphysics, morality, and aesthetics quite beyond such bounds; Wittgenstein was a philosopher who tried to set bounds to the sort of speech-acts which have a genuine relevance to the relations of things and persons in the empirical world that we all inhabit together, and to place the concerns of metaphysics, morality, and aesthetics securely beyond these, thereby tending gravely to discountenance the concerns in question.

In this Kantian endeavour, Wittgenstein found his work extraordinarily simplified by a constitutional personal solipsism, a strange constituent of his unusually charming person and character. This solipsism, this belief that 'the world is *my* world' and that 'this is manifest in the fact that the limits of *language* (of that language which alone I understand) mean the limits of *my* world' is stated in his first book, the *Tractatus Logico-philosophicus*, §5.62; though it is also said, in the same paragraph, that while what the solipsist *means* is quite correct, it also cannot be said, but has simply to show itself. And the *Blue Book*, a set of Notes circulated among Wittgenstein's students twelve years after the publication of his first book, continues the plea in favour of a solipsistic way of talking, as at least providing a different notation from the one which we follow in ordinary language, and which brings out analogies or differences among the matters we wish to speak of, to which ordinary speech fails to do justice (*Blue Book*, pp. 58–60). The solipsism of regarding the world as the speaker's world, and as somehow geared to what *he* alone can experience and talk of, is a profoundly interesting and unusual conscious stance, which many such as Descartes have nearly shared, but which none seems to have experienced so strongly as Wittgenstein. Very arguably, but also very controversially, in Wittgenstein's later work, despite his compensating stress on publicity, and his arguments against the possibility of a private language, linguistic solipsism always remains the explanatory background, unmentioned and to a growing extent unmentionable, of all his opinions and writings. For this solipsism means that he does not have to contend, as other philosophers usually have to contend, with a plurality of personal worlds, beyond which a single common world has to be constructed or postulated: the world of *his* experience is the only world there is, though there are of course a great number of behaving, talking persons in that world, of which he as a behaving talking person only is one, though occupying a curious central position in the system, that cannot very well be explained to the others. And the languages that he and his fellows speak are really all in a sense *his* languages, since they are all geared to the things and situations in *his* world, plus a fringe of private, personal feelings, evinced in highly special, highly derivative forms of speech and behaviour, and attributed both to himself, as a talking, behaving member of his world, and to others.

Wittgenstein's main works are the *Tractatus Logico-philosophicus* of 1921 and the *Philosophical Investigations*, which was published posthumously. Between these are the very interesting *Blue Book* and *Brown Book*, both first circulated as Notes for students, and in some ways a more arresting and successful presentation of his later views than the long, unfinished, wandering, hesitant *Philosophical Investigations*, his Opus Postumum. Some of his Lectures on the Philosophy of Mathematics given in 1939 are also of the highest interest and originality, and there is value in many of his posthumously published writings on mathematics, epistemology, ethics, and aesthetics. The doctrine of the *Tractatus*, his undoubted masterpiece, whose interpretation is of course highly controversial, is Kantian, in that it postulates the existence of an array of ultimate objects of reference which are certainly not to be found among the objects of ordinary encounter and experience. Like the substances of Leibniz and Kant's *Dissertation*, they are deeply *simple* and without any inner structure of parts, but, unlike those substances, they are without a distinct inner character of any sort — they are, roughly speaking, colourless (*Tractatus*, §2.0232) — and are capable only of what must be considered uniform, wholly external, wholly contingent relationships to other similar, wholly colourless units (§§2.01, 2.03, 2.061). On the number of the simples thus involved, and on the bonds which bind them together, whether directly or indirectly, into various groupings and dimensional arrangements, all the shapes, sizes, relative positions, and arrangements that we discern in complex, empirical objects in some manner depend, though in *what* manner they do so depend we are unable to say. But Wittgenstein holds that statements about the complex objects of ordinary experience must all refer, in some obscure and indirect manner, to the quite colourless arrangements among the quite colourless simples which in some manner underlie them, and that they depend for their truth and falsehood on the ultimate arrangements in question. Every statement about complexes, §2.0201 tells us, can be resolved into a statement about their constituents, and into the propositions which describe the complexes completely. Ordinary statements, with their many distinct but inseparable sides, must in fact be regarded as in some sense translations, into the language of complex, empirical macro-objectivity, of the micro-relationships which obtain among the ultimate simples which underlie them, and which could have been stated in an ultimate micro-language had there been any micro-speaker to make use of it. Statements in ordinary diction further involve many seemingly internal relations: one quality or shape can or cannot or must be combined with another, and so on. In the ultimate micro-language all such internalities would vanish: only the analytical truths of logic and mathematics would be irremovable, and these would merely connect one way of stating the ultimate facts with another. (These particular interpretations would be contested by many, who do not think that Wittgenstein was, in his earliest phase, thus rigorously analytic.)

According to Wittgenstein's view, all the macro-statements of ordinary life cover numberless bodies of alternative micro-statements that would make them true, and of which they are accordingly said to be the truth-functions, and there are likewise countless other bodies of alternative micro-statements that would make them false. They also entail, or exclude, or stand in other logical relations to other macro-statements, according as bodies of the micro-statements of which they each are truth-functions include, or are included by, or overlap, or exhaust, or are otherwise logically related to one another. To have insight into these underlying bodies of micro-statements would dispose of all the mysteries of entailment, exclusion, exhaustion, and so on, which do not always seem to be purely analytic. But, over the whole field of macro-statements, will preside a body of truths and falsehoods which are purely logical, the former being such that they are made true by *all* the possible, alternative groupings of micro-statements, and the latter by none of them. Logical truths seem to say a lot, because they are incompletely analysed, and logical falsehoods also seem to point to significant possibilities: in reality both are merely limiting cases of our macro-diction, to which no significantly limited assemblage of macro-alternatives can correspond. The penalty for employing macro-language is that it becomes possible to make statements that correspond to *no* micro-facts, and we are redeemed from this penalty by the logical truth of other macro-statements which are the precise negations of such macro-statements, and which are made true by *all* micro-facts. If we could have inhabited the paradise of micro-diction, we should never have been able to utter anything self-contradictory, and would have needed no redemptive logical tautologies to purge us from such utterances.

The views that Wittgenstein is here putting forward are in

many respects profoundly analogous to those of Kant, in that he locates a whole realm of unknowable, simple unities beneath the complex objects which appear before us empirically, and takes it that their relations are in some unknowable manner translated into the relations of empirical things. In referring to ordinary empirical objects, and their relations, in the manner in which our ordinary talk does refer to them, we also, in an indirect manner, refer to the unknowable relations among unknowable simple things of which our utterances are the truth-functions, and which must have, in their requisite groupings, an identity of logical form with our utterances. Wittgenstein, however, would differ from Kant in that his basic solipsism makes the realism of his object-theory and fact-theory a little questionable; possibly the micro-relations of simples, of which all our macro-statements are the truth-functions, are merely *postulated* relations among *postulated* existents, as Kant's Noumena, and their noumenal *Zusammenhänge*, certainly are not. The purely analytic character of the logical scaffolding which presides over our macro-diction, and which reflects an infinite contingency in its micro-structure, is likewise un-Kantian. The transcendental self of Wittgenstein passively reflects the macro-facts before it in its statements, and has not organized them by any prior exercise of the transcendental imagination. There are, further, no necessary, non-analytic categories, such as those of causal law, involved in the Wittgensteinian world-structure, though we, as scientific speakers and experimenters, always *look* for the most simple and uniform causal networks in which empirical material can be successfully cast, predicted, and controlled. That we have been successful so far in imposing certain interpretative networks on the empirical world certainly tells us something about that world, but it does not assure us that such success will always be possible (§§6.3–6.361). Everything that will be will be, and is in that empty sense determinate, but belief in an objective, non-logical, causal nexus is, according to Wittgenstein's view, purely superstitious (§§6.362–6.372; 5.136–5.1361). There can be no other necessity than logical necessity, and this, Wittgenstein claims to have shown, is wholly truistic and analytic. The profound gulf between Wittgenstein's radical contingency and inconsequent pragmatism, and Kant's *a priori*, synthetic necessity is here apparent.

The Transcendental Subject (§5.641) before whom the whole

empirical world makes its bow, is, as mentioned previously, a mere centre of co-ordination without empirical properties, like the self postulated in Kant's Transcendental Unity of Apperception, whose existence means little more than the existence of a unified world. But, since Wittgenstein's system is solipsistic, there are not for him a plurality of thinking selves with which a set of distinguishable empirical worlds can be correlated. Our transcendental self becomes, in fact, rather a redundancy, since there are no other selves to which it can be opposed: it therefore fades out in Wittgenstein's later theorizing, and becomes relegated to silence. There is also no need for inner, intentional acts by which the one phenomenal world is constituted by the subject: it is the most solid of givens, and requires no constitution by a conscious self. And the power of men, as creatures in the one world, to refer in their talk to objects and situations in it, depends presumably, though Wittgenstein in the *Tractatus* does not spell this out, on the palpable, phenomenal relations which connect words with phenomenal things and situations, and which then *indirectly* connect the latter, it must be supposed, with their ultimate basis in postulated simples, and the ultimate bonds among the latter. The inner thoughts of men then also become for Wittgenstein, at this early period, a mere set of more personal symbols, not fundamentally differing from those which they write or utter, by which they refer, by correlation of terms and identity of form, to the same macro-facts and their micro-foundations as do the symbols of their written or spoken language (§§5.541–5.5421). (All these statements of ours involve interpretations of Wittgenstein's condensed utterances which some would query, and which cannot be fully argued for in the present context.)

The profound obscurity of the relation of macro-statements to their inaccessible micro-equivalents leads, however, on the view of the *Tractatus*, to the construction of a large number of pseudo-statements which appear to say something significant, though they really say nothing, since the syntax of their construction, if developed in the direction of their micro-equivalents, is such that they correspond to nothing in the micro-realm. Traditional philosophy is full of such statements, which have no interpretation at the micro-level, and the philosophy which Wittgenstein recommends is one that must criticize statements and questions, and make it clear when they cannot be discussed or answered (see §§3.324; 4.003–4.0031; 4.111–4.115; 6.53). The procedure of Kant, in trying to show up the futility of metaphysical discussions and positions that go beyond what is epistemologically meaningful, or what has a relation to possible experience, is parallel to that of Wittgenstein: the simplicity of the soul, the freedom of the will, and the beginning of time are dealt with by Kant in a precisely similar manner. Kant, like Wittgenstein, attempts to dissolve his problems rather than to solve them, by showing that they have no relation to the sort of discourse that is phenomenally meaningful, and that can lead to knowledge.

Wittgenstein, however, like Kant, has his various transcendentals which, in the sort of speech that enables us to state the relations of ordinary empirical objects, cannot be spoken of at all, but which, since he does in fact speak of them, must be capable of being spoken of in some *other* manner. Kant's introduction of what can and must be thought of, but not known, is wholly parallel. The Wittgensteinian subject, or cosmic speaker, is such a transcendental; and so is the whole world conceived as a whole, whether in the abstract guise of logical space, the space of all possible micro-facts, or in the more concrete guise of 'everything that is the case', the totality of the macro-facts or micro-facts that there are (§§1–1.13; 6.44–6.45).

Wittgenstein, also, like Kant, places the roots of will and feeling, and the imperatives and values with which they enrich the world, beyond the realm of macro-facts, and micro-facts. If we know all that is the case, we know nothing about them. The freedom and invulnerability and deathlessness of the self are matters that cannot be spoken of in the sense in which empirical facts can be stated: in the world of fact everything is hemmed in and determinate, and we shall do whatever we shall do, and shall die and face ruin whenever we shall face them. Our freedom and deathlessness lie in another, non-factual dimension altogether. In the same way, the beauty of certain objects, and the excellence and blessedness of a certain way of life, and of the whole world seen in the light of these things, go beyond all the facts of the world, and belong to a mystical stratum that cannot be uttered as empirical facts are utterable (§§6.4–6.522). Wittgenstein in all these utterances is providing a close analogue to the practical postulations of Kant. It is an immense pity that those who have commented on the highly metaphysical and mystical *Tractatus* have, in the main, been deep-dyed barbarians as far as metaphysics and mysticism are concerned.

In Wittgenstein's later writings, on which it is not our task to comment fully here, since they are much less relevant to Kantianism, we have a more or less complete abandonment of talk about what cannot, in the ordinary empirical manner of discourse, be talked about. The simples of the *Tractatus* are elaborately criticized, and simplicity is made into a contextual and relativistic, not an absolute and metaphysical concept (*Investigations*, §§46–8). It is absurd to say that we cannot understand a sentence like 'Bring me a broom' without bringing in a reference to the broom's handle, brush, and other parts, and much less do we have to postulate the existence of countless unknowable simples which our sentence is supposed ultimately to mean (§60). The Transcendental Subject also goes by the board: though a solipsistic form of diction which relates everything to the self may provide relief from certain notational cramps, it is none the less a wholly idle innovation. For the word 'I' is a peculiar instrument of speech, which does not refer to some unique and mysterious and all-pervasive object: it is merely a means by which a speaker attracts attention to himself, and its use may be compared to the act of holding up one's hand (see *Blue Book*, pp. 58–68). And there is no room, in Wittgenstein's later work, for interior acts or experiences of attending, understanding, meaning, seeing, abstracting, expecting, intending, and so on. They are not needed as contributing to the whole *look* of the phenomenal world, which is simply treated as unquestionably and publicly there. It is presumed that, only when we have palpable mental 'pictures' of something, or 'feelings' which involve a noticeable disturbance, or queer quirks of association or mental procedure, do we have anything that deserves to be called a 'mental process' or an 'experience'. ('A pain's growing more and less; the hearing of a tune or a sentence: these are mental processes' (*Inv.*, §154).) Since such distinct images and feelings are not always noticeably present, and are almost always irrelevant to the intentional life of the mind, the latter is seen only in its vastly various outer public expressions, or in the mere readinesses for such expressions, in what we do or say, or are ready to do or say in certain circumstances. Thus, *expecting* a man to come to tea may be only fussing about in countless different ways and having some unimportant feelings (*Blue Book*, p. 20); attending to the shape of a vase may only be letting our eyes wander over it in a certain manner (*Inv.*, §33); understanding how to go on with a certain series may involve countless different, trivial performances on different occasions (*Inv.*, §151), and so forth.

Wittgenstein to some extent becomes conscious of these defects in his mental analyses, when he treats, in the last sections of the *Philosophical Investigations* (II. xi), of the variable 'aspects' in which things can be seen, but even there he tends to connect such aspects with rather queer cases from the psychological laboratory — ambiguous diagrams and such — and does not recognize that *all* seeing or thinking of objects is a seeing or thinking of them in certain aspects or conscious lights, *as* this or *as* that; and that our subjectivity, with its variable predications, emphases, backgrounds, modalities, and so on, is at *all* times writ large upon the phenomenal world, and does not require the assistance of language to make itself felt or/experienced, though language of course is infinitely important in sharpening and fixing it. Wittgenstein's philosophy of mind is built throughout on a denial of pre-linguistic meanings, for example, those of pastness, readiness, absence, and so forth, to which language gives expression, and which its learning always presupposes (see, e.g., *Brown Book*, §50). Kant's philosophy of mind is, on the other hand, built on a belief in such pre-linguistic meanings, in various basic imaginative and conceptual slantings, and so is Husserl's. We cannot in the present work argue for the entire correctness of this traditional approach, and for the total unacceptability of Wittgenstein's, however much the latter may have illuminated the many secondary complications in which the use of language is basic.

The later thought of Wittgenstein is further characterized by a continued onslaught on the questions and answers of traditional philosophy, all of which are held to ignore the manner in which words are actually *used*, and how such a use is actually taught. Philosophical problems arise when language goes on holiday, as Wittgenstein asserts in *Philosophical Investigations*, §38. Thus, Augustine wonders how any time can be long, since its parts never exist together, a puzzlement which would vanish if we simply concentrated on the procedures by which the length of time is estimated or measured, and by which the use of duration-terms is taught (*Blue Book*, p. 26). It is because the length of time is pictured as being like the length of a piece of tape that puzzles and antinomies arise. To concentrate on the actual situations in which we use temporal expressions, and were taught to use them, will lay all such difficulties to rest. We may likewise become puzzled by the use of the can-words and ability-words of ordinary diction, until we see how they are used, and how their use was taught: we then resist the view that an ability to do something is like a ghostly performance, or is a 'source' from which this 'springs'. All these issues are debated with great brilliance in the *Brown Book*, and in a more fatigued manner in the *Philosophical Investigations*. A set of 'language-games' is built up which attempts to cover any and every linguistic performance, for example, counting, greeting, narrating, describing, persuading, promising, and so on, in a manner which tries to remove everything mysterious and unobservable from their use or their teaching. It is the view of the present author that Wittgenstein's basic language-games are all covertly circular. Their teaching-situations presuppose an understanding of the meanings of, for example, duration, potency, number, and so on, that they are held to teach, and throw no light on them at all. The ultimate transcendentals involved in our understanding of ourselves, others, and the world remain as unassailably problematic, and as antinomic as ever.

Kant, however, tried to do away with philosophical theses, controversies, and antinomies in much the same manner as Wittgenstein, though Wittgenstein performed the slaughter more thoroughly than Kant. For, if Plato placed men in a cave from which egress was with effort possible, Kant placed them in a cave from which escape was impossible in this life, though it remained thinkable and desirable. Wittgenstein, however, constructed a habitation for hermits (or for a single hermit) from which escape was not only impossible, but neither thinkable nor desirable, except owing to a confusion. The importance of so radical a form of thought, and of the whole policy of dissolving rather than solving philosophical problems, is, however, incontestable, no matter how little one may feel willing to have one's problems removed by so drastic a therapy.

vii

From Wittgenstein we turn finally to consider Peter Strawson, whose *Bounds of Sense* (1966) is a most valuable critique of the *Critique of Pure Reason*, dealing at all times with the philosophical essentials of Kantian theory, and displaying throughout a much better understanding of its transcendently metaphysical ideas, which to Strawson are 'incoherent', than have many of those who have been more sympathetic to them. Here, in the Fourth Section of the book, we have a treatment entitled 'The Metaphysics of Transcendentalism', in which are arrayed, as in the glass bottles of a medical museum, all the organs which Strawson has excised from Kantian transcendentalism, as having no coherent or relevant meaning for a thought that wants to tie its concepts to clear empirical criteria.[1] And he has provided these excised organs with new names, and has divided them, or otherwise modified them, so as to make them more remotely like what he considers viable concepts. He has obligingly posited an A-relation, which is an analogue of 'causally affecting' or 'being causally affected': this A-relation holds among items known as Things-in-themselves without prejudice to the partial or complete identity of its terms, that is, to the partial or complete reflexivity of the A-relation. One term that is A-related, that is, the Transcendental Subject, is peculiar, in that it is at once A-affecting and A-affected. In the former capacity it is said to display understanding, a form-*producing* character, in the latter capacity it displays sensibility, a form-*yielding* character. There are other terms which enter into A-relations which may be said to be 'matter-producing' elements. Something called 'experience' is now held to be the outcome of this complex, quasi-causal transaction among A-terms, and such experience consists of 'intuitions', all of which have an order called temporality derived from one form-yielding element, whereas some also have a second order called spatiality derived from another form-yielding element. Intuitions further possess the character of being perceptions of a law-governed world of objects, due to the quasi-action of the form-producing element called understanding on the remaining form-yielding or matter-producing factors, and this law-governed world of objects is nothing apart from the perceptions which constitute it.

[1] The remainder of this chapter is a modified version of a part of my paper entitled 'Kant and Anglo-Saxon Criticism' given at the International Kant Conference in Rochester, NY, in 1970, and is printed here by kind permission of Professor Lewis Beck and the D. Reidel Publishing Company.

The contents of experience consist of two different sorts of appearances, which are also appearances in two totally different senses: the first, the appearances of the common A-term which exercises sensibility and understanding, are truly existent but wholly attributive elements, whereas the second, the appearances of physical nature, only *appear* to exist in the truly existent appearances just mentioned. Empirical knowledge is the outcome of all these factors, including those which are matter-producing. But there is also a knowledge of appearances which is independent of the matter-producing factors, and which is therefore said to be non-empirical or *a priori*. Such non-empirical knowledge is, however, restricted to possible appearances.

This remarkable sketch thus set forth, and involving fully interpretable as well as only semi-interpretable elements, is then put to the test, and Strawson decides, after long consideration, that the semi-interpretable elements in the 'model' do little or no significant work in it, and that Kant fails to provide a fully significant or even fully coherent account of the interplay of the various A-factors in the model with various empirical characters. And Kant, in his metaphysic of transcendental idealism has, Strawson holds, repeatedly violated one of his own most fundamental principles, a principle of which Strawson profoundly approves, and which he calls the principle of significance. This is the principle that there can be no legitimate or even meaningful employment of Ideas and concepts which does not relate them to the empirical or experiential conditions of their application. The connection of this principle with those of modern positivism and verificationism will of course be evident. It is, however, quite clear, as Strawson himself sometimes recognizes, that Kant's so-called principle of significance is really only a principle of *epistemological* significance. Kant throughout recognizes the value, even the indispensability, of employing certain Ideas and concepts which are *not* tied to any empirical conditions of application. He only refuses to regard them as, in such cases, making a contribution to knowledge.

After Strawson's careful excision of the mind's transcendental organs, it might be thought that Kant's critical philosophy would languish and die. The reverse is the case: the patient bounds from the operating table in an access of renewed vitality. The investigation of the limiting framework of Ideas and principles, the use and application of which are essential to empirical knowledge, and to any kind of being to which such knowledge is relevant, remains a supremely important task, to which, Strawson holds, Kant made fundamental contributions, and to whose carrying forward the various theses of his metaphysical transcendentalism have absolutely no relevance. (We reject the latter contention, holding, as we have argued, that meanings which are *not* epistemological are, for Kant, and also in truth, among the necessary background conditions of epistemological meanings.)

Strawson sees the contribution of Kant as embracing the following theses, all of which he finds acceptable: (i) that experience is essentially temporal; (ii) that there must be such unity among a temporally extended set of experiences as to make 'self-ascription' on the part of a subject of experience 'possible'; (iii) that experience must include an awareness of objects that can be judged about irrespective of the actual occurrence of particular experiences of them; (iv) that the objects thus judged about must be spatial; (v) that there must be one unified, spatio-temporal framework of empirical reality embracing all experience and its objects; and that (vi) certain principles of permanence and causality must be satisfied in the physical or objective world of things in space (*Bounds of Sense*, p. 24). Strawson further points out that Kant rightly holds that all the other theses stand in the most intimate logical relation to the thesis of the necessary unity of consciousness. Without objects, without things in space, without the principles of permanence and causality, there could be no such necessary unity. No one, he argues, could be conscious of a temporally extended series of experiences as his own, unless he could be aware of them as yielding knowledge of a unified objective world, through which his series of experiences forms just one subjective route.

It will be noted how Strawson qualifies and improves upon the exaggerations of the Transcendental Deductions. Like ourselves, he sees the unity of consciousness as a *necessary* condition of the presence to consciousness of a unified objective world, not simply as a *sufficient* condition of the latter, and of the categories of objectivity. Kant's genius, he says, and I agree with him, is nowhere more clearly shown than in his connection of the possibility of experience with the possibility of *contrasting* (not simply identifying) a subjectively perceptual route with an order which the objects of such perceptions independently possess, and in his recognition that this distinction must be revealed in the *content* of experience, since there can be no question of perceiving the pure framework of time itself. Strawson points out that it is not in the Transcendental Deductions alone, but only in their connection with the Aesthetic, the Analytic of Principles, and the Refutation of Idealism, that a coherent body of Kantian principles can be worked out and justified. The subject, in short, must *both* have a universal, law-discovering side, in virtue of which it can build up (with suitable aid from Things-in-themselves) an orderly picture of independent phenomenal reality in space and time; and *also* an element of selectivity within that reality, in part due to its position within the latter, and in part due to its own spontaneity, in virtue of which it carves out a specific route of appearances, both subjective and objective, within that total system. Strawson diverges from Kant in making the selection of a particular phenomenal route through the empirical world a more essential aspect in self-ascription than the constitution of the whole world through which this route runs. Both are, however, essential to self-ascription, since they are essential to one another, and bring each other out by their contrast. We are in complete agreement with Strawson on all of these points.

Some points in Strawson's treatment of the Kantian Analytic are particularly noteworthy. He points out that Kant does not simply write a reference to law-governed objectivity into his definition of experience, so that a phantasmagoria of impressions if such existed, would merely count as a non-experience. It would obviously be a very uninteresting proceeding simply to legislate verbally in this manner, and would moreover leave us open to the unremoved possibility of encountering disordered non-experiences at any moment for any length of time. The question, however, is whether there might not really be a consciousness which put disordered items together in a single confused picture, without there being a vestige of fixed rule in such a synthesis, a possibility which Kant at times seriously considers, and to which Strawson also gives an initial consideration. But Strawson here raises the difficulty that, in such a situation, it would be impossible to attach a sense to the notion of a single consciousness to which the successive presentations were supposed to belong: we seem, he says, to add nothing but a form of words to the hypothesis of an essentially disconnected set of impressions by stipulating that they should all belong to an identical consciousness. For such impressions to be truly connected and ascribable to a single consciousness, there would have to be some general feature that picked them out, and distinguished them as our own. But the possibility of such self-ascription, Strawson points out, involves a contrast: it would not be possible in the case of a mere rush of impressions. There would have to be features in that rush that enabled one to distinguish an objective sequence revealed by the impressions from the purely subjective sequence of the impressions themselves. This ground of distinction might not always be in evidence. There might be phantasmagoric 'trips' of great length. But not *all* experience could be of this phantasmagoric character if self-ascription were to be possible: there could be meaningful reference to a subject only if there were also the possibility of a contrasting reference to an object. And I do not think that Strawson would wish to deny that there could be a conscious series in which no *actual* self-ascription occurred, provided that such an ascription were *possible*. For the possibility of such a distinctive ascription must be there, if experience is to have that peculiar duplicity of aspect which is part of what we mean by calling it an 'experience'.

Strawson, however, feels that one must go further than Kant in developing the implications of possible self-ascription. He thinks that it is not sufficient to be able to ascribe all our experience to an 'abiding self', if this self remains vacuous and transcendental. He thinks that we can only give a full sense to such self-ascription if there are empirically applicable criteria of identity, by means of which a given self can be pinned down, and given a firm place among other selves, and among other realities in the space-time world. The subjective unity of self-consciousness can only make full sense if it can be regarded as *one* experiential route through the complexities of the objective world, beside which other objective routes are also possible. This means, though Strawson only spells it out elsewhere, that self-ascription always involves the possibility of other-ascription, that a social milieu, at least in possibility, is part and parcel of the possibility of experience. And he holds further, though again he only spells it out fully elsewhere, that self-ascription is only possible if there are objective criteria which enable one to pin this or that subject down, and oppose him to others, and these will, of course, have to be intersubjective, bodily criteria, and not merely subjective ones. We do not, indeed, identify our own subjective route of experience and ascribe it to ourselves, by making use of any criteria whatever, but we can only give full meaning to such an ascription if our self is also given a definite bodily location in the world, which renders it possible for both self and states to be given in other experiential routes, and for such other routes to appear in the route which is one's own. In some sense, then, a plurality of minds, and a plurality of embodied minds, able to identify one another in the world, are part and parcel of the necessary framework of experience.

Strawson has here extended Kant's transcendentalism in a manner that is at once deeply Kantian and also necessary. Kant's constant use of the pronoun 'We' instead of 'I' shows how, for him, sociality is built into the *a priori* structure of the world; and his criticism of the conception of a world of pure spirits, as it occurs in the early *Traüme eines Geistersehers*, and in a passage in the Postulates of Empirical Knowledge, shows him to be well on the way to agreeing with Strawson. I myself believe that the notion of a possible plurality of selves is in the deepest sense *a priori*, a part of the possibility of there being any consciousness or knowledge or being whatsoever, and that all the modern difficulties regarding our knowledge of other minds rest on the simple ignoring of this fact. I also agree with Strawson that embodiment and bodily identifiability are part of the developed notion of a system of selves, though I also believe that the bodies by which such selves are mutually identifiable may come to be the spiritual bodies of Saint Paul rather than the natural bodies of ordinary experience.

Strawson has, therefore, given us an interpretation of the Kantian Analytic which I cannot but regard with admiration. It is, however, followed by a treatment of the Dialectic, which I find less admirable, precisely because it bases itself on a principle of significance which Strawson fails to limit in the Kantian manner. Kant believed that we could not have knowledge of the unitary conscious subject which underlies experience, and is responsible for its unity; nor of the intricately interrelated system of Things-in-themselves, each simple and endowed with a unique individual nature, which appear to us in the space-time world; nor of the omnireal being which exists of necessity, since it covers all possibilities. But he also believed, as we have argued, that we can coherently *think* of these objects, and of certain of their essential features, and that such conceptions are necessary to the understanding of our scientific and practical life, and for its further extension and direction. There are, of course, great unclarities, and lapses into inconsistency, in Kant's exposition of these transcendent thoughts, but it is arguable that attempts to do without them, or anything like them, also involve similar unclarities and lapses into inconsistency. The greatness of Kant lies in his balanced concern with all that is in the cave of experience, and also with whatever must be thought of as lending intelligibility to its baffling assembly of disparate, ambiguous surface-shows, and thereby making our sojourn in it both intellectually and morally endurable. It is not to be conceived that the need for his peculiar sort of philosophical balance will ever become outmoded.

Bibliographical Note

The following are the full titles of the works of Kant that have been referred to in the text:

1747. *Gedanken von der wahren Schätzung der lebendigen Kräfte und Beurteilung der Beweise, deren sich Herr von Leibniz und andere Mechaniker in dieser Streitfragen bedient haben, nebst einigen vorhergehenden Betrachtungen welche die Kraft der Körper überhaupt betreffen* (*Thoughts on the True Estimation of Vis Viva or Active Force, and Assessment of the Proofs adduced by Herr von Leibniz and other Mechanical Physicists in regard to these Controversial Questions, together with some Introductory Treatments concerning Bodily Force in general*). Referred to as *The True Estimation of Vis Viva or Active Force.*

1755. *Allgemeine Naturgeschichte und Theorie des Himmels oder Versuch von der Verfassung und dem mechanischen Ursprunge des ganzen Weltgebaüdes, nach Newtonischen Grundsätzen abgehandelt* (*General Natural History and Theory of the Heavens: an Essay on the Constitution and Mechanical Origin of the whole World-structure, treated according to Newtonian principles*).

1755. *Principiorum Primorum Cognitionis Metaphysicae Nova Dilucidatio* (*A New Elucidation of the First Principles of Metaphysical Cognition*). Referred to as *Nova Dilucidatio.*

1756. *Metaphysicae cum Geometria iunctae Usus in Philosophia Naturali, cuius Specimen I continet Monadologiam Physicam* (*Joint Uses of Metaphysics and Geometry in Natural Philosophy, of which our first Specimen covers a Physical Monadology*). Referred to as *Physical Monadology.*

1758. *Neuer Lehrbegriff der Bewegung und Ruhe und her damit verknüpfter Folgerungen in den ersten Gründen der Naturwissenschaft* (*A new Doctrinal Concept of Motion and Rest and the Consequences which link it to the Prime Grounds of Natural Science*).

1762. *Die falsche Spitzfindigkeit der vier syllogistischen Figuren erwiesen* (*Proof of the Misleading Subtlety of the four Syllogistic Figures*).

1763. *Der einzig mögliche Beweisgrund zu einer Demonstration des Daseins Gottes* (*The only possible Ground on which a Proof of the Existence of God may be based*).

1763. *Versuch den Begriff der negativen Grössen in die Weltweisheit einzuführen* (*An Attempt to introduce the Notion of Negative Quantities into Philosophy*).

1764. *Beobachtungen über das Gefühl des Schönen und Erhabenen* (*Observations on the Feeling for the Beautiful and Sublime*).

1766. *Traüme eines Geistersehers, erlaütert durch Traüme der Metaphysik* (*Dreams of a Spirit-seer, seen in the light of the Dreams of Metaphysics*).

1770. *De Mundi Sensibilis atque Intelligibilis Forma et Principiis* (*On the Form and Principles of the Sensible and Intelligible World*). Generally referred to as *Dissertation*.

1781. *Kritik der reinen Vernunft* (*Critique of Pure Reason*), Edition I. Referred to as *CPR*, A.

1783. *Prolegomena zu einer jeden künftigen Metaphysik die als Wissenschaft wird auftreten können* (*Prolegomena to any future Metaphysic that can hope to rate as Science*). Referred to as *Prolegomena*.

1785. *Grundlegung zur Metaphysik der Sitten* (*Foundations of the Metaphysic of Morals*). Referred to as *Grundlegung*.

1786. *Metaphysische Anfangsgründe der Naturwissenschaft* (*Metaphysical Foundations of Natural Science*). Referred to as *MFNS*.

1787. *Kritik der reinen Vernunft* (*Critique of Pure Reason*), Edition II. Referred to as *CPR*, B.

1788. *Kritik der praktischen Vernunft* (*Critique of Practical Reason*). Referred to as *CPrR*.

1790. *Kritik der Urteilskraft* (*Critique of Judgement*). Its two parts are the Kritik der ästhetischen Urteilskraft (Critique of Aesthetic Judgement) and the Kritik der teleologischen Urteilskraft (Critique of Teleological Judgement).

1793. *Die Religion innerhalb der Grenzen der blossen Vernunft* (*Religion within the Bounds of mere Reason*). Generally referred to as *Religion*.

1797. *Die Metaphysik der Sitten* (*The Metaphysic of Morals*). Generally referred to as *Met. of Morals*, 1797. Its two parts are Die Rechslehre (Theory of Law or Right), and Metaphysische Anfangsgründe der Tugendlehre (Metaphysical Foundations of the Theory of Virtue).

1796–1803. *Opus Postumum*. This title is given to Kant's vast set of posthumously published jottings, assembled in thirteen packages or 'convolutes', and destined for use in a work on the Transition from Critical Philosophy to Physics. They are all to be found in the Prussian Academy Edition of Kant's complete works. Our dealings with this material have been mediated by Erich Adickes's ordering work in the 1920 Supplementary Volume of *Kant-Studien*.

I abstain from giving the full titles of Christian Wolff's German and Latin works. My references are *all* to his Latin, and *not* to his German works. My references to the writings of Crusius are sufficiently clear.

Index